GOGUEN CATEGORIES

TRENDS IN LOGIC
Studia Logica Library

VOLUME 25

Managing Editor
Ryszard Wójcicki, *Institute of Philosophy and Sociology, Polish Academy of Sciences, Warsaw, Poland*

Editors
Vincent F. Hendricks, *Department of Philosophy and Science Studies, Roskilde University, Denmark*
Daniele Mundici, *Department of Mathematics "Ulisse Dini", University of Florence, Italy*
Ewa Orłowska, *National Institute of Telecommunications, Warsaw, Poland*
Krister Segerberg, *Department of Philosophy, Uppsala University, Sweden*
Heinrich Wansing, *Institute of Philosophy, Dresden University of Technology, Germany*

SCOPE OF THE SERIES

Trends in Logic is a bookseries covering essentially the same area as the journal *Studia Logica* – that is, contemporary formal logic and its applications and relations to other disciplines. These include artificial intelligence, informatics, cognitive science, philosophy of science, and the philosophy of language. However, this list is not exhaustive, moreover, the range of applications, comparisons and sources of inspiration is open and evolves over time.

Volume Editor
Ewa Orłowska

The titles published in this series are listed at the end of this volume.

GOGUEN CATEGORIES

A Categorical Approach to L-fuzzy Relations

by

MICHAEL WINTER

Brock University,
St. Catharines,
ON, Canada

Springer

A C.I.P. Catalogue record for this book is available from the Library of Congress.

ISBN 978-90-481-7554-3

ISBN 978-1-4020-6164-6 (e-book)

Published by Springer
P.O. Box 17, 3300 AA Dordrecht, The Netherlands.

www.springer.com

Printed on acid-free paper

To my family

Contents

INTRODUCTION

In a wide variety of problems one has to treat uncertain or incomplete information. Some kind of exact science is needed to describe and understand existing methods, and to develop new attempts. Especially in applications of computer science, this is a fundamental problem. To handle such information, Zadeh [44], and simultaneously Klaua [22, 23], introduced the concept of fuzzy sets and relations. In contrast to usual sets, fuzzy sets are characterized by a membership relation taking its values from the unit interval $[0, 1]$ of the real numbers. After its introduction in 1965 the theory of fuzzy sets and relations was ranked to be some exotic field of research. The success during the past years even with consumer products involving fuzzy methods causes a rapidly growing interest of engineers and computer scientists in this field. Nevertheless, Goguen [12] generalized this concept in 1967 to $\mathcal{L}$-fuzzy sets and relations for an arbitrary complete Brouwerian lattice $\mathcal{L}$ instead of the unit interval $[0, 1]$ of the real numbers. He described one of his motivating examples as follows:

> A housewife faces a fairly typical optimization problem in her grocery shopping: she must select among all possible grocery bundles one that meets as well as several criteria of optimality, such as cost, nutritional value, quality, and variety. The *partial ordering* of the bundles is an intrinsic quality of this problem. (Goguen [12] 1967)

It seems to be unnatural – comparing apples to oranges – to describe the criteria of optimality by a linear ordering as the unit interval. Why should the nutritional value of a given product be described by 0.6 (instead of 0.65, or any other value from $[0, 1]$), and why should a product with a high nutritional value be better than a product with high quality since those criteria are usually incomparable?

This observation has led to the theory of *multiobjective* or *multicriteria* optimization problems (cf. [13]). Instead of combining several criteria into a single number, and choosing the highest value, the concept of *Pareto optimailty* is used. In this approach the elements that are not dominated are taken for further considerations. Here an element x is said to dominate an element y if the value x_i for each objective i is greater than or equal to the corresponding value y_i of y. Traditional techniques of optimization and search have been applied in this area. Recently, even genetic algorithms have been used to search for multicriteria optima (e.g., [30, 31]).

One important notion within fuzzy theory is 0-1 crispness. A 0-1 crisp set or relation is described by the property that their characteristic function supplies either the least element 0 or the greatest element 1 of the unit interval $[0, 1]$ or more general the complete Brouwerian lattice $\mathcal{L}$. The class of 0-1 crisp fuzzy sets or relations may be seen as the subclass of regular sets or relations within the fuzzy world. Especially in applications, this notion is fundamental. We want to demonstrate this by considering two examples.

In fuzzy decision theory the basic problem is to select a specific element from a fuzzy set of alternatives. Therefore, several cuts are used [9, 24]. Basically, an α-cut of a fuzzy set M is a set N such that an element x is in N if, and only if, x is in M with a degree $\geq \alpha$. Analogously, an α-cut of a fuzzy relation R is a crisp relation S such that a pair of elements is related in S if, and only if, they are related in R with a degree $\geq \alpha$. Some variants of this notion may also be used. By definition, these cut operations are strongly connected to the notion of crispness. In particular, using the notion of crispness, one may define cut operations, and a cut operation naturally implies a notion of crispness.

Another example might be the development of a fuzzy controller. Usually the output of the controller has to be a 0-1 crisp value since it is used to control some nonfuzzy physical or software system. Therefore, a procedure, called defuzzification, is applied to transform the fuzzy output into some 0-1 crisp value. This list of examples may be continued. The bottom line is that a convenient theory for $\mathcal{L}$-fuzzy relations should be able to express the notion of crispness.

Today, fuzzy theory as well as its application is usually formulated as a variation of set theory or some kind of many-valued logic (e.g., cf. [2, 14, 26]). Although many algebraic laws are developed, these formalizations are not algebraic themselves. But an algebraic description would have several advantages. Applications of fuzzy theory may be described by simple terms in this language. In this way, we get in some sense a denotational semantics of the application, and, hence, a mathematical theory to reason about notions as correctness. One may prove such properties using the calculus of the algebraic theory, which is quite often more or less equational. Furthermore, this denotational semantics may be used to get a prototype of the application.

On the other hand, the calculus of binary relations has been investigated since the middle of the nineteenth century as an algebraic theory for logic and set theory [36, 37]. A first adequate development of such algebras was given by de Morgan and Peirce. Their work has been taken up and systematically extended by Schröder in [34]. More than 40 years later, Tarski started with the exhaustive study of relation algebras [35], and more generally, Boolean algebras with operators [17].

The papers above deal with relational algebras presented in their classical form. Elements of such algebras might be called *quadratic* or *homogeneous*; relations over a fixed universe. Usually a relation acts between two different kinds of objects, e.g., between customers and products. Therefore, a variant of the theory of binary relations has evolved that treats relations as *heterogeneous* or *rectangular*. A convenient framework to describe such kind of typing is given by category theory [3, 10, 27, 28, 32, 33].

There are some attempts to extend the calculus of relations to the fuzzy world. In [21] the concept of fuzzy relation algebras was introduced as an algebraic formalization of fuzzy relations with sup-min composition. These algebras are equipped with a semiscalar multiplication, i.e., an operation mapping an element from $[0, 1]$ and a fuzzy relation to a fuzzy relation. In the standard model this is done by componentwise multiplication of the real values. Fuzzy relation algebras and their categorical counterpart [11], so-called Zadeh categories, constitute a convenient algebraic theory for fuzzy relations. Using the semiscalar multiplication it is also possible to characterize 0-1 crisp relations. Unfortunately, there is no way to extend or modify this approach for $\mathcal{L}$-fuzzy relations since for an arbitrary complete Brouwerian lattice such a semiscalar multiplication may not exist.

Another approach is based on Dedekind categories and was introduced in [27]. It was shown that the class of $\mathcal{L}$-fuzzy relations constitutes such a category. Unfortunately, the notion of 0-1 crispness causes some problems. Using the notion of scalar elements, i.e., a set of partial identities corresponding to the lattice $\mathcal{L}$, several notions of crispness in an arbitrary Dedekind category were introduced in [11, 20]. It was shown that the notion of s-crispness as well as the notion of l-crispness coincides with 0-1 crispness under an assumption concerning the underlying lattice. This assumption is fulfilled by all linear orderings, e.g., the unit interval. Unfortunately, it was also shown that both classes of crisp relations are trivial if the underlying lattice is a Boolean lattice. Actually, it can be shown (Theorem 5.1) that the notion of 0-1 crispness cannot be formalized in the language of Dedekind categories, i.e., this theory is too weak to express this property. Therefore, an extended theory is needed: the theory of Goguen categories.

In this book, we want to focus on Goguen categories introduced in [40] and some weaker structures as a convenient algebraic/categorical framework for $\mathcal{L}$-fuzzy relations and their application in computer science. In particular, we are interested in the development process of fuzzy controllers using the method of Mamdani [25]. One major problem is to ensure totality of the controller, i.e., the controller should produce an output value for each input. If the controller is described by a relation R within a Goguen category, this property can be proved by showing $\mathbb{I} \sqsubseteq R; R^{\smile}$, where $\mathbb{I}$ is the identity relation, ; is composition of relations, and $R^{\smile}$ is the converse of R. In most applications the controller is constructed by several components, which are combined using t-norms and t-conorms. The actual choice of the norms and their parameters is often done by experts using their experiences. Especially in complex applications, such a development process might easily lead to "holes" in the domain of the controller, i.e., to a partially defined controller. On the other hand, the relational description R of the controller can be parametric in those norms. From a generic proof of R being total (which is necessarily parametric too) we can generate a set of conditions that have to be satisfied in order to ensure the totality of R. The expert may now select a convenient set of norms and parameters fulfilling these conditions. The controller generated is guaranteed to be total. We will give an example of the development process sketched above in Chapter 6.

This book is organized as follows. In Chapters 1 and 2, we will introduce several mathematical notions as sets and lattices. The basic properties of $\mathcal{L}$-fuzzy relations are investigated in Chapter 3. Afterwards, we will concentrate on the categorical description of relations, i.e., we will introduce several categories of relations in Chapter 4. Furthermore, their basic properties are proved, and their connections to $\mathcal{L}$-fuzzy relations are studied. Chapter 5 is dedicated to Goguen categories and several weaker structures. We will prove some basic properties of those kinds of categories, focus on their representation theory, concentrate on derived connectives from a generalized notion of t-norms and t-conorms, and investigate the validity of equations in the substructure of crisp relations. In the last chapter we will give an applications of Goguen categories in computer science. We want to construct an $\mathcal{L}$-fuzzy controller with respect to a given set of rules. This controller is not based on the unit interval. Furthermore, we will construct the controller without deciding in advance which norms and parameters should be used. From a generic proof of the totality of the controller we derive properties that can be used by an engineer to finally decide about those parameters.

The writing of this book extended over almost 5 years. The early version grew out of the Habilitation thesis of the author in Munich, in 2003. In the following years several parts were revised and extended. In particular, Sections 5.1–5.4 were added in order to provide a more detailed overview of categories of $\mathcal{L}$-fuzzy relations.

The author would like to thank Gunther Schmidt and Yasuo Kawahara for their constant support during the Habilitation. Ivo Düntsch has to be thanked not only as a colleague, but also as a source of suggestions and advice.

The RelMiCS (Relational Methods in Computer Science) community was not only a source of useful comments and criticism, but also of friendship.

The first draft of this book was written in Munich. The author would like to thank the Department of Computer Science of the University of the Federal Armed Forces, Munich, Germany, for its support during this phase. The revision and the writing of the final version took place in St. Catharines. The author would like to thank the Department of Computer Science of Brock University, St. Catharines, Canada, for its support during the later phase.

Last but not least, a special thanks goes to Ewa Orlowska, who suggested to publish the result of the Habilitation in a book.

1
SETS, RELATIONS, AND FUNCTIONS

Sets are fundamental in mathematics. In this chapter we briefly introduce the concepts and notations from set theory we will use throughout the book. We assume that the reader is familiar with the basic concepts of set theory. He may use some kind of naive set theory or a formal theory as ZF or ZFC [18], i.e., the Zermelo-Fraenkel axioms of set theory. As usual, we denote the fact that "x is an element of a set A" by $x \in A$. The set with no elements is called the *empty set*, and is denoted by $\emptyset$. If every element of a set A is also an element of the set B, we say A is a *subset* of B denoted by $A \subseteq B$.

The *set comprehension* "the set of all elements of a set A fulfilling a predicate $\mathfrak{P}$" is denoted by $\{x \in A \mid \mathfrak{P}(x)\}$. If it is clear from the context or if it is insignificant which A is meant, we simply write $\{x \mid \mathfrak{P}(x)\}$.

Union, intersection, and set difference are defined as usual:

$$\begin{array}{lll} \textit{union} & A \cup B & := \{x \mid x \in A \text{ or } x \in B\}, \\ \textit{intersection} & A \cap B & := \{x \mid x \in A \text{ and } x \in B\}, \\ \textit{set difference} & A \setminus B & := \{x \mid x \in A \text{ and } x \notin B\}. \end{array}$$

The *complement* $\overline{A}$ of a set A in respect to a set $B \supseteq A$ is just the set difference $B \setminus A$. The binary operations union and intersection may be generalized to an arbitrary set of sets as argument. Suppose A_i for $i \in I$ are sets. Then,

$$\begin{array}{lll} \text{union} & \bigcup_{i \in I} A_i & := \{x \mid \exists i \in I : x \in A_i\}, \\ \text{intersection} & \bigcap_{i \in I} A_i & := \{x \mid \forall i \in I : x \in A_i\}. \end{array}$$

The *Cartesian product* of two sets A and B is the set of all pairs (x, y) with $x \in A$ and $y \in B$, and is denoted by $A \times B$. The set of all subsets of A is called the *power set* of A, and is denoted by $\mathcal{P}(A)$.

A *binary relation* R between two sets A and B is an element of $\mathcal{P}(A \times B)$. A is called the *source* and B the *target* of R. If $A = B$, the relation R is also called an *endorelation* or *homogeneous*. To indicate that a binary relation R has source A and target B we usually write $R : A \to B$.

Apart from the set theoretic operations, we consider two further operations on binary relations. Let R be a relation between A and B and S between B and C. Then we define

$$\begin{array}{lrcl} \textit{conversion} & R^{\mathsf{T}} & := & \{(y,x) \mid (x,y) \in R\}, \\ \textit{composition} & R \circ S & := & \{(x,z) \mid \exists y \in B : (x,y) \in R \text{ and } (y,z) \in S\}. \end{array}$$

Due to the definition above, a composition $Q \circ R$ has to be read from the left to the right, i.e., first Q, and then R. We usually write $R(x, y)$ instead of $(x, y) \in R$. Notice that $R^{\mathsf{T}^{\mathsf{T}}} = R$, and that composition is *associative*, i.e., for all relation $Q : A \to B, R : B \to C$ and $S : C \to D$ we have $(Q \circ R) \circ S = Q \circ (R \circ S)$. The *identity relation* $\mathbb{I}_A$ on a set A is defined as the set $\{(x, x) \mid x \in A\}$. Then for all relations $R : A \to B$ we have $R = \mathbb{I}_A \circ R = R \circ \mathbb{I}_B$.

The *range* or *image* $\mathrm{ran}(R)$ of a relation $R : A \to B$ is defined as the set $\{y \in B \mid \exists x \in A : R(x, y)\}$. Dually, the *domain* $\mathrm{dom}(R)$ of R is defined as the set $\{x \in A \mid \exists y \in B : R(x, y)\}$. Obviously, we have $\mathrm{dom}(R) = \mathrm{ran}(R^{\mathsf{T}})$ and $\mathrm{ran}(R) = \mathrm{dom}(R^{\mathsf{T}})$.

A function f from A to B is a binary relation $f : A \to B$ which is

univalent $f(x, y_1)$ and $f(x, y_2)$ implies $y_1 = y_2$ for all $x \in A$ and $y_1, y_2 \in B$,
total for all $x \in A$ there exists some $y \in B$ so that $f(x, y)$.

Both properties may be expressed using the relational constructions. The first property is equivalent to $f^{\mathsf{T}} \circ f \subseteq \mathbb{I}_B$, and the second to $\mathbb{I}_A \subseteq f \circ f^{\mathsf{T}}$. The image of a function $f : A \to B$ will also be denoted by $f(A)$. As indicated above, arbitrary binary relations are denoted by uppercase and functions by lowercase letters. If f is a function, we usually write $f(x)$ to indicate the (necessarily unique) y so that $f(x, y)$. The set of all functions from A to B will be denoted by $A \to B$.

A relation $R : A \to B$ is called

(1) *injective* iff[1] $R(x_1, y)$ and $R(x_2, y)$ implies $x_1 = x_2$ for all $x_1, x_2 \in A$ and $y \in B$,

(2) *surjective* iff for all $y \in B$ there exists some $x \in A$ so that $R(x, y)$,

(3) *bijective* iff it is injective and surjective.

[1]We use the phrase "iff" as an abbreviation for "if and only if."

Obviously, a relation is injective iff R^{T} is univalent, surjective iff R^{T} is total, and bijective iff R^{T} is a function. A bijective function is also called a bijection. For historical reasons, the converse of a bijection f is denoted by f^{-1}. Notice that we have

$$f^{-1}(f(x)) = x \quad \text{and} \quad f(f^{-1}(y)) = y$$

for all bijections $f : A \to B$ and $x \in A, y \in B$.

The cartesian product construction is associative up to a bijection, i.e., the function $\alpha_{A,B,C} : (A \times B) \times C \to A \times (B \times C)$ defined by $\alpha_{A,B,C}((a,b),c) = (a,(b,c))$ is bijective for arbitrary sets A, B, and C. We define n-ary products by iterating binary products. Due to the associativity this is well-defined.

Given an n-ary function $f : A_1 \times \cdots \times A_n \to B$ we will use the extended set comprehension scheme $\{f(x_1,\ldots,x_n) \mid x_1 \in A_1,\ldots,x_n \in A_n\}$ as an abbreviation for

$$\{y \mid \exists x_1 \in A_1 \cdots \exists x_n \in A_n : y = f(x_1,\ldots,x_n)\}.$$

The concept of a Cartesian product of sets may be further generalized using functions. Let A_i for $i \in I$ be sets. The *I-indexed product* $\prod\limits_{i\in I} A_i$ of the sets A_i is defined as the set of all functions f from I to $\bigcup\limits_{i\in I} A_i$ so that $f(i) \in A_i$ for all $i \in I$. For a finite set $I = \{1,\ldots,n\}$ we get the usual n-ary product of $A_1,\ldots,A_n$. Notice, if $A_i = A_j =: A$ for all $i,j \in I$, i.e., all components of the product are equal, $\prod\limits_{i\in I} A_i$ is just $I \to A$.

We introduce some notations for commonly known sets:

$\mathbb{B}$	set of Boolean values $\{\mathbf{t},\mathbf{f}\}$ or $\{0,1\}$ ($\mathbf{t} = 1 \mathrel{\hat=} \text{true}$, $\mathbf{f} = 0 \mathrel{\hat=} \text{false}$),
$\mathbb{N}$	set of the natural numbers $\{0,1,2,\ldots\}$,
$\mathbb{N}^{\infty}$	set of the natural numbers with an additional greatest element ∞,
$\mathbb{R}$	set of real numbers,

$[0,1] = \{x \in \mathbb{R} \mid 0 \le x \le 1\}$ unit interval of real numbers.

The concept of a homomorphism between structured sets, i.e., sets with some operations and/or relations defined on them, is usually somewhat informal. One may obtain a formal definition using the theory of universal algebras. In this book a homomorphism is a function reflecting the structure of the corresponding sets. For example, a homomorphism between the semigroups $(G_1,+_1,0_1)$ and $(G_2,+_2,0_2)$ is a function $f : G_1 \to G_2$ respecting the group operation $+$ and the neutral element 0, i.e., $f(x +_1 y) = f(x) +_2 f(y)$ for all $x, y \in G_1$ and $f(0_1) = 0_2$. As usual, a bijective homomorphism f so that f^{-1} is also a homomorphism is called an isomorphism. In this situation the source and the target of f are called isomorphic.

2
LATTICES

In this chapter we want to introduce basic concepts from lattice theory we will need throughout this book. For a comprehensive introduction to this theory we refer to [4, 16, 29].

A very natural concept is a (partially) ordered set (or poset). Elements of such a set may be related to each other by notion of "being smaller or equal." Formally, a *poset* is a set P with a binary relation $\leq$ on it so that

reflexive	$x \leq x$ for all $x \in P$,
transitive	if $x \leq y$ and $y \leq z$, then $x \leq z$ for all $x, y, z \in P$,
antisymmetric	if $x \leq y$ and $y \leq x$, then $x = y$ for all $x, y \in P$.

A poset P is called *linear* iff $x \leq y$ or $y \leq x$ holds for all $x, y \in P$. The set of real numbers $\mathbb{R}$ with the usual ordering is a linear poset. Obviously, the unit interval $[0, 1]$ of the real numbers is also a linear poset. The power set $\mathcal{P}(A)$ of a set A with more than one element together with set-inclusion $\subseteq$ is a standard example of a nonlinear poset.

Finite posets are often visualized by their Hasse diagrams. A Hasse diagram is a drawing of the transitive reduction of the partial order, i.e., each element of the set is represented as a vertex, and the order relationship by upward oriented edges. The graph has an edge from x to y if $x \leq y$ and $x \neq y$, and there is no z with $z \neq x$ and $z \neq y$ such that $x \leq z \leq y$. In this case, y is said to cover x, or y is an immediate successor of x. Figure 2.1 shows the Hasse diagram of

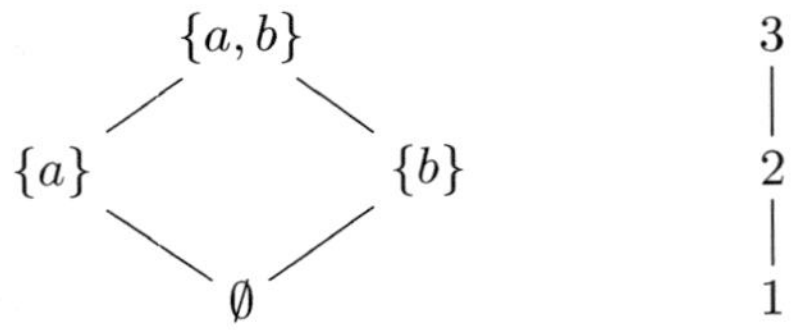

Figure 2.1. Two Hasse diagrams.

the powerset of $\{a, b\}$ and the linear order of the subset $\{1, 2, 3\}$ of the natural numbers.

If we define $x \preceq y$ iff $y \leq x$ for a poset P, we will obtain a new poset, called the *reversed ordering* on P.

A function f between two posets P_1 and P_2 is called *monotone* iff $x \leq y$ implies $f(x) \leq f(y)$. Notice that the symbol $\leq$ in the previous property refers to different partial orderings, namely to that of P_1 and P_2, respectively. Monotone functions are the homomorphisms between posets as introduced in the previous chapter. We will denote the set of monotone functions from P_1 to P_2 by $P_1 \overset{\leq}{\to} P_2$. Dually, an *antitone function* f between two posets P_1 and P_2 is a function so that $x \leq y$ implies $f(y) \leq f(x)$ for all $x, y \in P_1$. Therefore, an antitone function is a monotone function from P_1 to the reversed ordering on P_2. The set of antitone functions from P_1 to P_2 is denoted by $P_1 \overset{\geq}{\to} P_2$. Since monotone and antitone functions are defined dually, many properties hold for both sets of functions. Therefore, we will refer to either the set of monotone or the set of antitone functions by $P_1 \overset{*}{\to} P_2$.

Consider the powerset $\mathcal{P}(A)$ of the set $A = \{a, b\}$, the linear poset $P = \{1, 2, 3, 4\}$ and the function $f : \mathcal{P}(A) \to P$ visualized in Figure 2.2. This function is monotone. Furthermore, f is also bijective, but its converse $f^{-1} : P \to \mathcal{P}(A)$ is not monotone. Indeed, we have $2 \leq 3$ but $f^{-1}(2) = \{b\} \not\subseteq \{a\} = f^{-1}(3)$.

The cartesian product of posets can be ordered componentwise. Figure 2.3 shows the Hasse diagram of the product of the posets from Figure 2.1.

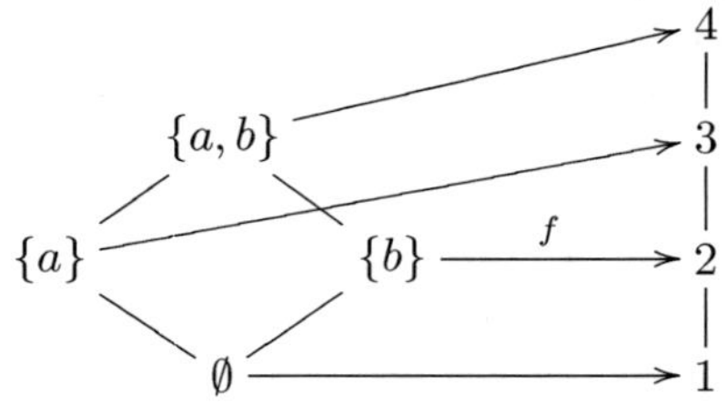

Figure 2.2. A monotone function.

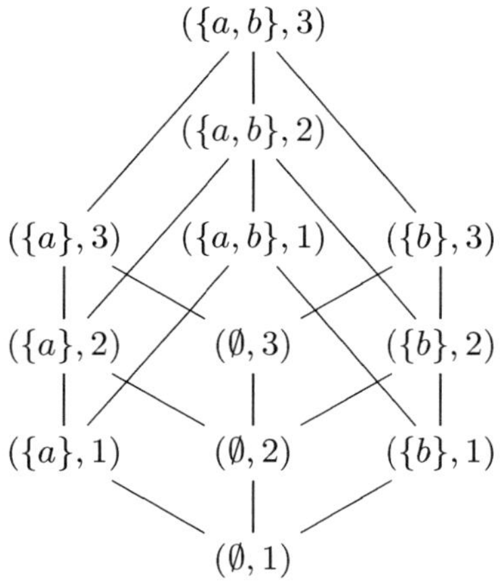

Figure 2.3. Hasse diagram of product of the posets from Figure 2.1.

Theorem 2.1 *Let P_i be posets for $i \in I$. Then $\prod_{i\in I} P_i$ together with the relation*

$$f \leq g \iff \forall i \in I : f(i) \leq g(i)$$

is again a poset.

The proof of the theorem above is an easy exercise and, therefore, omitted. Notice that n-ary products and the set of all functions from I to a poset P are special cases of the previous theorem.

An *upper bound* of a subset M of a poset P is an element $u \in P$ so that $x \leq u$ for all $x \in M$, and dually a *lower bound* of M is an element $l \in P$ so that $l \leq x$ for all $x \in M$. A *greatest element* of M is an element of M, which is also an upper bound of M. Dually, a *least element* of M is defined as an element of M, which is also a lower bound of M. It is easy to verify that greatest and least elements are unique (if they exist) so that we can refer to them as the greatest and the least element of M. The *least upper bound* of M is the least element of the set of upper bounds of M, and the *greatest lower bound* of M is the greatest element of the set of lower bounds of M.[1]

Figure 2.4 shows two posets with a subset M and its lower bounds. Notice that the second order has exactly one additional element. As a consequence, the first ordering does not provide a greatest lower bound of M whereas the second does.

Definition 2.2 *A lower semilattice $\mathcal{L}$ is a poset so that every pair of elements x and y has a greatest lower bound or meet denoted by $x \wedge y$. It is called complete*

[1]The least upper bound and the greatest lower bound of M may not exist. But, if they exist, they are unique since they are defined as greatest resp. least elements.

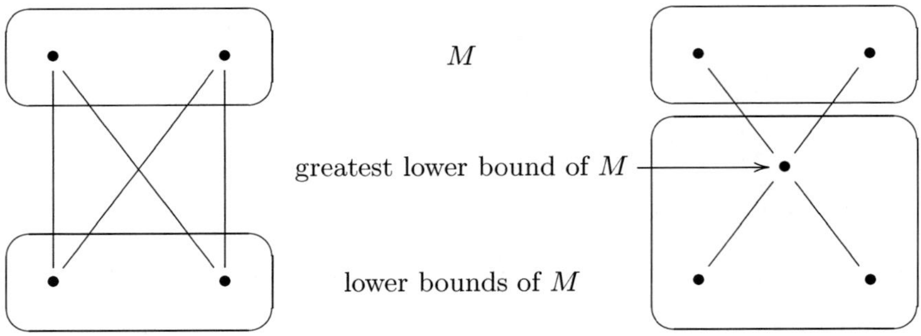

Figure 2.4. Example of lower bounds.

iff every subset $M \neq \emptyset$ of $\mathcal{L}$ has a greatest lower bound denoted by $\bigwedge M$. A subset $\mathcal{L}'$ of a (complete) lower semilattice $\mathcal{L}$ is called a (complete) lower subsemilattice of $\mathcal{L}$ iff $\mathcal{L}'$ is closed under $\wedge$ resp. $\bigwedge$, i.e., for all $x, y \in \mathcal{L}'$ we have $x \wedge y \in \mathcal{L}'$ resp. for all subsets $M \neq \emptyset$ of $\mathcal{L}'$ we have $\bigwedge M \in \mathcal{L}'$. Dually, an upper semilattice $\mathcal{L}$ is a poset so that every pair of elements x and y has a least upper bound or join denoted by $x \vee y$. It is called complete iff every subset $M \neq \emptyset$ of $\mathcal{L}$ has a least upper bound denoted by $\bigvee M$. A subset $\mathcal{L}'$ of a (complete) upper semilattice $\mathcal{L}$ is called a (complete) upper subsemilattice of $\mathcal{L}$ iff $\mathcal{L}'$ is closed under $\vee$ resp. $\bigvee$, i.e., for all $x, y \in \mathcal{L}'$ we have $x \vee y \in \mathcal{L}'$ resp. for all subsets $M \neq \emptyset$ of $\mathcal{L}'$ we have $\bigvee M \in \mathcal{L}'$.

Notice that a complete lower semilattice has a least element $0 = \bigwedge \mathcal{L}$. Dually, a complete upper semilattice has a greatest element $1 = \bigvee \mathcal{L}$.

The posets of Figure 2.1 and 2.3 are lower semilattices as well as upper semilattices, and the posets of Figure 2.4 are not. Another example of a complete lattice is the powerset of a set A. In this example, the greatest lower bound of a set of subsets of A is given by the intersection, and the least upper bound by the union of the sets.

An element x of a lower semilattice $\mathcal{L}$ with least element 0 is called *linear* iff $x \wedge y = 0$ implies $y = 0$ for all $y \in \mathcal{L}$. Notice that iff $\mathcal{L}$ has at least two elements 0 is not linear.

In a linear poset every nonzero element is linear. The converse is, in general, not true. In the nonlinear lower semilattice $\{0, a, b, c\}$ induced by Figure 2.5 all nonzero elements are linear.

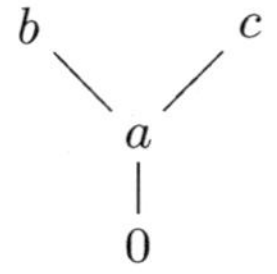

Figure 2.5. A semilattice so that all nonzero elements are linear.

The binary operations $\wedge$ and $\vee$ of the corresponding semilattices fulfill the following properties:

idempotent	$x \wedge x = x,$	$x \vee x = x,$
commutative	$x \wedge y = y \wedge x,$	$x \vee y = y \vee x,$
associative	$x \wedge (y \wedge z) = (x \wedge y) \wedge z,$	$x \vee (y \vee z) = (x \vee y) \vee z,$
consistent	$x \wedge y = x \;\Leftrightarrow\; x \leq y,$	$x \vee y = y \;\Leftrightarrow\; x \leq y,$
monotone $\forall y \leq z:$	$x \wedge y \leq x \wedge z,$	$x \vee y \leq x \vee z.$

The proof of the properties above is an easy exercise, and, therefore, omitted. Furthermore, the formulas above may be used to get an algebraic definition of semilattices, e.g., every set with a binary operation $\wedge$, which is idempotent, commutative, and associative is a lower semilattice by defining $x \leq y$ iff $x \wedge y = x$.

A monotone function f between two upper/lower semilattices $\mathcal{L}_1$ and $\mathcal{L}_2$ fulfills $f(x \wedge y) \leq f(x) \wedge f(y)$ resp. $f(x) \vee f(y) \leq f(x \vee y)$ since $f(x \wedge y) \leq f(x)$ and $f(x \wedge y) \leq f(y)$ resp. $f(x) \leq f(x \vee y)$ and $f(y) \leq f(x \vee y)$. Dually, for an antitone function g we have $g(x \vee y) \leq g(x) \wedge g(y)$ resp. $g(x) \vee g(y) \leq g(x \wedge y)$. If $\mathcal{L}_1$ and $\mathcal{L}_2$ are complete lower/upper semilattices, the more general inequalities $f(\bigwedge M) \leq \bigwedge\limits_{x \in M} f(x)$ resp. $\bigvee\limits_{x \in M} f(x) \leq f(\bigvee M)$ for all $\emptyset \neq M \subseteq \mathcal{L}_1$ follow. Dually, for an antitone function we have $f(\bigvee M) \leq \bigwedge\limits_{x \in M} f(x)$ and $\bigvee\limits_{x \in M} f(x) \leq f(\bigwedge M)$ for all $\emptyset \neq M \subseteq \mathcal{L}_1$.

Theorem 2.3 *Let $\mathcal{L}_i$ be (complete) lower/upper semilattices for $i \in I$. Then the poset $\prod\limits_{i \in i} \mathcal{L}_i$ together with either the operation*

$$\begin{aligned} &(f \wedge g)(i) := f(i) \wedge g(i), \\ \textit{or} \quad &(f \vee g)(i) := f(i) \vee g(i) \end{aligned}$$

is again a (complete) lower/upper semilattice, respectively. Furthermore, for a poset P and a (complete) lower/upper semilattice $\mathcal{L}$ the posets $P \stackrel{*}{\rightarrow} \mathcal{L}$ are (complete) lower/upper subsemiattices of $P \rightarrow \mathcal{L}$, respectively.

Proof. We just prove that $P \stackrel{\leq}{\rightarrow} \mathcal{L}$ is a lower subsemilattice of $P \rightarrow \mathcal{L}$ for a poset P and a lower semilattice $\mathcal{L}$. Recall, that $P \rightarrow \mathcal{L}$ is a special case of a product of semilattices. Suppose f and g are monotone and $x \leq y$. Then we have

$$(f \wedge g)(x) = f(x) \wedge g(x) \leq f(y) \wedge g(y) = (f \wedge g)(y)$$

by the monotonicity of $\wedge$, and, hence, $f \wedge g$ monotone. □

A function f between two lower semilattices $\mathcal{L}_1$ and $\mathcal{L}_2$ fulfilling $f(x \wedge y) = f(x) \wedge f(y)$ is called a *lower semilattice homomorphism. Upper semilattice homomorphisms* are defined dually. Since $x \leq y$ iff $x \wedge y = x$, resp. $x \leq y$ iff $x \vee y = y$, all lower/upper semilattice homomorphisms are monotone.

With respect to antitone functions we call a function f between a lower semilattice $\mathcal{L}_1$ and an upper semilattice $\mathcal{L}_2$ with $f(x \wedge y) = f(x) \vee f(y)$ a *lower co-semilattice homomorphism*. Again, *upper co-semilattice homomorphisms* are defined dually. A similar argument shows that these functions are antitone.

A *complete lower/upper semilattice homomorphism* f between two complete lower/upper semilattices $\mathcal{L}_1$ and $\mathcal{L}_2$ is a function fulfilling

$$f\left(\bigwedge M\right) = \bigwedge_{x\in M} f(x) \quad \text{resp.} \quad f\left(\bigvee M\right) = \bigvee_{x\in M} f(x)$$

for all subsets $M \neq \emptyset$ of $\mathcal{L}_1$. Obviously, every complete lower/upper semilattice homomorphism is a lower/upper semilattice homomorphism. Complete upper semilattice homomorphisms are also called continuous.

Complete lower/upper co-semilattice homomorphisms are defined similarly. They have to fulfill

$$f\left(\bigwedge M\right) = \bigvee_{x\in M} f(x) \quad \text{resp.} \quad f\left(\bigvee M\right) = \bigwedge_{x\in M} f(x).$$

The function f from Figure 2.2 is neither a lower nor an upper semilattice homomorphism since

$$f(\{a\} \cap \{b\}) = f(\emptyset) = 1 \neq 2 = 2 \wedge 3 = f(\{a\} \wedge f(\{b\})$$
$$\text{and } f(\{a\} \cup \{b\}) = f(\{a,b\}) = 4 \neq 3 = 2 \vee 3 = f(\{a\} \vee f(\{b\}).$$

Definition 2.4 *A lattice $\mathcal{L}$ is a poset that is a lower and an upper semilattice. A subset $\mathcal{L}'$ of $\mathcal{L}$ is a called a sublattice of $\mathcal{L}$ iff $\mathcal{L}'$ is a lower and an upper subsemilattice of $\mathcal{L}$.*

Before we define complete lattices we want to prove the following lemma:

Lemma 2.5 *Let $\mathcal{L}$ be a lattice. Then we have the following:*

(1) If $\mathcal{L}$ has a greatest element 1 *and is complete as a lower semilattice, then it is complete as an upper semilattice.*

(2) If $\mathcal{L}$ has a least element 0 *and is complete as an upper semilattice, then it is complete as a lower semilattice.*

Proof. We just prove (1) since (2) is shown dually. Suppose M is a subset of $\mathcal{L}$. Let N be the set of upper bounds of M. Then $N \neq \emptyset$ since $1 \in N$ so that $x := \bigwedge N$ is well-defined. Furthermore, x is an upper bound of M since it is a meet of upper bounds of M. Last but not least, by definition it is the least upper bound of M. □

The previous lemma motivates the following definition of complete lattices:

Definition 2.6 *A lattice $\mathcal{L}$ is called complete iff it is either a complete lower semilattice with a greatest element or a complete upper semilattice with a least element. A subset $\mathcal{L}'$ of $\mathcal{L}$ is called a complete sublattice of $\mathcal{L}$ iff it is a complete lower and a complete upper subsemilattice.*

Notice that complete lattices have a least element 0 and a greatest element 1. They fulfill $0 = \bigwedge \mathcal{L} = \bigvee \emptyset$ and $1 = \bigvee \mathcal{L} = \bigwedge \emptyset$.

The binary operations $\wedge$ and $\vee$ fulfill the following absorption laws:

$$x \wedge (y \vee x) = x \quad \text{and} \quad x \vee (y \wedge x) = x$$

for all x and y. Again, the proof is an easy exercise, and, therefore, omitted.

The standard example of a complete lattice is the powerset $\mathcal{P}(A)$ of a set A with the usual operations $\cap$ and $\cup$. Furthermore, the unit interval $[0,1]$ is also a complete lattice with minimum as meet and maximum as join. The real numbers itself do not constitute a complete lattice since there is no least and greatest element. Nevertheless, they form a lattice.

Theorem 2.7 *Let $\mathcal{L}_i$ for $i \in I$ be (complete) lattices. Then the poset $\prod_{i \in I} \mathcal{L}_i$ is again a (complete) lattice. Furthermore, for a poset P and a (complete) lattice $\mathcal{L}$ the posets $P \overset{*}{\rightarrow} \mathcal{L}$ are (complete) sublattices of $P \rightarrow \mathcal{L}$.*

Again, the proof of the theorem above is omitted.

A *lattice homomorphism* is a function that is a lower and an upper semilattice homomorphism. In the case of completeness the defining equations are also required for $M = \emptyset$, i.e., a *complete lattice homomorphism* is a function $f : \mathcal{L}_1 \rightarrow \mathcal{L}_2$ so that

$$f\left(\bigvee M\right) = \bigvee_{x \in M} f(x), \text{ and } f\left(\bigwedge M\right) = \bigwedge_{x \in M} f(x)$$

for all subsets M of $\mathcal{L}_1$. Notice that we have $f(1) = f(\bigwedge \emptyset) = \bigwedge \emptyset = 1$ and $f(0) = f(\bigvee \emptyset) = \bigvee \emptyset = 0$. Again, every complete lattice homomorphism is a lattice homomorphism.

Later on, complete upper co-semilattice homomorphisms with $f(0) = 1$ will play an important role. As an abbreviation we call them antimorphisms. Notice that we could equivalently extend the defining equation for complete upper co-semilattice homomorphisms to the case $M = \emptyset$ instead of requiring $f(0) = 1$.

Sometimes, we are interested in subsets of complete lattices, which are given as an image of a special class of functions.

Definition 2.8 *Let $f : P \rightarrow P$ be an endofunction on a poset P. Suppose f fulfills*

(monotone)	*f is monotone,*
(idempotent)	*$f(f(x)) = f(x)$ for all $x \in P$.*

Then f is called a closure operation iff $x \leq f(x)$ (extensive), and a kernel or coclosure operation iff $f(x) \leq x$ (contractive) for all $x \in P$.

The following properties are stated for closure operations. By duality, a version of the corresponding properties for kernel operations is obvious.

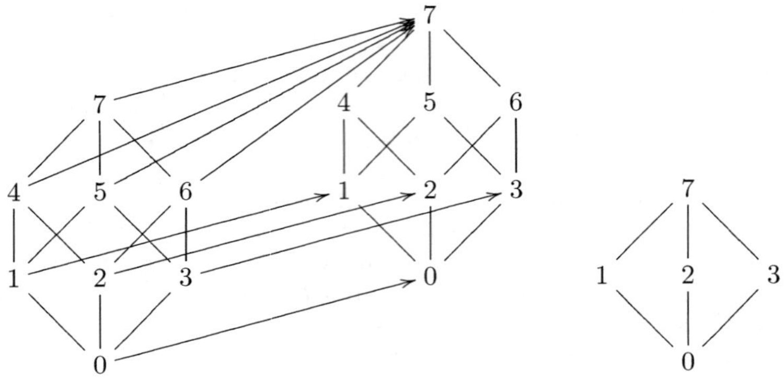

Figure 2.6. A closure operation and the lattice of closed elements.

A closure operation induces a substructure of the given lattice. Figure 2.6 shows a closure operation and the lower subsemilattice of closed elements. Notice that this structure is, in fact, a lattice (cf. Theorem 2.10) but not a sublattice. The join of the elements 1 and 2 in the original lattice is 4 whereas their join among the closed elements is 7.

Lemma 2.9 *Let $\mathcal{L}$ be a complete lattice and f a closure operation. Then $f(\mathcal{L})$ is a complete lower subsemilattice.*

Proof. Let M be a subset of $f(\mathcal{L})$. Then for every $y \in M$ there is an x so that $y = f(x)$. This implies $f(y) = f(f(x)) = f(x) = y$ since f is idempotent. We conclude that

$$\begin{aligned} f\Big(\bigwedge M\Big) &\leq \bigwedge_{x \in M} f(x) && f \text{ is monotone} \\ &= \bigwedge M && \text{computation above} \\ &\leq f\Big(\bigwedge M\Big), && f \text{ extensive} \end{aligned}$$

which shows $f(\bigwedge M) = \bigwedge M$, and, hence, $\bigwedge M \in f(\mathcal{L})$. □

Since f is extensive $1 \in f(\mathcal{L})$. The previous lemma together with Lemma 2.5 imply that $f(\mathcal{L})$ is a complete lattice. The next theorem gives us a little more insight into the structure, i.e., the join operation, of this lattice.

Theorem 2.10 *If $\mathcal{L}$ is a complete lattice and f a closure operation, then the image $f(\mathcal{L})$ of f together with $\wedge$ and $x \mathbin{\dot\vee} y := f(x \vee y)$ is a complete lattice.*

Proof. By Lemma 2.9 it remains to show that $f(\bigvee M)$ is the least upper bound of M in $f(\mathcal{L})$. Since f is monotone it is an upper bound. Suppose y is an element of $f(\mathcal{L})$ and another upper bound of M. Then there is an x with $f(x) = y$, and we have $\bigvee M \leq y$ since $\bigvee M$ is the least upper bound of M in $\mathcal{L}$. We get $f(\bigvee M) \leq f(y) = f(f(x)) = f(x) = y$, and, hence, the assertion. □

Last but not least, we want to prove a lemma about isomorphisms. Some properties of f^{-1} follow from the corresponding properties of f and vice versa. This gives us some flexibility in proving properties of bijective functions.

Lemma 2.11 *Let $\mathcal{L}_1$ and $\mathcal{L}_2$ be (complete) lattices and $f : \mathcal{L}_1 \to \mathcal{L}_2$ a bijection so that*

(1) either f or f^{-1} is a (complete) lower semilattice homomorphism, and

(2) either f or f^{-1} is a (complete) upper semilattice homomorphism.

Then f is an isomorphism.

Proof. We just prove that f^{-1} is an upper semilattice homomorphism implies that f is as well. The other properties are shown analogously. Consider the computation

$$\begin{aligned} f(x \vee y) &= f(f^{-1}(f(x)) \vee f^{-1}(f(y))) && f \text{ bijective} \\ &= f(f^{-1}(f(x) \vee f(y))) && f^{-1} \text{ is an upper semilattice} \\ & && \text{homomorphism} \\ &= f(x) \vee f(y). && f \text{ bijective} \end{aligned}$$

In the case of completeness the assertion is proved similarly. □

2.1 GALOIS CORRESPONDENCES AND RESIDUATED OPERATIONS

We now describe a fundamental construction, which arises from pairs of functions between posets. This notion originates from a revolutionary method introduced by Galois. He related every field extension to a group in order to study properties of the field extension by studying the properties of the related group. We shall have nothing further to say about this connection, called the Galois correspondence. Our attention is devoted to connections between functions in a much broader setting.

Definition 2.12 *Let P_1 and P_2 be posets. A pair of functions $f : P_1 \to P_2$ and $g : P_2 \to P_1$ is called a Galois correspondence between P_1 and P_2 iff*

$$f(x) \leq y \iff x \leq g(y)$$

for all $x \in P_1$ and $y \in P_2$. f is called the lower and g the upper adjoint of the Galois correspondence.

Notice that the definition of a Galois correspondence found in the literature [4] often requires

$$y \leq f(x) \iff x \leq g(y).$$

Our notion is in fact a Galois correspondence between P_1 and the reversed ordering on P_2 in the sense above. Since all Galois correspondences considered in this book are of this special form we use this slightly modified definition.

We will see later that Galois correspondences and resituated operations (cf. Definition 2.16) arise naturally in certain lattices so that we do not provide an explicit example.

Lemma 2.13 *Let P_1 and P_2 be posets and (f, g) a Galois correspondence between P_1 and P_2. Then we have*

(1) $x \leq g(f(x))$ *and* $f(g(y)) \leq y$ *for all* $x \in P_1$ *and* $y \in P_2$,

(2) f *and* g *are monotone,*

(3) $f(x) = f(g(f(x)))$ *and* $g(y) = g(f(g(y)))$ *for all* $x \in P_1$ *and* $y \in P_2$,

(4) $f \circ g$, *i.e., the operation* $x \mapsto g(f(x))$, *is a closure and* $g \circ f$, *i.e., the operation* $x \mapsto f(g(x))$, *is a kernel operation.*

Proof.

(1) By definition $x \leq g(f(x))$ is equivalent to $f(x) \leq f(x)$, and $f(g(y)) \leq y$ is equivalent to $g(y) \leq g(y)$.

(2) Suppose $x_1 \leq x_2$. Then by (1) we have $x_1 \leq x_2 \leq g(f(x_2))$, and, hence, $f(x_1) \leq f(x_2)$. The second assertion is shown analogously.

(3) We just show the first assertion. The inclusion $\geq$ follows from (1), and $\leq$ from (1) and (2).

(4) Again, we just show the first assertion. $f \circ g$ is monotone since f and g are. Furthermore, it is extensive by (1) and idempotent by (3). □

Property (2) can be strengthened if P_1 and P_2 are lattices.

Lemma 2.14 *Let (f, g) be a Galois correspondence between two lattices. Then f is an upper and g a lower semilattice homomorphism.*

Proof. The first assertion follows from

$$\begin{aligned} f(x \vee y) \leq u &\Leftrightarrow x \vee y \leq g(u) && \text{Galois correspondence} \\ &\Leftrightarrow x \leq g(u) \quad \text{and} \quad y \leq g(u) \\ &\Leftrightarrow f(x) \leq u \quad \text{and} \quad f(y) \leq u && \text{Galois correspondence} \\ &\Leftrightarrow f(x) \vee f(y) \leq u, \end{aligned}$$

and the second follows analogously. □

The previous lemma motivates an interesting characterization of Galois correspondences within complete lattices. The corresponding properties provide also necessary and sufficient conditions for the existence of an upper or lower adjoint of a given function.

Theorem 2.15 *Let $\mathcal{L}_1$ and $\mathcal{L}_2$ be complete lattices, and let $f : \mathcal{L}_1 \to \mathcal{L}_2$ and $g : \mathcal{L}_2 \to \mathcal{L}_1$ be functions. Then the following properties are equivalent:*

(1) (f, g) is a Galois correspondence,

(2) f is a complete upper semilattice homomorphism and

$$g(y) = \bigvee\{u \in \mathcal{L}_1 \mid f(u) \leq y\},$$

(3) g is a complete lower semilattice homomorphism and

$$f(x) = \bigwedge\{v \in \mathcal{L}_2 \mid x \leq g(v)\}.$$

Proof. (1)⇒(2): Let M be a subset of $\mathcal{L}_1$. The inclusion $f(\bigvee M) \geq \bigvee_{x \in M} f(x)$ is trivial since f is monotone by Lemma 2.13 (2). Let $u := \bigvee_{x \in M} f(x)$. Then we have $f(y) \leq u$, and, hence, $y \leq g(u)$ for all $y \in M$. This implies $\bigvee M \leq g(u)$, which is equivalent to $f(\bigvee M) \leq \bigvee_{x \in M} f(x)$. The second assertion follows from $\bigvee\{u \in \mathcal{L}_1 \mid f(u) \leq y\} = \bigvee\{u \in \mathcal{L}_1 \mid u \leq g(y)\} = g(y)$.

(2)⇒(1): We have to show

$$f(x) \leq y \quad \Longleftrightarrow \quad x \leq \bigvee\{u \in \mathcal{L}_1 \mid f(u) \leq y\}.$$

Suppose $f(x) \leq y$. Then we immediately conclude that $x \leq \bigvee\{u \in \mathcal{L}_1 \mid f(u) \leq y\}$. On the other hand, $x \leq \bigvee\{u \in \mathcal{L}_1 \mid f(u) \leq y\}$ implies

$$f(x) \leq f\Big(\bigvee\{u \in \mathcal{L}_1 \mid f(u) \leq y\}\Big) = \bigvee\{f(u) \in \mathcal{L}_1 \mid f(u) \leq y\} \leq y$$

since f is an upper semilattice homomorphism.

(1)⇔(3) is shown analogously. □

The notion of a pair of residuated operations is a slight generalization of the notion of a Galois correspondence.

Definition 2.16 *Let P_1, P_2 and P_3 be posets. A triple of functions $f : P_1 \times P_2 \to P_3, g_l : P_3 \times P_2 \to P_1$ and $g_r : P_1 \times P_3 \to P_2$ is called a triple of residuated operations iff*

$$f(u, v) \leq w \quad \Longleftrightarrow \quad u \leq g_l(w, v) \quad \Longleftrightarrow \quad v \leq g_r(u, w)$$

for all $u \in P_1, v \in P_2$ and $w \in P_3$.

Obviously, if f, g_l and g_r constitute a triple of residuated operations, then for $u \in P_1$ and $v \in P_2$ the pair of functions $h_u(x) := f(u, x)$ and $k_u(y) := g_r(u, y)$ resp. $l_v(x) := f(x, v)$ and $m_v(y) := g_l(y, v)$ are Galois correspondences. Therefore, we call f the lower, g_l the upper left and g_r the upper right adjoint of the triple of residuated operations. Furthermore, for all $w \in P_3$ the pair of functions $r_w(x) := g_l(w, x)$ and $s_w(y) := g_r(y, w)$ constitutes a Galois correspondence between P_2 and the reversed order on P_1. These observations give us the following corollary:

Corollary 2.17 *Let P_1, P_2 and P_3 be posets and (f, g_l, g_r) a triple of residuated operations. Then we have*

(1) $v \leq g_r(u, f(u, v))$ and $f(u, g_r(u, w)) \leq w$ for all $u \in P_1, v \in P_2$ and $w \in P_3$,

(2) $u \leq g_l(f(u, v), v)$ and $f(g_l(w, v), v) \leq w$ for all $u \in P_1, v \in P_2$ and $w \in P_3$,

(3) $v \leq g_r(g_l(w, v), w)$ and $u \leq g_l(w, g_r(u, w))$ for all $u \in P_1, v \in P_2$ and $w \in P_3$,

(4) f is monotone in both arguments,

(5) g_l is monotone in the first and antitone in the second argument,

(6) g_r is antitone in the first and monotone in the second argument.

Obviously, there is a version of Lemma 2.14 for residuated operations.

Corollary 2.18 *Let (f, g_l, g_r) be a triple of residuated operations between lattices. Then f is an upper semilattice homomorphism in both arguments, g_l is a lower semilattice homomorphism in the first and an upper co-semilattice homomorphism in the second argument and g_r is an upper co-semilattice homomorphism in the first and a lower semilattice homomorphism in the second argument.*

As above, we obtain an interesting characterization of residuated triples within complete lattices.

Corollary 2.19 *Let $\mathcal{L}_1, \mathcal{L}_2$ and $\mathcal{L}_3$ be complete lattices, and let $f : \mathcal{L}_1 \times \mathcal{L}_2 \to \mathcal{L}_3, g_l : \mathcal{L}_3 \times \mathcal{L}_2 \to \mathcal{L}_1$ and $g_r : \mathcal{L}_1 \times \mathcal{L}_3 \to \mathcal{L}_2$ be functions. Then the following properties are equivalent:*

(1) (f, g_l, g_r) is a triple of residuated operations,

(2) f is a complete upper semilattice homomorphism in both arguments,
$g_l(w, v) = \bigvee\{u \in \mathcal{L}_1 \mid f(u, v) \leq w\}$ *and*
$g_r(u, w) = \bigvee\{v \in \mathcal{L}_2 \mid f(u, v) \leq w\}$,

(3) g_l is a complete lower semilattice homomorphism in the first and a complete upper co-semilattice homomorphism in the second argument,
$f(u, v) = \bigwedge\{w \in \mathcal{L}_3 \mid u \leq g_l(w, v)\}$ *and*
$g_r(u, w) = \bigvee\{v \in \mathcal{L}_2 \mid u \leq g_l(w, v)\}$,

(4) g_r is a complete upper co-semilattice homomorphism in the first and a complete lower semilattice homomorphism in the second argument,
$f(u, v) = \bigwedge\{w \in \mathcal{L}_3 \mid u \leq g_r(u, w)\}$ *and*
$g_l(u, w) = \bigvee\{u \in \mathcal{L}_1 \mid v \leq g_r(u, w)\}$.

If f is commutative, i.e., $P_1 = P_2$ and $f(u, v) = f(v, u)$ for all $u, v \in P_1$, then $g_l(w, v) = g_r(v, w) =: g(v, w)$ and we call g just the upper adjoint.

2.2 DISTRIBUTIVE LATTICES

In the next three chapters, we want to focus on special classes of lattices. The first class we are interested in is the class of distributive lattices. First of all, there is a weak version of distributivity, which is valid in all lattices.

Lemma 2.20 *Let $\mathcal{L}$ be a lattice. Then we have for all elements $u, v, w \in \mathcal{L}$*

(1) $u \wedge (v \vee w) \geq (u \wedge v) \vee (u \wedge w)$,

(2) $u \vee (v \wedge w) \leq (u \vee v) \wedge (u \vee w)$.

Proof. We just prove (1). Obviously, $u \wedge v \leq u$ and $u \wedge v \leq v \leq v \vee w$, and, hence, $u \wedge v \leq u \wedge (v \vee w)$. Analogously, we get $u \wedge w \leq u \wedge (v \vee w)$, which implies the assertion. □

An important class of lattices is defined by the law of distributivity, i.e., where the inequalities of the previous lemma are replaced by equalities.

Lemma 2.21 *In any lattice $\mathcal{L}$, the following identities are equivalent:*

(1) $u \wedge (v \vee w) = (u \wedge v) \vee (u \wedge w)$ *for all* $u, v, w \in \mathcal{L}$,

(2) $u \vee (v \wedge w) = (u \vee v) \wedge (u \vee w)$ *for all* $u, v, w \in \mathcal{L}$.

Proof. We prove that (1) implies (2). The converse implication is shown analogously. For all $u, v, w \in \mathcal{L}$, we have

$$\begin{aligned}
(u \vee v) \wedge (u \vee w) &= ((u \vee v) \wedge u) \vee ((u \vee v) \wedge w) && \text{by (1)} \\
&= u \vee (w \wedge (u \vee v)) && \text{absorption and} \\
& && \text{commutative law} \\
&= u \vee ((w \wedge u) \vee (w \wedge v)) && \text{by (1)} \\
&= (u \vee (w \wedge u)) \vee (w \wedge v) && \text{associative law} \\
&= u \vee (w \wedge v). && \text{absorption law}
\end{aligned}$$

□

It is easy to verify that the identities of the previous lemma do not hold in all lattices.

Definition 2.22 *A lattice $\mathcal{L}$ is called distributive iff Lemma 2.21(1) (or equivalently Lemma 2.21 (2)) holds. A complete lattice is called completely upward-distributive iff it is distributive and* $x \wedge \bigvee M = \bigvee_{y \in M} (x \wedge y)$ *and completely downward-distributive iff it is distributive and* $x \vee \bigwedge M = \bigwedge_{y \in M} (x \vee y)$ *holds for all* $x \in \mathcal{L}$ *and* $M \subseteq \mathcal{L}$. *A completely distributive lattice is a lattice that is completely upward- and downward-distributive.*

Notice that the generalized distribution laws given in the previous definition are not equivalent.

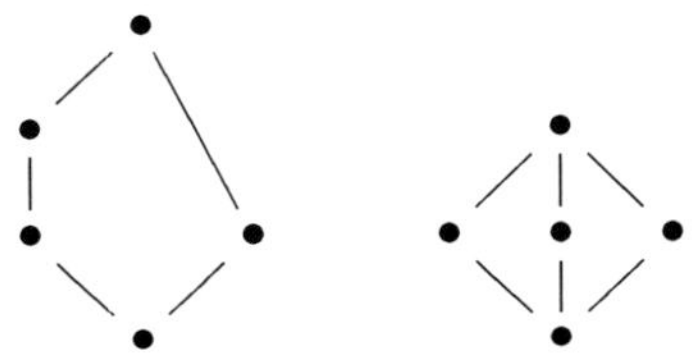

Figure 2.7. Two nondistributive lattices.

Figure 2.7 shows two nondistributive lattices. It can be shown that those lattices actually characterize the class of nondistributive lattices. However, the weak version of distributivity (cf. Lemma 2.20) is valid, of course.

Completely upward-distributive lattices are also called complete Brouwerian lattices or complete Heyting algebras. Usually, Brouwerian lattices or Heyting algebras are defined via relative pseudo-complements. Later on, we will establish the connection between completely upward-distributive and complete Brouwerian lattices. Notice that with a distributive complete lattice we refer to a lattice, which is distributive and complete but neither necessarily completely upward- nor downward-distributive.

The power set of a set as well as the unit interval $[0, 1]$ is a completely distributive lattice.

Theorem 2.23 *Let $\mathcal{L}_i$ for $i \in I$ be (completely upward-/downward-) distributive lattices. Then so is $\prod_{i\in I} \mathcal{L}_i$.*

Again, the proof of the theorem above is an easy exercise, and, therefore, omitted.

Notice that the (complete) sublattices $P \overset{*}{\to} \mathcal{L}$ for a poset P and a (completely upward-/downward-) distributive lattice $\mathcal{L}$ are again (completely upward-/downward-) distributive. This follows immediately from the fact that the required properties are true in $P \to \mathcal{L}$.

2.3 BROUWERIAN LATTICES

Another important class of lattices is motivated by the possibility to use complements or negation, i.e., elements similar to the complement $\overline{A}$ of a set A. First, we want to consider a weak version of relative complements.

Definition 2.24 *Let $\mathcal{L}$ be a lattice and $x, y \in \mathcal{L}$. A relative pseudo-complement $y{:}x$ of x in y is an element so that*

$$u \leq y{:}x \iff x \wedge u \leq y$$

for all $u \in \mathcal{L}$. A lattice in which for every pair of elements the relative pseudo-complement exist is called a Brouwerian lattice or a Heyting algebra.

Notice that $\wedge$ and $:$ induces a triple of residuated operations since $\wedge$ is commutative. Furthermore, any Brouwerian lattice has a greatest element.

Consider $x{:}x$ for an element x. Then $y \leq x{:}x$ iff $x \wedge y \leq x$, which is true for all elements y.

A Brouwerian lattice homomorphism f is a lattice homomorphism between Brouwerian lattices so that $f(y{:}x) = f(y){:}f(x)$ for all x and y.

As mentioned above, completely upward-distributive lattices are also called complete Brouwerian lattices or complete Heyting algebras. The reason for that is given by the next theorem.

Theorem 2.25 *(1) Every Brouwerian lattice is distributive.*

(2) A complete lattice is a Brouwerian lattice iff it is completely upward-distributive.

Proof.

(1) For elements $u, v, w \in \mathcal{L}$ define $x := (u \wedge v) \vee (u \wedge w)$, and consider $x{:}u$. Since $u \wedge v \leq x$ and $u \wedge w \leq x$ we have $v \leq x{:}u$ and $w \leq x{:}u$. We conclude that $u \wedge (v \vee w) \leq u \wedge (x{:}u) \leq x = (u \wedge v) \vee (u \wedge w)$. By Lemma 2.20 the assertion follows immediately.

(2) If $\mathcal{L}$ is a complete Brouwerian lattice, we have

$$u \wedge v \leq w \iff v \leq w{:}u \iff u \leq w{:}v.$$

Therefore, $\wedge$ and $:$ induce a triple of residuated operations. By Corollary 2.19 (1)$\Rightarrow$(2) $\wedge$ is a complete upper semilattice homomorphism, and, hence, $\mathcal{L}$ completely upward-distributive. For the other implication, assume $\wedge$ is a complete upper semilattice homomorphism. Then we define $w{:}u := \bigvee\{v \in \mathcal{L} \mid u \wedge v \leq w\}$. Corollary 2.19 (2)$\Rightarrow$(1) implies the assertion. $\square$

The previous theorem also shows that every finite distributive lattice is actually a Brouwerian lattice. Figure 2.8 gives an example of such a lattice. If we want to compute the relative pseudo-complement of 2 in 1, we have to consider the inclusion $2 \wedge x \leq 1$. Since $2 \wedge 0 = 2 \wedge 1 = 2 \wedge 3 = 0$ and $2 \wedge 2 = 2 \wedge 4 = 2 \wedge 5 = 2 \not\leq 1$ the inclusion is satisfied for the elements from the set $\{0, 1, 3\}$. The join of those elements is 3 so that we obtain $1{:}2 = 3$.

Unfortunately, not every complete lattice homomorphism between complete Brouwerian lattices is a complete Brouwerian lattice homomorphism but we

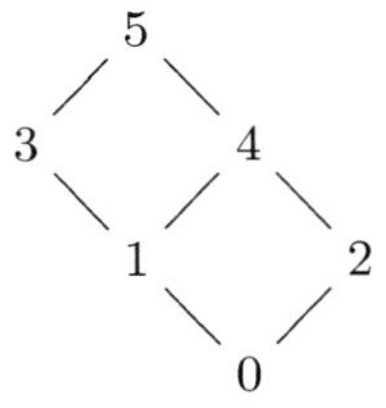

Figure 2.8. A finite distributive lattice.

have

$$
\begin{aligned}
f(y{:}x) &= f\Big(\bigvee\{u \in \mathcal{L}_1 \mid x \wedge u \le y\}\Big) \\
&= \bigvee\{f(u) \mid x \wedge u \le y\}) && f \text{ complete lattice homomorphism} \\
&\le \bigvee\{f(u) \mid f(x) \wedge f(u) \le f(y)\} && f \text{ lower semilattice homomorphism} \\
&= \bigvee\{v \in f(\mathcal{L}_1) \mid f(x) \wedge v \le f(y)\} \\
&\le \bigvee\{v \in \mathcal{L}_2 \mid f(x) \wedge v \le f(y)\} && f(\mathcal{L}_1) \subseteq \mathcal{L}_2 \\
&= f(y){:}f(x).
\end{aligned}
$$

The computation above also shows that if f is bijective, it is indeed a Brouwerian lattice homomorphism. Furthermore, consider the computation

$$
\begin{aligned}
f^{-1}(y{:}x) &= f^{-1}((f(f^{-1}(x))){:}(f(f^{-1}(y))) \\
&= f^{-1}(f(f^{-1}(x){:}f^{-1}(y))) && f \text{ homomorphism} \\
&= f^{-1}(x){:}f^{-1}(y).
\end{aligned}
$$

This implies that the notions of complete lattice isomorphisms and complete Brouwerian lattice isomorphisms are equivalent.

If there is a least element 0, the relative pseudo-complement $0{:}x$ of x in 0 is called the pseudo-complement of x, and denoted by $\neg x$.

Notice that by definition an element x of a Brouwerian lattice is linear iff $\neg x = 0$.

2.4 BOOLEAN ALGEBRAS

The unit interval $[0, 1]$ is a Brouwerian lattice since it is completely upward-distributive. In this lattice we have $\neg x = 0$, and, hence, $x \vee \neg x = x$ for all elements $x \neq 0$. This shows that a Brouwerian lattice need not be complemented, i.e., need not be a Boolean algebra. Another example is the lattice from Figure 2.8. In this lattice we have $\neg 1 = 2$ but $1 \vee \neg 1 = 1 \vee 2 = 4 \neq 5$.

Definition 2.26 *A Brouwerian lattice $\mathcal{L}$ with least element* 0 *and a greatest element* 1 *is called a Boolean algebra iff $x \vee \neg x = 1$ for all elements $x \in \mathcal{L}$. The element $\neg x$ is called the complement of x, and denoted by $\overline{x}$.*

Notice that in a Boolean algebra $y{:}x = \overline{x} \vee y$ since $x \wedge (\overline{x} \vee y) = (x \wedge \overline{x}) \vee (x \wedge y) = x \wedge y \le y$ and $x \wedge u \le y$ implies $u \le \overline{x} \vee u = (\overline{x} \vee x) \wedge (\overline{x} \vee u) = \overline{x} \vee (x \wedge u) \le \overline{x} \vee y$. Furthermore, $\overline{x}$ is the unique element u so that $x \wedge u = 0$ and $x \vee u = 1$ since we have

$$
\begin{aligned}
u &= u \wedge 1 \\
&= u \wedge (\overline{x} \vee x) \\
&= (u \wedge \overline{x}) \vee (u \wedge x) && \text{distributivity} \\
&= (u \wedge \overline{x}) \vee (x \wedge \overline{x}) && x \wedge u = 0 = x \wedge \overline{x} \\
&= (u \vee x) \wedge \overline{x} && \text{distributivity} \\
&= \overline{x}. && x \vee u = 1
\end{aligned}
$$

The set $\mathbb{B}$ of Boolean values with $\mathbf{f} \leq \mathbf{t}$ is a simple example of a (complete) Boolean algebra. Furthermore, the power set of a set A also forms a complete Boolean algebra with $\overline{B}$ as complement of B. Any nontrivial linear ordering, i.e., a poset with more than two elements, is not a Boolean algebra.

Theorem 2.27 (DeMorgan) *In every Boolean algebra $\mathcal{L}$ we have for all elements $x, y \in \mathcal{L}$*

(1) $\overline{x \wedge y} = \overline{x} \vee \overline{y}$,

(2) $\overline{x \vee y} = \overline{x} \wedge \overline{y}$.

Proof. We just prove (1). We immediately conclude that

$$
\begin{aligned}
(x \wedge y) \wedge (\overline{x} \vee \overline{y}) &= (x \wedge y \wedge \overline{x}) \vee (x \wedge y \wedge \overline{y}) && \text{distributivity} \\
&= 0, \\
(x \wedge y) \vee (\overline{x} \vee \overline{y}) &= (x \vee \overline{x} \vee \overline{y}) \wedge (y \vee \overline{x} \vee \overline{y}) && \text{distributivity} \\
&= 1,
\end{aligned}
$$

and, hence, the assertion. □

As mentioned above, the Boolean algebra of a power set of a set A is completely distributive. This is an application of the following theorem:

Theorem 2.28 *Every complete Boolean algebra is completely distributive.*

Proof. Suppose $\mathcal{L}$ is a complete Boolean algebra. By Theorem 2.25 (2) it remains to show that $x \vee \bigwedge M = \bigwedge_{y \in M} (x \vee y)$ for all $x \in \mathcal{L}$ and $M \subseteq \mathcal{L}$. Since $\vee$ is monotone the inclusion $\leq$ is trivial. Let $u := \bigwedge_{y \in M} (x \vee y)$. Then we have $u \leq x \vee y$ for all $y \in M$. This implies

$$
\begin{aligned}
u \wedge \overline{x} &\leq (x \vee y) \wedge \overline{x} \\
&= (x \wedge \overline{x}) \vee (y \wedge \overline{x}) && \text{distributivity} \\
&= y \wedge \overline{x} \\
&\leq y.
\end{aligned}
$$

We conclude that $u \wedge \overline{x} \leq \bigwedge M$, and, hence,

$$\begin{aligned} u &\leq x \vee u \\ &= (x \vee u) \wedge (x \vee \overline{x}) \\ &= x \vee (u \wedge \overline{x}) && \text{distributivity} \\ &\leq x \vee \bigwedge M. \end{aligned}$$

□

Now, Theorem 2.27 may be generalized for complete Boolean algebras.

Theorem 2.29 (DeMorgan) *In every complete Boolean algebra $\mathcal{L}$ we have for all subsets $M \subseteq \mathcal{L}$*

(1) $\overline{\bigwedge M} = \bigvee_{x \in M} \overline{x}$,

(2) $\overline{\bigvee M} = \bigwedge_{x \in M} \overline{x}$.

In the proof of Theorem 2.27 the distribution laws are essential. The theorem above may be shown analogously using the generalized distribution laws.

2.5 SPECIAL ELEMENTS

The prime numbers are of special interest within the natural numbers. They are characterized by the fact that they cannot be generated by other elements using the binary operation of multiplication. In a lattice we may have an analogous situation.

Definition 2.30 *An element $x \neq 0$ of a lattice $\mathcal{L}$ with least element 0 is called irreducible iff $y \vee z = x$ implies $x = y$ or $x = z$.*

Consider again the lattice from Figure 2.8. The irreducible elements are given by $\{1, 2, 3\}$. The elements 4 is not irreducible since $4 = 1 \vee 2$.

In a complete lattice we may switch to a more restricted notion of irreducibility.

Definition 2.31 *An element x of a complete lattice $\mathcal{L}$ is called completely irreducible iff for all subsets of $M \subseteq \mathcal{L}$ the property $\bigvee M = x$ implies $x \in M$.*

Notice that 0 is not completely irreducible since $0 = \bigvee \emptyset$. Furthermore, every completely irreducible element is irreducible but not vice versa. The element 1 of the unit interval $[0, 1]$ is irreducible since if 1 is the maximum of two elements x and y, then 1 is either x or y. On the other hand, 1 is not included in the set $\{1 - \frac{1}{n} \mid n \in \mathbb{N} \setminus \{0\}\} \subseteq [0, 1]$, but it is its least upper bound.

Definition 2.32 *An element $a \neq 0$ of a lattice $\mathcal{L}$ with least element 0 is called an atom of $\mathcal{L}$ iff $x \leq a$ implies $x = a$ or $x = 0$. The set of all atoms of*

$\mathcal{L}$ is denoted by $\mathrm{At}(\mathcal{L})$. *Furthermore, a complete lattice is called atomic iff* $x = \bigvee\{a \in \mathrm{At}(\mathcal{L}) \mid a \leq x\}$ *holds for all* $x \in \mathcal{L}$.

In the power set of a set A the singleton sets $\{x\}$ with $x \in A$ are the atoms. Furthermore, every upper neighbor of 0, i.e., every element x so that $x \neq 0$, and there is no element $y \neq 0$ and $y \neq x$ with $0 \leq y \leq x$, is an atom. Therefore, every finite lattice with at least two elements has at least one atom.

Obviously, every atom is completely irreducible but not vice versa. Let $\mathbb{N}^\infty$ be the complete linear lattice of natural numbers with an additional greatest element ∞. Then all elements except 0 and ∞ are completely irreducible, but 1 is the unique atom of $\mathbb{N}^\infty$. Nevertheless, the observation above implies that every finite lattice has at least one completely irreducible element.

2.6 FIXED POINTS

We will describe several operations on lattices using fixed points of suitable endofunctions. Furthermore, later on we will use an induction principle to conclude properties of such fixed points, called the principle of fixed point induction.

The proof of the existence of a fixed point given in this chapter is somewhat more complex than the usual one. The reason is that we obtain the principle of fixed point induction as an application of the notions to be introduced.

Definition 2.33 *Let* $f : P \to P$ *be an endofunction on a poset* P *and* $a \in P$. *Then an element* $\mu_f(a) \in P$ *is called the least fixed point of* f *greater or equal to* a *iff* $f(\mu_f(a)) = \mu_f(a)$ *and for all elements* $b \in P$ *the properties* $f(b) = b$ *and* $a \leq b$ *imply* $\mu_f(a) \leq b$.

$\mu_f(a)$ does not exist in general. Therefore, in the rest of this section we suppose that $\mathcal{L}$ is a complete lattice, $f : \mathcal{L} \to \mathcal{L}$ is a monotone endofunction, and a is an element of $\mathcal{L}$ with $a \leq f(a)$.

Definition 2.34 *A subset* M *of* $\mathcal{L}$ *is called an* f, a*-closed set iff*

(1) $a \in M$,

(2) if $x \in M$, *then so is* $f(x)$,

(3) if $\emptyset \neq N \subseteq M$, *then* $\bigvee N \in M$.

Obviously, $\mathcal{L}$ is an f, a-closed set.

Lemma 2.35 *The intersection of* f, a*-closed sets is again* f, a*-closed.*

Proof. Suppose $\mathcal{X}$ is a set of f, a-closed sets. Then we obtain the following:

(1) $a \in \bigcap \mathcal{X}$ since a is in every element of $\mathcal{X}$.

(2) If $x \in \bigcap \mathcal{X}$, then $x \in M$ for all $M \in \mathcal{X}$, which implies $f(x) \in M$ for all M, and, hence, $f(x) \in \bigcap \mathcal{X}$.

(3) Suppose $\emptyset \neq N \subseteq \bigcap \mathcal{X}$. Then $\emptyset \neq N \subseteq M$ for all $M \in \mathcal{X}$. This implies $\bigvee N \in M$, and, hence, $\bigvee N \in \bigcap \mathcal{X}$.

The computation above shows that $\bigcap \mathcal{X}$ is f, a-closed. □

Now, let $X_{f,a} := \bigcap\{M \mid M \text{ is } f, a\text{-closed}\}$. From the previous lemma we conclude that $X_{f,a}$ is f, a-closed.

Theorem 2.36 (Fixed point Theorem) *Let $\mathcal{L}$ be a complete lattice, $f : \mathcal{L} \to \mathcal{L}$ a monotone endofunction and a an element of $\mathcal{L}$ with $a \leq f(a)$. Then $\mu_f(a)$ exists, and we have $\mu_f(a) = \bigvee X_{f,a}$.*

Proof. Let $c := \bigvee X_{f,a}$ and $E := \{x \mid x \leq f(x) \text{ and } a \leq x\}$. We want to show that E is f, a-closed.

(1) $a \in E$ since $a \leq a$ and $a \leq f(a)$ by the assumption.

(2) Suppose $x \in E$. Then we have $f(x) \leq f(f(x))$ and $a \leq f(a) \leq f(x)$ since f is monotone.

(3) If $\emptyset \neq N \subseteq E$, then $a \leq \bigvee N$ is trivial, and we have

$$\begin{aligned} \bigvee N &\leq \bigvee_{y \in N} f(y) && \text{since } y \in E \\ &\leq f\Big(\bigvee N\Big). && f \text{ monotone} \end{aligned}$$

We conclude $X_{f,a} \subseteq E$, and, hence, $c \in E$, which implies $c \leq f(c)$. Since $f(c)$ is an element of $X_{f,a}$ and $c = \bigvee X_{f,a}$ we get $f(c) \leq c$, and, hence, that c is a fixed point of f greater or equal to a. It remains to show that c is indeed the least fixed point with that property.

Suppose b is another fixed point of f greater or equal to a. Let $B := \{x \mid a \leq x \leq b\}$. Again, we want to show that B is f, a-closed.

(1) $a \in B$ is trivial.

(2) If $x \in B$, then $a \leq f(a) \leq f(x) \leq f(b) = b$ since f is monotone and b is a fixed point of f.

(3) Suppose $\emptyset \neq N \subseteq B$. Then $a \leq \bigvee N \leq b$, and, hence, $\bigvee N \in B$.

We conclude that $X_{f,a} \subseteq B$, and, hence, $c \in B$, which is equivalent to $c \leq b$. □

As mentioned above, we are interested in an induction principle in order to prove properties of $\mu_f(a)$. Unfortunately, the principle of fixed point induction is not valid for arbitrary predicates.

Definition 2.37 *A predicate $\mathfrak{P}$ on a complete lattice $\mathcal{L}$ is called admissible (or continuous) iff for every nonempty set $M \subseteq \mathcal{L}$ the property $\mathfrak{P}(x)$ for all $x \in M$ implies $\mathfrak{P}(\bigvee M)$.*

Notice that we may use n-ary predicates by taking the n-ary product of the underlying lattices.

Theorem 2.38 (Fixed point Induction) *Let $\mathcal{L}$ be a complete lattice, $f : \mathcal{L} \to \mathcal{L}$ a monotone endofunction, a an element of $\mathcal{L}$ with $a \leq f(a)$, and $\mathfrak{P}$ be an admissible predicate on $\mathcal{L}$. Then the properties*

Base case: *$\mathfrak{P}(a)$,*

Induction step: *$\mathfrak{P}(b)$ implies $\mathfrak{P}(f(b))$ for all $b \in \mathcal{L}$,*

imply $\mathfrak{P}(\mu_f(a))$.

Proof. Let $M_{\mathfrak{P}} := \{x \mid \mathfrak{P}(x)\}$. Then $M_{\mathfrak{P}}$ is an f, a-closed set since property (1) corresponds to the base case, (2) to the induction step, and (3) to the continuity of $\mathfrak{P}$. We conclude $X_{f,a} \subseteq M_{\mathfrak{P}}$, and, hence, $\mu_f(a) \in M_{\mathfrak{P}}$. □

Notice that the principle of fixed point induction is equivalent to a special case of transfinite induction on the class of ordinal numbers. Since we did not introduce ordinal numbers we just want to sketch this connection. For a monotone endofunction f on a complete lattice $\mathcal{L}$ and an element a with $a \leq f(a)$ one may define

$$\begin{aligned} f^0(a) &:= a, \\ f^{x+1}(a) &:= f(f^x(a)) && \text{for successor ordinals } x+1, \\ f^y(a) &:= \bigvee_{x<y} f^x(a) && \text{for limiting ordinals } y. \end{aligned}$$

Since the class of ordinals is not a set but $\mathcal{L}$ is, it can be shown that there is a least ordinal u with $f^u(a) = f^{u+1}(a)$, which implies that $f^u(a)$ is the least fixed point of f greater or equal to a. Now, the principle of fixed point induction states that $\mathfrak{P}$ holds for $f^x(a)$ for all ordinals x, and, hence, for that least fixed point. The base case and the induction step of the fixed point induction are exactly the base case and the induction step for successor ordinals of the transfinite induction. The property of being admissible implies the induction step for limiting ordinals.

2.7 THE COMPLETE BROUWERIAN LATTICE OF ANTIMORPHISMS

Later on, we will see that antimorphisms play an important role within our approach to fuzzy theory. In this chapter, we want to study the structure of the set of antimorphisms $\mathcal{L}_1 \overset{\text{anti}}{\to} \mathcal{L}_2$ between two complete lattices.

Given an element $u \in \mathcal{L}_2$ we will identify u with the constant function $u : \mathcal{L}_1 \to \mathcal{L}_2$ defined by $u(x) := u$ for all $x \in \mathcal{L}_1$. This function is antitone, but in general not an antimorphism. Therefore, the quasi constant antimorphism induced by u is defined by

$$\dot{u}(x) = \begin{cases} 1 \text{ iff } x = 0, \\ u \text{ iff } x \neq 0. \end{cases}$$

The set of all antimorphisms $\mathcal{L}_1 \overset{\text{anti}}{\to} \mathcal{L}_2$ need not be a (complete) sublattice of $\mathcal{L}_1 \to \mathcal{L}_2$ or $\mathcal{L}_1 \overset{\geq}{\to} \mathcal{L}_2$. Nevertheless, it contains the greatest function $\dot{1}$.

Lemma 2.39 *The meet of a set of antimorphisms is again an antimorphism.*

Proof. The assertion follows immediately from the following computation:

$$\begin{aligned}
\Big(\bigwedge_{i\in I} f_i\Big)\Big(\bigvee M\Big) &= \bigwedge_{i\in I} f_i\Big(\bigvee M\Big) && \text{definition of } \wedge \text{ for functions}\\
&= \bigwedge_{i\in I}\bigwedge_{x\in M} f_i(x) && f_i \text{ antimorphism}\\
&= \bigwedge_{x\in M}\bigwedge_{i\in I} f_i(x) &&\\
&= \bigwedge_{x\in M}\Big(\bigwedge_{i\in I} f_i\Big)(x). && \text{definition of } \wedge \text{ for functions} \quad \square
\end{aligned}$$

The previous lemma induces the following closure operation:

$$\tau(f) := \bigwedge\{h \mid f \leq h \text{ and } h \text{ antimorphism}\}.$$

Notice that the antimorphism closure $\tau(u)$ of the constant function u is equal to $\dot{u}$. This follows from $\dot{u}(\bigvee\emptyset) = \dot{u}(0) = 1 = \bigwedge\emptyset$ and $M \setminus \{0\} \neq \emptyset$ implies

$$\bigwedge_{x\in M} \dot{u}(x) = \bigwedge_{x\in M\setminus\{0\}} \dot{u}(x) = \bigwedge_{x\in M\setminus\{0\}} u(x) = u = u\Big(\bigvee M\setminus\{0\}\Big) = \dot{u}\Big(\bigvee M\Big).$$

Lemma 2.40 *Let $\mathcal{L}_1$ and $\mathcal{L}_2$ be complete lattices. Then τ is a closure operation on $\mathcal{L}_1 \to \mathcal{L}_2$ so that the image of τ is the set of antimorphisms $\mathcal{L}_1 \overset{\text{anti}}{\to} \mathcal{L}_2$.*

Proof. First of all, by Lemma 2.39 $\tau(f)$ is an antimorphism for every function f. On the other hand, any antimorphism g is greater or equal to itself so that $\tau(g) = g$ follows. Now, we want to show the three properties of a closure operation.

(1) Suppose $f \leq g$. Then the set $\{h \mid g \leq h \text{ and } h \text{ antimorphism}\}$ is a subset of $\{h \mid f \leq h \text{ and } h \text{ antimorphism}\}$, which implies $\tau(f) \leq \tau(g)$.

(2) τ is extensive since any element of $\{h \mid f \leq h \text{ and } h \text{ antimorphism}\}$, and, hence, its meet is greater or equal to f.

(3) We have already shown that $\tau(g) = g$ for all antimorphisms g so that $\tau(\tau(f)) = \tau(f)$ follows. □

Now, by Theorem 2.10, we may establish the fact that $\mathcal{L}_1 \overset{\text{anti}}{\to} \mathcal{L}_2$ is indeed a complete lattice. In the rest of this chapter, we want to show that it is a complete Brouwerian lattice if $\mathcal{L}_1$ and $\mathcal{L}_2$ are.

Corollary 2.41 *Let $\mathcal{L}_1$ and $\mathcal{L}_2$ be complete lattices. Then the set $\mathcal{L}_1 \overset{\text{anti}}{\to} \mathcal{L}_2$ together with meet and join $f \curlyvee g := \tau(f \vee g)$ is again a complete lattice.*

Unfortunately, the definition of τ gives us no information about the image of $\tau(f)$ for a given value $x \in \mathcal{L}_1$. Therefore, consider the following operation:

$$\varphi(f)(x) := \bigvee_{\substack{M \subseteq \mathcal{L}_1 \\ \bigvee M = x}} \bigwedge_{y \in M} f(y).$$

We will show that $\tau(f)$ is indeed the least fixed point $\mu_\varphi(f)$ of φ greater or equal to f in the complete lattice of antitone function from $\mathcal{L}_1$ to $\mathcal{L}_2$. Then we may prove properties of τ by using φ and the principle of fixed point induction.

Later on, we will use a slightly modified definition of φ.

Lemma 2.42 *Let $\mathcal{L}_1$ be a complete Brouwerian lattice, $\mathcal{L}_2$ a complete lattice and $f : \mathcal{L}_1 \to \mathcal{L}_2$ be antitone. Then we have*

$$\varphi(f)(x) = \bigvee_{\substack{M \subseteq \mathcal{L}_1 \\ \bigvee M \geq x}} \bigwedge_{y \in M} f(y).$$

Proof. The inclusion $\leq$ is trivial. Suppose M is a subset of $\mathcal{L}_1$ so that $\bigvee M \geq x$. Then define $M_x := \{x \wedge y \mid y \in M\}$ and conclude that

$$\bigvee M_x = \bigvee_{y \in M} (x \wedge y) = x \wedge \bigvee M = x$$

since $\mathcal{L}_1$ is a complete Brouwerian lattice. Furthermore, $x \wedge y \leq y$, and, hence, $f(y) \leq f(x \wedge y)$. This implies $\bigwedge_{y \in M} f(y) \leq \bigwedge_{z \in M_x} f(z)$, and, hence,

$$\bigvee_{\bigvee M \geq x} \bigwedge_{y \in M} f(y) \leq \bigvee_{\bigvee M = x} \bigwedge_{y \in M} f(y) = \varphi(f)(x). \qquad \square$$

In the next lemma we have summarized some basic properties of φ.

Lemma 2.43 *(1) φ is monotone on $\mathcal{L}_1 \to \mathcal{L}_2$.*

(2) $f \leq \varphi(f)$ for all $f \in \mathcal{L}_1 \to \mathcal{L}_2$.

(3) If f is an antimorphism, then $\varphi(f) = f$.

Proof.

(1) Suppose $f \leq g$. Then we have $f(y) \leq g(y)$ for all $y \in \mathcal{L}_1$, which implies $\bigwedge_{y \in M} f(y) \leq \bigwedge_{y \in M} g(y)$ for all subsets M of $\mathcal{L}_1$. We obtain $\bigvee_{\bigvee M = x} \bigwedge_{y \in M} f(y) \leq \bigvee_{\bigvee M = x} \bigwedge_{y \in M} g(y)$, and, hence, $\varphi(f) \leq \varphi(g)$.

(2) We immediately conclude that

$$f(x) = \bigwedge_{y \in \{x\}} f(y) \leq \bigvee_{\bigvee M = x} \bigwedge_{y \in M} f(y) = \varphi(f)(x).$$

(3) The assertion follows from

$$\begin{aligned}
\varphi(f)(x) &= \bigvee_{\bigvee M = x} \bigwedge_{y \in M} f(y) \\
&= \bigvee_{\bigvee M = x} f\left(\bigvee M\right) && f \text{ is an antimorphism} \\
&= \bigvee_{\bigvee M = x} f(x) && \bigvee M = x \\
&= f(x).
\end{aligned}$$

□

The previous lemma implies that for every f there is a least fixed point $\mu_\varphi(f)$ of φ greater or equal to f.

Lemma 2.44 *Let $\mathcal{L}_1$ be a complete Brouwerian lattice and $\mathcal{L}_2$ a complete lattice. Then f is antitone implies $\varphi(f)$ is antitone and $\mu_\varphi(f)$ is an antimorphism.*

Proof. Suppose $x \leq y$ and M is a subset of $\mathcal{L}_1$ so that $\bigvee M = y$. Consider the set $M_x := \{x \wedge u \mid u \in M\}$. Then we have

$$\bigvee M_x = \bigvee_{u \in M} (x \wedge u) = x \wedge \bigvee M = x \wedge y = x$$

since $\mathcal{L}_1$ is a Brouwerian lattice. Furthermore, for every $u \in M$ we have $f(u) \leq f(u \wedge x)$ since f is antitone, and, hence, $\bigwedge_{u \in M} f(u) \leq \bigwedge_{v \in M_x} f(v)$. Now, we get the first assertion from

$$\begin{aligned}
\varphi(f)(y) &= \bigvee_{\bigvee M = y} \bigwedge_{u \in M} f(u) \\
&\leq \bigvee_{\bigvee M = y} \bigwedge_{v \in M_x} f(v) && \text{computation above} \\
&\leq \bigvee_{\bigvee N = x} \bigwedge_{v \in N} f(v) \\
&= \varphi(f)(x).
\end{aligned}$$

Now, let $\mathfrak{P}$ be the predicate of being antitone, i.e.,

$$\mathfrak{P}(g) \quad :\Leftrightarrow \quad \forall x, y \in \mathcal{L}_1 : \; x \leq y \Rightarrow g(y) \leq g(x).$$

This predicate is admissible since $\mathfrak{P}(g_i)$ for all $i \in I$ implies $\bigvee_{i \in I} g_i(y) \leq \bigvee_{i \in I} g_i(x)$ for all $x, y \in \mathcal{L}_1$ with $x \leq y$, and, hence, $\mathfrak{P}(\bigvee_{i \in I} g_i)$.

The base case $\mathfrak{P}(f)$ is trivial since f is antitone. Suppose $\mathfrak{P}(g)$, i.e., g is antitone. As shown above, we conclude that $\varphi(g)$ is antitone, and, hence, $\mathfrak{P}(\varphi(g))$. The principle of fixed point induction shows that $\mu_\varphi(f)$ is antitone.

It remains to show that $\mu_\varphi(f)$ is an antimorphism. Since $\mu_\varphi(f)$ is antitone we conclude that $\mu_\varphi(f)(\bigvee N) \leq \bigwedge_{y \in N} \mu_\varphi(f)(y)$. The other inclusion follows from

$$\begin{aligned}
\mu_\varphi(f)\Big(\bigvee N\Big) &= \varphi(\mu_\varphi(f))\Big(\bigvee N\Big) && \mu_\varphi(f) \text{ is a fixed point} \\
&= \bigvee_{\bigvee M = \bigvee N} \bigwedge_{y \in M} \mu_\varphi(f)(y) \\
&\geq \bigwedge_{y \in N} \mu_\varphi(f)(y).
\end{aligned}$$

□

Now, we are ready to establish the connection between φ and τ.

Theorem 2.45 *Let $\mathcal{L}_1$ be a complete Brouwerian lattice, $\mathcal{L}_2$ a complete lattice, and $f : \mathcal{L}_1 \to \mathcal{L}_2$ be antitone. Then we have $\tau(f) = \mu_\varphi(f)$.*

Proof. Since $\tau(f)$ is an antimorphism it is also a fixed point of φ by Lemma 2.43 (3). Furthermore, $\tau(f)$ is greater or equal to f. This implies $\mu_\varphi(f) \leq \tau(f)$ since $\mu_\varphi(f)$ is the least fixed point of φ greater or equal to f. The other inclusion follows immediately from the fact that $\mu_\varphi(f)$ is an antimorphism by Lemma 2.44 and $f \leq \mu_\varphi(f)$ since $\tau(f)$ is the least antimorphism greater or equal to f. □

As mentioned above, by Theorem 2.45 we may use the principle of fixed point induction in order to prove properties of τ on the subset of antitone functions. As a first example we obtain the next lemma.

Lemma 2.46 *Let $\mathcal{L}_1$ and $\mathcal{L}_2$ be complete Brouwerian lattices, and $f, g : \mathcal{L}_1 \xrightarrow{\geq} \mathcal{L}_2$. Then we have the following:*

(1) $\tau(f) \wedge g \leq \tau(f \wedge g)$,

(2) $\tau(f) \wedge \tau(g) = \tau(f \wedge g)$.

Proof.

(1) We prove the assertion by fixed point induction. Therefore, we define the following predicate:

$$\mathfrak{P}(h, k) \quad :\Leftrightarrow \quad h \wedge g \leq k.$$

Suppose $\{(h_i, k_i) \mid i \in I\}$ is a set so that $\mathfrak{P}(h_i, k_i)$, and, hence, $h_i \wedge g \leq k_i$ holds for all $i \in I$. Then we conclude that $\bigvee_{i \in I} (h_i \wedge g) \leq \bigvee_{i \in I} k_i$. Since $\mathcal{L}_1 \rightarrow \mathcal{L}_2$ is a complete Brouwerian lattice by Theorem 2.23 we have $(\bigvee_{i \in I} h_i) \wedge g \leq \bigvee_{i \in I} k_i$, and, hence, $\mathfrak{P}(\bigvee_{i \in I} h_i, \bigvee_{i \in I} k_i)$.

The base case of the fixed point induction is trivial since $\mathfrak{P}(f, f \wedge g)$ holds. Now, suppose $\mathfrak{P}(h, k)$. Then we conclude that

$$\begin{aligned}
(\varphi(h) \wedge g)(x) &= \varphi(h)(x) \wedge g(x) && \text{definition of } \wedge \\
&= \left(\bigvee_{\bigvee M = x} \bigwedge_{y \in M} h(y) \right) \wedge g(x) \\
&= \bigvee_{\bigvee M = x} \bigwedge_{y \in M} (h(y) \wedge g(x)) && \mathcal{L}_1 \rightarrow \mathcal{L}_2 \text{ is a complete Brouwerian lattice} \\
&\leq \bigvee_{\bigvee M = x} \bigwedge_{y \in M} (h(y) \wedge g(y)) && g \text{ is antitone and } y \leq x \\
&= \bigvee_{\bigvee M = x} \bigwedge_{y \in M} (h \wedge g)(y) \\
&\leq \bigvee_{\bigvee M = x} \bigwedge_{y \in M} k(y) && \text{induction hypothesis} \\
&= \varphi(k)(x),
\end{aligned}$$

and, hence, $\mathfrak{P}(\varphi(h), \varphi(k))$. By the principle of fixed point induction we get

$$\mathfrak{P}(\mu_\varphi(f), \mu_\varphi(f \wedge g)) \quad \Leftrightarrow \quad \tau(f) \wedge g \leq \tau(f \wedge g).$$

(2) The inclusion $\tau(f \wedge g) \leq \tau(f) \wedge \tau(g)$ is trivial since τ is monotone. The other inclusion follows from

$$\begin{aligned}
\tau(f) \wedge \tau(g) &\leq \tau(f \wedge \tau(g)) && \text{by (1)} \\
&\leq \tau^2(f \wedge g) && \text{by (1)} \\
&= \tau(f \wedge g).
\end{aligned}$$

□

We aim at the following theorem:

Theorem 2.47 *Let $\mathcal{L}_1$ and $\mathcal{L}_2$ be complete Brouwerian lattices. Then $\mathcal{L}_1 \overset{\text{anti}}{\rightarrow} \mathcal{L}_2$ is again a complete Brouwerian lattice.*

Proof. By Theorem 2.25 (2) and Corollary 2.41 it is sufficient to show that

(1) $(f \wedge g) \veebar h = (f \veebar h) \wedge (g \veebar h)$ for all antimorphisms f, g, h,

(2) $f \wedge \dot{\bigvee}_{i\in I} g_i = \dot{\bigvee}_{i\in I} (f \wedge g_i)$ for all $i \in I$ and $f, g_i : \mathcal{L}_1 \overset{\text{anti}}{\to} \mathcal{L}_2$.

The first assertion follows from

$$\begin{aligned}
(f \wedge g) \dot{\vee} h &= \tau((f \wedge g) \vee h) \\
&= \tau((f \vee h) \wedge (g \vee h)) && \mathcal{L}_1 \to \mathcal{L}_2 \text{ is distributive} \\
&= \tau(f \vee h) \wedge \tau(g \vee h) && \text{Lemma 2.46 (2)} \\
&= (f \dot{\vee} h) \wedge (g \dot{\vee} h)
\end{aligned}$$

and the second from

$$\begin{aligned}
f \wedge \dot{\bigvee}_{i\in I} g_i &= f \wedge \tau\Big(\bigvee_{i\in I} g_i\Big) \\
&= \tau\Big(f \wedge \bigvee_{i\in I} g_i\Big) && \text{Lemma 2.46(2) since } \tau(f) = f \\
&= \tau\Big(\bigvee_{i\in I} (f \wedge g_i)\Big) && \mathcal{L}_1 \to \mathcal{L}_2 \text{ is a complete Brouwerian lattice} \\
&= \dot{\bigvee}_{i\in I} (f \wedge g_i).
\end{aligned}$$

□

2.8 FILTERS

We may use the φ operation and the principle of fixed point induction in order to prove properties of τ. But, in general, we are not able to compute $\tau(f)(x)$ for a given x explicitly. Unfortunately, later on we will need this value in connection with validity of equations within crisp and noncrisp relations.

If x is completely irreducible, we obtain

$$\varphi(f)(x) = \bigvee_{\bigvee M = x} \bigwedge_{y \in M} f(y) = f(x)$$

for all antitone f since $x \in M$ for all sets M with $\bigvee M = x$. A simple verification shows[2] that this implies $\tau(f)(x) = \mu_\varphi(f)(x) = f(x)$, and, hence, that the problem mentioned above is trivial for completely irreducible elements. In other words, if x is completely irreducible, we are able to compute $\tau(f)(x)$ explicitly since the result is $f(x)$. Unfortunately, there are complete Brouwerian lattices without such elements.

In this chapter, we focus on the problem to find for some given complete Brouwerian lattice $\mathcal{L}$ a suitable complete Brouwerian lattice $\mathcal{L}'$ with at least one completely irreducible element so that for all complete lattices $\mathcal{L}''$ the τ operation on $\mathcal{L}' \overset{\geq}{\to} \mathcal{L}''$ is a canonical extension of the τ operation on $\mathcal{L} \overset{\geq}{\to} \mathcal{L}''$.

[2]This property is shown by fixed point induction using the predicate $\mathfrak{P}(g) :\Leftrightarrow g(x) = f(x)$.

The question arises what is a canonical extension, i.e., which property should be satisfied. Let ϑ be the mapping from $\mathcal{L} \overset{\geq}{\to} \mathcal{L}''$ to $\mathcal{L}' \overset{\geq}{\to} \mathcal{L}''$. Then the following property:

$$\text{(ext)} \qquad \tau(\vartheta(\tau(f))) = \tau(\vartheta(f))$$

will be suitable. It allows us to compute the value of the image of the antimorphism closure of f within $\mathcal{L}' \overset{\geq}{\to} \mathcal{L}''$ by using just the image of f and the corresponding τ operation. Then we may conclude that $\tau(\vartheta(\tau(f)))(x) = \tau(\vartheta(f))(x) = \vartheta(f)(x)$ for all completely irreducible elements in $\mathcal{L}'$. Notice that τ on the left-hand side of (ext) refers to two different τ operations, namely the outer one to the operation on $\mathcal{L}' \overset{\geq}{\to} \mathcal{L}''$ and the inner one to that on $\mathcal{L} \overset{\geq}{\to} \mathcal{L}''$.

Unfortunately, the usual embedding of $\mathcal{L}$ into the power set of all prime filters does not work. This embedding is not necessarily (upward) continuous so that the least upper bound of a subset $M \subseteq \mathcal{L}$ and the union of the image of M need not coincide. As a consequence, φ resp. τ on $\mathcal{L}' \overset{\geq}{\to} \mathcal{L}''$ is not a canonical extension of φ resp. τ for $\mathcal{L} \overset{\geq}{\to} \mathcal{L}''$ in the sense mentioned above. We have to switch to the special class of complete prime filters.

Definition 2.48 *A subset F of a lattice $\mathcal{L}$ is called a filter of $\mathcal{L}$ iff the following properties hold:*

(1) If $x \in F$ and $y \in F$, then $x \wedge y \in F$,

(2) If $x \in F$ and $y \in \mathcal{L}$, then $x \vee y \in F$.

In the next lemma we give an alternative definition of a filter, which is useful to compare the notion of a filter with the notions given later.

Lemma 2.49 *A subset F of a lattice $\mathcal{L}$ is a filter iff*

(1) $x \in F$ and $y \in F$ iff $x \wedge y \in F$,

(2) If $x \in F$ or $y \in F$, then $x \vee y \in F$.

Proof. Obviously, every set fulfilling (1) and (2) is a filter. Now, suppose F is a filter and $x \wedge y \in F$. By property (2) of a filter we have $x = x \vee (x \wedge y) \in F$ and $y = y \vee (x \wedge y) \in F$. The second property is trivial. □

Filters that are generated by a single element are of special interest.

Definition 2.50 *For all elements $x \in \mathcal{L}$ the set $[x] := \{y \in \mathcal{L} \mid x \leq y\}$ is called the principal filter induced by x.*

The definition above naturally leads to the following lemma:

Lemma 2.51 *A principal filter is a filter.*

Proof. Suppose $y, z \in [x]$. Then we have $x \leq y$ and $x \leq z$, which implies $x \leq y \wedge z$, and, hence, $y \wedge z \in [x]$. Now, suppose $y \in F$ and $z \in \mathcal{L}$. Then we get $x \leq y \leq y \vee z$, and, hence, $y \vee z \in [x]$. □

As mentioned above, a special class of filters is used to show that a distributive lattice may be embedded into a power set.

Definition 2.52 *A subset F of a lattice $\mathcal{L}$ with least element 0 is called a prime filter of $\mathcal{L}$ iff for all $x, y \in \mathcal{L}$ the following properties hold:*

(1) $0 \notin F$,

(2) $x \wedge y \in F$ *iff* $x \in F$ *and* $y \in F$,

(3) $x \vee y \in F$ *iff* $x \in F$ *or* $y \in F$.

Using Lemma 2.49 it is obvious that any prime filter is a filter. That the other implication is not true is shown by the next lemma.

Lemma 2.53 *Let $\mathcal{L}$ be a distributive lattice and $x \in \mathcal{L}$. Then the principal filter $[x]$ is a prime filter iff x is irreducible.*

Proof. $\Rightarrow$: Suppose $y \vee z = x$. Since $x \in [x]$ we may assume without loss of generality $y \in [x]$. We conclude that $y \leq x$ since $y \leq y \vee z = x$ and $x \leq y$ from $y \in [x]$.

$\Leftarrow$: First of all, $x \neq 0$ by definition, and, hence, $0 \notin [x]$. Furthermore, suppose $y \vee z \in [x]$ and define $y' := x \wedge y$ and $z' := x \wedge z$. Then we have $y' \vee z' = (x \wedge y) \vee (x \wedge z) = x \wedge (y \vee z) = x$ since $x \leq y \vee z$. Without loss of generality we get $x = y' = x \wedge y$, which implies $x \leq y$, and, hence, $y \in [x]$. □

On the other hand, the maximal elements within the set of filters are of special interest.

Definition 2.54 *A filter $F \subseteq \mathcal{L}$ of lattice $\mathcal{L}$ with least element 0 is called a maximal filter or an ultrafilter iff it is maximal with respect to the property $0 \notin F$.*

As above, there is a connection between ultrafilters and a set of special elements.

Lemma 2.55 *Let $\mathcal{L}$ be a lattice and $x \in \mathcal{L}$. Then the principal filter $[x]$ is an ultrafilter iff x is an atom.*

Proof. $\Rightarrow$: Suppose $y \leq x$. If $y \in [x]$, we conclude that $x = y$. On the other hand, if $y \notin [x]$, the principal filter $[y]$ is a proper superset of $[x]$, which implies $0 \in [y]$ since $[x]$ is maximal. We get $y = 0$.

$\Leftarrow$: Suppose F is a filter so that $0 \notin F$ and $[x] \subseteq F$. For $y \in F$ we have $x \wedge y \in F$. Since x is an atom and $0 \notin F$ we obtain $x \wedge y = x$, which immediately implies $x \leq y$, and, hence, $y \in [x]$. □

The maximality of ultrafilters implies a nice property for pairs of elements $x, \overline{x}$ of a Boolean algebra.

Lemma 2.56 *Let $\mathcal{L}$ be a Boolean algebra and F an ultrafilter. Then for every element $x \in \mathcal{L}$ exactly one of $x, \overline{x}$ belongs to F.*

Proof. Suppose, neither x nor $\overline{x}$ belongs to F. Define $F' := \{z \mid \exists y \in F : z \geq x \wedge y\}$. We show that

(1) F' is a filter,

(2) $x \in F'$,

(3) $0 \notin F'$,

(4) $F \subseteq F'$.

The existence of such an F' contradicts the maximality of F, and, hence, either $x \in F$ or $\overline{x} \in F$.

(1) Let $u, v \in F'$ and compute $u \wedge v \geq (x \wedge y_1) \wedge (x \wedge y_2) = x \wedge (y_1 \wedge y_2)$ for suitable elements $y_1, y_2 \in F$. This shows that $u \wedge v \in F'$ since $y_1 \wedge y_2 \in F$. Now, suppose $u \in F$ and $v \in \mathcal{L}$. Then $u \geq x \wedge y$ for a $y \in F$. We get $u \vee v \geq (x \wedge y) \vee v = (x \vee v) \wedge (y \vee v) \geq x \wedge (y \vee v)$, which implies $u \vee v \in F'$ since $y \vee v \in F$.

(2) This follows immediately from $x = x \wedge 1$ and $1 \in F$.

(3) Suppose $0 \in F'$. Then there is an element $y \in F$ so that $x \wedge y = 0$. This implies $y \leq \overline{x}$. Since F is a filter we conclude that $\overline{x} = y \vee \overline{x} \in F$, a contradiction.

(4) This follows immediately from $y \geq x \wedge y$ for all $y \in F$.

Suppose $x \in F$ and $\overline{x} \in F$ then we obtain $x \wedge \overline{x} = 0 \in F$, a contradiction. □

Using the previous lemma, we are able to show that ultrafilters within a Boolean algebra may be defined just by properties of their elements. A quantification over all subsets of the Boolean algebra, or at least over all filters, is not needed.

Lemma 2.57 *Let $\mathcal{L}$ be a Boolean algebra. A filter F is a prime filter iff F is an ultrafilter.*

Proof. $\Rightarrow$: Suppose F' is a filter so that $0 \notin F'$ and $F \subseteq F'$. For $x \in F'$ we have $x \vee \overline{x} = 1 \in F$. This implies either $x \in F$ or $\overline{x} \in F$. In the second case we conclude that $x \wedge \overline{x} = 0 \in F'$, a contradiction, since $x \in F'$ and $\overline{x} \in F \subseteq F'$.

$\Leftarrow$: It is sufficient to show that $x \vee y \in F$ implies $x \in F$ or $y \in F$. Consider $(x \vee y) \wedge (\overline{x} \wedge \overline{y}) = 0 \notin F$. Since F is a filter we get $\overline{x} \wedge \overline{y} \notin F$, and, hence, $\overline{x} \notin F$ or $\overline{y} \notin F$. Using Lemma 2.56 we obtain $x \in F$ or $y \in F$. □

The next lemma is in some sense a generalization of Lemma 2.55.

Lemma 2.58 *Let $\mathcal{L}$ be a complete Boolean algebra and F an ultrafilter. Then $\bigwedge F$ equals 0 or is an atom.*

Proof. Suppose $x \leq \bigwedge F$ and consider the principal filter $[x]$. Then we have $F \subseteq [x]$, which implies $F = [x]$ or $0 \in [x]$ by the maximality of F. In the first case we conclude $x = \bigwedge F$ and in the second case $x = 0$. □

As mentioned at the beginning of this section, we will need a special class of prime filters. We may motivate this new notion also by the following fact: As shown in the previous lemmata properties of principal filters are related to properties of the generating element. So far we have encountered the following relationships:

class of filters		class of elements
principal filter	$\hat{=}$	arbitrary element
principal prime filter	$\hat{=}$	irreducible element
principal ultrafilter	$\hat{=}$	atom

A class of filters corresponding to completely irreducible elements is still missing. Since those elements are defined using arbitrary unions it is not surprising that the corresponding class of filters requires such a property as well.

Definition 2.59 *A subset $F \subseteq \mathcal{L}$ of a complete Brouwerian lattice $\mathcal{L}$ is called a complete prime filter iff for all $x, y \in \mathcal{L}$ and all subsets $M \subseteq \mathcal{L}$ the following properties hold:*

(1) $0 \notin F$,

(2) $x \wedge y \in F$ *iff* $x \in F$ *and* $y \in F$,

(3) $\bigvee M \in F$ *iff* $\exists y \in M : y \in F$.

We will denote the set of all complete prime filters of $\mathcal{L}$ by $\mathcal{F}_{\mathcal{L}}$. If $\mathcal{F}_{\mathcal{L}} \neq \emptyset$, we call $\mathcal{L}$ proper.

Again, there is a connection between complete prime filters and a set of special elements.

Lemma 2.60 *Let $\mathcal{L}$ be a complete Brouwerian lattice and $x \in \mathcal{L}$. Then the principal filter $[x]$ is a complete prime filter iff x is completely irreducible.*

Proof. $\Rightarrow$: Suppose $\bigvee M = x \in [x]$. Then there is a $y \in M \cap [x]$ since $[x]$ is a complete prime filter. We conclude $y \leq x$ from $y \in M$ and $x \leq y$ from $y \in [x]$. This implies $x = y \in M$.

$\Leftarrow$: It is sufficient to show that $\bigvee M \in [x]$ implies that there is a $y \in M$ with $x \leq y$. Define $M_x := \{x \wedge y \mid y \in M\}$. Then we have $\bigvee M_x = \bigvee_{y \in M} (x \wedge y) = x \wedge \bigvee M = x$ since $\mathcal{L}$ is a complete Brouwerian lattice. This implies $x \in M_x$ since x is completely irreducible. We conclude that $x = x \wedge y \leq y$ for a suitable $y \in M$. □

We will prove property (ext) for proper lattices. But first, we want to study this class of lattices.

Theorem 2.61 *(1) Every linear ordering is proper.*

(2) If a lattice has at least one completely irreducible element, then it is proper.

(3) The class of proper lattices is closed under arbitrary products.

(4) A complete atomless Boolean algebra is not proper.

Proof.

(1) The set $F := \mathcal{L} \setminus \{0\}$ for a linear ordering $\mathcal{L}$ is obviously a complete prime filter.

(2) If x is completely irreducible, then the principal filter $[x]$ is a complete prime filter by Lemma 2.60.

(3) Let $\mathcal{L}_i$ for $i \in I$ be proper lattices. Suppose for all $i \in I$ the set F_i is a complete prime filter of $\mathcal{L}_i$. Then define $F := \prod\limits_{i \in I} F_i$. It is easy to verify that F is a complete prime filter of $\prod\limits_{i \in I} \mathcal{L}_i$.

(4) Suppose F is a complete prime filter of a complete atomless Boolean algebra $\mathcal{L}$. Then F is a prime filter, and, hence, an ultrafilter of $\mathcal{L}$ by Lemma 2.57. Furthermore, by Lemma 2.58 we have $\bigwedge F$ equals 0 or is an atom. Since $\mathcal{L}$ is atomless $\bigwedge F = 0$ follows. Define $\overline{F} := \{\overline{x} \mid x \in F\}$. Then $F \cap \overline{F} = \emptyset$ by Lemma 2.56. Last but not least, we have $\bigvee \overline{F} = \bigvee\limits_{x \in F} \overline{x} = \overline{\bigwedge F} = 1 \in F$, which shows that F is not a complete prime filter. □

Notice that property (2) of the previous theorem implies that every finite lattice and every power set is proper. Furthermore, from (1) we conclude that the unit interval $[0,1]$ of the real numbers is also proper.

Now, we define a function $\psi : \mathcal{L} \to \mathcal{P}(\mathcal{F}_{\mathcal{L}})$ by $\psi(x) := \{F \in \mathcal{F}_{\mathcal{L}} \mid x \in F\}$. Notice that ψ is defined similar to the function used in the representation theorem of Boolean algebras by Stone. However, ψ is not necessarily injective. But we have the following:

Lemma 2.62 *(1)* $\psi(x \wedge y) = \psi(x) \cap \psi(y)$,

(2) $\psi(\bigvee M) = \bigcup\limits_{y \in M} \psi(y)$.

Proof.

(1) Consider the following computation:

$$\begin{aligned} F \in \psi(x \wedge y) &\Leftrightarrow x \wedge y \in F \\ &\Leftrightarrow x \in F \text{ and } y \in F && F \text{ is a prime filter} \\ &\Leftrightarrow F \in \psi(x) \text{ and } F \in \psi(y) \\ &\Leftrightarrow F \in \psi(x) \cap \psi(y). \end{aligned}$$

(2) The assertion follows immediately from

$$\begin{aligned} F \in \psi(\bigvee M) &\Leftrightarrow \bigvee M \in F \\ &\Leftrightarrow \exists y \in M : y \in F && F \text{ is a complete prime filter} \\ &\Leftrightarrow \exists y \in M : F \in \psi(y) \\ &\Leftrightarrow F \in \bigcup_{y \in M} \psi(y). \end{aligned}$$

□

Using ψ we may extend a function $f : \mathcal{L}_1 \to \mathcal{L}_2$ to a function $\vartheta(f) : \mathcal{P}(\mathcal{F}_{\mathcal{L}_1}) \to \mathcal{L}_2$ by

$$\vartheta(f)(\mathfrak{M}) := \bigvee_{\substack{x \in \mathcal{L}_1 \\ \mathfrak{M} \subseteq \psi(x)}} f(x).$$

In the next lemma we have summarized some basic properties of ϑ.

Lemma 2.63 *Let $\mathcal{L}_1$ and $\mathcal{L}_2$ be complete Brouwerian lattices. For all antitone functions $f, g, f_i : \mathcal{L}_1 \overset{\geq}{\to} \mathcal{L}_2$ for all $i \in I$ we have*

(1) $\vartheta(f)$ is antitone,

(2) $\bigvee_{i \in I} \vartheta(f_i) = \vartheta(\bigvee_{i \in I} f_i)$,

(3) $\vartheta(f \wedge g) = \vartheta(f) \wedge \vartheta(g)$,

(4) $\vartheta(f)(\{F\}) = \bigvee_{x \in F} f(x)$.

Proof.

(1) If $\mathfrak{M} \subseteq \mathfrak{N}$, we obtain $\{x \mid \mathfrak{N} \subseteq \psi(x)\} \subseteq \{x \mid \mathfrak{M} \subseteq \psi(x)\}$, and, hence,

$$\vartheta(f)(\mathfrak{N}) = \bigvee_{\mathfrak{N} \subseteq \psi(x)} f(x) \leq \bigvee_{\mathfrak{M} \subseteq \psi(x)} f(x) = \vartheta(f)(\mathfrak{M}).$$

(2) Consider the following computation:

$$\begin{aligned} \Big(\bigvee_{i \in I} \vartheta(f_i)\Big)(\mathfrak{M}) &= \bigvee_{i \in I} \vartheta(f_i)(\mathfrak{M}) && \text{definition of } \vee \\ &= \bigvee_{i \in I} \bigvee_{\mathfrak{M} \subseteq \psi(x)} f_i(x) && \text{definition of } \vartheta \\ &= \bigvee_{\mathfrak{M} \subseteq \psi(x)} \bigvee_{i \in I} f_i(x) \\ &= \bigvee_{\mathfrak{M} \subseteq \psi(x)} \Big(\bigvee_{i \in I} f_i\Big)(x) && \text{definition of } \vee \\ &= \Big(\vartheta\Big(\bigvee_{i \in I} f_i\Big)\Big)(\mathfrak{M}). && \text{definition of } \vartheta \end{aligned}$$

(3) First, we show that $\bigvee\limits_{\mathfrak{M}\subseteq\psi(x)} (f(x) \wedge g(x)) = (\bigvee\limits_{\mathfrak{M}\subseteq\psi(x)} f(x)) \wedge (\bigvee\limits_{\mathfrak{M}\subseteq\psi(x)} g(x))$. The inclusion $\leq$ is trivial. Suppose $\mathfrak{M} \subseteq \psi(x)$ and $\mathfrak{M} \subseteq \psi(y)$. Then $\mathfrak{M} \subseteq \psi(x) \cap \psi(y) = \psi(x \wedge y)$. Furthermore, $f(x) \wedge g(y) \leq f(x \wedge y) \wedge g(x \wedge y)$ since f and g are antitone. We conclude that

$$\begin{aligned}
&\Big(\bigvee_{\mathfrak{M}\subseteq\psi(x)} f(x)\Big) \wedge \Big(\bigvee_{\mathfrak{M}\subseteq\psi(x)} g(x)\Big) \\
&= \bigvee_{\mathfrak{M}\subseteq\psi(x)} \Big(f(x) \wedge \Big(\bigvee_{\mathfrak{M}\subseteq\psi(x)} g(x)\Big)\Big) && \mathcal{L}_1 \to \mathcal{L}_2 \text{ is a complete Brouwerian lattice} \\
&= \bigvee_{\mathfrak{M}\subseteq\psi(x)} \bigvee_{\mathfrak{M}\subseteq\psi(y)} (f(x) \wedge g(y)) && \mathcal{L}_1 \to \mathcal{L}_2 \text{ is a complete Brouwerian lattice} \\
&\leq \bigvee_{\mathfrak{M}\subseteq\psi(x\wedge y)} (f(x \wedge y) \wedge g(x \wedge y)) && \text{computation above} \\
&= \bigvee_{\mathfrak{M}\subseteq\psi(x)} (f(x) \wedge g(x)).
\end{aligned}$$

Now, consider the following computation:

$$\begin{aligned}
(\vartheta(f \wedge g))(\mathfrak{M}) &= \bigvee_{\mathfrak{M}\subseteq\psi(x)} (f \wedge g)(x) && \text{definition of } \vartheta \\
&= \bigvee_{\mathfrak{M}\subseteq\psi(x)} (f(x) \wedge g(x)) && \text{definition of } \wedge \\
&= \Big(\bigvee_{\mathfrak{M}\subseteq\psi(x)} f(x)\Big) \wedge \Big(\bigvee_{\mathfrak{M}\subseteq\psi(x)} g(x)\Big) && \text{computation above} \\
&= \vartheta(f)(\mathfrak{M}) \wedge \vartheta(g)(\mathfrak{M}) && \text{definition of } \vartheta \\
&= (\vartheta(f) \wedge \vartheta(g))(\mathfrak{M}). && \text{definition of } \wedge
\end{aligned}$$

(4) We immediately conclude that

$$\vartheta(f)(\{F\}) = \bigvee_{\{F\}\subseteq\psi(x)} f(x) = \bigvee_{F\in\psi(x)} f(x) = \bigvee_{x\in F} f(x). \qquad \Box$$

Notice that (2) as well as (3) of the previous lemma implies that ϑ is monotone.

The next lemma will show the key property (ext) introduced above. Notice that in the proof of this lemma it is essential that ψ is continuous.

Lemma 2.64 *If $f : \mathcal{L}_1 \to \mathcal{L}_2$ is antitone, then we have $\tau(\vartheta(\tau(f))) = \tau(\vartheta(f))$.*

Proof. $\leq$: Since $f \leq \tau(f)$ we get $\vartheta(f) \leq \vartheta(\tau(f))$ by Lemma 2.63 (2), and, hence, $\tau(\vartheta(f)) \leq \tau(\vartheta(\tau(f)))$.

$\geq$: Consider the property

$$(*) \qquad \vartheta(\tau(f)) \leq \tau(\vartheta(f)).$$

From $(*)$ we immediately conclude that $\tau(\vartheta(\tau(f))) \leq \tau^2(\vartheta(f)) = \tau(\vartheta(f))$. We prove $(*)$ by fixed point induction. Therefore, we define the predicate

$$\mathfrak{P}(h) \quad :\Leftrightarrow \quad \vartheta(h) \leq \tau(\vartheta(f))$$

This predicate is admissible since $\mathfrak{P}(h_i)$ for all $i \in I$ implies $\bigvee_{i\in I} \vartheta(h_i) \leq \tau(\vartheta(f))$, and, hence, $\vartheta(\bigvee_{i\in I} h_i) \leq \tau(\vartheta(f))$ by Lemma 2.63 (2), which is equivalent to $\mathfrak{P}(\bigvee_{i\in I} h_i)$.

The base case $\mathfrak{P}(f)$ is trivial. Let $\mathfrak{M}$ be a subset of $\mathcal{F}_{\mathcal{L}}, x$ so that $\mathfrak{M} \subseteq \psi(x)$ and M a set with $\bigvee M = x$. Then we define $P_M := \{\mathfrak{M} \cap \psi(y) \mid y \in M\}$. Using Lemma 2.62 (2) we conclude that

$$\bigcup P_M = \bigcup_{y\in M} (\mathfrak{M} \cap \psi(y)) = \mathfrak{M} \cap \bigcup_{y\in M} \psi(y) = \mathfrak{M} \cap \psi(\bigvee M) = \mathfrak{M}.$$

Furthermore, we have $h(y) \leq \bigvee_{\mathfrak{M}\cap\psi(y)\subseteq\psi(z)} h(z)$ for all $y \in M$, which implies $\bigwedge_{y\in M} h(y) \leq \bigwedge_{\mathfrak{N}\in P_M} \bigvee_{\mathfrak{N}\subseteq\psi(z)} h(z)$. We obtain

$$(**) \qquad \bigvee_{\mathfrak{M}\subseteq\psi(x)} \bigvee_{\bigvee M=x} \bigwedge_{y\in M} h(y) \leq \bigvee_{\bigcup P=\mathfrak{M}} \bigwedge_{\mathfrak{N}\in P} \bigvee_{\mathfrak{N}\subseteq\psi(z)} h(z).$$

Now, the induction step follows from

$$\begin{aligned}
\vartheta(\varphi(h))(\mathfrak{M}) &= \bigvee_{\mathfrak{M}\subseteq\psi(x)} \varphi(h)(x) && \text{definition of } \vartheta \\
&= \bigvee_{\mathfrak{M}\subseteq\psi(x)} \bigvee_{\bigvee M=x} \bigwedge_{y\in M} h(y) && \text{definition of } \varphi \\
&\leq \bigvee_{\bigcup P=\mathfrak{M}} \bigwedge_{\mathfrak{N}\in P} \bigvee_{\mathfrak{N}\subseteq\psi(z)} h(z) && \text{by } (**) \\
&= \bigvee_{\bigcup P=\mathfrak{M}} \bigwedge_{\mathfrak{N}\in P} \vartheta(h)(\mathfrak{N}) && \text{definition of } \vartheta \\
&\leq \bigvee_{\bigcup P=\mathfrak{M}} \bigwedge_{\mathfrak{N}\in P} \tau(\vartheta(f))(\mathfrak{N}) && \text{induction hypothesis} \\
&= \varphi(\tau(\vartheta(f)))(\mathfrak{M}) && \text{definition of } \varphi \\
&= \tau(\vartheta(f))(\mathfrak{M}). && \tau(f) \text{ fixed point of } \varphi
\end{aligned}$$

From the principle of fixed point induction we obtain property $(*)$. □

We summarize Lemma 2.64 and 2.63 (4) and compute

$$\tau(\vartheta(\tau(f)))(\{F\}) = \tau(\vartheta(f))(\{F\}) = \vartheta(f)(\{F\}) = \bigvee_{x\in F} f(x).$$

2.9 LATTICE-ORDERED SEMIGROUPS

In fuzzy theory t-norms and t-conorms are essential for defining new operations for fuzzy sets and/or relations. The corresponding notion for $\mathcal{L}$-fuzzy relations is given by complete lattice-ordered semigroups introduced in [12].

Definition 2.65 *Let $\mathcal{L}$ be a distributive lattice with least element 0 and greatest element 1, $*$ a binary operation on $\mathcal{L}$ and $e, z \in \mathcal{L}$. Then $(\mathcal{L}, *, e, z)$ is called a lattice-ordered operator set, abbreviated loos, iff*

(1) $*$ is monotone in both arguments,

(2) e is a left and right neutral element for $*$, i.e., $x * e = e * x = x$ for all $x \in \mathcal{L}$,

(3) z is a left and right zero for $*$, i.e., $x * z = z * x = z$ for all $x \in \mathcal{L}$.

If $*$ is associative, $(\mathcal{L}, *, e, z)$ is called a lattice-ordered semigroup (losg). Furthermore, if $\mathcal{L}$ is a complete Brouwerian lattice and $*$ is continuous (distributes over nonempty unions) in both arguments, i.e.,

$$x * \left(\bigvee_{i\in I} y_i\right) = \bigvee_{i\in I}(x * y_i) \quad \text{and} \quad \left(\bigvee_{i\in I} y_i\right) * x = \bigvee_{i\in I}(y_i * x)$$

for all nonempty sets I, $(\mathcal{L}, *, e, z)$ is called a complete lattice-ordered operator set/semigroup (cloos/closg). Finally, the structures defined above are called commutative if $*$ is.

As usual, e and z are unique. Suppose e' is another left and right neutral element and z' is another left and right zero for $*$. Then we conclude that

$$\begin{aligned} e &= e * e' && e' \text{ right neutral} \qquad & z &= z * z' && z \text{ left zero} \\ &= e', && e \text{ left neutral} & &= z'. && z' \text{ right zero} \end{aligned}$$

Notice that for $\mathcal{L} = [0, 1]$, $e = 1$ and $z = 0$ we get the usual definition of t-norms and for $e = 0$ and $z = 1$ of t-conorms. For example, the product norm, i.e., $(x, y) \mapsto xy$, is a commutative closg.

Further examples of commutative losgs are $(\mathcal{L}, \wedge, 1, 0)$, $(\mathcal{L}, \vee, 0, 1)$. In addition, we may define the following operations:

$$x \circledast y := \begin{cases} x & \text{iff} \quad y = 1, \\ y & \text{iff} \quad x = 1, \\ 0 & \text{otherwise.} \end{cases} \qquad x \boxplus y := \begin{cases} x & \text{iff} \quad y = 0, \\ y & \text{iff} \quad x = 0, \\ 1 & \text{otherwise.} \end{cases}$$

Again, $(\mathcal{L}, \circledast, 1, 0)$ and $(\mathcal{L}, \boxplus, 0, 1)$ are commutative losgs.

Lemma 2.66 *Let $(\mathcal{L}, *, 1, z)$ be a loos. Then we have the following:*

(1) $z = 0$, i.e., $x * 0 = 0 * x = 0$ for all $x \in \mathcal{L}$,

(2) $x \circledast y \leq x * y \leq x \wedge y$ for all $x, y \in \mathcal{L}$,

(3) $* = \wedge$ iff $u * u = u$ for all $u \in \mathcal{L}$.

Proof.

(1) $x * 0 \leq 1 * 0 = 0$ and $0 * x \leq 0 * 1 = 0$, and, hence, $z = 0$.

(2) The second inclusion follows immediately from $x * y \leq x * 1 = x$ and $x * y \leq 1 * y = y$. Suppose $x \circledast y \neq 0$. Then $x = 1$ or $y = 1$, and, hence, $x \circledast y = 1 \circledast y = y = 1 * y = x * y$ resp. $x \circledast y = x \circledast 1 = x = x * 1 = x * y$.

(3) $\Rightarrow$ is trivial, and $\Leftarrow$ follows from 2. and $x \wedge y = (x \wedge y) * (x \wedge y) \leq x * y$.□

If the identity 1 of $(\mathcal{L}, *, 1, z)$ in the previous lemma is replaced by 0, a dual version may be proved.

Lemma 2.67 *Let $(\mathcal{L}, *, 0, z)$ be a loos. Then we have the following:*

(1) $z = 1$, i.e., $x * 1 = 1 * x = 1$ for all $x \in \mathcal{L}$,

(2) $x \vee y \leq x * y \leq x \boxplus y$ for all $x, y \in \mathcal{L}$,

(3) $* = \vee$ iff $u * u = u$ for all $u \in \mathcal{L}$.

Proof. Similar to Lemma 2.66. □

3
L-FUZZY RELATIONS

As mentioned in the introduction, for a complete Brouwerian lattice $\mathcal{L}$ an $\mathcal{L}$-fuzzy relation R between two nonempty sets A and B is a function from $A \times B$ to $\mathcal{L}$. Notice, if $\mathcal{L} = \mathbb{B}$, we get the set of regular binary relations between A and B. Therefore, we also use the denotation $R : A \to B$ to indicate that an $\mathcal{L}$-fuzzy relation R has source A and target B.

3.1 BASIC OPERATIONS AND PROPERTIES

Let $Q, R : A \to B$ and $S : B \to C$ be $\mathcal{L}$-fuzzy relations. Then we may introduce several operations as follows:

$$\begin{aligned}
(Q \cap R)(x,y) &:= Q(x,y) \wedge R(x,y), \\
(Q \cup R)(x,y) &:= Q(x,y) \vee R(x,y), \\
Q^{\mathsf{T}}(x,y) &:= Q(y,x), \\
(Q \circ S)(x,z) &:= \bigvee_{y \in B} (Q(x,y) \wedge S(y,z)).
\end{aligned}$$

Notice that these operations are generalizations of those defined for regular (crisp) binary relations, i.e, for $\mathcal{L} = \mathbb{B}$ they coincide with the corresponding set-theoretic operations defined in Chapter 1. Furthermore, the inclusion $\subseteq$, which is induced by the intersection or union of $\mathcal{L}$-fuzzy relations, has to be read as follows:

$$Q \subseteq R \iff \forall x \in A, y \in B : Q(x,y) \leq R(x,y).$$

Again, this is a generalization of $\subseteq$ defined for regular relations.

By Theorems 2.7, 2.23, and 2.25 (2) the set of all $\mathcal{L}$-fuzzy relations between A and B is again a complete Brouwerian lattice with least and greatest element defined by

$$\perp\!\!\!\perp_{AB}(x,y) := 0, \qquad \top\!\!\!\top_{AB}(x,y) := 1.$$

Furthermore, one may define the identity relation on the set A by

$$\mathbb{I}_A(x,y) := \begin{cases} 1 & \text{iff } x = y, \\ 0 & \text{else.} \end{cases}$$

Theorem 3.1 *Let $\mathcal{L}$ be a complete Brouwerian lattice. Then for all $\mathcal{L}$-fuzzy relations $Q, Q', Q_i : A \to B, R, R_i : B \to C, S : C \to D$ for $i \in I$ and $T : A \to C$ we have*

(1) $Q \circ \mathbb{I}_B = Q$ *and* $\mathbb{I}_B \circ R = R$,

(2) $(Q \circ R) \circ S = Q \circ (R \circ S)$,

(3) $(Q \cap Q')^{\mathrm{T}} = Q^{\mathrm{T}} \cap Q'^{\mathrm{T}}$,

(4) $(Q \circ R)^{\mathrm{T}} = R^{\mathrm{T}} \circ Q^{\mathrm{T}}$,

(5) $(Q^{\mathrm{T}})^{\mathrm{T}} = Q$,

(6) $Q \circ (\bigcap_{i\in I} R_i) \subseteq \bigcap_{i\in I} (Q \circ R_i)$ *and* $(\bigcap_{i\in I} Q_i) \circ R \subseteq \bigcap_{i\in I} (Q_i \circ R)$,

(7) $Q \circ R \cap T \subseteq Q \circ (R \cap Q^{\mathrm{T}} \circ T)$,

(8) $Q \circ \perp\!\!\!\perp_{BC} = \perp\!\!\!\perp_{AC}$,

(9) $Q \circ (\bigcup_{i\in I} R_i) = \bigcup_{i\in I} (Q \circ R_i)$ *and* $(\bigcup_{i\in I} Q_i) \circ R = \bigcup_{i\in I} (Q_i \circ R)$,

Proof. Throughout this proof, $(*)$ refers to the fact that $\mathcal{L}$ is completely upward-distributive.

(1) We just show the first assertion. This follows immediately from

$$\begin{aligned}
(Q \circ \mathbb{I}_B)(u,w) &= \bigvee_{v\in B} (Q(u,v) \wedge \mathbb{I}_B(v,w)) && \text{definition of } \circ \\
&= Q(u,w) \wedge 1 && \text{definition of } \mathbb{I}_B \\
&= Q(u,w).
\end{aligned}$$

(2) The following computation shows the assertion:

$$\begin{aligned}
((Q \circ R) \circ S)(u,x) &= \bigvee_{w \in C} ((Q \circ R)(u,w) \wedge S(w,x)) \\
&= \bigvee_{w \in C} \left(\left(\bigvee_{v \in B} (Q(u,v) \wedge R(v,w)) \right) \wedge S(w,x) \right) \\
&= \bigvee_{w \in C} \bigvee_{v \in B} (Q(u,v) \wedge R(v,w) \wedge S(w,x)) && \text{by } (*) \\
&= \bigvee_{v \in B} \bigvee_{w \in C} (Q(u,v) \wedge R(v,w) \wedge S(w,x)) \\
&= \bigvee_{v \in B} \left(Q(u,v) \wedge \left(\bigvee_{w \in C} (R(v,w) \wedge S(w,x)) \right) \right) && \text{by } (*) \\
&= \bigvee_{v \in B} \left(Q(u,v) \wedge (R \circ S)(v,x) \right) \\
&= (Q \circ (R \circ S)(u,x)).
\end{aligned}$$

(3) Again, the following computation shows the assertion:

$$\begin{aligned}
(Q \cap Q')^{\mathsf{T}}(u,v) &= (Q \cap Q')(v,u) \\
&= Q(v,u) \wedge Q'(v,u) \\
&= Q^{\mathsf{T}}(u,v) \wedge Q'^{\mathsf{T}}(u,v) \\
&= (Q^{\mathsf{T}} \cap Q'^{\mathsf{T}})(u,v).
\end{aligned}$$

(4) The assertion is shown as follows:

$$\begin{aligned}
(Q \circ R)^{\mathsf{T}}(u,w) &= (Q \circ R)(w,u) \\
&= \bigvee_{v \in B} (Q(w,v) \wedge R(v,u)) \\
&= \bigvee_{v \in B} (R^{\mathsf{T}}(u,v) \wedge Q^{\mathsf{T}}(v,w)) \\
&= (R^{\mathsf{T}} \circ Q^{\mathsf{T}})(u,w).
\end{aligned}$$

(5) follows immediately from

$$(Q^{\mathsf{T}})^{\mathsf{T}}(u,v) \;=\; Q^{\mathsf{T}}(v,u) \;=\; Q(u,v).$$

(6) We just show the first assertion. Therefore, consider the following computation:

$$\begin{aligned}
\left(Q \circ \left(\bigcap_{i \in I} R_i \right) \right)(u,w) &= \bigvee_{v \in B} \left(Q(u,v) \wedge \left(\bigcap_{i \in I} R_i \right)(v,w) \right) \\
&= \bigvee_{v \in B} \left(Q(u,v) \wedge \bigwedge_{i \in I} R_i(v,w) \right)
\end{aligned}$$

$$
\begin{aligned}
&= \bigvee_{v \in B} \bigwedge_{i \in I} (Q(u,v) \wedge R_i(v,w)) \\
&\leq \bigwedge_{i \in I} \bigvee_{v \in B} (Q(u,v) \wedge R_i(v,w)) \\
&= \bigwedge_{i \in I} (Q \circ R_i)(u,w) \\
&= \left(\bigcap_{i \in I} (Q \circ R_i) \right) (u,w)
\end{aligned}
$$

(7) Again, consider the following computation:

$$
\begin{aligned}
&(Q \circ R \cap T)(u,w) \\
&= (Q \circ R)(u,w) \wedge T(u,w) \\
&= \left(\bigvee_{v \in B} (Q(u,v) \wedge R(v,w)) \right) \wedge T(u,w) \\
&= \bigvee_{v \in B} (Q(u,v) \wedge R(v,w) \wedge T(u,w)) && \text{by } (*) \\
&= \bigvee_{v \in B} (Q(u,v) \wedge R(v,w) \wedge Q(u,v) \wedge T(u,w)) \\
&\leq \bigvee_{v \in B} \left(Q(u,v) \wedge R(v,w) \wedge \left(\bigvee_{u' \in A} (Q(u',v) \wedge T(u',w)) \right) \right) \\
&= \bigvee_{v \in B} (Q(u,v) \wedge R(v,w) \wedge (Q^{\mathsf{T}} \circ T)(v,w)) \\
&= \bigvee_{v \in B} (Q(u,v) \wedge (R \cap Q^{\mathsf{T}} \circ T)(v,w)) \\
&= (Q \circ (R \cap Q^{\mathsf{T}} \circ T))(u,w).
\end{aligned}
$$

(8) The assertion follows immediately from

$$
(Q \circ \perp\!\!\!\perp_{BC})(u,w) \;=\; \bigvee_{v \in B} (Q(u,v) \wedge \perp\!\!\!\perp_{BC}(v,w)) = 0 = \perp\!\!\!\perp_{AC}(u,w).
$$

(9) We just show the first assertion. It follows from

$$
\begin{aligned}
\left(Q \circ \left(\bigcup_{i \in I} R_i \right) \right) (u,w) &= \bigvee_{v \in B} (Q(u,v) \wedge \left(\bigcup_{i \in I} R_i \right) (v,w)) \\
&= \bigvee_{v \in B} \left(Q(u,v) \wedge \left(\bigvee_{i \in I} R_i(v,w) \right) \right) \\
&= \bigvee_{v \in B} \bigvee_{i \in I} (Q(u,v) \wedge R_i(v,w)) && \text{by } (*)
\end{aligned}
$$

$$= \bigvee_{i \in I} \bigvee_{v \in B} (Q(u,v) \wedge R_i(v,w))$$

$$= \bigvee_{i \in I} (Q \circ R_i)(u,w)$$

$$= \left(\bigcup_{i \in I} (Q \circ R_i) \right)(u,w). \qquad \square$$

Notice that (9) of the previous lemma implies that $\circ$ is a lower adjoint of a triple of residuated operations. The upper left adjoint is denoted by $S \mathbin{.\!\dot{}\,} R$ and the upper right adjoint by $Q \mathbin{\dot{}\!.} S$. The next lemma shows the componentwise definition of the residuals.

Lemma 3.2 *Let $\mathcal{L}$ be a complete Brouwerian lattice. Then for all $\mathcal{L}$-fuzzy relations $Q : A \to B, R : B \to C$, and $S : A \to C$ we have*

(1) $(Q \mathbin{\dot{}\!.} S)(u,w) = \bigwedge_{v \in A} (S(v,w){:}Q(v,u))$,

(2) if $Q \subseteq \mathbb{I}_A$, *then* $(Q \mathbin{\dot{}\!.} S)(v,w) = S(v,w){:}Q(v,v)$,

(3) $(S \mathbin{.\!\dot{}\,} R)(v,u) = \bigwedge_{w \in C} (S(v,w){:}R(u,w))$,

(4) if $R \subseteq \mathbb{I}_B$, *then* $(S \mathbin{.\!\dot{}\,} R)(v,u) = S(v,w){:}R(u,u)$.

Proof.

(1) Define a relation U by the right-hand side of the assumption, i.e., we define $U(u,w) := \bigwedge_{v \in A} (S(v,w){:}Q(v,u))$, and suppose $(Q \mathbin{\dot{}\!.} S)(u,w) = x$. First of all, we have

$$\begin{aligned} Q(v,u) \wedge U(u,w) &= Q(v,u) \wedge \bigwedge_{v' \in A} S(v',w){:}Q(v',u) && \text{definition } U \\ &\leq Q(v,u) \wedge S(v,w){:}Q(v,u) \\ &\leq S(v,w) && \text{definition :} \end{aligned}$$

such that $\bigvee_{u \in B} (Q(v,u) \wedge U(u,w)) \leq S(v,w)$ follows. This implies $Q \circ U \subseteq S$, and, hence, $U \subseteq Q \mathbin{\dot{}\!.} S$ by the definition of the residual. The previous inclusion shows $\bigwedge_{v \in A} (S(v,w){:}Q(v,u)) \leq x$. The property $Q \circ (Q \mathbin{\dot{}\!.} S) \subseteq S$ implies $Q(v,u) \wedge x \leq S(v,w)$ for all $v \in A$. We obtain $x \leq S(v,w){:}Q(v,u)$ for all $v \in A$, and, hence, $x \leq \bigwedge_{v \in A} (S(v,w){:}Q(v,u))$.

(2) The assertion follows immediately from (1) since $x{:}0 = 1$.

(3) and (4) are shown analogously. $\square$

3.2 CRISPNESS

As mentioned in the introduction, crispness is a fundamental notion within fuzzy theory. An $\mathcal{L}$-fuzzy relation Q is called *0–1 crisp*, iff $Q(x,y) = 0$ or $Q(x,y) = 1$ for all x and y. If we identify **f** and 0 resp. **t** and 1 and regular binary relations with $\mathbb{B}$-fuzzy relations, we may regard 0–1 crisp relations over an arbitrary complete Brouwerian lattice $\mathcal{L}$ as regular relations. Obviously, the set of 0–1 crisp relations is closed under all operations defined above. Furthermore, under the identification of 0–1 crisp and regular relations introduced above they coincide with the set-theoretic operations. Therefore, we will use the set-theoretic notations and definitions also for 0–1 crisp relations, e.g., we write $Q(x,y)$ instead of $Q(x,y) = 1$ and

$$\begin{array}{rrcl} & (Q \circ R)(u,w) & \Longleftrightarrow & \exists v : Q(u,v) \text{ and } R(v,w) \\ \text{instead of} & (Q \circ R)(u,w) = 1 & \Longleftrightarrow & \bigvee_{v}(Q(u,v) \wedge R(v,w)) = 1 \end{array}$$

for 0–1 crisp relations Q and R.

There are several possibilities to identify a class of $\mathcal{L}$-fuzzy relations with the lattice $\mathcal{L}$ itself, e.g., one could choose ideal elements. In our approach we will take scalar relations. An $\mathcal{L}$-fuzzy relation $\alpha_A^u : A \to A$ is called a *scalar* on A induced by $u \in \mathcal{L}$ iff

$$\alpha_A^u(x,y) = \begin{cases} u & \text{iff } x = y, \\ 0 & \text{else.} \end{cases}$$

Obviously, the set of scalars on A is closed under arbitrary intersections and unions and is isomorphic to $\mathcal{L}$. The induced isomorphism is an isomorphism of complete Brouwerian lattices since it is surjective in respect to the set of scalars on A.

A *u-cut* of an $\mathcal{L}$-fuzzy relation is defined as the following 0–1 crisp relation:

$$R_u(x,y) := \begin{cases} 1 & \text{iff } R(x,y) \geq u, \\ 0 & \text{else.} \end{cases}$$

The special cut with 1 will be denoted by $R^{\downarrow}$. It is the greatest 0–1 crisp relation R contains. On the other hand, we may define

$$R^{\uparrow}(x,y) := \begin{cases} 1 & \text{iff } R(x,y) \neq 0 \\ 0 & \text{else.} \end{cases}$$

$R^{\uparrow}$ is the least 0–1 crisp relation containing R. In fuzzy theory the relations $R^{\uparrow}$ and $R^{\downarrow}$ are called the support and the kernel of R, respectively.

In the next lemma we have summarized some properties of the operations defined above.

Lemma 3.3 *Let $\mathcal{L}$ be a complete Brouwerian lattice, and $Q, R : A \to B$ and $S : B \to C$ be $\mathcal{L}$-fuzzy relations. Then we have*

(1) *Q is 0-1 crisp iff $Q^{\uparrow} = Q$ iff $Q^{\downarrow} = Q$,*

(2) *$(^{\uparrow}, ^{\downarrow})$ is a Galois correspondence,*

(3) $(R^{\mathsf{T}} \circ S^{\downarrow})^{\uparrow} = R^{\uparrow\mathsf{T}} \circ S^{\downarrow}$,

(4) $(Q \cap R^{\downarrow})^{\uparrow} = Q^{\uparrow} \cap R^{\downarrow}$,

(5) *if $u \neq 0$, then $\alpha_A^{u\uparrow} = \mathbb{I}_A$,*

(6) $Q_u = (\alpha_A^u \because Q)^{\downarrow}$.

Proof.

(1) The assertion follows immediately from the definition of $^{\uparrow}$ and $^{\downarrow}$.

(2) Suppose $R^{\uparrow} \subseteq S$ and $R^{\uparrow}(x,y) \neq 0$. Then by the definition of $^{\uparrow}$ we have $1 = R^{\uparrow}(x,y) \leq S(x,y)$, and, hence, $R(x,y) \leq 1 = S^{\downarrow}(x,y)$. The other implication is shown analogously.

(3) Define two operations $^{\uparrow}, ^{\downarrow} : \mathcal{L} \to \mathcal{L}$ on the lattice $\mathcal{L}$ by $x^{\uparrow} = 0$ if $x = 0$ and $x^{\uparrow} = 1$ otherwise, and by $x^{\downarrow} = 1$ if $x = 1$ and $x^{\downarrow} = 0$ otherwise, respectively. Then we have

(a) $R^{\uparrow}(x,y) = (R(x,y))^{\uparrow}$,

(b) $R^{\downarrow}(x,y) = (R(x,y))^{\downarrow}$.

Furthermore, the operations satisfy

(c) $(x \wedge y^{\downarrow})^{\uparrow} = x^{\uparrow} \wedge y^{\downarrow}$ for all $x, y \in \mathcal{L}$,,

(d) $(\bigvee M)^{\uparrow} = \bigvee\limits_{x \in M} x^{\uparrow}$ for all subset M of $\mathcal{L}$.

Finally, we obtain

$$\begin{aligned}
(R^{\mathsf{T}} \circ S^{\downarrow})^{\uparrow}(u,w) &= ((R^{\mathsf{T}} \circ S^{\downarrow})(u,w))^{\uparrow} && \text{(a)}\\
&= \Big(\bigvee_v (R^{\mathsf{T}}(u,v) \wedge S^{\downarrow}(u,w))\Big)^{\uparrow} && \text{definition of } \circ\\
&= \Big(\bigvee_v (R(v,u) \wedge (S(u,w))^{\downarrow})\Big)^{\uparrow} && \text{(b) and definition of } ^{\mathsf{T}}\\
&= \bigvee_v ((R(v,u) \wedge (S(u,w))^{\downarrow})^{\uparrow}) && \text{(d)}\\
&= \bigvee_v ((R(v,u))^{\uparrow} \wedge (S(u,w))^{\downarrow}) && \text{(c)}\\
&= \bigvee_v (R^{\uparrow}(v,u) \wedge S^{\downarrow}(u,w)) && \text{(a) and (b)}\\
&= \bigvee_v (R^{\uparrow\mathsf{T}}(u,v) \wedge S^{\downarrow}(v,w)) && \text{definition of } ^{\mathsf{T}}\\
&= (R^{\uparrow\mathsf{T}} \circ S^{\downarrow})(u,w). && \text{definition of } \circ
\end{aligned}$$

(4) Using the operations defined in (3) the assertion follows from

$$\begin{aligned}
(Q \sqcap R^{\downarrow})^{\uparrow}(u,v) &= ((Q \sqcap R^{\downarrow})(u,v))^{\uparrow} && \text{(3a)}\\
&= (Q(u,v) \wedge R^{\downarrow}(u,v))^{\uparrow} && \text{definition of } \sqcap\\
&= (Q(u,v) \wedge R(u,v)^{\downarrow})^{\uparrow} && \text{(3b)}\\
&= Q(u,v)^{\uparrow} \wedge R(u,v)^{\downarrow} && \text{(3c)}\\
&= Q^{\uparrow}(u,v) \wedge R^{\downarrow}(u,v) && \text{(3a) and (3b)}\\
&= (Q^{\uparrow} \sqcap R^{\downarrow})(u,v). && \text{definition of } \sqcap
\end{aligned}$$

(5) By the definition of $^{\uparrow}$ we have for every $u \neq 0$

$$\alpha_A^{u\,\uparrow}(x,y) = \left\{ \begin{array}{l} 1 \text{ iff } x = y \\ 0 \text{ iff } x \neq y \end{array} \right\} = \mathbb{I}_A(x,y).$$

(6) We will show the following property, which implies immediately the assertion:

$$(\alpha_A^u \because Q)^{\downarrow}(x,y) = 1 \quad \Longleftrightarrow \quad Q(x,y) \geq u.$$

Therefore, we define a crisp relation $U_{x,y} : A \to B$ by

$$U_{x,y}(x',y') := \begin{cases} 1 & \text{iff } x' = x \text{ and } y' = y \\ 0 & \text{otherwise.} \end{cases}$$

Then we conclude

$$\begin{aligned}
(\alpha_A^u \because Q)^{\downarrow}(x,y) = 1 &\Leftrightarrow U_{x,y} \sqsubseteq (\alpha_A^u \because Q)^{\downarrow} && \text{by definition of } U_{x,y}\\
&\Leftrightarrow U_{x,y} \sqsubseteq \alpha_A^u \because Q && \text{(2) and } U \text{ is crisp}\\
&\Leftrightarrow \alpha_A^u \circ U_{x,y} \sqsubseteq Q\\
&\Leftrightarrow u \leq Q(x,y),
\end{aligned}$$

where the last equivalence follows from $(\alpha_A^u \circ U_{x,y})(x,y) = u$ and $(\alpha_A^u \circ U_{x,y})(x',y') = 0$ if $x' \neq x$ or $y' \neq y$. □

Notice that (5) of the previous lemma implies that the induced function f_R from $\mathcal{L}$ to the set of 0–1 crisp relations defined by $f_R(u) := R_u$ is an antimorphism. In the case of the unit interval f_R is also called a tower resp. a chain of relations [9]. Furthermore, we have the following theorem:

Theorem 3.4 *Let $\mathcal{L}$ be a complete Brouwerian lattice and $R : A \to B$ a $\mathcal{L}$-fuzzy relation. Then we have*

$$R = \bigsqcup_{u \in \mathcal{L}} (\alpha_A^u \circ R_u).$$

Proof. The assertion follows immediately from

$$\begin{aligned}
\Big(\bigcup_{u\in\mathcal{L}}(\alpha_A^u \circ R_u)\Big)(w,y) &= \bigvee_{u\in\mathcal{L}}(\alpha_A^u \circ R_u)(w,y) && \text{definition } \cup \\
&= \bigvee_{u\in\mathcal{L}}\bigvee_{x\in A}(\alpha_A^u(w,x) \wedge R_u(x,y)) && \text{definition } \circ \\
&= \bigvee_{u\in\mathcal{L}}(u \wedge R_u(w,y)) && \text{definition of } \alpha_A^u \\
&= \bigvee_{\substack{u\in\mathcal{L}\\ R(w,y)\geq u}} u && \text{definition of } R_u \\
&= R(w,y).
\end{aligned}$$

□

The theorem above is known as the α-cut Theorem in fuzzy theory. On the other hand, the collection of the R_u is the least collection fulfilling the equation above. Notice that in the next lemma we identify **Rel** with the 0–1 crisp relations from $\mathcal{L}$-**Rel**.

Lemma 3.5 *Let $f : \mathcal{L} \stackrel{\text{anti}}{\to} \mathbf{Rel}[A,B]$ be an antimorphism, $R : A \to B$ an $\mathcal{L}$-fuzzy relation with $R \subseteq \bigcup_{u\in\mathcal{L}}(\alpha_A^u \circ f(u))$. Then we have $R_v \subseteq f(v)$ for all $v \in \mathcal{L}$.*

Proof. Suppose $R_v(x,y) = 1$. By definition we have $v \leq (\bigcup_{u\in\mathcal{L}}(\alpha_A^u \circ f(u)))(x,y)$. Now, let M be the set of all $w \in \mathcal{L}$ such that $f(w)(x,y) = 1$ holds. Then we have

$$\begin{aligned}
v &\leq \Big(\bigcup_{u\in\mathcal{L}}(\alpha_A^u \circ f(u))\Big)(x,y) \\
&= \bigvee_{u\in\mathcal{L}}(\alpha_A^u \circ f(u))(x,y) && \text{definition of } \cup \\
&= \bigvee_{u\in\mathcal{L}}\bigvee_{w\in A}(\alpha_A^u(x,w) \wedge f(u)(w,y)) && \text{definition of } \circ \\
&= \bigvee_{u\in\mathcal{L}}(u \wedge f(u)(x,y)) && \text{definition of } \alpha_A^u \\
&= \bigvee M. && \text{definition of } M \text{ and } f(u) \text{ is crisp}
\end{aligned}$$

Now, let $M' := \{v \wedge u \mid u \in M\}$. Then we get $\bigvee M' = \bigvee_{u\in M}(v \wedge u) = v \wedge \bigvee M = v$ since $\mathcal{L}$ is completely upward-distributive. Every element $w \in M'$ is less or equal to an element u of M. Since f is antitone we get $f(u) \subseteq f(w)$, and, hence, $f(w)(x,y) = 1$ for all $w \in M'$ by the definition of M. Finally, we conclude that

$$\begin{aligned}
1 &= \bigcap_{w \in M'} f(w)(x,y) \\
&= f\Big(\bigvee M'\Big)(x,y) && f \text{ antimorphism} \\
&= f(v)(x,y). && \text{computation above}
\end{aligned}$$

□

3.3 OPERATIONS DERIVED FROM LATTICE-ORDERED SEMIGROUPS

Within applications of fuzzy theory, usually union, meet and composition operators derived from t-norms resp. t-conorms, or more general from commutative complete lattice-ordered semigroups (commutative closg) as introduced in section 2.9, are used.

Definition 3.6 *Let $Q, R : A \to B$ and $S : B \to C$ be $\mathcal{L}$-fuzzy relations, and $(\mathcal{L}, *, e, z)$ be a lattice-ordered operator set (loos). Then we define*

(1) $(Q \sqcap_* R)(x,y) := Q(x,y) * R(x,y)$,

(2) $(Q \circ_* S)(x,z) := \bigvee_{y \in B} (Q(x,y) * S(y,z))$.

We want to show that the operations above may be defined in a component-free manner. Later on, this gives us the possibility to compare these operations with abstract defined $*$-based connectives.

Theorem 3.7 *Let $Q, R : A \to B$ and $S : B \to C$ be $\mathcal{L}$-fuzzy relations, and $(\mathcal{L}, *, e, z)$ be a loos. Then we have*

(1) $Q \sqcap_* R = \bigsqcup_{x,y \in \mathcal{L}} (\alpha_A^{x*y} \circ ((\alpha_A^x \because Q)^\downarrow \sqcap (\alpha_A^y \because R)^\downarrow))$,

(2) $Q \circ_* S = \bigsqcup_{x,y \in \mathcal{L}} (\alpha_A^{x*y} \circ (\alpha_A^x \because Q)^\downarrow \circ (\alpha_B^y \because R)^\downarrow)$.

Proof.

(1) First of all, we have

$$\begin{aligned}
&((\alpha_A^x \because Q)^\downarrow \sqcap (\alpha_A^y \because R)^\downarrow)(u,v) \\
\Leftrightarrow\ & (\alpha_A^u \because Q)^\downarrow(u,v) \text{ and } (\alpha_A^y \because R)^\downarrow(u,v) && \text{definition } \sqcap \text{ for crisp relations} \\
\Leftrightarrow\ & Q(u,v) \geq x \text{ and } R(u,v) \geq y. && \text{Lemma 3.3 (5)}
\end{aligned}$$

This immediately implies

$$\begin{aligned}
&\Big(\bigcup_{x,y\in\mathcal{L}}(\alpha_A^{x*y}\circ((\alpha_A^x \because Q)^{\downarrow}\cap(\alpha_A^y \because R)^{\downarrow}))\Big)(u,v) \\
&= \bigvee_{x,y\in\mathcal{L}} (\alpha_A^{x*y}\circ((\alpha_A^x \because Q)^{\downarrow}\cap(\alpha_A^y \because R)^{\downarrow}))(u,v) && \text{definition } \cup \\
&= \bigvee_{\substack{x,y\in\mathcal{L} \\ ((\alpha_A^x \because Q)^{\downarrow}\cap(\alpha_A^y \because R)^{\downarrow})(u,v)}} \alpha_A^{x*y}(u,u) && \text{definition } \circ \text{ with a scalar and a crisp argument} \\
&= \bigvee_{\substack{x,y\in\mathcal{L} \\ ((\alpha_A^x \because Q)^{\downarrow}\cap(\alpha_A^y \because R)^{\downarrow})(u,v)}} x*y && \text{definition } \alpha_A^{x*y} \\
&= \bigvee_{\substack{x,y\in\mathcal{L} \\ Q(u,v)\geq x \text{ and } R(u,v)\geq y}} x*y && \text{see above} \\
&= Q(x,y)*R(x,y). && \text{monotonicity of } *
\end{aligned}$$

(2) Again, we obtain

$$\begin{aligned}
&((\alpha_A^x \because Q)^{\downarrow}\circ(\alpha_A^y \because R)^{\downarrow})(u,w) \\
&\Leftrightarrow \exists v\in B:\ (\alpha_A^u \because Q)^{\downarrow}(u,v) \text{ and } (\alpha_A^y \because R)^{\downarrow}(v,w) && \text{definition } \circ \text{ for crisp relations} \\
&\Leftrightarrow \exists v\in B:\ Q(u,v)\geq x \text{ and } R(v,w)\geq y. && \text{Lemma 3.3 (5)}
\end{aligned}$$

This implies

$$\begin{aligned}
&\Big(\bigcup_{x,y\in\mathcal{L}}(\alpha_A^{x*y}\circ(\alpha_A^x \because Q)^{\downarrow}\circ(\alpha_B^y \because S)^{\downarrow})\Big)(u,w) \\
&= \bigvee_{x,y\in\mathcal{L}} (\alpha_A^{x*y}\circ(\alpha_A^x \because Q)^{\downarrow}\circ(\alpha_B^y \because S)^{\downarrow})(u,w) && \text{definition } \cup \\
&= \bigvee_{\substack{x,y\in\mathcal{L} \\ ((\alpha_A^x \because Q)^{\downarrow}\circ(\alpha_B^y \because S)^{\downarrow})(u,w)}} \alpha_A^{x*y}(u,u) && \text{definition } \circ \text{ with a scalar and a crisp argument} \\
&= \bigvee_{\substack{x,y\in\mathcal{L} \\ ((\alpha_A^x \because Q)^{\downarrow}\circ(\alpha_B^y \because S)^{\downarrow})(u,w)}} x*y && \text{definition } \alpha_A^{x*y} \\
&= \bigvee_{\substack{x,y\in\mathcal{L} \\ \exists v\in B:\ Q(u,v)\geq x \text{ and } S(v,w)\geq y}} x*y && \text{see above} \\
&= \bigvee_{v\in B} (Q(u,v)*S(v,w)),
\end{aligned}$$

where the last equality is shown as follows: Suppose $Q(u,v) \geq x$ and $S(v,w) \geq y$. Then we immediately conclude that $x*y \leq Q(u,v)*S(v,w) \leq \bigvee_{v\in B}(Q(u,v)*S(v,w))$, and, hence,

$$\bigvee_{\substack{x,y\in\mathcal{L}\\ \exists v\in B:\ Q(u,v)\geq x \text{ and } S(v,w)\geq y}} x*y \leq \bigvee_{v\in B}(Q(u,v)*S(v,w)).$$

On the other hand, for all $v \in B$ we have

$$Q(u,v)*S(v,w) \leq \bigvee_{\substack{x,y\in\mathcal{L}\\ \exists v\in B:\ Q(u,v)\geq x \text{ and } S(v,w)\geq y}} x*y$$

since $Q(u,v) \leq Q(u,v)$ and $S(v,w) \leq S(v,w)$. □

Notice that the lemma above is true for arbitrary loos, i.e., whatever the neutral element e is. As mentioned in Chapter 2, a commutative losg $(\mathcal{L}, \times, 1, 0)$ is a generalized version of a t-norm, and analogously a commutative losg $(\mathcal{L}, +, 0, 1)$ a generalized version of a t-conorm. In this context we may define the following meet and union operations on $\mathcal{L}$-fuzzy relations $Q, R : A \to B$ by

$$Q \wedge_\times R := Q \sqcap_\times R, \qquad Q \vee_+ R := Q \sqcap_+ R.$$

In the case $\mathcal{L} = [0,1]$, these definitions are exactly the usual definitions of t-norm based meet, resp. t-conorm, based union of fuzzy relations.

For the moment, we dispense with a further investigation of the properties of the $*$-based operations defined above. This will be done in section 5.10.

4
CATEGORIES OF RELATIONS

Usually a binary relation acts between two different sets. Therefore, an algebraic theory for relations should reflect this kind of typing, i.e., the theory should have a suitable notion of source and target of its elements. A convenient framework for that is given by category theory.

4.1 CATEGORIES

In this chapter we will introduce some basic notions from category theory. For a comprehensive introduction to this theory, especially for computer scientists, we refer to [1].

Definition 4.1 *A category $\mathcal{C}$ consists of*

(1) a class of objects $\mathrm{Obj}_{\mathcal{C}}$,

(2) for every pair of objects A and B a class of morphisms $\mathcal{C}[A,B]$,

(3) an associative binary (partial) operation ; mapping each pair of morphisms f in $\mathcal{C}[A,B]$ and g in $\mathcal{C}[B,C]$ to a morphism $f;g$ in $\mathcal{C}[A,C]$,

(4) for every object A a morphism $\mathbb{I}_A$ such that for all f in $\mathcal{C}[A,B]$ and g in $\mathcal{C}[C,A]$ we have $\mathbb{I}_A;f = f$ and $g;\mathbb{I}_A = g$.

If f is a morphism in $\mathcal{C}[A,B]$, we will denote it by $f : A \to B$.

The following table lists some common categories by specifying their objects and morphisms:

Category	Objects	Morphisms
Set	sets	functions
Rel	sets	relations
$[0,1]$-**Rel**	nonempty sets	fuzzy relations
$\mathcal{L}$-**Rel**	nonempty sets	$\mathcal{L}$-fuzzy relations
PO	posets	monotone functions
$\mathbf{Vct}_{\mathbb{F}}$	vector spaces over the field $\mathbb{F}$	linear functions
ZF	models of Zermelo-Fraenkel set theory	$\in$-preserving functions, i.e., $x \in A$ implies $f(x) \in f(A)$

Theorem 3.1 (1) and (2) show that **Rel**, $[0,1]$-**Rel**, and $\mathcal{L}$-**Rel** are indeed categories.

Notice that the class of objects as well as the class of morphisms need not to be a set. For example, in **ZF** every class of morphisms $\mathbf{ZF}[A,B]$ as well as the class of objects is indeed a class and not a set. Also, in **Set** or **Rel** the class of objects is not a set but all classes of morphisms $\mathbf{Set}[A,B]$ or $\mathbf{Rel}[A,B]$ are indeed sets. Such a category is called *locally small.*

The natural notion of a homomorphism between categories is given by functors.

Definition 4.2 *A functor F between two categories $\mathcal{C}_1$ and $\mathcal{C}_2$ is a pair of functions $(F_{\mathrm{Obj}}, F_{\mathrm{Mor}})$ such that*

(1) F_{Obj} maps the objects of $\mathcal{C}_1$ to the objects $\mathcal{C}_2$,

(2) F_{Mor} maps morphisms of $\mathcal{C}_1$ to morphisms of $\mathcal{C}_2$ such that for all morphisms $f : A \to B$ and objects A and B of $\mathcal{C}_1$ the image $F_{\mathrm{Mor}}(f)$ is a morphism from $F_{\mathrm{Obj}}(A)$ to $F_{\mathrm{Obj}}(B)$ in $\mathcal{C}_2$,

(3) $F_{\mathrm{Mor}}(f); F_{\mathrm{Mor}}(g) = F_{\mathrm{Mor}}(f;g)$ for all morphisms $f : A \to B$ and $g : B \to C$ and objects A, B, and C in $\mathcal{C}_1$,

(4) $F_{\mathrm{Mor}}(\mathbb{I}_A) = \mathbb{I}_{F_{\mathrm{Obj}}(A)}$ for all objects A in $\mathcal{C}_1$.

A functor F is called faithful iff F_{Mor} is injective. It is called full iff for all objects A and B and morphisms $g : F_{\mathrm{Mor}}(A) \to F_{\mathrm{Mor}}(B)$ there is a morphism $f : A \to B$ such that $F_{\mathrm{Mor}}(f) = g$.

A full functor may be seen as a functor such that F_{Mor} is surjective on the image of F_{Obj}. As usual, an isomorphism between categories is a functor, which is bijective on objects and morphisms and $F^{-1} := (F_{\mathrm{Obj}}^{-1}, F_{\mathrm{Mor}}^{-1})$ is again a functor.

We will omit the subscripts Obj and Mor as it is always clear from the context whether the functor is meant to operate on objects or morphisms.

For technical reasons we call a pair of functions $(F_{\mathrm{Obj}}, F_{\mathrm{Mor}})$ fulfilling (1) and (2) of Definition 4.2 a pre-functor.

Lemma 4.3 *A pre-functor $F : \mathcal{C}_1 \to \mathcal{C}_2$, which is full, faithful, and bijective on objects is an isomorphism iff either F or F^{-1} respects composition, i.e., fulfills (3) of Definition 4.2.*

Proof. Without loss of generality suppose F respects composition. The computation

$$\begin{aligned}
F(\mathbb{I}_A) &= F(\mathbb{I}_A); \mathbb{I}_{F(A)} && F \text{ surjective on objects}\\
&= F(\mathbb{I}_A); F(F^{-1}(\mathbb{I}_{F(A)})) && F \text{ is full and faithful}\\
&= F(\mathbb{I}_A; F^{-1}(\mathbb{I}_{F(A)})) && \text{property (3) of a functor}\\
&= F(F^{-1}(\mathbb{I}_{F(A)})) && \\
&= \mathbb{I}_{F(A)} && F \text{ is full and faithful}
\end{aligned}$$

shows that F is a functor. It remains to show that F^{-1} preserves identities and composition. Suppose A is an object of $\mathcal{C}_2$. Since F is bijective on objects we have $F(F^{-1}(A)) = A$. We obtain

$$F^{-1}(\mathbb{I}_A) = F^{-1}(\mathbb{I}_{F(F^{-1}(A))}) = F^{-1}(F(\mathbb{I}_{F^{-1}(A)})) = \mathbb{I}_{F^{-1}(A)}$$

since F is a functor. Now, suppose A, B, and C are objects of $\mathcal{C}_2$ and $f : A \to B$ and $g : B \to C$. Again, we have $F(F^{-1}(A)) = A$, $F(F^{-1}(B)) = B$, $F(F^{-1}(C)) = C$, $F(F^{-1}(f)) = f$, and $F(F^{-1}(g)) = g$ since F is full, faithful, and bijective on objects. This implies

$$\begin{aligned}
F^{-1}(f; g) &= F^{-1}(F(F^{-1}(f)); F(F^{-1}(g))) && \text{computation above}\\
&= F^{-1}(F(F^{-1}(f); F^{-1}(g))) && F \text{ is a functor}\\
&= F^{-1}(f); F^{-1}(g). && F \text{ is full and faithful} \quad \square
\end{aligned}$$

4.2 ALLEGORIES

Throughout this book, phrases like "the class $\mathcal{R}[A, B]$ is a lattice" should not imply that $\mathcal{R}[A, B]$ is a set. It just states that there are several operations fulfilling the corresponding algebraic laws. On the other hand, if we refer to $\mathcal{R}[A, B]$ as some complete structure, we implicitly mean that it is a set since the notion of a subset is essential for complete structures.

Definition 4.4 *An allegory $\mathcal{R}$ is a category satisfying the following:*

(1) For all objects A and B the class $\mathcal{R}[A, B]$ is a lower semilattice. Meet and the induced ordering are denoted by $\sqcap, \sqsubseteq$, respectively. The elements in $\mathcal{R}[A, B]$ are called relations.

(2) There is a monotone operation $\breve{}$ *(called the converse operation) such that for all relations* $Q, R : A \to B$ *and* $S : B \to C$ *the following holds:*

$$(Q;S)^{\smile} = S^{\smile};Q^{\smile} \quad \text{and} \quad (Q^{\smile})^{\smile} = Q.$$

(3) For all relations $Q : A \to B$, $R, S : B \to C$ *we have* $Q;(R \sqcap S) \sqsubseteq Q;R \sqcap Q;S$.

(4) For all relations $Q : A \to B, R : B \to C$ *and* $S : A \to C$ *the modular law* $Q;R \sqcap S \sqsubseteq Q;(R \sqcap Q^{\smile};S)$ *holds.*

Notice that [10] requires $(Q \sqcap R)^{\smile} = Q^{\smile} \sqcap R^{\smile}$ instead of the monotonicity of $.^{\smile}$. Obviously, the property above implies monotonicity and the other implication is shown as follows:

$$\begin{aligned}
X \sqsubseteq Q^{\smile} \sqcap R^{\smile} &\Leftrightarrow X \sqsubseteq Q^{\smile} \quad \text{and} \quad X \sqsubseteq R^{\smile} \\
&\Leftrightarrow X^{\smile} \sqsubseteq Q \quad \text{and} \quad X^{\smile} \sqsubseteq R \qquad {}^{\smile} \text{ monotone and (2b)} \\
&\Leftrightarrow X^{\smile} \sqsubseteq Q \sqcap R \\
&\Leftrightarrow X \sqsubseteq (Q \sqcap R)^{\smile}. \qquad {}^{\smile} \text{ monotone and (2b)}
\end{aligned}$$

A homomorphism $F : \mathcal{R}_1 \to \mathcal{R}_2$ between allegories is a functor, which preserves the converse operation and, restricted to every $\mathcal{R}_1[A, B]$, is a lower semilattice homomorphism. An allegory $\mathcal{R}$, as well as the structures defined later, is called representable iff there is an embedding into **Rel**, i.e., there is a faithful homomorphism F (of convenient type) from $\mathcal{R}$ to **Rel**.

By Theorem 3.1 (1)–(7), the category $\mathcal{L}$-**Rel** of $\mathcal{L}$-fuzzy relations with meet $\cap$ and conversion ^{T} is an allegory.

Lemma 4.5 *Let* $\mathcal{R}$ *be an allegory,* A, B, C *objects of* $\mathcal{R}$ *and* $Q, R : A \to B$, $S : B \to C$, $T : A \to C$, *and* $U, V : A \to A$. *Then we have*

(1) $\mathbb{I}_A^{\smile} = \mathbb{I}_A$,

(2) $(Q \sqcap R);S \sqsubseteq Q;S \sqcap R;S$,

(3) ; *is monotone in both arguments,*

(4) $Q;S \sqcap T \sqsubseteq (Q \sqcap T;S^{\smile});S$,

(5) $Q;S \sqcap T \sqsubseteq (Q \sqcap T;S^{\smile});(S \sqcap Q^{\smile};T)$,

(6) $Q \sqsubseteq Q;Q^{\smile};Q$,

(7) $\mathbb{I}_A \sqcap (U \sqcap V);(U \sqcap V)^{\smile} = \mathbb{I}_A \sqcap U;V^{\smile} = \mathbb{I}_A \sqcap V;U^{\smile}$,

(8) $Q = (\mathbb{I}_A \sqcap Q;Q^{\smile});Q = Q;(\mathbb{I}_B \sqcap Q^{\smile};Q)$.

Proof.

(1) The assertion follows from

$$\begin{aligned} \mathbb{I}_A &= (\mathbb{I}_A^\smile)^\smile && \text{axiom (2b)} \\ &= (\mathbb{I}_A;\mathbb{I}_A^\smile)^\smile && \text{identity law} \\ &= (\mathbb{I}_A^\smile)^\smile;\mathbb{I}_A^\smile && \text{axiom (2a)} \\ &= \mathbb{I}_A;\mathbb{I}_A^\smile && \text{axiom (2b)} \\ &= \mathbb{I}_A^\smile && \text{identity law} \end{aligned}$$

(2) Consider the following computation:

$$\begin{aligned} (Q \sqcap R);S &= (((Q \sqcap R);S)^\smile)^\smile && \text{axiom (2b)} \\ &= (S^\smile;(Q^\smile \sqcap R^\smile))^\smile && \text{axiom (2a)} \\ &\sqsubseteq (S^\smile;Q^\smile \sqcap S^\smile;R^\smile)^\smile && \text{(1) and axiom (3)} \\ &= ((Q;S \sqcap R;S)^\smile)^\smile && \text{axiom (2a)} \\ &= Q;S \sqcap R;S. && \text{axiom (2b)} \end{aligned}$$

(3) The assertion follows immediately from (2) and axiom (3).

(4) is shown similar to (2).

(5) The assertion is shown as follows:

$$\begin{aligned} Q;S \sqcap T &= (Q;S \sqcap T) \sqcap T \\ &\sqsubseteq (Q \sqcap T;S^\smile);S \sqcap T && \text{(4)} \\ &\sqsubseteq (Q \sqcap T;S^\smile);(S \sqcap (Q \sqcap T;S^\smile)^\smile;T) && \text{axiom (4)} \\ &\sqsubseteq (Q \sqcap T;S^\smile);(S \sqcap Q^\smile;T). && {}^\smile \text{ monotone and (3)} \end{aligned}$$

(6) Again, consider the following computation:

$$\begin{aligned} Q &= Q;\mathbb{I}_B \sqcap Q && \text{identity law} \\ &\sqsubseteq Q;(\mathbb{I}_B \sqcap Q^\smile;Q) && \text{axiom (4)} \\ &\sqsubseteq Q;Q^\smile;Q. && \text{(3)} \end{aligned}$$

(7) First of all, we have $\mathbb{I}_A \sqcap (U \sqcap V);(U \sqcap V)^\smile \sqsubseteq \mathbb{I}_A \sqcap U;V^\smile$. The other inclusion follows from

$$\begin{aligned} \mathbb{I}_A \sqcap U;V^\smile &= \mathbb{I}_A \sqcap (\mathbb{I}_A \sqcap (\mathbb{I}_A \sqcap U;V^\smile)) \\ &\sqsubseteq \mathbb{I}_A \sqcap (\mathbb{I}_A \sqcap (\mathbb{I}_A;V \sqcap U);V^\smile) && \text{modular law} \\ &= \mathbb{I}_A \sqcap (\mathbb{I}_A \sqcap (U \sqcap V);V^\smile) && \text{identity law} \\ &\sqsubseteq \mathbb{I}_A \sqcap (U \sqcap V);((U \sqcap V)^\smile;\mathbb{I}_A \sqcap V^\smile) && \text{modular law} \\ &= \mathbb{I}_A \sqcap (U \sqcap V);(U \sqcap V)^\smile. \end{aligned}$$

The second assertion is shown analogously.

(8) We just show the first assertion, which follows immediately from

$$\begin{aligned}(\mathbb{I}_A \sqcap Q;Q^\smile);Q &\sqsubseteq Q \\ &= \mathbb{I}_A;Q \sqcap Q \\ &\sqsubseteq (\mathbb{I}_A \sqcap Q;Q^\smile);Q. \qquad (4)\end{aligned}$$

□

In the remainder of this book we will use the properties (1)–(6) of the previous lemma without mentioning.

An important class of relations is given by mappings.

Definition 4.6 *Let $\mathcal{R}$ be an allegory and $Q : A \to B$. Then we call*

(1) Q univalent iff $Q^\smile;Q \sqsubseteq \mathbb{I}_B$,

(2) Q total iff $\mathbb{I}_A \sqsubseteq Q;Q^\smile$,

(3) Q a map iff Q is univalent and total,

(4) Q injective iff $Q^\smile$ is univalent,

(5) Q surjective iff $Q^\smile$ is total,

(6) Q bijective iff $Q^\smile$ is a map,

(7) Q a bijection iff Q is a bijective map.

Notice that in **Rel** the definitions above correspond to the set-theoretic definitions. As usual, we will denote mappings by lowercase letters.

Since the notions of univalent and injective relations as well as the notions of total and surjective relations are dual via conversion we just state properties of univalent and/or total relations.

The class of univalent relations, the class of total relations, and, hence, the class of mappings is closed under composition. This may be seen as follows:

$$\begin{aligned}(Q;R)^\smile;Q;R &= R^\smile;Q^\smile;Q;R \\ &\sqsubseteq R^\smile;R && Q \text{ univalent} \\ &\sqsubseteq \mathbb{I}_C, && R \text{ univalent} \\ Q;R;(Q;R)^\smile &= Q;R;R^\smile;Q^\smile \\ &\sqsupseteq Q;Q^\smile && R \text{ total} \\ &\sqsupseteq \mathbb{I}_A. && Q \text{ total}\end{aligned}$$

On the other hand, if $Q;R$ is total, then so is Q. This follows from

$$\begin{aligned}\mathbb{I}_A &= \mathbb{I}_A \sqcap Q;R;(Q;R)^\smile && Q;R \text{ total} \\ &= \mathbb{I}_A \sqcap Q;R;R^\smile;Q^\smile \\ &\sqsubseteq (Q;\sqcap Q;R;R^\smile);Q^\smile && \text{modular law} \\ &\sqsubseteq Q;Q^\smile.\end{aligned}$$

Some other interesting properties of univalent relations are summarized in the next lemma.

Lemma 4.7 *Let $\mathcal{R}$ be an allegory, $Q : A \to B$ be univalent and $R, S : B \to C$, $T : C \to A$, and $U : C \to B$. Then we have*

(1) $Q;(R \sqcap S) = Q;R \sqcap Q;S$,

(2) $T;Q \sqcap U = (T \sqcap U;Q^{\smile});Q$.

Proof.

(1) It remains to show that $Q;R \sqcap Q;S \sqsubseteq Q;(R \sqcap S)$. Therefore, consider the following computation:

$$\begin{aligned} Q;R \sqcap Q;S &\sqsubseteq Q;(R \sqcap Q^{\smile};Q;S) && \text{modular law} \\ &\sqsubseteq Q;(R \sqcap S). && Q \text{ univalent} \end{aligned}$$

(2) The assertion is shown as follows:

$$\begin{aligned} (T \sqcap U;Q^{\smile});Q &\sqsubseteq T;Q \sqcap U;Q^{\smile};Q \\ &\sqsubseteq T;Q \sqcap U && Q \text{ univalent} \\ &\sqsubseteq (T \sqcap U;Q^{\smile});Q. && \text{modular law} \end{aligned}$$
□

Now, suppose f is a concrete map, i.e., a set-theoretic function. Then we may state the following property of functions: The image of a set A under f is included in a set B iff A is included in the inverse image of B or, alternatively, the operations $Q \mapsto Q;f$ and $R \mapsto R;f^{\smile}$ form a Galois correspondence. The next lemma shows that this property is valid in all allegories.

Lemma 4.8 *Let $\mathcal{R}$ be an allegory, $Q : A \to B, R : A \to C$, $S : D \to B$ be relations, and $f : B \to C$ and $g : A \to D$ be mappings. Then we have*

(1) $Q;f \sqsubseteq R$ *iff* $Q \sqsubseteq R;f^{\smile}$,

(2) $g^{\smile};Q \sqsubseteq S$ *iff* $Q \sqsubseteq g;S$.

Proof.

(1) Suppose $Q;f \sqsubseteq R$. Then we get $Q \sqsubseteq Q;f;f^{\smile} \sqsubseteq R;f^{\smile}$ since f is total. Now, suppose $Q \sqsubseteq R;f^{\smile}$ and compute $Q;f \sqsubseteq R;f^{\smile};f \sqsubseteq R$ since f is univalent.

(2) follows from (1) using converse. □

In the view of scalars, *partial identities*, i.e., relations $R : A \to A$ with $R \sqsubseteq \mathbb{I}_A$ are of special interest.

Lemma 4.9 *Let $\mathcal{R}$ be an allegory, $S, T : B \to B$ partial identities and $Q, U : A \to B$ and $R, V : B \to C$ arbitrary relations. Then we have*

(1) $S^{\smile} = S$,

(2) $S;S = S$,

(3) $S;T = S \sqcap T$,

(4) $Q;(S \sqcap T) = Q;S \sqcap Q;T$ *and* $(S \sqcap T);R = S;R \sqcap T;R$,

(5) $(Q \sqcap U);(S \sqcap T) = Q;S \sqcap U;T$ *and* $(S \sqcap T);(R \sqcap V) = S;R \sqcap T;V$.

Proof.

(1) Consider the following computation:

$$\begin{aligned} S &\sqsubseteq S;S^{\smile};S && \text{Lemma 4.5 (6)} \\ &\sqsubseteq \mathbb{I}_B;S^{\smile};\mathbb{I}_B && S \text{ partial identity} \\ &= S^{\smile}. \end{aligned}$$

The other inclusion is shown analogously.

(2) The following computation shows the assertion:

$$\begin{aligned} S &\sqsubseteq S;S^{\smile};S && \text{Lemma 4.5 (6)} \\ &\sqsubseteq S;\mathbb{I}_B;S && S \text{ partial identity} \\ &= S;S \\ &\sqsubseteq S;\mathbb{I}_B && S \text{ partial identity} \\ &= S. \end{aligned}$$

(3) First, we have $S;T \sqsubseteq S;\mathbb{I}_B = S$ and $S;T \sqsubseteq \mathbb{I}_B;T = T$, and, hence, $S;T \sqsubseteq S \sqcap T$. The other inclusion is shown as follows:

$$\begin{aligned} S \sqcap T &= (S \sqcap T);(S \sqcap T) && \text{(2) since } S \sqcap T \text{ is a partial identity} \\ &\sqsubseteq S;T \end{aligned}$$

(4) We just show the first assertion, where the inclusion $\sqsubseteq$ is trivial. The other inclusion follows from

$$\begin{aligned} &Q;S \sqcap Q;T \\ &\sqsubseteq Q;(S \sqcap Q^{\smile};Q;T) && \text{modular law} \\ &= Q;(S \sqcap \mathbb{I}_B \sqcap Q^{\smile};Q;T) && S \sqsubseteq \mathbb{I}_B \\ &= Q;(S \sqcap \mathbb{I}_B \sqcap Q^{\smile};Q;T^{\smile}) && (1) \\ &= Q;(S \sqcap \mathbb{I}_B \sqcap (Q^{\smile};Q \sqcap T);(Q^{\smile};Q \sqcap T)^{\smile}) && \text{Lemma 4.5 (7)} \\ &\sqsubseteq Q;(S \sqcap \mathbb{I}_B \sqcap T;T^{\smile}) \\ &= Q;(S \sqcap \mathbb{I}_B \sqcap T) && \text{(1) and (2)} \\ &= Q;(S \sqcap T). && S \sqsubseteq \mathbb{I}_B \end{aligned}$$

(5) Notice that the relations S and $S \sqcap T$ are univalent. Again, we just show the first assertion, which follows from

$$\begin{aligned}
&Q; S \sqcap U; T \\
&= (Q \sqcap U; T; S^{\smile}); S && \text{Lemma 4.7 (2)} \\
&= (Q \sqcap U; (S \sqcap T)); S && \text{(1) and (3)} \\
&= (Q \sqcap U; (S \sqcap T); (S \sqcap T)); S && \text{(2)} \\
&= (Q; (S \sqcap T)^{\smile} \sqcap U; (S \sqcap T)); (S \sqcap T); S && \text{Lemma 4.7 (2)} \\
&= (Q; (S \sqcap T) \sqcap U; (S \sqcap T)); (S \sqcap T) && \text{(1) and (3)} \\
&= (Q; \sqcap U); (S \sqcap T); (S \sqcap T) && \text{Lemma 4.7 (1)} \\
&= (Q; \sqcap U); (S \sqcap T). && \text{(2)}
\end{aligned}$$

□

As for lattices, a convenient allegory of antimorphism is embedded into an allegory of antitone functions, which is defined as follows:

Theorem 4.10 *Let $\mathcal{R}$ be an allegory and P a poset. Then the structure $\mathcal{R}^P_{\geq}$ defined by*

(1) the objects of $\mathcal{R}^P_{\geq}$ are the objects of $\mathcal{R}$,

(2) $\mathcal{R}^P_{\geq}[A, B]$ is the lower semilattice $P \stackrel{\geq}{\to} \mathcal{R}[A, B]$,

(3) all other operations and constants are defined componentwise, i.e.,

$$\mathbb{I}_A(x) := \mathbb{I}_A, \quad (f; g)(x) := f(x); g(x), \quad f^{\smile}(x) := (f(x))^{\smile}$$

is again an allegory.

Proof. We just show that $f; g$ and $f^{\smile}$ are antitone. The rest of the proof follows immediately since all operations and constants are defined componentwise and the axioms of an allegory are equational. Suppose $x \sqsubseteq y$. Then we have $(f; g)(y) = f(y); g(y) \sqsubseteq f(x); g(x) = (f; g)(x)$ and $f^{\smile}(y) = (f(y))^{\smile} \sqsubseteq (f(x))^{\smile} = f^{\smile}(x)$. □

4.3 DISTRIBUTIVE ALLEGORIES

Consider the collection of binary relations on a fixed set. This structure constitutes a distributive lattice with a least element. This is our motivation to switch from lower semilattices to distributive lattices as the basic order structure.

Definition 4.11 *A distributive allegory $\mathcal{R}$ is an allegory satisfying the following:*

(1) The classes $\mathcal{R}[A, B]$ are distributive lattices with a least element. Union and the least element are denoted by $\sqcup, \perp\!\!\!\perp_{AB}$, respectively.

(2) For all relations $Q : A \to B$ *we have* $Q; \perp\!\!\!\perp_{BC} = \perp\!\!\!\perp_{AC}$.

(3) For all relations $Q : A \to B$, $R, S : B \to C$ *we have* $Q; (R \sqcup S) = Q; R \sqcup Q; S$.

Obviously, a homomorphism between distributive allegories is a homomorphism, which is also an upper semilattice homomorphism for every pair of objects.

Again, Theorem 3.1 (8) and (9) show that the allegory $\mathcal{L}$-**Rel** of $\mathcal{L}$-fuzzy relations with union $\cup$ is a distributive allegory.

Lemma 4.12 *Let* $\mathcal{R}$ *be a distributive allegory. Then for all* $Q, R : A \to B$ *and* $S : B \to C$ *we have*

(1) $\perp\!\!\!\perp_{AB}^{\smile} = \perp\!\!\!\perp_{BA}$,

(2) $\perp\!\!\!\perp_{CA}; Q = \perp\!\!\!\perp_{CB}$,

(3) $(Q \sqcup R)^{\smile} = Q^{\smile} \sqcup R^{\smile}$,

(4) $(Q \sqcup R); S = Q; S \sqcup R; S$.

Proof.

(1) Suppose $X : B \to A$. Then we have $\perp\!\!\!\perp_{AB} \sqsubseteq X^{\smile}$, and, hence, $\perp\!\!\!\perp_{AB}^{\smile} \sqsubseteq X$.

(2) We immediately conclude that $\perp\!\!\!\perp_{CA}; Q = (Q^{\smile}; \perp\!\!\!\perp_{CA}^{\smile})^{\smile} = (Q^{\smile}; \perp\!\!\!\perp_{AC})^{\smile} = \perp\!\!\!\perp_{BC}^{\smile} = \perp\!\!\!\perp_{CB}$ by (1) and axiom (2).

(3) The inclusion $\sqsupseteq$ is trivial since $^{\smile}$ is monotone. The other inclusion follows from

$$\begin{aligned}(Q \sqcup R)^{\smile} \sqsubseteq Q^{\smile} \sqcup R^{\smile} &\Leftrightarrow Q \sqcup R \sqsubseteq (Q^{\smile} \sqcup R^{\smile})^{\smile} \\ &\Leftrightarrow Q \sqsubseteq (Q^{\smile} \sqcup R^{\smile})^{\smile} \quad \text{and} \quad R \sqsubseteq (Q^{\smile} \sqcup R^{\smile})^{\smile} \\ &\Leftrightarrow Q^{\smile} \sqsubseteq Q^{\smile} \sqcup R^{\smile} \quad \text{and} \quad R^{\smile} \sqsubseteq Q^{\smile} \sqcup R^{\smile}.\end{aligned}$$

(4) Consider the following computation:

$$\begin{aligned}(Q \sqcup R); S &= (S^{\smile}; (Q \sqcup R)^{\smile})^{\smile} \\ &= (S^{\smile}; (Q^{\smile} \sqcup R^{\smile}))^{\smile} && \text{by (3)} \\ &= (S^{\smile}; Q^{\smile} \sqcup S^{\smile}; R^{\smile})^{\smile} && \text{axiom (4)} \\ &= (Q; S^{\smile} \sqcup R; S^{\smile})^{\smile} \\ &= Q; S \sqcup R; S. && \text{by (3)}\end{aligned}$$

□

By Theorem 2.23 the structure $P \overset{\geq}{\rightrightarrows} \mathcal{R}[A, B]$ is a distributive lattice for all A and B. This motivates the following theorem:

Theorem 4.13 *Let $\mathcal{R}$ be a distributive allegory and P a poset. Then the allegory $\mathcal{R}^P_{\geq}$ is again a distributive allegory.*

The axioms of a distributive allegory are equational and all new operations and constants are defined componentwise. Therefore, we omit the proof of the previous theorem.

4.4 DIVISION ALLEGORIES

The next step in the hierarchy of allegories are division allegories. They are characterized by the fact that ; is a lower adjoint.

Definition 4.14 *A division allegory $\mathcal{R}$ is a distributive allegory such that ; has an upper left adjoint, i.e., for all relations $R : B \to C$ and $S : A \to C$ there is a relation $S/R : A \to B$ (called the left residual of S and R) such that for all $Q : A \to B$ the following holds:*

$$Q;R \sqsubseteq S \iff Q \sqsubseteq S/R.$$

As before, a homomorphism F between division allegories is a homomorphism between distributive allegories, which reflects the residual operation, i.e., $F(S/R) = F(S)/F(R)$ for all $R : B \to C$ and $S : A \to C$.

Again, as mentioned after Theorem 3.1 $\mathcal{L}$-**Rel** is a division allegory with $S \mathbin{.\!\!\cdot} R$ as residual.

The computation

$$\begin{aligned} Q;R \sqsubseteq S &\Leftrightarrow R^{\smile};Q^{\smile} \sqsubseteq S^{\smile} \\ &\Leftrightarrow R^{\smile} \sqsubseteq S^{\smile}/Q^{\smile} \\ &\Leftrightarrow R \sqsubseteq (S^{\smile}/Q^{\smile})^{\smile} \end{aligned}$$

shows that in a division allegory there is also an upper right adjoint $(S^{\smile}/Q^{\smile})^{\smile}$ for ;, which will be denoted by $Q\backslash S$ and called the right residual of S and Q. A symmetric version, called the symmetric quotient, of the residuals may be defined as $\mathrm{syQ}(Q,R) := (Q\backslash R) \sqcap (Q^{\smile}/R^{\smile})$. By definition, this relation is the greatest solution X of the inclusions

$$Q;X \sqsubseteq R \quad \text{and} \quad X;R^{\smile} \sqsubseteq Q^{\smile}.$$

From the Corollaries 2.17 and 2.18 on triples of residuated operations we get the following:

Corollary 4.15 *Let $\mathcal{R}$ be a division allegory and $Q, Q_1, Q_2 : A \to B$, $R, R_1, R_2 : B \to C$, and $S, S_1, S_2 : A \to C$. Then we have*

(1) $Q \sqsubseteq (Q;R)/R$ *and* $R \sqsubseteq Q\backslash(Q;R)$,

(2) $(S/R);R \sqsubseteq S$ *and* $Q;(Q\backslash S) \sqsubseteq S$,

(3) $S/(Q\backslash S) \sqsubseteq Q$ *and* $(S/R)\backslash S \sqsubseteq R$,

(4) $Q_2 \sqsubseteq Q_1, R_2 \sqsubseteq R_1$ *and* $S_1 \sqsubseteq S_2$ *implies* $S_1/R_1 \sqsubseteq S_2/R_2$ *and* $Q_1\backslash S_1 \sqsubseteq Q_2\backslash S_2$,

(5) $(S_1 \sqcap S_2)/R = (S_1/R) \sqcap (S_2/R)$ *and* $Q\backslash(S_1 \sqcap S_2) = (Q\backslash S_1) \sqcap (Q\backslash S_2)$,

(6) $S/(R_1 \sqcup R_2) = (S/R_1) \sqcap (S/R_2)$ *and* $(Q_1 \sqcup Q_2)\backslash S = (Q_1\backslash S) \sqcap (Q_2\backslash S)$,

Notice that the properties (1), (2), and (5) may also be used as axioms for the residuals. This shows that the notion of division allegories may also be defined equationally.

In the next lemma we have summarized further properties of the residuals.

Lemma 4.16 *Let* $\mathcal{R}$ *be a division allegory and* $Q : A \to B$, $R : B \to C$, $S : A \to C$, $F : D \to A$, *and* $G : C \to E$. *Then we have*

(1) $S/\mathbb{I}_C = S$ *and* $\mathbb{I}_A\backslash S = S$,

(2) $F;(S/R) \sqsubseteq (F;S)/R$ *and* $(Q\backslash S);G \sqsubseteq Q\backslash(S;G)$,

(3) if F *and* $G^\smile$ *are mappings, then the inclusions in (2) are equalities,*

(4) $S/R \sqsubseteq (S;G)/(R;G)$ *and* $Q\backslash S \sqsubseteq (F;Q)\backslash(F;S)$,

(5) if $F^\smile$ *and* G *are total and injective, then the inclusions in (4) are equalities.*

Proof. In all cases we just show the first assertion.

(1) Corollary 4.15 (1) implies $S \sqsubseteq (S;\mathbb{I}_C)/\mathbb{I}_C = S/\mathbb{I}_C$ and we conclude $S/\mathbb{I}_C = (S/\mathbb{I}_C);\mathbb{I}_C \sqsubseteq S$ using Corollary 4.15 (2).

(2) Again, Corollary 4.15 (2) implies $F;(S/R);R \sqsubseteq F;S$, which is equivalent to $F;(S/R) \sqsubseteq (F;S)/R$.

(3) We immediately conclude that

$$\begin{aligned}
(F;S)/R &\sqsubseteq F;F^\smile;((F;S)/R) && F \text{ total}\\
&\sqsubseteq F;((F^\smile;F;S)/R) && (2)\\
&\sqsubseteq F;(S/R). && F \text{ univalent and Corollary 4.15 (4)}
\end{aligned}$$

(4) Consider the following computation:

$$\begin{aligned}
X \sqsubseteq S/R &\Leftrightarrow X;R \sqsubseteq S && \text{definition of } /\\
&\Rightarrow X;R;G \sqsubseteq S;G\\
&\Leftrightarrow X \sqsubseteq (S;G)/(R;G), && \text{definition of } /
\end{aligned}$$

which implies the assertion.

(5) The assertion follows from

$$\begin{aligned} X \sqsubseteq (S;G)/(R;G) &\Leftrightarrow X;R;G \sqsubseteq S;G && \text{definition of } / \\ &\Rightarrow X;R;G;G^{\smile} \sqsubseteq S;G;G^{\smile} \\ &\Leftrightarrow X;R \sqsubseteq S && G;G^{\smile} = \mathbb{I}_C \text{ by the assumption} \\ &\Leftrightarrow X \sqsubseteq S/R. \end{aligned}$$

□

In the next lemma we have summarized some basic properties of symmetric quotients.

Lemma 4.17 *Let* $\mathcal{R}$ *be a division allegory,* $Q : A \to B$, $R : A \to C$, $S : A \to D$ *be relations, and* $f : D \to A$ *be a mapping. Then we have*

(1) $f;\mathrm{syQ}(Q,R) = \mathrm{syQ}(Q;f^{\smile},R)$,

(2) $\mathrm{syQ}(Q,R)^{\smile} = \mathrm{syQ}(R,Q)$,

(3) $\mathrm{syQ}(Q,R);\mathrm{syQ}(R,S) \sqsubseteq \mathrm{syQ}(Q,S)$.

Proof.

(1) The following computation shows the assertion:

$$\begin{aligned} & X \sqsubseteq f;\mathrm{syQ}(Q,R) \\ \Leftrightarrow\ & f^{\smile};X \sqsubseteq \mathrm{syQ}(Q,R) && \text{Lemma 4.8 (2)} \\ \Leftrightarrow\ & Q;f^{\smile};X \sqsubseteq R \text{ and } f^{\smile};X;R^{\smile} \sqsubseteq Q^{\smile} && \text{definition syQ} \\ \Leftrightarrow\ & Q;f^{\smile};X \sqsubseteq R \text{ and } X;R^{\smile} \sqsubseteq f;Q^{\smile} && \text{Lemma 4.8 (2)} \\ \Leftrightarrow\ & X \sqsubseteq \mathrm{syQ}(Q;f^{\smile},R). && \text{definition syQ} \end{aligned}$$

(2) We immediately conclude that

$$\begin{aligned} & X \sqsubseteq \mathrm{syQ}(Q,R)^{\smile} \\ \Leftrightarrow\ & X^{\smile} \sqsubseteq \mathrm{syQ}(Q,R) \\ \Leftrightarrow\ & Q;X^{\smile} \sqsubseteq R \text{ and } X^{\smile};R^{\smile} \sqsubseteq Q^{\smile} && \text{definition syQ} \\ \Leftrightarrow\ & X;Q^{\smile} \sqsubseteq R^{\smile} \text{ and } R;X \sqsubseteq Q \\ \Leftrightarrow\ & X \sqsubseteq \mathrm{syQ}(R,Q). && \text{definition syQ} \end{aligned}$$

(3) The assertion follows from

$$\begin{aligned} & \mathrm{syQ}(Q,R);\mathrm{syQ}(R,S) \\ =\ & ((Q\backslash R) \sqcap (Q^{\smile}/R^{\smile}));((R\backslash S) \sqcap (R^{\smile}/S^{\smile})) && \text{definition syQ} \\ \sqsubseteq\ & (Q\backslash R);(R\backslash S) \sqcap (Q^{\smile}/R^{\smile});(R^{\smile}/S^{\smile}) \\ \sqsubseteq\ & (Q\backslash S) \sqcap (Q^{\smile}/S^{\smile}) \\ =\ & \mathrm{syQ}(Q,S), && \text{definition syQ} \end{aligned}$$

where the second inclusion is shown as follows: We have $(Q\backslash R);(R\backslash S);S \sqsubseteq (Q\backslash R);R \sqsubseteq Q$ by Corollary 4.15 (2), and, hence, $(Q\backslash R);(R\backslash S) \sqsubseteq Q\backslash S$. $(Q^{\smile}/R^{\smile});(R^{\smile}/S^{\smile}) \sqsubseteq Q^{\smile}/S^{\smile}$ is shown analogously. □

Unfortunately, for antitone functions f and g, the function $(f/g)(x) := f(x)/g(x)$ is not antitone since $/$ itself is antitone in the second argument. Therefore, $\mathcal{R}^{P}_{\geq}$ is not necessarily a division allegory. We will get a convenient theorem in the case of completeness, i.e., for Dedekind categories in the next chapter.

The axioms of a division allegory are not independent. This is shown by the next lemma.

Theorem 4.18 *A category $\mathcal{R}$ is a division allegory iff the following holds:*

(1) For all objects A and B the collection $\mathcal{R}[A,B]$ is a distributive lattice with $Q;\perp\!\!\!\perp_{BC} = \perp\!\!\!\perp_{AC}$ for all relations $Q : A \to B$,

(2) $^{\smile}$ is a monotone operation with $(Q;R)^{\smile} = R^{\smile};Q^{\smile}$ and $(Q^{\smile})^{\smile} = Q$ for all relations $Q : A \to B$ and $R : B \to C$.

(3) The modular law is valid.

(4) The left residual exists.

Proof. The implication $\Rightarrow$ is trivial. For the other implication we have to show

(1) $Q;(R \sqcap S) \sqsubseteq Q;R \sqcap Q;S$,

(2) $Q;(R \sqcup S) = Q;R \sqcup Q;S$.

The second assertion follows from Corollary 2.18 since ; is a lower adjoint of a triple of residuated operations. Therefore, ; is monotone in the second argument, which implies the first assertion. □

4.5 DEDEKIND CATEGORIES

Now, we will switch to complete structures. Remember, that this will imply that the corresponding categories are locally small.

Definition 4.19 *A Dedekind category $\mathcal{R}$ is a division allegory so that every $\mathcal{R}[A,B]$ is a complete Brouwerian lattice. The greatest element in $\mathcal{R}[A,B]$ is denoted by $\top\!\!\!\top_{AB}$.*

A homomorphism between Dedekind categories is a homomorphism between division allegories, which is a complete Brouwerian lattice homomorphism for any pair of objects.

Lemma 4.20 *Let $F : \mathcal{R}_1 \to \mathcal{R}_2$ be a pre-functor between Dedekind categories, which is full, faithful, and bijective on objects. Furthermore, suppose*

(1) either F or F^{-1} respects composition,

(2) either F or F^{-1} respects the converse operation,

(3) either F or F^{-1} is a complete lower semilattice homomorphism for every pair of objects, and

(4) either F or F^{-1} is an upper semilattice homomorphism for every pair of objects.

Then F is an isomorphism.

Proof. By Lemma 4.3 F is an isomorphism of categories. Suppose without loss of generality that F respects the converse operation. Then we have

$$\begin{aligned} F^{-1}(Q^{\smile}) &= F^{-1}(F(F^{-1}(Q))^{\smile}) && F \text{ bijective on relations} \\ &= F^{-1}(F(F^{-1}(Q)^{\smile})) && F \text{ respects } {}^{\smile} \\ &= F^{-1}(Q)^{\smile}. && F \text{ bijective on relations} \end{aligned}$$

By Lemma 2.11 and the observation after Theorem 2.25 it is sufficient to show that F and F^{-1} preserve residuals. This follows immediately from the following computations:

$$\begin{aligned} F(Q/R) &= F\left(\bigsqcup\{X \mid X;R \sqsubseteq Q\}\right) \\ &= \bigsqcup\{F(X) \mid X;R \sqsubseteq Q\} && F \text{ complete lattice homo.} \\ &= \bigsqcup\{F(X) \mid F(X);F(R) \sqsubseteq F(Q)\} && F \text{ homomorphism and bijective} \\ &= \bigsqcup\{Y \mid Y;F(R) \sqsubseteq F(Q)\} && F \text{ bijective} \\ &= F(Q)/F(R), \\ F^{-1}(S/T) &= F^{-1}(F(F^{-1}(S))/F(F^{-1}(T))) && F \text{ bijective on relations} \\ &= F^{-1}(F(F^{-1}(S)/F^{-1}(T))) && F \text{ homomorphism} \\ &= F^{-1}(S)/F^{-1}(T). && F \text{ bijective on relations} \end{aligned}$$

□

As mentioned in Chapter 3, every $\mathcal{L}$-**Rel**$[A, B]$ is a complete Brouwerian lattice, and, hence, $\mathcal{L}$-**Rel** is a Dedekind category. Now, we want to state some properties of the greatest elements within Dedekind categories.

Lemma 4.21 *Let $\mathcal{R}$ be a Dedekind category and A and B objects of $\mathcal{R}$. Then we have*

(1) $\mathbb{T}_{AB}^{\smile} = \mathbb{T}_{BA}$,

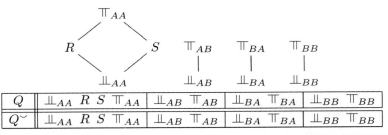

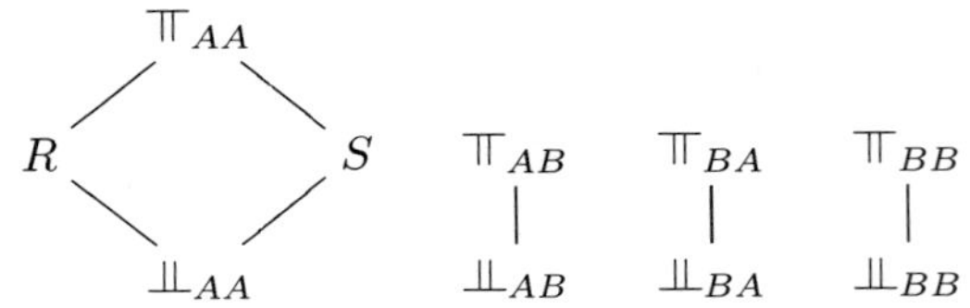

Q	$\bot\!\!\bot_{AA}$	R	S	$\top\!\!\top_{AA}$	$\bot\!\!\bot_{AB}$	$\top\!\!\top_{AB}$	$\bot\!\!\bot_{BA}$	$\top\!\!\top_{BA}$	$\bot\!\!\bot_{BB}$	$\top\!\!\top_{BB}$
$Q^\smile$	$\bot\!\!\bot_{AA}$	R	S	$\top\!\!\top_{AA}$	$\bot\!\!\bot_{AB}$	$\top\!\!\top_{AB}$	$\bot\!\!\bot_{BA}$	$\top\!\!\top_{BA}$	$\bot\!\!\bot_{BB}$	$\top\!\!\top_{BB}$

;	$\bot\!\!\bot_{AA}$	R	S	$\top\!\!\top_{AA}$	$\bot\!\!\bot_{AB}$	$\top\!\!\top_{AB}$	$\bot\!\!\bot_{BA}$	$\top\!\!\top_{BA}$	$\bot\!\!\bot_{BB}$	$\top\!\!\top_{BB}$
$\bot\!\!\bot_{AA}$	$\bot\!\!\bot_{AA}$	$\bot\!\!\bot_{AA}$	$\bot\!\!\bot_{AA}$	$\bot\!\!\bot_{AA}$	$\bot\!\!\bot_{AB}$	$\bot\!\!\bot_{AB}$				
R	$\bot\!\!\bot_{AA}$	R	$\bot\!\!\bot_{AA}$	R	$\bot\!\!\bot_{AB}$	$\top\!\!\top_{AB}$				
S	$\bot\!\!\bot_{AA}$	$\bot\!\!\bot_{AA}$	S	S	$\bot\!\!\bot_{AB}$	$\bot\!\!\bot_{AB}$				
$\top\!\!\top_{AA}$	$\bot\!\!\bot_{AA}$	R	S	$\top\!\!\top_{AA}$	$\bot\!\!\bot_{AB}$	$\bot\!\!\bot_{AB}$				
$\bot\!\!\bot_{AB}$							$\bot\!\!\bot_{AA}$	$\bot\!\!\bot_{AA}$	$\bot\!\!\bot_{AB}$	$\bot\!\!\bot_{AB}$
$\top\!\!\top_{AB}$							$\bot\!\!\bot_{AA}$	R	$\bot\!\!\bot_{AB}$	$\top\!\!\top_{AB}$
$\bot\!\!\bot_{BA}$	$\bot\!\!\bot_{BA}$	$\bot\!\!\bot_{BA}$	$\bot\!\!\bot_{BA}$	$\bot\!\!\bot_{BA}$	$\bot\!\!\bot_{BB}$	$\bot\!\!\bot_{BB}$				
$\top\!\!\top_{BA}$	$\bot\!\!\bot_{BA}$	$\top\!\!\top_{BA}$	$\bot\!\!\bot_{BA}$	$\top\!\!\top_{BA}$	$\bot\!\!\bot_{BB}$	$\top\!\!\top_{BB}$				
$\bot\!\!\bot_{BB}$							$\bot\!\!\bot_{BA}$	$\bot\!\!\bot_{BA}$	$\bot\!\!\bot_{BB}$	$\bot\!\!\bot_{BB}$
$\top\!\!\top_{BB}$							$\bot\!\!\bot_{BA}$	$\top\!\!\top_{BA}$	$\bot\!\!\bot_{BB}$	$\top\!\!\top_{BB}$

Figure 4.1. A Dedekind category with $\top\!\!\top_{AB};\top\!\!\top_{BA} \neq \top\!\!\top_{AA}$.

(2) $\top\!\!\top_{AA};\top\!\!\top_{AB} = \top\!\!\top_{AB};\top\!\!\top_{BB} = \top\!\!\top_{AB}$,

(3) $\top\!\!\top_{AB} = \top\!\!\top_{AB};\top\!\!\top_{BA};\top\!\!\top_{AB}$.

Proof.

(1) Suppose $X : B \to A$. Then we have $X^\smile \sqsubseteq \top\!\!\top_{AB}$, and, hence, $X \sqsubseteq \top\!\!\top_{AB}^\smile$.

(2) We have $\top\!\!\top_{AB} = \top\!\!\top_{AB};\mathbb{I}_{BB} \sqsubseteq \top\!\!\top_{AB};\top\!\!\top_{BB}$. Analogously, we obtain $\top\!\!\top_{AB} = \mathbb{I}_{AA};\top\!\!\top_{AB} \sqsubseteq \top\!\!\top_{AA};\top\!\!\top_{AB}$.

(3) The assertion follows immediately from (1) and Lemma 4.5 (6). □

Notice that the general property $\top\!\!\top_{AB};\top\!\!\top_{BC} = \top\!\!\top_{AC}$ is not valid. Consider the four (finite) lattices with converse and composition defined in Figure 4.1.

In this Dedekind category we have $\top\!\!\top_{AB};\top\!\!\top_{BA} = R \neq \top\!\!\top_{AA}$. This counterexample can also be found in [39].

We will call a Dedekind category *uniform* iff the equation $\top\!\!\top_{AB};\top\!\!\top_{BC} = \top\!\!\top_{AC}$ is true for all objects A, B and C with $\mathbb{I}_B \neq \bot\!\!\bot_{BB}$.

The so-called Tarski-rule

$$R \neq \bot\!\!\bot_{BC} \quad \Longrightarrow \quad \top\!\!\top_{AB};R;\top\!\!\top_{CD} = \top\!\!\top_{AD}$$

implies that $\mathcal{R}$ is uniform. The Dedekind category of $\mathcal{L}$-fuzzy relations is uniform. But, if the lattice $\mathcal{L}$ has at least three elements, the converse implication does not hold. Let $u \in \mathcal{L}$ be an element with $0 \neq u \neq 1$. Then we have $\mathbb{I}_A \neq \perp\!\!\!\perp_{AA}$, $\alpha_A^u \neq \perp\!\!\!\perp_{AA}$ and $(\top\!\!\!\top_{AA};\alpha_A^u;\top\!\!\!\top_{AA})(x) = u$ for all $x \in A$, which shows that $\top\!\!\!\top_{AA};\alpha_A^u;\top\!\!\!\top_{AA} \neq \top\!\!\!\top_{AA}$.

According to the equivalence of the Tarski-rule to a generalized version of the notion of simplicity known from universal algebra, we call a Dedekind category *simple* iff the Tarski-rule is valid.

Corollary 2.19 for residuated triples gives us the following:

Corollary 4.22 *Let $\mathcal{R}$ be a Dedekind category $Q, Q_i : A \to B$, $R, R_i : B \to C$ and $S, S_i : A \to C$ for $i \in I$. Then we have*

(1) $Q;(\bigsqcup_{i\in I} R_i) = \bigsqcup_{i\in I}(Q;R_i)$ *and* $(\bigsqcup_{i\in I} Q_i);R = \bigsqcup_{i\in I}(Q_i;R)$

(2) $Q;(\bigsqcap_{i\in I} R_i) \sqsubseteq \bigsqcap_{i\in I}(Q;R_i)$ *and* $(\bigsqcap_{i\in I} Q_i);R \sqsubseteq \bigsqcap_{i\in I}(Q_i;R)$,

(3) $\bigsqcap_{i\in I}(S_i/R) = (\bigsqcap_{i\in I} S_i)/R$ *and* $\bigsqcap_{i\in I}(Q\backslash S_i) = Q\backslash(\bigsqcap_{i\in I} S_i)$,

(4) $\bigsqcap_{i\in I}(S/R_i) = S/(\bigsqcup_{i\in I} R_i)$ *and* $\bigsqcap_{i\in I}(Q_i\backslash S) = (\bigsqcup_{i\in I} Q_i)\backslash S$.

In the next lemma we have summarized some other properties valid in Dedekind categories.

Lemma 4.23 *Let $\mathcal{R}$ be a Dedekind category $Q : A \to B$, $R : B \to C$, $S : A \to D$, and $T : D \to C$. Then we have*

(1) $(Q \sqcap S;\top\!\!\!\top_{DB});R = Q;R \sqcap S;\top\!\!\!\top_{DC}$ *and* $Q;(R \sqcap \top\!\!\!\top_{BD};T) = Q;R \sqcap \top\!\!\!\top_{AD};T$,

(2) $\mathbb{I}_A \sqcap Q;Q^{\smile} = \mathbb{I}_A \sqcap Q;\top\!\!\!\top_{BA} = \mathbb{I}_A \sqcap \top\!\!\!\top_{AB};Q^{\smile}$,

(3) if Q and $R^{\smile}$ are univalent, then the inclusions in Corollary 4.22 (2) are equalities.

(4) Q is total iff $Q;\top\!\!\!\top_{BC} = \top\!\!\!\top_{AC}$ for all objects C.

Proof. In all cases we just show the first assertion.

(1) Consider the following computation:

$$\begin{aligned}(Q \sqcap S;\top\!\!\!\top_{DB});R &\sqsubseteq Q;R \sqcap S;\top\!\!\!\top_{DB};R\\ &\sqsubseteq Q;R \sqcap S;\top\!\!\!\top_{DC}\\ &\sqsubseteq (Q \sqcap S;\top\!\!\!\top_{DC};R^{\smile});R &&\text{modular law}\\ &\sqsubseteq (Q \sqcap S;\top\!\!\!\top_{DB});R.\end{aligned}$$

(2) Again, consider the following computation:

$$\begin{aligned}\mathbb{I}_A \sqcap Q;\mathbb{T}_{BA} &= \mathbb{I}_A \sqcap Q;\mathbb{T}_{AB}^{\smile} \\ &= \mathbb{I}_A \sqcap (Q \sqcap \mathbb{T}_{AB});(Q \sqcap \mathbb{T}_{AB})^{\smile} \qquad \text{Lemma 4.5 (7)} \\ &= \mathbb{I}_A \sqcap Q;Q^{\smile}.\end{aligned}$$

(3) We just show the first assertion. Since Q is univalent, $\bigsqcap_{i\in I}(Q;R_i) \sqsubseteq Q;R_i$ implies $Q^{\smile};(\bigsqcap_{i\in I}(Q;R_i)) \sqsubseteq Q^{\smile};Q;R_i \sqsubseteq R_i$ for all $i \in I$. We immediately conclude that $Q^{\smile};(\bigsqcap_{i\in I}(Q;R_i)) \sqsubseteq \bigsqcap_{i\in I} R_i$, and, hence,

$$(*) \qquad Q;Q^{\smile};\left(\bigsqcap_{i\in I}(Q;R_i)\right) \sqsubseteq Q;\left(\bigsqcap_{i\in I} R_i\right).$$

We obtain

$$\begin{aligned}\bigsqcap_{i\in I}(Q;R_i) &= \bigsqcap_{i\in I}(Q;R_i \sqcap Q;\mathbb{T}_{BC}) \\ &= \left(\bigsqcap_{i\in I}(Q;R_i)\right) \sqcap Q;\mathbb{T}_{BC} \\ &= (\mathbb{I}_A \sqcap Q;\mathbb{T}_{BA});\left(\bigsqcap_{i\in I}(Q;R_i)\right) && (1) \\ &= (\mathbb{I}_A \sqcap Q;Q^{\smile});\left(\bigsqcap_{i\in I}(Q;R_i)\right) && (2) \\ &\sqsubseteq Q;Q^{\smile};\left(\bigsqcap_{i\in I}(Q;R_i)\right) \\ &\sqsubseteq Q;\left(\bigsqcap_{i\in I} R_i\right). && (*)\end{aligned}$$

(4) Suppose Q is total. Then we have $\mathbb{T}_{AC} = \mathbb{I}_A;\mathbb{T}_{AC} \sqsubseteq Q;Q^{\smile};\mathbb{T}_{AC} \sqsubseteq Q;\mathbb{T}_{BC}$. Now, suppose $Q;\mathbb{T}_{BC} = \mathbb{T}_{AC}$. Then $\mathbb{I}_A \sqcap Q;Q^{\smile} = \mathbb{I}_A \sqcap Q;\mathbb{T}_{BA} = \mathbb{I}_A \sqcap \mathbb{T}_{AA} = \mathbb{I}_A$ follows. □

Within Dedekind categories there are several further properties of partial identities. These are collected in the next lemma.

Lemma 4.24 *Let $\mathcal{R}$ be a Dedekind category, $S, T, S_i : A \to A$ for all $i \in I$ partial identities and $R : C \to A, U : A \to B$. Then we have*

(1) $S = \mathbb{I}_A \sqcap S;\mathbb{T}_{AA} = \mathbb{I}_A \sqcap \mathbb{T}_{AA};S$,

(2) $R;S = R \sqcap \mathbb{T}_{CA};S$ *and* $S;U = U \sqcap S;\mathbb{T}_{AB}$,

(3) $\bigsqcap_{i\in I}(\mathbb{T}_{CA};S_i) = \mathbb{T}_{CA};(\bigsqcap_{i\in I} S_i)$, *and* $\bigsqcap_{i\in I}(S_i;\mathbb{T}_{AB}) = (\bigsqcap_{i\in I} S_i);\mathbb{T}_{AB}$,

(4) $\bigsqcap_{i\in I}(R;S_i) = R;(\bigsqcap_{i\in I} S_i)$, *and* $\bigsqcap_{i\in I}(S_i;U) = (\bigsqcap_{i\in I} S_i);U$.

Proof. In all cases we just show the first assertion.

(1) By Lemma 4.9 (1) and (2) we have $S = \mathbb{I}_A \sqcap S;S^{\smile}$. From Lemma 4.23 (2) we conclude the assertion.

(2) Consider the following computation:

$$\begin{aligned} R;S &= R;(\mathbb{I}_A \sqcap \mathbb{T}_{AA};S) && (1) \\ &= R \sqcap \mathbb{T}_{CA};S && \text{Lemma 4.23 (1)} \end{aligned}$$

(3) It is sufficient to show $\sqsubseteq$. This follows from

$$\begin{aligned} \bigsqcap_{i\in I}(\mathbb{T}_{CA};S_i) &= \mathbb{T}_{CA} \sqcap \bigsqcap_{i\in I}(\mathbb{T}_{CA};S_i) \\ &\sqsubseteq \mathbb{T}_{CA} \sqcap \mathbb{T}_{CC};\bigsqcap_{i\in I}(\mathbb{T}_{CA};S_i) && \mathbb{I}_C \sqsubseteq \mathbb{T}_{CC} \\ &= \mathbb{T}_{CA};\left(\mathbb{I}_A \sqcap \mathbb{T}_{AC};\bigsqcap_{i\in I}(\mathbb{T}_{CA};S_i)\right) && \text{Lemma 4.23 (1)} \\ &\sqsubseteq \mathbb{T}_{CA};\left(\mathbb{I}_A \sqcap \bigsqcap_{i\in I}(\mathbb{T}_{AC};\mathbb{T}_{CA};S_i)\right) \\ &\sqsubseteq \mathbb{T}_{CA};\left(\mathbb{I}_A \sqcap \bigsqcap_{i\in I}(\mathbb{T}_{AA};S_i)\right) \\ &= \mathbb{T}_{CA};\left(\bigsqcap_{i\in I}(\mathbb{I}_A \sqcap \mathbb{T}_{AA};S_i)\right) \\ &= \mathbb{T}_{CA};\left(\bigsqcap_{i\in I} S_i\right). && (1) \end{aligned}$$

(4) We immediately conclude that

$$\begin{aligned} \bigsqcap_{i\in I}(R;S_i) &= \bigsqcap_{i\in I}(R \sqcap \mathbb{T}_{CA};S_i) && (2) \\ &= R \sqcap \bigsqcap_{i\in I}(\mathbb{T}_{CA};S_i) \\ &= R \sqcap \mathbb{T}_{CA};\left(\bigsqcap_{i\in I} S_i\right) && (3) \\ &= R;\left(\bigsqcap_{i\in I} S_i\right). && (2) \end{aligned}$$

□

In contrast to division allegories, which are not necessarily complete, the residuals in $\mathcal{R}^P_{\geq}$ can be constructed if $\mathcal{R}$ is complete.

Theorem 4.25 *Let $\mathcal{R}$ be a Dedekind category and P a poset. Then the allegory $\mathcal{R}^P_{\geq}$ is again a Dedekind category.*

Proof. First of all, $\mathcal{R}^P_{\geq}[A,B]$ is a complete Brouwerian lattice by Theorem 2.23 and Theorem 2.25 (2). The residuals exist by Corollary 2.19 since ; is defined componentwise and, therefore, an upper semilattice homomorphism in both arguments. □

Last but not least, we want to introduce a special endo-isomorphism of Dedekind categories. We will need this isomorphism for the motivation of Goguen categories.

Lemma 4.26 *Let $\mathcal{R}$ be a Dedekind category, and $\{f_A \mid A \text{ object of } \mathcal{R}\}$ be a class of bijections $f_A : A \to A$. Then F defined by $F(A) := A$ and $F(g) := f_A^{\smile}; R; f_B$ for $R : A \to B$ is an isomorphism.*

Proof. Suppose $F(R) = F(S)$. Then we conclude $R = f_A; f_A^{\smile}; R; f_B; f_B^{\smile} = f_A; F(R); f_B^{\smile} = f_A; F(S); f_B^{\smile} = f_A; f_A^{\smile}; S; f_B; f_B^{\smile} = S$ since f_A and f_B are bijections. Obviously, $f_A; Q; f_B^{\smile}$ is mapped to Q by F such that F is full, faithful, and bijective on objects. Using Lemma 4.20 the assertion follows from Corollary 4.22 (1) and Lemma 4.23 (3) since $F^{-1}(Q) = f_A; Q; f_B^{\smile}$. □

4.6 RELATIONAL CONSTRUCTIONS IN DEDEKIND CATEGORIES

In applications of Dedekind categories, especially in computer science, one often wants to use abstract counterparts of set-theoretic constructions as disjoint union of sets, Cartesian product of sets or subsets. Later on, we will give some examples in connection with the interpretation of fuzzy controllers within a Goguen category. In this chapter, we want to introduce those constructions.

The abstract counterpart of a disjoint union of sets is called a relational sum. It is characterized by the injections in the following way:

Definition 4.27 *Let $\{A_i \mid i \in I\}$ be a set of objects of a Dedekind category indexed by some set I. An object $\sum\limits_{i\in I} A_i$, together with relations $\iota_j \in \mathcal{R}[A_j, \sum\limits_{i\in I} A_i]$ for all $j \in I$, is called a relational sum of $\{A_i \mid i \in I\}$ iff for all $i,j \in I$ with $i \neq j$ the following holds:*

$$\iota_i;\iota_i^{\smile} = \mathbb{I}_{A_i}, \qquad \iota_i;\iota_j^{\smile} = \perp\!\!\!\perp_{A_iA_j}, \qquad \bigsqcup_{i\in I}(\iota_i^{\smile};\iota_i) = \mathbb{I}_{\sum\limits_{i\in I} A_i}.$$

$\mathcal{R}$ has relational sums iff for every set of objects the relational sum does exist.

A relational sum is unique up to isomorphism. We do not need that property so we omit the proof.

$\mathcal{L}$-**Rel** has relational sums, which are given by the disjoint union and the corresponding (crisp) set-theoretic injections. This is easy to verify and, therefore, we omit the proof.

The dual notion of a sum is the notion of a product.

Definition 4.28 *Let A and B be objects of a Dedekind category. An object $A \times B$, together with two relations $\pi : A \times B \to A$ and $\rho : A \times B \to B$, is called* *a relational product of A and B iff the following holds:*

$$\pi^{\smile};\pi \sqsubseteq \mathbb{I}_A, \qquad \rho^{\smile};\rho \sqsubseteq \mathbb{I}_B, \qquad \pi^{\smile};\rho = \mathbb{T}_{AB}, \qquad \pi;\pi^{\smile} \sqcap \rho;\rho^{\smile} = \mathbb{I}_{A\times B}.$$

$\mathcal{R}$ has relational products iff for every pair of objects a relational product does exist.

Again, this construction is unique up to isomorphism. Furthermore, $\mathcal{L}$-**Rel** has relational products, which are given by the Cartesian products of sets and the corresponding set-theoretic projections. As above, we omit the proofs.

There is also an abstract notion of singleton sets, called a unit.

Definition 4.29 *An object* I *is called a unit iff* $\mathbb{I}_{\mathrm{I}} = \mathbb{T}_{\mathrm{II}}$ *and* $\mathbb{T}_{A\mathrm{I}}$ *is total for all objects A.*

Again, units are unique up to isomorphism. In $\mathcal{L}$-**Rel** every singleton set is a unit.

A subset M of a set N may be described by the canonical injection $f : M \to N$. Furthermore, the set of equivalence classes of an equivalence relation is fully determined by the function mapping each element to its equivalence class. Combining both concept we aim at the notion of a splitting.

Definition 4.30 *Let* $Q : A \to A$ *be a symmetric idempotent relation, i.e.,* $Q^{\smile} = Q$ *and* $Q;Q = Q$*. An object B together with a relation* $R : B \to A$ *is called a splitting of Q (or R splits Q) iff* $R;R^{\smile} = \mathbb{I}_B$ *and* $R^{\smile};R = Q$*.*

As before, a splitting is unique up to isomorphism. If Q is a partial identity, the object B of the splitting corresponds to the subset given by Q. Analogously, if Q is an equivalence relation, B corresponds to the set of equivalence classes. This shows that in $\mathcal{L}$-**Rel** every symmetric idempotent splits.

We have seen that $\mathcal{L}$-**Rel** offers all relational constructions introduced in this chapter. Furthermore, the corresponding relations, i.e., the projections, injections, and splittings of crisp relations, are crisp. Later on, we will see that there may also be noncrisp versions of these constructions. This causes a problem within the application of the theory since it is usually supposed that they are crisp. In Section 5.9 we will focus on that problem.

4.7 THE DEDEKIND CATEGORY OF ANTIMORPHISMS

In Theorem 2.47 we have shown that the collection of antimorphisms $\mathcal{L}_1 \overset{\text{anti}}{\to} \mathcal{L}_2$ is a complete Brouwerian lattice if $\mathcal{L}_1$ and $\mathcal{L}_2$ are. Now, we want to extend this theorem to Dedekind categories.

Throughout this chapter let $\mathcal{R}$ be a Dedekind category and $\mathcal{L}$ a complete Brouwerian lattice such that $\mathcal{R}^{\mathcal{L}}_{\geq}$ is again a Dedekind category.

Lemma 4.31 *For all antitone functions* $f, f_i : \mathcal{L} \overset{\geq}{\to} \mathcal{R}[A,B]$*,* $g, g_i : \mathcal{L} \overset{\geq}{\to} \mathcal{R}[B,C]$ *for all* $i \in i$ *and* $h : \mathcal{L} \overset{\geq}{\to} \mathcal{R}[C,D]$ *we have*

(1) $\tau(f);g \sqsubseteq \tau(f;g)$ *and* $f;\tau(g) \sqsubseteq \tau(f;g)$*,*

(2) $\tau(\tau(f);g) = \tau(f;g)$ *and* $\tau(f;\tau(g)) = \tau(f;g)$,

(3) $\tau(\tau(\bigsqcup_{i\in I} f_i);g) = \tau(\bigsqcup_{i\in I} \tau(f_i;g))$ *and* $\tau(f;\tau(\bigsqcup_{i\in I} g_i)) = \tau(\bigsqcup_{i\in I} \tau(f;g_i))$.

Proof. In all cases we just prove the first assertion.

(1) We prove the assertion using fixed point induction. Therefore, we define the following predicate:

$$\mathfrak{P}(k,l) \quad :\Longleftrightarrow \quad k;g \sqsubseteq l.$$

This predicate is admissible since $\mathfrak{P}(k_i,l_i)$, which is equivalent to $k_i;g \sqsubseteq l_i$ for all $i \in I$, implies $\bigsqcup_{i\in I}(k_i;g) \sqsubseteq \bigsqcup_{i\in I} l_i$, which is equivalent to $(\bigsqcup_{i\in I} k_i);g \sqsubseteq \bigsqcup_{i\in I} l_i$ and $\mathfrak{P}(\bigsqcup_{i\in I} k_i, \bigsqcup_{i\in I} l_i)$.

The base case $\mathfrak{P}(f,f;g)$ is trivial. Now, suppose $\mathfrak{P}(k,l)$. Then we have

$$\begin{aligned}
(\varphi(k);g)(x) &= \varphi(k)(x);g(x) && \text{definition of ;}\\
&= \left(\bigsqcup_{\bigvee M = x}\ \bigsqcap_{y\in M} k(y)\right);g(x) && \text{definition of } \varphi\\
&= \bigsqcup_{\bigvee M = x}\left(\bigsqcap_{y\in M} k(y)\right);g(x) &&\\
&\sqsubseteq \bigsqcup_{\bigvee M = x}\ \bigsqcap_{y\in M} (k(y);g(x)) &&\\
&\sqsubseteq \bigsqcup_{\bigvee M = x}\ \bigsqcap_{y\in M} (k(y);g(y)) && k \text{ and } g \text{ antitone}\\
&= \bigsqcup_{\bigvee M = x}\ \bigsqcap_{y\in M} (k;g)(y) && \text{definition of ;}\\
&\sqsubseteq \bigsqcup_{\bigvee M = x}\ \bigsqcap_{y\in M} l(y) && \text{induction hypothesis}\\
&= \varphi(l)(x). && \text{definition of } \varphi
\end{aligned}$$

The principle of fixed point induction gives us $\mathfrak{P}(\mu_\varphi(f), \mu_\varphi(f;g))$, and, hence, $\tau(f);g \sqsubseteq \tau(f;g)$.

(2) Using (1) we conclude that $\tau(\tau(f);g) \sqsubseteq \tau^2(f;g) = \tau(f;g) \sqsubseteq \tau(\tau(f);g)$.

(3) Since $\tau(f_i;g) \sqsubseteq \tau(\tau(\bigsqcup_{i\in I} f_i);g)$ for all $i \in I$ we get

$$\tau\left(\bigsqcup_{i\in I} \tau(f_i;g)\right) \sqsubseteq \tau^2(\tau\left(\bigsqcup_{i\in I} f_i\right);g) = \tau(\tau\left(\bigsqcup_{i\in I} f_i\right);g).$$

The other inclusion follows from

$$\tau\left(\tau\left(\bigsqcup_{i\in I} f_i\right);g\right) = \tau\left(\left(\bigsqcup_{i\in I} f_i\right);g\right) \qquad (2)$$

$$= \tau\left(\bigsqcup_{i\in I}(f_i;g)\right) \qquad \text{; defined componentwise}$$

$$\sqsubseteq \tau\left(\bigsqcup_{i\in I}\tau(f_i;g)\right). \qquad \square$$

In the next lemma we have summarized some properties of the converse operation in $\mathcal{R}^{\mathcal{L}}_{\geq}$.

Lemma 4.32 *For all $f : \mathcal{L} \overset{\text{anti}}{\to} \mathcal{R}[A,B]$ and $g : \mathcal{L} \overset{\text{anti}}{\to} \mathcal{R}[B,C]$ we have*

(1) $f^{\smile}$ is an antimorphism from $\mathcal{L}$ to $\mathcal{R}[B,A]$,

(2) $\tau(f;g)^{\smile} = \tau(g^{\smile};f^{\smile})$.

Proof.

(1) The assertion follows from

$$f^{\smile}\left(\bigvee M\right) = \left(f\left(\bigvee M\right)\right)^{\smile} \qquad \text{definition of } {}^{\smile}$$

$$= \left(\prod_{x\in M} f(x)\right)^{\smile} \qquad f \text{ antimorphism}$$

$$= \prod_{x\in M} (f(x))^{\smile}$$

$$= \prod_{x\in M} f^{\smile}(x). \qquad \text{definition of } {}^{\smile}$$

(2) The assertion is shown by fixed point induction. Define the following predicate:

$$\mathfrak{P}(h,k) \quad :\Longleftrightarrow \quad h^{\smile} = k.$$

This predicate is admissible since $\mathfrak{P}(h_i,k_i)$, which is equivalent to $h_i^{\smile} = k_i$ for all $i \in I$, implies $\bigsqcup_{i\in I} h_i^{\smile} = \bigsqcup_{i\in I} k_i$, and, hence, $(\bigsqcup_{i\in I} h_i)^{\smile} = \bigsqcup_{i\in I} k_i$ and $\mathfrak{P}(\bigsqcup_{i\in I} h_i, \bigsqcup_{i\in I} k_i)$.

The base case $\mathfrak{P}(f;g, g^{\smile};f^{\smile})$ is trivial. Now, suppose $\mathfrak{P}(h,k)$. Then we have

$$\varphi(h)^{\smile}(x) = \varphi(h)(x)^{\smile}$$

$$= \left(\bigsqcup_{\bigvee M = x}\prod_{y\in M} h(y)\right)^{\smile} \qquad \text{definition of } \varphi$$

$$= \bigsqcup_{\bigvee M = x}\prod_{y\in M} (h(y))^{\smile}$$

$$
\begin{aligned}
&= \bigsqcup_{\bigvee M = x} \bigsqcap_{y \in M} h^{\smile}(y) && \text{definition of } {}^{\smile} \\
&= \bigsqcup_{\bigvee M = x} \bigsqcap_{y \in M} k(y) && \text{induction hypothesis} \\
&= \varphi(k)(x). && \text{definition of } \varphi
\end{aligned}
$$

From the principle of fixed point induction we get $\mathfrak{P}(\mu_\varphi(f;g), \mu_\varphi(g^{\smile};f^{\smile}))$, and, hence, $\tau(f;g)^{\smile} = \tau(g^{\smile};f^{\smile})$. □

Now, we are able to prove the main theorem of this section.

Theorem 4.33 *Let $\mathcal{R}$ be a Dedekind category and $\mathcal{L}$ a complete Brouwerian lattice. Then the structure $\mathcal{R}^{\mathcal{L}}$ defined by*

(1) the objects of $\mathcal{R}^{\mathcal{L}}$ are the objects of $\mathcal{R}$,

(2) $\mathcal{R}^{\mathcal{L}}[A,B]$ is the complete Brouwerian lattice $\mathcal{L} \overset{\text{anti}}{\to} \mathcal{R}[A,B]$ of antimorphisms,

(3) the converse operation is defined componentwise,

(4) composition is defined by $f \mathbin{\dot{;}} g := \tau(f;g)$ with identity $\dot{\mathbb{I}}$ is again a Dedekind category.

Proof. First, we want to show that $\mathcal{R}^{\mathcal{L}}$ is a category. Associativity follows from

$$
\begin{aligned}
f \mathbin{\dot{;}} (g \mathbin{\dot{;}} h) &= \tau(f;\tau(g;h)) && \text{definition of } \dot{;} \\
&= \tau(f;(g;h)) && \text{Lemma 4.31 (2)} \\
&= \tau((f;g);h) && ;\ \text{defined componentwise} \\
&= \tau(\tau(f;g);h) && \text{Lemma 4.31 (2)} \\
&= (f \mathbin{\dot{;}} g) \mathbin{\dot{;}} h. && \text{definition of } \dot{;}
\end{aligned}
$$

Furthermore, we have $f \mathbin{\dot{;}} \dot{\mathbb{I}}_B = \tau(f;\tau(\mathbb{I}_B)) = \tau(f;\mathbb{I}_B) = \tau(f) = f$ by Lemma 4.31 (2). $\dot{\mathbb{I}}_A \mathbin{\dot{;}} f = f$ follows analogously.

By Theorem 2.47 every $\mathcal{R}^{\mathcal{L}}[A,B]$ is a complete Brouwerian lattice, and Lemma 4.32 shows the properties of the converse operation. The modular law follows from

$$
\begin{aligned}
(f \mathbin{\dot{;}} g) \sqcap h &= \tau(f;g) \sqcap h && \text{definition of } \dot{;} \\
&= \tau(f;g) \sqcap \tau(h) && h \text{ is an antimorphism} \\
&= \tau(f;g \sqcap h) && \text{Lemma 2.46 (2)} \\
&\sqsubseteq \tau(f;(g \sqcap f^{\smile};h)) && ;\ \text{and } \sqcap \text{ defined componentwise} \\
&\sqsubseteq \tau(f;(g \sqcap \tau(f^{\smile};h))) && \tau \text{ closure operation} \\
&= f \mathbin{\dot{;}} (g \sqcap f^{\smile} \mathbin{\dot{;}} h). && \text{definition of } \dot{;}
\end{aligned}
$$

Since ';' is a complete upper semilattice homomorphism by Lemma 4.31 (3) the residuals may be defined using Theorem 2.19. Finally, from Theorem 4.18 we conclude the assertion. □

4.8 SCALARS AND CRISPNESS IN DEDEKIND CATEGORIES

In some sense a relation of a Dedekind category may be seen as an $\mathcal{L}$-fuzzy relation. The lattice $\mathcal{L}$ may equivalently be characterized by the ideal relations, i.e., a relation $J_{AB} : A \to B$ satisfying $\mathbb{T}_{AA}; J_{AB}; \mathbb{T}_{BB} = J_{AB}$, or by the scalar relations.

Definition 4.34 *A relation $\alpha_A : A \to A$ is called a scalar on A iff $\alpha_A \sqsubseteq \mathbb{I}_A$ and $\mathbb{T}_{AA}; \alpha_A = \alpha_A; \mathbb{T}_{AA}$. The set of all scalars on A is denoted by $\mathrm{Sc}_{\mathcal{R}}(A)$.*

The notion of ideals was introduced by Jónsson and Tarski [17] and the notion of scalars by Furusawa and Kawahara [20].

Lemma 4.35 *$\mathrm{Sc}_{\mathcal{R}}(A)$ is a complete Brouwerian lattice. The pseudo-complement of α_A in $\mathrm{Sc}_{\mathcal{R}}(A)$ is denoted by $\neg{:}\alpha_A$.*

Proof. We have to show that $\mathrm{Sc}_{\mathcal{R}}(A)$ is closed under arbitrary meet and union. This follows immediately from Lemma 4.24 (3). □

Consequently, we call a scalar linear iff it is linear in $\mathrm{Sc}_{\mathcal{R}}(A)$. As mentioned in Section 2.3 this is equivalent to $\neg{:}\alpha_A = \mathbb{\perp}_{AA}$. Notice that $\mathbb{I}_A \neq \mathbb{\perp}_{AA}$ implies that $\mathbb{I}_A$ is linear since $\mathbb{I}_A$ is the greatest element in $\mathrm{Sc}_{\mathcal{R}}(A)$.

Lemma 4.36 *Let $Q : A \to B$ be a relation. Then we have*

(1) $\mathbb{T}_{AA}; Q; \mathbb{T}_{BA}$ is an ideal element,

(2) $\mathbb{I}_A \sqcap \mathbb{T}_{AA}; Q; \mathbb{T}_{BA}$ is a scalar on A,

(3) $Q = \mathbb{\perp}_{AB}$ iff the relation from (1) equals zero iff the relation from (2) equals zero.

Proof.

(1) Using Lemma 4.21 (2) we immediately get $\mathbb{T}_{CC}; (\mathbb{T}_{CA}; Q; \mathbb{T}_{BD}); \mathbb{T}_{DD} = \mathbb{T}_{CA}; Q; \mathbb{T}_{BD}$.

(2) First of all, this relation is a partial identity. The following computation shows that it is indeed a scalar:

$$
\begin{aligned}
&\mathbb{T}_{AA}; (\mathbb{I}_A \sqcap \mathbb{T}_{AA}; Q; \mathbb{T}_{BA}) \\
&= \mathbb{T}_{AA} \sqcap \mathbb{T}_{AA}; Q; \mathbb{T}_{BA} && \text{Lemma 4.23 (1)} \\
&= (\mathbb{I}_A \sqcap \mathbb{T}_{AA}; Q; \mathbb{T}_{BA}); \mathbb{T}_{AA}. && \text{Lemma 4.23 (1)}
\end{aligned}
$$

(3) Obviously, $Q = \perp\!\!\!\perp_{AB}$ implies $\top\!\!\!\top_{AA};Q;\top\!\!\!\top_{BA} = \perp\!\!\!\perp_{AB}$ and the latter implies $\mathbb{I}_A \sqcap \top\!\!\!\top_{AA};Q;\top\!\!\!\top_{BA} = \perp\!\!\!\perp_{AA}$. Now, suppose $\mathbb{I}_A \sqcap \top\!\!\!\top_{AA};Q;\top\!\!\!\top_{BA} = \perp\!\!\!\perp_{AA}$. Then we have

$$\begin{aligned} Q &\sqsubseteq \top\!\!\!\top_{AA};Q;\top\!\!\!\top_{BB} \\ &= \top\!\!\!\top_{AB} \sqcap \top\!\!\!\top_{AA};Q;\top\!\!\!\top_{BB} \\ &= (\mathbb{I}_A \sqcap \top\!\!\!\top_{AA};Q;\top\!\!\!\top_{BA});\top\!\!\!\top_{AB} && \text{Lemma 4.23 (1)} \\ &= \perp\!\!\!\perp_{AA};\top\!\!\!\top_{AB} \\ &= \perp\!\!\!\perp_{AB}, \end{aligned}$$

which completes the proof. □

The next lemma shows that we may use ideal elements instead of scalars. We have chosen scalars since they provide a nice algebraic term for cuts (cf. Lemma 3.3 (5)).

Lemma 4.37 *The mappings $\phi(J) := \mathbb{I}_A \sqcap J$ and $\phi^{-1}(\alpha) := \alpha;\top\!\!\!\top_{AA}$ constitute a bijection between the set of ideal elements on A and $\mathrm{Sc}_{\mathcal{R}}(A)$.*

Proof. The assertion follows immediately from

$$\begin{aligned} \phi^{-1}(\phi(J)) &= (\mathbb{I}_A \sqcap J);\top\!\!\!\top_{AA} \\ &= (\mathbb{I}_A \sqcap J;\top\!\!\!\top_{AA});\top\!\!\!\top_{AA} && J \text{ ideal element} \\ &= (\top\!\!\!\top_{AA} \sqcap J;\top\!\!\!\top_{AA}) && \text{Lemma 4.23 (1)} \\ &= \top\!\!\!\top_{AA} \sqcap J && J \text{ ideal element} \\ &= J, \\ \phi(\phi^{-1}(\alpha)) &= \mathbb{I}_A \sqcap \alpha;\top\!\!\!\top_{AA} \\ &= \mathbb{I}_A;\alpha && \text{Lemma 4.24 (2)} \\ &= \alpha. \end{aligned}$$

□

Within $\mathcal{L}$-fuzzy relations the sets $\mathrm{Sc}_{\mathcal{L}\text{-}\mathbf{Rel}}(A)$ and $\mathrm{Sc}_{\mathcal{L}\text{-}\mathbf{Rel}}(B)$ are isomorphic for arbitrary sets A and B. Unfortunately, that is not true for all Dedekind categories. Consider the following computation:

$$\begin{aligned} &\top\!\!\!\top_{AB};(\top\!\!\!\top_{BA};\alpha_A;\top\!\!\!\top_{AB} \sqcap \mathbb{I}_B);\top\!\!\!\top_{BA} \sqcap \mathbb{I}_A \\ &= \top\!\!\!\top_{AA};\alpha_A;\top\!\!\!\top_{AA} \sqcap \top\!\!\!\top_{AB};\top\!\!\!\top_{BA} \sqcap \mathbb{I}_A && \text{Lemma 4.23 (1)} \\ &= \alpha_A \sqcap \top\!\!\!\top_{AB};\top\!\!\!\top_{BA}. && \text{Lemma 4.24 (1)} \end{aligned}$$

For $\alpha_A = \mathbb{I}_A$ this shows that the sets of scalars are isomorphic iff $\mathcal{R}$ is uniform. Consequently, a suitable abstract categorical description of $\mathcal{L}$-fuzzy relations should be a uniform Dedekind category.

Using the scalars, there are two notions of crispness in an arbitrary Dedekind category.

Definition 4.38 *A relation $R : A \to B$ is called l-crisp/s-crisp iff $\alpha_A;Q \sqsubseteq R$ implies $Q \sqsubseteq R$ for all linear/nonzero scalars α_A and all relations $Q : A \to B$.*

Obviously, $\mathbb{T}_{AB}$ is s-crisp as well as l-crisp. Furthermore, we have the following lemma:

Lemma 4.39 *Let $R_i : A \to B$ for $i \in I$ be (l-crisp) s-crisp relations. Then $\bigsqcap_{i\in I} R_i$ is (l-crisp) s-crisp.*

Proof. Suppose $\alpha_A;Q \sqsubseteq \bigsqcap_{i\in I} R_i$ for a relation $Q : A \to B$ and a (linear) nonzero scalar α_A. Then we obtain $\alpha_A;Q \sqsubseteq R_i$, and, hence, $Q \sqsubseteq R_i$ for all $i \in I$, which implies $Q \sqsubseteq \bigsqcap_{i\in I} R_i$. □

Again, this gives us the possibility to define closure operations mapping every relation $R : A \to B$ to the least s-crisp resp. l-crisp relation it is contained

$$R^s := \bigsqcap\{Q : A \to B \mid R \sqsubseteq Q \text{ and } Q \text{ is } s\text{-crisp}\},$$
$$R^l := \bigsqcap\{Q : A \to B \mid R \sqsubseteq Q \text{ and } Q \text{ is } l\text{-crisp}\}.$$

Obviously, s-crispness implies l-crispness, and, hence, $R^l \sqsubseteq R^s$.

As for τ there is another possibility to characterize R^s resp. R^l. Consider the functions

$$\Phi_s(R) := \bigsqcup_{\substack{\alpha_A \in \mathrm{Sc}_{\mathcal{G}}(A)\\ \alpha_A \neq \perp\!\!\!\perp_{AA}}} (\alpha_A \backslash R),$$
$$\Phi_l(R) := \bigsqcup_{\substack{\alpha_A \in \mathrm{Sc}_{\mathcal{G}}(A)\\ \alpha_A \text{ linear}}} (\alpha_A \backslash R).$$

Notice that the unions on the right-hand side of the definitions above are nonempty if $\mathbb{I}_A \neq \perp\!\!\!\perp_{AA}$ since the $\mathbb{I}_A$ is linear.

Lemma 4.40 *(1) Φ_s and Φ_l are monotone,*

(2) $R \sqsubseteq \Phi_s(R)$ and $R \sqsubseteq \Phi_l(R)$ for all $R : A \to B$,

Proof.

(1) The assertion follows immediately from the fact that $\backslash$ is monotone in the second argument by Corollary 4.15 (4).

(2) If there is no nonzero scalar, we conclude $\perp\!\!\!\perp_{AA} = \mathbb{I}_A$, which implies $Q = \perp\!\!\!\perp_{AB}$ for all relations $Q : A \to B$, and, hence, $\perp\!\!\!\perp_{AB} = R = \Phi_s(R) = \Phi_l(R) = R^s = R^l$. Now, suppose $\mathbb{I}_A \neq \perp\!\!\!\perp_{AA}$ and consider the following computation:

$$\begin{aligned} R &= \mathbb{I}_A \backslash R && \text{Lemma 4.16 (1)} \\ &\sqsubseteq \alpha_A \backslash R, && \text{Corollary 4.15 (4)} \end{aligned}$$

which implies the assertion. □

The previous lemma and Theorem 2.36 shows that for every R there exists a least fixed point $\mu_{\Phi_s}(R)$ of Φ_s and a least fixed point $\mu_{\Phi_l}(R)$ of Φ_l greater than R.

Theorem 4.41 *Let $\mathcal{R}$ be a Dedekind category. Then we have $R^s = \mu_{\Phi_s}(R)$ and $R^l = \mu_{\Phi_l}(R)$ for all relations R.*

Proof. $\sqsubseteq$: It is sufficient to show that $\mu_{\Phi_s}(R)$ is s-crisp and $\mu_{\Phi_l}(R)$ is l-crisp. Suppose there is a nonzero resp. linear scalar α_A and a relation Q such that $\alpha_A;Q \sqsubseteq \mu_{\Phi_s}(R)$ resp. $\alpha_A;Q \sqsubseteq \mu_{\Phi_l}(R)$. Then we have

$$\begin{aligned} Q &\sqsubseteq \alpha_A\backslash\mu_{\Phi_s}(R) && \text{definition } \backslash \\ &\sqsubseteq \bigsqcup_{\alpha_A \neq \perp\!\!\!\perp_{AA}} (\alpha_A\backslash\mu_{\Phi_s}(R)) \\ &= \Phi_s(\mu_{\Phi_s}(R)) && \text{definition } \Phi_s \\ &= \mu_{\Phi_s}(R) && \text{fixed point property} \end{aligned}$$

and $Q \sqsubseteq \mu_{\Phi_l}(R)$ analogously.
$\sqsupseteq$: It is sufficient to show that $\Phi_s(R^s) \sqsubseteq R^s$ resp. $\Phi_l(R^l) \sqsubseteq R^l$ since then R^s resp. R^l is a fixed point of Φ_s resp. Φ_l by Lemma 4.40 (2). For every nonzero/linear scalar α_A we have $\alpha_A\backslash R^s \sqsubseteq R^s$ and $\alpha_A\backslash R^l \sqsubseteq R^l$, respectively, since $\alpha_A;(\alpha_A\backslash R^s) \sqsubseteq R^s$ and R^s is s-crisp resp. $\alpha_A;(\alpha_A\backslash R^l) \sqsubseteq R^l$ and R^l is l-crisp. This implies $\Phi_s(R^s) = \bigsqcup_{\alpha_A \neq \perp\!\!\!\perp_{AA}} (\alpha_A\backslash R^s) \sqsubseteq R^s$ and $\Phi_l(R^l) = \bigsqcup_{\alpha_A \text{ linear}} (\alpha_A\backslash R^l) \sqsubseteq R^l$. □

First, we want to concentrate on s-crispness. Unfortunately, $\perp\!\!\!\perp_{AB}$ may be not s-crisp. Dedekind categories in which $\perp\!\!\!\perp_{AB}$ is s-crisp are characterized by the following lemma:

Lemma 4.42 *In a Dedekind category $\mathcal{R}$ the following statements are equivalent:*

(1) All nonzero scalars are linear.

(2) $\perp\!\!\!\perp_{AB}$ is s-crisp.

(3) For every $R : A \to B$, its pseudo-complement $\neg R$ is s-crisp.

Proof. (1)⇒(2): Suppose $\alpha_A;Q \sqsubseteq \perp\!\!\!\perp_{AB}$ for a relation $Q : A \to B$ and a nonzero scalar α_A. Then we get

$$\begin{aligned} \alpha_A \sqcap (\top\!\!\!\top_{AA};Q;\top\!\!\!\top_{BA} \sqcap \mathbb{I}_A) &= \alpha_A;(\top\!\!\!\top_{AA};Q;\top\!\!\!\top_{BA} \sqcap \mathbb{I}_A) && \text{Lemma 4.24 (2)} \\ &\sqsubseteq \alpha_A;\top\!\!\!\top_{AA};Q;\top\!\!\!\top_{BA} \\ &= \top\!\!\!\top_{AA};\alpha_A;Q;\top\!\!\!\top_{BA} && \alpha_A \text{ scalar} \\ &\sqsubseteq \top\!\!\!\top_{AA};\perp\!\!\!\perp_{AB};\top\!\!\!\top_{BA} && \text{assumption} \\ &= \perp\!\!\!\perp_{AA}. \end{aligned}$$

Since $\mathbb{T}_{AA};Q;\mathbb{T}_{BA} \sqcap \mathbb{I}_A$ is a scalar by Lemma 4.36 (2) and α_A is linear by the assumption we conclude that $\mathbb{T}_{AA};Q;\mathbb{T}_{BA} \sqcap \mathbb{I}_A \sqsubseteq \neg{:}\alpha_A = \perp\!\!\!\perp_{AA}$. Lemma 4.36 (3) shows $Q = \perp\!\!\!\perp_{AB}$.
(2)⇒(3): Suppose $\alpha_A;Q \sqsubseteq \neg R$ for a relation $Q : A \to B$ and a nonzero scalar α_A. Then we obtain $\alpha_A;Q \sqcap R \sqsubseteq \perp\!\!\!\perp_{AB}$, and, hence,

$$\begin{aligned} \alpha_A;(Q \sqcap R) &= \alpha_A;Q \sqcap \alpha_A;R && \text{Lemma 4.9 (4)} \\ &\sqsubseteq \alpha_A;Q \sqcap R && \alpha_A \sqsubseteq \mathbb{I}_A \\ &\sqsubseteq \perp\!\!\!\perp_{AB}. \end{aligned}$$

Since $\perp\!\!\!\perp_{AB}$ is s-crisp we have $Q \sqcap R \sqsubseteq \perp\!\!\!\perp_{AB}$, and, hence, $Q \sqsubseteq \neg R$.
(3)⇒(1): First of all, $\perp\!\!\!\perp_{AA}$ is s-crisp by (3) since $\neg\mathbb{T}_{AB} = \perp\!\!\!\perp_{AB}$. Now, suppose $\alpha_A \neq \perp\!\!\!\perp_{AA}$ and β_A is a scalar such that $\alpha_A \sqcap \beta_A = \perp\!\!\!\perp_{AA}$. This implies $\alpha_A;\beta_A = \alpha_A \sqcap \beta_A \sqsubseteq \perp\!\!\!\perp_{AA}$ by Lemma 4.9 (3), and, hence, $\beta_A \sqsubseteq \perp\!\!\!\perp_{AA}$ since $\perp\!\!\!\perp_{AA}$ is s-crisp. □

The next lemma shows that in the situation not described by the previous lemma the notion of s-crispness is trivial.

Lemma 4.43 *Let A be an object of a Dedekind category. If there is a nonzero and nonlinear scalar α_A on A, then there is no s-crisp relation $R : A \to B$ except $\mathbb{T}_{AB}$ for all objects B.*

Proof. Suppose $R : A \to B$ is s-crisp and α_A, β_A are nonzero scalars such that $\alpha_A \sqcap \beta_A = \perp\!\!\!\perp_{AA}$ holds. Then $\alpha_A;(\beta_A;\mathbb{T}_{AB}) = (\alpha_A \sqcap \beta_A);\mathbb{T}_{AB} = \perp\!\!\!\perp_{AB} \sqsubseteq R$ by Lemma 4.9 (3). We conclude that $\beta_A;\mathbb{T}_{AB} \sqsubseteq R$ and further $\mathbb{T}_{AB} \sqsubseteq R$ since R is s-crisp. □

Considering $\mathcal{L}$-fuzzy relations we have the following connection between 0–1 and s-crispness:

Lemma 4.44 *In $\mathcal{L}$-**Rel** all s-crisp relations are 0–1 crisp.*

Proof. Suppose $R : A \to B$ is s-crisp and assume that $R(x_0, y_0) = u \neq 0$ for a pair $(x_0, y_0) \in A \times B$. Consider the scalar $\alpha_A^u : A \to A$ on A induced by u and the relation $Q : A \to B$ defined by $Q(x, y) := R(x, y){:}u$. Then we have $(\alpha_A^u;Q)(x, y) = (\alpha_A^u;\mathbb{T}_{AB} \sqcap Q)(x, y) = u \wedge (R(x, y){:}u) \leq R(x, y)$. Since R is s-crisp we get $Q \sqsubseteq R$, and, hence, $1 = u{:}u = R(x_0, y_0){:}u = Q(x_0, y_0) \leq R(x_0, y_0)$, which shows that R is 0–1 crisp. □

The converse is, in general, not true. A property of the underlying lattice $\mathcal{L}$ equivalent for $\mathcal{L}$-fuzzy relations to Lemma 4.42 (1) is required.

Lemma 4.45 *In $\mathcal{L}$-**Rel** the following properties are equivalent:*

(1) All 0–1 crisp relations are s-crisp.

(2) All nonzero elements of $\mathcal{L}$ are linear.

Proof. (1)⇒(2): Let be $0 \neq u \in \mathcal{L}$ and $v \in \mathcal{L}$ with $u \wedge v = 0$. Then the scalar α^u_A on A induced by u is nonzero and we have $\alpha^u_A ; \alpha^v_A = \alpha^u_A \sqcap \alpha^v_A = \perp\!\!\!\perp_{AA}$. Since $\perp\!\!\!\perp_{AA}$ is s-crisp by the assumption we conclude that $\alpha^v_A = \perp\!\!\!\perp_{AA}$, and, hence, $v = 0$.
(2)⇒(1): Suppose that $\alpha^u_A ; Q \sqsubseteq R$ for $0 \neq u \in \mathcal{L}$, $Q : A \to B$ is a relation and $R : A \to B$ is a 0–1 crisp relation. To prove that R is s-crisp it is sufficient to show that $R(x, y) = 0$ implies $Q(x, y) = 0$ since R is 0–1 crisp. Suppose $R(x, y) = 0$. Then we have $0 = R(x, y) \sqsupseteq (\alpha^u_A ; Q)(x, y) = u \wedge Q(x, y)$. The assumption gives us $Q(x, y) = 0$ since u is nonzero and linear. □

We have seen that the notion of s-crispness coincides with 0–1 crispness under an assumption on $\mathcal{L}$. In the rest of this chapter, we want to study the notion of l-crispness.

Considering $\mathcal{L}$-fuzzy relations we have the following connection between l-crispness and 0–1 crispness:

Lemma 4.46 *In* $\mathcal{L}$-**Rel** *all 0–1 crisp relations are l-crisp.*

Proof. Suppose that $\alpha^u_A ; Q \sqsubseteq R$ for a linear scalar α^u_A, $Q : A \to B$ is a relation and $R : A \to B$ is a 0–1 crisp relation. Then u is also linear. In order to prove that R is l-crisp it is sufficient to show that $R(x, y) = 0$ implies $Q(x, y) = 0$ since R is 0–1 crisp. Suppose $R(x, y) = 0$. Then we have $0 = R(x, y) \sqsupseteq (\alpha^u_A ; Q)(x, y) = u \wedge Q(x, y)$. This implies $Q(x, y) = 0$ since u is linear. □

Notice that the previous lemma shows that $\perp\!\!\!\perp_{AB}$ is l-crisp.

The converse of the previous lemma is, in general, not true. The same property as in Lemma 4.45 is needed.

Lemma 4.47 *In* $\mathcal{L}$-**Rel** *following properties are equivalent:*

(1) All l-crisp relations are 0–1 crisp.

(2) All nonzero elements of $\mathcal{L}$ are linear.

Proof. (1)⇒(2): Suppose there is a nonlinear element $u \in \mathcal{L}$, i.e., $\neg u \neq 0$. We have to show that there is an l-crisp relation R, which is not 0–1 crisp. Define $R : A \to B$ by $R(x, y) := \neg u$ and suppose $\alpha^v_A ; Q \sqsubseteq R$ for linear scalar α^v_A and a relation $Q : A \to B$. First of all, v is linear since $\mathrm{Sc}_{\mathcal{L}\text{-}\mathbf{Rel}}(A)$ and $\mathcal{L}$ are isomorphic as complete Brouwerian lattices. Then we conclude $v \wedge Q(x, y) = (\alpha^v_A ; Q)(x, y) \leq R(x, y) = \neg u$. This implies $v \wedge (Q(x, y) \wedge u) = 0$, and, hence, $Q(x, y) \wedge u = 0$ since v is linear. The previous property gives us $Q(x, y) \leq \neg u = R(x, y)$, which shows that R is l-crisp. But R is not 0–1 crisp since $\neg u \neq 0$ by the assumption and $\neg u \neq 1$ since otherwise we have $0 = u \wedge \neg u = u \wedge 1 = u$, a contradiction to $u \neq 0$.
(2)⇒(1): If all nonzero elements of $\mathcal{L}$ are linear, then all nonzero scalars are linear, and, hence, the notions of s-crispness and l-crispness coincide. By Lemma 4.44 we conclude (1). □

The previous lemma shows that the notion of l-crispness as well as the notion of s-crispness coincides with 0-1 crispness just in the case that all nonzero elements of $\mathcal{L}$ are linear.

Furthermore, if $\mathcal{L}$ is a Boolean algebra, no scalar is linear, and, therefore, the notion of s-crispness by Lemma 4.43 as well as the notion of l-crispness is trivial.

4.9 SCHRÖDER CATEGORIES

Last but not least, we want to switch from complete Brouwerian lattices to complete Boolean algebras as the underlying lattice structure of relations.

Definition 4.48 *A Schröder category is a Dedekind category in which every $\mathcal{R}[A, B]$ is a (complete) Boolean algebra.*

The Dedekind category $\mathcal{L}$-**Rel** is, in general, not a Schröder category. It is iff the lattice $\mathcal{L}$ is a Boolean algebra. On the other hand, the substructure of crisp relations constitutes a Schröder category since $\overline{0} = 1$ and $\overline{1} = 0$ is valid in any Brouwerian lattice.

The next theorem states a version of the so-called Schröder equivalences. Notice that these equivalences and the modular law are equivalent in the presence of the other axioms of a Schröder category.

Theorem 4.49 (Schröder equivalences) *Let $\mathcal{R}$ be a Schröder category, $Q : A \to B$, $R : B \to C$, and $S : A \to C$. Then we have*

$$Q;R \sqsubseteq S \iff Q^{\smile};\overline{S} \sqsubseteq \overline{R} \iff \overline{S};R^{\smile} \sqsubseteq \overline{Q}$$

Proof. We just show "$\Rightarrow$" of the first equivalence. All other implication follow similarly. Assume $Q;R \sqsubseteq S$, which is equivalent to $Q;R \sqcap \overline{S} = \perp\!\!\!\perp_{AC}$. Then we conclude

$$\begin{aligned} Q^{\smile};\overline{S} \sqcap R &\sqsubseteq Q^{\smile};(\overline{S} \sqcap Q;R) && \text{modular law} \\ &= Q^{\smile};\perp\!\!\!\perp_{AC} && \text{see above} \\ &= \perp\!\!\!\perp_{BC}, \end{aligned}$$

and, hence, $Q^{\smile};\overline{S} \sqsubseteq \overline{R}$. □

As an application of the previous theorem we want to show that the residuals are given by expression involving complements.

Lemma 4.50 *Let $\mathcal{R}$ be a Schröder category, $Q : A \to B$, $R : B \to C$, and $S : A \to C$. Then we have*

(1) $Q\backslash S = \overline{Q^{\smile};\overline{S}}$,

(2) $S/R = \overline{\overline{S};R^{\smile}}$.

Proof. The first assertion follows immediately from

$$\begin{aligned} X \sqsubseteq Q\backslash S &\Leftrightarrow Q;X \sqsubseteq S && \text{residual} \\ &\Leftrightarrow Q^{\smile};\overline{S} \sqsubseteq \overline{R} && \text{Theorem 4.49} \\ &\Leftrightarrow X \sqsubseteq \overline{Q^{\smile};\overline{S}}. \end{aligned}$$

The second is shown analogously. □

4.10 FORMAL LANGUAGES OF RELATIONAL CATEGORIES

Later on, we will compare the validity of several formulae in the relational categories introduced so far. Therefore, we have to define formal languages over those categories. We require a set of object variables and a set of typed relation variables, i.e., every relation variable is of the form $r : a \to b$ where a and b are object variables. Now, general terms and formulae are defined as follows:

Definition 4.51 *The set of terms of type $a \to b$ and the set of formulae are defined inductively as follows:*

(1) Every relation variable $r : a \to b$ is a term of type $a \to b$.

(2) If a is an object variable, then $\mathbb{I}_a$ is a term of type $a \to a$.

(3) If t is a term of type $a \to b$, then $t^{\smile}$ is a term of type $b \to a$.

(4) If t_1 and t_2 are terms of type $a \to b$, then $t_1 \sqcap t_2$ is a term of type $a \to b$.

(5) If t_1 and t_2 are terms of type $a \to b$ resp. $b \to c$, then $t_1;t_2$ is a term of type $a \to c$.

(6) If a and b are object variables, then $\mathbb{O}_{ab}$ is a term of type $a \to b$.

(7) If t_1 and t_2 are terms of type $a \to b$, then $t_1 \sqcup t_2$ is a term of type $a \to b$.

(8) If a and b are object variables, then $\mathbb{T}_{ab}$ is a term of type $a \to b$.

(9) If t_1 and t_2 are terms of type $a \to c$ resp. $b \to c$, then t_1/t_2 is a term of type $a \to b$.

(10) If Θ is a formula and $r : a \to b$ a relation variable, then $\bigsqcup\{r : a \to b \mid \Theta\}$ and $\bigsqcap\{r : a \to b \mid \Theta\}$ are terms of type $a \to b$.

(11) If t_1 and t_2 are terms of type $a \to b$, then $t_1 = t_2$ is a formula.

(12) If Θ_1 and Θ_2 are formulas, then $\Theta_1 \wedge \Theta_2$ is a formula.

(13) If Θ is a formula, then $\neg\Theta$ is a formula.

(14) If Θ is a formula and $r : a \to b$ is a relation variable, then $(\forall r : a \to b)\Theta$ is a formula.

(15) If Θ is a formula and a is an object variable, then $(\forall a)\Theta$ is a formula.

The terms in the language of allegories are given by those terms that are built up by (1)–(5). Analogously, the terms of the language of distributive allegories are given by (1)–(7), of distributive allegories with greatest elements by (1)–(8), of division allegories by (1)–(9), and of Dedekind categories by (1)–(10). Notice that within the language of Dedekind categories (4)–(8) may be dropped since they are special cases of (10) in the following way:

$$\begin{aligned}
t_1 \sqcap t_2 &\hat{=} \bigsqcap \{r : a \to b \mid r = t_1 \vee r = t_2\},\\
t_1 \sqcup t_2 &\hat{=} \bigsqcup \{r : a \to b \mid r = t_1 \vee r = t_2\},\\
\perp\!\!\!\perp_{ab} &\hat{=} \bigsqcap \{r : a \to b \mid r = r\},\\
\top\!\!\!\top_{ab} &\hat{=} \bigsqcup \{r : a \to b \mid r = r\},\\
t_1 / t_2 &\hat{=} \bigsqcup \{r : a \to b \mid t_2 ; r \sqcup t_1 = t_1\}.
\end{aligned}$$

A formula in the language of a specific relational category is a formula such that all terms are terms in the language of this kind of a relational category. Finally, a set of equations is a set of formulae of the form (11).

In the rest of this chapter we will prove several properties of terms and formulae within specific classes of relational categories. This is usually done by structural induction. In all cases, we will be careful that we just use properties of the most general kind of relational categories, which may be concerned. For example, if we prove a property of terms t by structural induction and we are considering the case $t = t_1 \sqcap t_2$, we will just use theorems valid in all allegories. This implies that the corresponding theorem is valid for all relational categories and their corresponding languages.

Given a relational category $\mathcal{R}$, an environment σ over $\mathcal{R}$ is a function mapping each object variable a to an object A of $\mathcal{R}$ and each relation variable $r : a \to b$ to a relation $R : \sigma(a) \to \sigma(b)$. The update $\sigma[A/a]$ resp. $\sigma[R/r : a \to b]$ of σ at the object variable a resp. at the relation variable $r : a \to b$ with the object A resp. with the relation $R : \sigma(a) \to \sigma(b)$ is defined by

$$\begin{aligned}
\sigma[A/a](b) &:= \begin{cases} \sigma(b) & \text{iff } a \neq b,\\ A & \text{iff } a = b,\end{cases}\\
\sigma[A/a](r : c \to d) &:= \begin{cases} \perp\!\!\!\perp_{A\sigma(d)} & \text{iff } a = c,\\ \perp\!\!\!\perp_{\sigma(c)A} & \text{iff } a = d,\\ \sigma(r : c \to d) & \text{iff } a \neq c \wedge a \neq d,\end{cases}\\
\sigma[R/r : a \to b](c) &:= \sigma(c),\\
\sigma[R/r : a \to b](s : c \to d) &:= \begin{cases} \sigma(s : c \to d) & \text{iff } r : a \to b \neq s : c \to d,\\ R & \text{iff } r : a \to b = s : c \to d.\end{cases}
\end{aligned}$$

Notice that the update of an environment is again an environment. As usual we denote a sequence of updates $\sigma[A/a][B/b][R/r : a \to b]$ of an environment σ by $\sigma[A/a, B/b, R/r : a \to b]$.

The value of a term and the validity of a formula are defined as usual. In order to avoid confusion we give here the formal definition.

Definition 4.52 *The value $\mathcal{V}_{\mathcal{R}}(t)(\sigma)$ of a term t of type $a \to b$ and the validity $\mathcal{R} \models_\sigma \Theta$ of a formula Θ in a suitable relational category $\mathcal{R}$ under an environment σ is defined inductively as follows:*

(1) $\mathcal{V}_{\mathcal{R}}(r : a \to b)(\sigma) := \sigma(r : a \to b)$,

(2) $\mathcal{V}_{\mathcal{R}}(\mathbb{I}_a)(\sigma) := \mathbb{I}_{\sigma(a)}$,

(3) $\mathcal{V}_{\mathcal{R}}(t^{\smile})(\sigma) := (\mathcal{V}_{\mathcal{R}}(t)(\sigma))^{\smile}$,

(4) $\mathcal{V}_{\mathcal{R}}(t_1 \sqcap t_2)(\sigma) := \mathcal{V}_{\mathcal{R}}(t_1) \sqcap \mathcal{V}_{\mathcal{R}}(t_2)$,

(5) $\mathcal{V}_{\mathcal{R}}(t_1; t_2)(\sigma) := \mathcal{V}_{\mathcal{R}}(t_1)(\sigma); \mathcal{V}_{\mathcal{R}}(t_2)(\sigma)$,

(6) $\mathcal{V}_{\mathcal{R}}(\perp\!\!\!\perp_{ab})(\sigma) := \perp\!\!\!\perp_{\sigma(a)\sigma(b)}$,

(7) $\mathcal{V}_{\mathcal{R}}(t_1 \sqcup t_2)(\sigma) := \mathcal{V}_{\mathcal{R}}(t_1) \sqcup \mathcal{V}_{\mathcal{R}}(t_2)$,

(8) $\mathcal{V}_{\mathcal{R}}(\top\!\!\!\top_{ab})(\sigma) := \top\!\!\!\top_{\sigma(a)\sigma(b)}$,

(9) $\mathcal{V}_{\mathcal{R}}(t_1/t_2)(\sigma) := \mathcal{V}_{\mathcal{R}}(t_1)(\sigma)/\mathcal{V}_{\mathcal{R}}(t_2)(\sigma)$,

(10) $\mathcal{V}_{\mathcal{R}}(\bigsqcup\{r : a \to b \mid \varphi\})(\sigma) := \bigsqcup\{R \mid \mathcal{R} \models_{\sigma[R/r:a\to b]} \varphi\}$,

(11) $\mathcal{V}_{\mathcal{R}}(\bigsqcap\{r : a \to b \mid \varphi\})(\sigma) := \bigsqcap\{R \mid \mathcal{R} \models_{\sigma[R/r:a\to b]} \varphi\}$,

(12) $\mathcal{R} \models_\sigma t_1 = t_2$ *iff* $\mathcal{V}_{\mathcal{R}}(t_1)(\sigma) = \mathcal{V}_{\mathcal{R}}(t_2)(\sigma)$,

(13) $\mathcal{R} \models_\sigma \Theta_1 \land \Theta_2$ *iff* $\mathcal{R} \models_\sigma \Theta_1$ *and* $\mathcal{R} \models_\sigma \Theta_2$,

(14) $\mathcal{R} \models_\sigma \neg\Theta$ *iff* $\mathcal{R} \not\models_\sigma \Theta$,

(15) $\mathcal{R} \models_\sigma (\forall r : a \to b)\Theta$ *iff* $\mathcal{R} \models_{\sigma[R/r:a\to b]} \Theta$ *for all* $R : \sigma(a) \to \sigma(b)$,

(16) $\mathcal{R} \models_\sigma (\forall a)\Theta$ *iff* $\mathcal{R} \models_{\sigma[A/a]} \Theta$ *for all objects* A.

The set of relational variables $\mathrm{RV}(t)$ of a term t is defined as the set of all relational variables occurring in t. Furthermore, the set $\mathrm{OV}(t)$ of object variables of t is defined as the set of object variables a such that there is a relational variable in $\mathrm{RV}(t)$ typed with a, i.e., there is a variable in $\mathrm{RV}(t)$ of the form $r : a \to b$ or $r : c \to a$. Obviously, the occurrences of an object variable within a term are completely determined by the occurrences of the relational variables.

An occurrence of a relational variable $r : a \to b$ in a formula Θ is called *bounded* iff it is within a subformula of Θ of the form $(\forall r : a \to b)\Theta'$ and free otherwise. With $\mathrm{RV}(\Theta)$ we denote the free relational variables of Θ, i.e., the relational variables, which have at least one free occurrence in Θ. Analogously, an occurrence of an object variable a in Θ is called bounded iff it is within a subformula of the form $(\forall a)\Theta'$ and free otherwise. Again, $\mathrm{OV}(\Theta)$ we denote the set of free object variables of Θ, i.e., the object variables, which have at least one free occurrence in Θ.

We will use the notation $\mathrm{RV}(S)$ resp. $\mathrm{OV}(S)$ also for a set of equations $S = \{t_1^i = t_2^i \mid i \in I\}$ denoting the relational resp. object variables within the terms of S. Formally, we have $\mathrm{RV}(S) = \bigcup_{i\in I} \mathrm{RV}(t_1^i) \cup \bigcup_{i\in I} \mathrm{RV}(t_2^i)$ resp. $\mathrm{OV}(S) = \bigcup_{i\in I} \mathrm{OV}(t_1^i) \cup \bigcup_{i\in I} \mathrm{OV}(t_2^i)$.

Theorem 4.53 *Let t be a term and Θ a formula in the language of Dedekind categories. Furthermore, let $\mathcal{R}$ be a Dedekind category and σ_1 and σ_2 environments over $\mathcal{R}$. Then we have the following:*

(1) if $\sigma_1(r : a \to b) = \sigma_2(r : a \to b)$ for all $r : a \to b \in RV(t)$ and $\sigma_1(a) = \sigma_2(a)$ for all $a \in OV(t)$, then $\mathcal{V}_\mathcal{R}(t)(\sigma_1) = \mathcal{V}_\mathcal{R}(t)(\sigma_2)$,

(2) if $\sigma_1(r : a \to b) = \sigma_2(r : a \to b)$ for all $r : a \to b \in RV(\Theta)$ and $\sigma_1(a) = \sigma_2(a)$ for all $a \in OV(\Theta)$, then $\mathcal{R} \models_{\sigma_1} \Theta$ iff $\mathcal{R} \models_{\sigma_2} \Theta$.

The proof of the previous theorem is a straightforward structural induction and, therefore, omitted.

As mentioned above, the previous lemma is also valid for allegories, distributive and division allegories.

Given a functor $F : \mathcal{R}_1 \to \mathcal{R}_2$ and an environment σ we denote with $F(\sigma)$ the environment defined by

(1) $F(\sigma)(a) = F(\sigma(a))$ for all object variables a,

(2) $F(\sigma)(r : a \to b) := F(\sigma(r : a \to b))$ for all relation variables $r : a \to b$.

Notice that $F(\sigma)$ is indeed an environment. Since σ is an environment we have $\sigma(r : a \to b) : \sigma(a) \to \sigma(b)$. This implies $F(\sigma(r : a \to b)) : F(\sigma(a)) \to F(\sigma(b))$ since F is a functor, and, hence, $F(\sigma)(r : a \to b) : F(\sigma)(a) \to F(\sigma)(b)$.

Consider the following computation with $r : a \to b \neq s : c \to d$:

$$\begin{aligned}
F(\sigma[R/r : a \to b])(r : a \to b) &= F(\sigma[R/r : a \to b](r : a \to b)) \\
&= F(R) \\
&= F(\sigma)[F(R)/r : a \to b](r : a \to b), \\
\text{and} \quad F(\sigma[R/r : a \to b])(s : c \to d) &= F(\sigma[R/r : a \to b](s : c \to d)) \\
&= F(\sigma(s : c \to d)) \\
&= F(\sigma)[F(R)/r : a \to b](s : c \to d),
\end{aligned}$$

which shows that $F(\sigma[R/r : a \to b]) = F(\sigma)[F(R)/r : a \to b]$. Analogously, we obtain $F(\sigma[A/a]) = F(\sigma)[F(A)/a]$. Furthermore, if F is an isomorphism, the function $\sigma \mapsto F(\sigma)$ is a bijection on the class of environments.

Lemma 4.54 *Let t, t_1, t_2 be a term of type $a \to b$ and Θ a formula in the language of division allegories. Furthermore, let $\mathcal{R}_1$ and $\mathcal{R}_2$ be division allegories,*

σ an environment over $\mathcal{R}_1$ and $F : \mathcal{R}_1 \to \mathcal{R}_2$ a homomorphism of division allegories. Then the following holds:

(1) $F(\mathcal{V}_{\mathcal{R}_1}(t)(\sigma)) = \mathcal{V}_{\mathcal{R}_2}(t)(F(\sigma))$,

(2) $\mathcal{R}_1 \models_\sigma t_1 = t_2$ *iff* $\mathcal{R}_2 \models_{F(\sigma)} t_1 = t_2$.

Proof.

(1) The assertion is shown by structural induction as follows:

$$\begin{aligned}
F(\mathcal{V}_{\mathcal{R}_1}(r : a \to b)(\sigma)) &= F(\sigma(r : a \to b)) && \text{def. of value}\\
&= F(\sigma)(r : a \to b) && \text{def. of } F(\sigma)\\
&= \mathcal{V}_{\mathcal{R}_2}(r : a \to b)F(\sigma), && \text{def. of value}\\
F(\mathcal{V}_{\mathcal{R}_1}(\mathbb{I}_a)(\sigma)) &= F(\mathbb{I}_{\sigma(a)}) && \text{def. of value}\\
&= \mathbb{I}_{F(\sigma(a))} && F \text{ functor}\\
&= \mathbb{I}_{F(\sigma)(a)} && \text{def. of } F(\sigma)\\
&= \mathcal{V}_{\mathcal{R}_2}(\mathbb{I}_a)F(\sigma), && \text{def. of value}\\
F(\mathcal{V}_{\mathcal{R}_1}(t^{\smile})(\sigma)) &= F((\mathcal{V}_{\mathcal{R}_1}(t)(\sigma))^{\smile}) && \text{def. of value}\\
&= F(\mathcal{V}_{\mathcal{R}_1}(t)(\sigma))^{\smile} && F \text{ homo.}\\
&= (\mathcal{V}_{\mathcal{R}_2}(t)(F(\sigma)))^{\smile} && \text{ind. hyp.}\\
&= \mathcal{V}_{\mathcal{R}_2}(t^{\smile})(F(\sigma)), && \text{def. of value}\\
F(\mathcal{V}_{\mathcal{R}_1}(t_1 \sqcap t_2)(\sigma)) &= F(\mathcal{V}_{\mathcal{R}_1}(t_1)(\sigma) \sqcap \mathcal{V}_{\mathcal{R}_1}(t_2)(\sigma)) && \text{def. of value}\\
&= F(\mathcal{V}_{\mathcal{R}_1}(t_1)(\sigma)) \sqcap F(\mathcal{V}_{\mathcal{R}_1}(t_2)(\sigma)) && F \text{ homo.}\\
&= \mathcal{V}_{\mathcal{R}_2}(t_1)(F(\sigma)) \sqcap \mathcal{V}_{\mathcal{R}_2}(t_2)(F(\sigma)) && \text{ind. hyp.}\\
&= \mathcal{V}_{\mathcal{R}_2}(t_1 \sqcap t_2)(F(\sigma)) && \text{def. of value}\\
F(\mathcal{V}_{\mathcal{R}_1}(t_1;t_2)(\sigma)) &= F(\mathcal{V}_{\mathcal{R}_1}(t_1)(\sigma);\mathcal{V}_{\mathcal{R}_1}(t_2)(\sigma)) && \text{def. of value}\\
&= F(\mathcal{V}_{\mathcal{R}_1}(t_1)(\sigma)); F(\mathcal{V}_{\mathcal{R}_1}(t_2)(\sigma)) && F \text{ functor}\\
&= \mathcal{V}_{\mathcal{R}_2}(t_1)(F(\sigma)); \mathcal{V}_{\mathcal{R}_2}(t_2)(F(\sigma)) && \text{ind. hyp.}\\
&= \mathcal{V}_{\mathcal{R}_2}(t_1;t_2)(F(\sigma)) && \text{def. of value}\\
F(\mathcal{V}_{\mathcal{R}_1}(\perp\!\!\!\perp_{ab})(\sigma)) &= F(\perp\!\!\!\perp_{\sigma(a)\sigma(b)}) && \text{def. of value}\\
&= \perp\!\!\!\perp_{F(\sigma(a))F(\sigma(b))} && F \text{ homo.}\\
&= \perp\!\!\!\perp_{F(\sigma)(a)F(\sigma)(b)} && \text{def. of } F(\sigma)\\
&= \mathcal{V}_{\mathcal{R}_2}(\perp\!\!\!\perp_{ab})(F(\sigma)), && \text{def. of value}\\
F(\mathcal{V}_{\mathcal{R}_1}(t_1 \sqcup t_2)(\sigma)) &= F(\mathcal{V}_{\mathcal{R}_1}(t_1)(\sigma) \sqcup \mathcal{V}_{\mathcal{R}_1}(t_2)(\sigma)) && \text{def. of value}\\
&= F(\mathcal{V}_{\mathcal{R}_1}(t_1)(\sigma)) \sqcup F(\mathcal{V}_{\mathcal{R}_1}(t_2)(\sigma)) && F \text{ homo.}\\
&= \mathcal{V}_{\mathcal{R}_2}(t_1)(F(\sigma)) \sqcup \mathcal{V}_{\mathcal{R}_2}(t_2)(F(\sigma)) && \text{ind. hyp.}\\
&= \mathcal{V}_{\mathcal{R}_2}(t_1 \sqcup t_2)(F(\sigma)) && \text{def. of value}
\end{aligned}$$

$$\begin{aligned} F(\mathcal{V}_{\mathcal{R}_1}(t_1/t_2)(\sigma)) &= F(\mathcal{V}_{\mathcal{R}_1}(t_1)(\sigma)/\mathcal{V}_{\mathcal{R}_1}(t_2)(\sigma)) && \text{def. of value}\\ &= F(\mathcal{V}_{\mathcal{R}_1}(t_1)(\sigma))/F(\mathcal{V}_{\mathcal{R}_1}(t_2)(\sigma)) && F \text{ homo.}\\ &= \mathcal{V}_{\mathcal{R}_2}(t_1)(F(\sigma))/\mathcal{V}_{\mathcal{R}_2}(t_2)(F(\sigma)) && \text{ind. hyp.}\\ &= \mathcal{V}_{\mathcal{R}_2}(t_1/t_2)(F(\sigma)) && \text{def. of value} \end{aligned}$$

(2) The assertion follows immediately from (1). □

Again, the previous lemma is also valid for allegories and distributive and their formal languages.

If F is an isomorphism, the previous lemma may be strengthened.

Lemma 4.55 *Let t be a term of type $a \to b$ and Θ a formula in the language of Dedekind categories. Furthermore, let $\mathcal{R}_1$ and $\mathcal{R}_2$ be Dedekind categories, σ an environment over $\mathcal{R}_1$ and $F : \mathcal{R}_1 \to \mathcal{R}_2$ an isomorphism of Dedekind categories. Then the following holds:*

(1) $F(\mathcal{V}_{\mathcal{R}_1}(t)(\sigma)) = \mathcal{V}_{\mathcal{R}_2}(t)(F(\sigma))$,

(2) $\mathcal{R}_1 \models_\sigma \Theta$ iff $\mathcal{R}_2 \models_{F(\sigma)} \Theta$.

Proof. The assertions are shown simultaneously by structural induction. Using Lemma 4.54 (1) it remains to show that (1) holds for arbitrary unions and meets. This follows from the computation:

$$\begin{aligned} &F(\mathcal{V}_{\mathcal{R}_1}(\bigsqcup\{r : a \to b \mid \Theta\})(\sigma))\\ &= F\left(\bigsqcup\{R \mid \mathcal{R}_1 \models_{\sigma[R/r:a\to b]} \Theta\}\right) && \text{def. of value}\\ &= \bigsqcup\{F(R) \mid \mathcal{R}_1 \models_{\sigma[R/r:a\to b]} \Theta\}) && F \text{ homo.}\\ &= \bigsqcup\{F(R) \mid \mathcal{R}_2 \models_{F(\sigma[R/r:a\to b])} \Theta\}) && \text{ind. hyp.}\\ &= \bigsqcup\{F(R) \mid \mathcal{R}_2 \models_{F(\sigma)[F(R)/r:a\to b]} \Theta\})\\ &= \bigsqcup\{S \mid \mathcal{R}_2 \models_{F(\sigma)[S/r:a\to b]} \Theta\}) && F \text{ iso.}\\ &= \mathcal{V}_{\mathcal{R}_2}\left(\bigsqcup\{r : a \to b \mid \Theta\}\right)(\sigma) && \text{def. of value} \end{aligned}$$

and a similar computation for meet. If Θ is an equality, (1) gives us the assertion. The remaining cases are shown as follows:

$$\begin{aligned} \mathcal{R}_1 \models_\sigma \Theta_1 \wedge \Theta_2 &\iff \mathcal{R}_1 \models_\sigma \Theta_1 \text{ and } \mathcal{R}_1 \models_\sigma \Theta_2 && \text{def. of validity}\\ &\iff \mathcal{R}_2 \models_{F(\sigma)} \Theta_1 \text{ and } \mathcal{R}_2 \models_{F(\sigma)} \Theta_2 && \text{ind. hyp.}\\ &\iff \mathcal{R}_2 \models_{F(\sigma)} \Theta_1 \wedge \Theta_2, && \text{def. of validity}\\ \mathcal{R}_1 \models_\sigma \neg\Theta &\iff \mathcal{R}_1 \not\models_\sigma \Theta && \text{def. of validity}\\ &\iff \mathcal{R}_2 \not\models_{F(\sigma)} \Theta && \text{ind. hyp.}\\ &\iff \mathcal{R}_1 \models_\sigma \neg\Theta, && \text{def. of validity} \end{aligned}$$

$$\begin{array}{lll}
\mathcal{R}_1 \models_\sigma (\forall r : a \to b)\Theta & & \\
\qquad \iff \mathcal{R}_1 \models_{\sigma[R/r:a\to b]} \Theta \text{ for all } R & & \text{def. of validity} \\
\qquad \iff \mathcal{R}_2 \models_{F(\sigma[R/r:a\to b])} \Theta \text{ for all } R & & \text{ind. hyp.} \\
\qquad \iff \mathcal{R}_2 \models_{F(\sigma)[F(R)/r:a\to b])} \Theta \text{ for all } R & & \\
\qquad \iff \mathcal{R}_2 \models_{F(\sigma)[S/r:a\to b])} \Theta \text{ for all } S & & F \text{ iso.} \\
\qquad \iff \mathcal{R}_2 \models_{F(\sigma)} (\forall r : a \to b)\Theta & & \text{def. of validity} \\
\mathcal{R}_1 \models_\sigma (\forall a)\Theta \iff \mathcal{R}_1 \models_{\sigma[A/a]} \Theta \text{ for all } A & & \text{def. of validity} \\
\qquad \iff \mathcal{R}_2 \models_{F(\sigma[A/a])} \Theta \text{ for all } A & & \text{ind. hyp.} \\
\qquad \iff \mathcal{R}_2 \models_{F(\sigma)[F(A)/a])} \Theta \text{ for all } A & & \\
\qquad \iff \mathcal{R}_2 \models_{F(\sigma)[B/a])} \Theta \text{ for all } B & & F \text{ iso.} \\
\qquad \iff \mathcal{R}_2 \models_{F(\sigma)} (\forall a)\Theta. & & \text{def. of validity} \quad \Box
\end{array}$$

Notice that the last lemma is also valid for allegories, distributive and division allegories, and their formal languages.

5
CATEGORIES OF L-FUZZY RELATIONS

The notion of crispness is a basic property of $\mathcal{L}$-fuzzy relations and sets such that a suitable algebraic theory should be able to express this property. We have shown that there are some notions of crispness within Dedekind categories, which grasp the notion of 0–1 crispness under an assumption on the underlying lattice. Unfortunately, a general notion, which coincides with 0–1 crispness has not yet been given.

Theorem 5.1 *There is no formula Θ in the language of Dedekind categories such that we have for all complete Brouwerian lattices $\mathcal{L}$ and $\mathcal{L}$-fuzzy relations $R : A \to B$*

$$\mathcal{L}\textbf{-Rel} \models_{\sigma[A/a,B/b,R/r:a\to b]} \Theta \text{ for all environments } \sigma \quad \Longleftrightarrow \quad R \text{ is 0–1 crisp.}$$

Proof. Consider the Boolean algebra $B_4 := \mathcal{P}(\{a,b\})$, i.e., the power set of the set $\{a,b\}$. Let $X = \{x\}$ and $Y = \{x,y\}$ be sets. Consider the $\mathcal{L}$-fuzzy relation $f : Y \to Y$ defined by

$$f := \begin{pmatrix} \{a\} & \{b\} \\ \{b\} & \{a\} \end{pmatrix}$$

and the 0–1 crisp relation $R : X \to Y$ defined by

$$R := \begin{pmatrix} \{a,b\} & \emptyset \end{pmatrix}.$$

A simple verification of the properties

$$f^{\smile} = f, \quad f \circ f = \begin{pmatrix} \{a,b\} & \emptyset \\ \emptyset & \{a,b\} \end{pmatrix} = \mathbb{I}_Y.$$

shows that f is bijection in B_4-**Rel**$[Y,Y]$. Obviously, the class consisting of f for Y and the identity on all other sets Z is a class of bijections. Now, take the isomorphism F induced by that class (cf. Lemma 4.26) and suppose such a formula Θ to exist. Then we have $B_4\text{-}\mathbf{Rel} \models_{\sigma[X/a,Y/b,R/r:a\to b]} \Theta$ for all environments σ since R is 0–1 crisp. Lemma 4.55 implies that $B_4\text{-}\mathbf{Rel} \models_{F(\sigma[X/a,Y/b,R/r:a\to b])} \Theta$, and, hence, $B_4\text{-}\mathbf{Rel} \models_{F(\sigma)[X/a,Y/b,F(R)/r:a\to b])} \Theta$ since $F(X) = X$ and $F(Y) = Y$. Since F is an isomorphism, we conclude $B_4\text{-}\mathbf{Rel} \models_{\sigma'[X/a,Y/b,F(R)/r:a\to b])} \Theta$ for all environments σ', and, hence, $F(R) = R; f$ is 0–1 crisp. But, this is a contradiction since

$$F(R) = \begin{pmatrix} \{a,b\} & \emptyset \end{pmatrix} \circ \begin{pmatrix} \{a\} & \{b\} \\ \{b\} & \{a\} \end{pmatrix} = \begin{pmatrix} \{a\} & \{b\} \end{pmatrix},$$

which shows that $F(R)$ is not 0–1 crisp. □

The previous theorem shows that the theory of Dedekind categories is too weak to express crispness. This gives us the motivation to define extended algebraic structures for $\mathcal{L}$-fuzziness, called arrow categories and Goguen categories.

5.1 ARROW CATEGORIES

In the previous theorem we have shown that we need an additional concept to define a suitable algebraic theory of $\mathcal{L}$-fuzzy relations. Our approach introduces two operations mapping every relation to its support and kernel, respectively. In other terms, those operations map the relation to the greatest 0–1 crisp relation it contains and to the least 0–1 crisp relation it is included in. We now give an abstract definition.

Definition 5.2 *An arrow category $\mathcal{A}$ is a Dedekind category with $\mathbb{T}_{AB} \neq \mathbb{L}_{AB}$ for all objects A and B together with two operations $^{\uparrow}$ and $^{\downarrow}$ satisfying the following:*

(1) $R^{\uparrow}, R^{\downarrow} : A \to B$ *for all* $R : A \to B$.

(2) $({}^{\uparrow}, {}^{\downarrow})$ *is a Galois correspondence.*

(3) $(R^{\smile}; S^{\downarrow})^{\uparrow} = R^{\uparrow\smile}; S^{\downarrow}$ *for all* $R : B \to A$ *and* $S : B \to C$.

(4) $(Q \sqcap R^{\downarrow})^{\uparrow} = Q^{\uparrow} \sqcap R^{\downarrow}$ *for all* $Q, R : A \to B$.

(5) If $\alpha_A \neq \mathbb{L}_{AA}$ *is a nonzero scalar, then* $\alpha_A^{\uparrow} = \mathbb{I}_A$.

Furthermore, an arrow category is called linear iff all nonzero scalars are linear, and it is called Boolean iff it is a Schröder category.

A homomorphism F between arrow categories is a homomorphism between Dedekind categories preserving $^\uparrow$ and $^\downarrow$, i.e, $F(R^\uparrow) = F(R)^\uparrow$ and $F(R^\downarrow) = F(R)^\downarrow$ for all $R : A \to B$. Consequently, we call an arrow category $\mathcal{A}$ representable iff there is an embedding of arrow categories into $\mathcal{L}$-**Rel** for a suitable complete Brouwerian lattice $\mathcal{L}$.

The obvious definition of $^\uparrow$ and $^\downarrow$ introduced in Chapter 3 for $\mathcal{L}$-fuzzy relations gives the standard model.

Theorem 5.3 *Let $\mathcal{L}$ be a complete Brouwerian lattice with $0 \neq 1$. Then $\mathcal{L}$-**Rel** together with $^\uparrow$ and $^\downarrow$ is an arrow category.*

Proof. First of all, we have $\mathbb{T}_{AB} \neq \mathbb{\perp}_{AB}$ for all nonempty sets since $0 \neq 1$. Axiom (1) is trivial, and the axioms (2)–(5) were already shown in Lemma 3.3 (2)–(5). □

According to the standard model and Lemma 3.3 (1), we define crispness in an arbitrary arrow category as follows:

Definition 5.4 *A relation $R : A \to B$ of an arrow category $\mathcal{A}$ is called crisp iff $R^\uparrow = R$. The crisp fragment $\mathcal{A}^\uparrow$ of $\mathcal{A}$ is defined as the collection of all crisp relations of $\mathcal{A}$.*

From Lemma 2.13 and Lemma 2.15 we get the following corollary:

Corollary 5.5 *Let $\mathcal{A}$ be an arrow category and $R, R_i : A \to B$ for $i \in I$. Then we have*

(1) $^\uparrow$ *and* $^\downarrow$ *are monotone,*

(2) $R \sqsubseteq R^{\uparrow\downarrow}$ *and* $R^{\downarrow\uparrow} \sqsubseteq R$,

(3) $R^\uparrow = R^{\uparrow\downarrow\uparrow}$ *and* $R^\downarrow = R^{\downarrow\uparrow\downarrow}$,

(4) $(\bigsqcup_{i\in I} R_i)^\uparrow = \bigsqcup_{i\in I} R_i^\uparrow$ *and* $(\bigsqcap_{i\in I} R_i)^\downarrow = \bigsqcap_{i\in I} R^\downarrow{}_i$.

In the next lemma we have summarized some basic properties of arrow categories.

Lemma 5.6 *Let $\mathcal{A}$ be an arrow category and $Q, R : A \to B, S : B \to C, T : A \to C$. Then we have*

(1) $\mathbb{I}_A^\uparrow = \mathbb{I}_A \neq \mathbb{\perp}_{AA}$,

(2) $R^{\downarrow\uparrow} = R^\downarrow$,

(3) $R^{\uparrow\downarrow} = R^\uparrow$,

(4) $^\uparrow$ *is a closure and* $^\downarrow$ *a kernel operation,*

(5) $R = R^\uparrow$ *iff* $R^\downarrow = R^\uparrow$ *iff* $R^\downarrow = R$,

(6) $\perp\!\!\!\perp^{\uparrow}_{AB} = \perp\!\!\!\perp_{AB}$ *and* $\top\!\!\!\top^{\downarrow}{}_{AB} = \top\!\!\!\top_{AB}$,

(7) $(R^{\smile};S^{\uparrow})^{\uparrow} = R^{\uparrow\smile};S^{\uparrow}$,

(8) $R^{\smile\uparrow} = R^{\uparrow\smile}$ *and* $R^{\smile\downarrow} = R^{\downarrow\smile}$,

(9) $(R;S^{\downarrow})^{\uparrow} = R^{\uparrow};S^{\downarrow}$ *and* $(R^{\downarrow};S)^{\uparrow} = R^{\downarrow};S^{\uparrow}$,

(10) $(R;S^{\uparrow})^{\uparrow} = R^{\uparrow};S^{\uparrow}$ *and* $(R^{\uparrow};S)^{\uparrow} = R^{\uparrow};S^{\uparrow}$,

(11) $(Q \sqcap R^{\uparrow})^{\uparrow} = Q^{\uparrow} \sqcap R^{\uparrow}$,

(12) *For all nonzero ideal relations* $J^{\uparrow} = \top\!\!\!\top_{AB}$ *holds,*

(13) $R^{\downarrow}{:}Q^{\uparrow} = (R{:}Q^{\uparrow})^{\downarrow} \sqsubseteq (R{:}Q)^{\downarrow}$ *and* $(R{:}Q)^{\uparrow} \sqsubseteq R^{\uparrow}{:}Q^{\downarrow}$,

(14) $Q^{\uparrow}\backslash T^{\downarrow} = (Q^{\uparrow}\backslash T)^{\downarrow} \sqsubseteq (Q\backslash T)^{\downarrow}$ *and* $(Q\backslash T)^{\uparrow} \sqsubseteq Q^{\downarrow}\backslash T^{\uparrow}$,

(15) $T^{\downarrow}/S^{\uparrow} = (T/S^{\uparrow})^{\downarrow} \sqsubseteq (T/S)^{\downarrow}$ *and* $(T/S)^{\uparrow} \sqsubseteq T^{\uparrow}/S^{\downarrow}$.

Proof.

(1) Suppose $\mathbb{I}_A = \perp\!\!\!\perp_{AA}$. Then we obtain $\top\!\!\!\top_{AB} = \mathbb{I}_A;\top\!\!\!\top_{AB} = \perp\!\!\!\perp_{AA};\top\!\!\!\top_{AB} = \perp\!\!\!\perp_{AB}$, a contradiction. Axiom (5) implies $\mathbb{I}^{\uparrow}_A = \mathbb{I}_A$.

(2) The following computation shows the assertion:

$$
\begin{aligned}
R^{\downarrow\uparrow} &= (\mathbb{I}^{\smile}_A;R^{\downarrow})^{\uparrow} \\
&= \mathbb{I}^{\uparrow}{}^{\smile}_A;R^{\downarrow} && \text{Axiom (3)} \\
&= R^{\downarrow}. && (1)
\end{aligned}
$$

(3) $R^{\uparrow} = R^{\uparrow\downarrow\uparrow} = R^{\uparrow\downarrow}$ by (2).

(4) First of all, we have $R \sqsubseteq R^{\uparrow\downarrow} = R^{\uparrow}$ and $R^{\uparrow} = R^{\uparrow\downarrow\uparrow} = R^{\uparrow\uparrow}$ using (2) and (3). Since $^{\uparrow}$ is monotone, it is a closure operation. The second assertion is shown analogously.

(5) Suppose $R^{\uparrow} = R$. Then we have $R^{\uparrow\downarrow} = R^{\downarrow}$ and by (3) $R^{\uparrow} = R^{\downarrow}$. Analogously, from $R^{\downarrow} = R$ we get $R^{\downarrow\uparrow} = R^{\uparrow}$ and by (2) $R^{\downarrow} = R^{\uparrow}$. Now, suppose $R^{\downarrow} = R^{\uparrow}$. Then we conclude from (4) $R \sqsubseteq R^{\uparrow} = R^{\downarrow} \sqsubseteq R$, and, hence, $R^{\downarrow} = R$ and $R^{\uparrow} = R$.

(6) The assertion follows immediately from (4) and (5).

(7) We immediately conclude that $(R^{\smile};S^{\uparrow})^{\uparrow} = (R^{\smile};S^{\uparrow\downarrow})^{\uparrow} = R^{\uparrow\smile};S^{\uparrow\downarrow} = R^{\uparrow\smile};S^{\uparrow}$.

(8) Using (7) we obtain $R^{\smile\uparrow} = (R^{\smile};\mathbb{I}_A)^{\uparrow} = (R^{\smile};\mathbb{I}_A^{\uparrow})^{\uparrow} = R^{\uparrow\smile};\mathbb{I}_A^{\uparrow} = R^{\uparrow\smile};\mathbb{I}_A = R^{\uparrow\smile}$. The other assertion follows from

$$\begin{aligned} X \sqsubseteq R^{\smile\downarrow} &\iff X^{\uparrow} \sqsubseteq R^{\smile} && \text{Galois correspondence} \\ &\iff X^{\uparrow\smile} \sqsubseteq R && \\ &\iff X^{\smile\uparrow} \sqsubseteq R && \text{see above} \\ &\iff X^{\smile} \sqsubseteq R^{\downarrow} && \text{Galois correspondence} \\ &\iff X \sqsubseteq R^{\downarrow\smile}. && \end{aligned}$$

(9) We immediately conclude that

$$\begin{aligned} (R;S^{\downarrow})^{\uparrow} &= (R^{\smile\smile};S^{\downarrow})^{\uparrow} && \\ &= R^{\smile\uparrow\smile};S^{\downarrow} && \text{Axiom (3)} \\ &= R^{\uparrow\smile\smile};S^{\downarrow} && (8) \\ &= R^{\uparrow};S^{\downarrow}. && \end{aligned}$$

The second assertion follows from the first one by using conversion twice and (8).

(10) This is shown analogously to (9) using (7) and (8).

(11) We immediately conclude $(Q \sqcap R^{\uparrow})^{\uparrow} = (Q \sqcap R^{\uparrow\downarrow})^{\uparrow} = Q^{\uparrow} \sqcap R^{\uparrow\downarrow} = Q^{\uparrow} \sqcap R^{\uparrow}$ using Axiom (4) and (3) of this lemma.

(12) Suppose $J \neq \perp\!\!\!\perp_{AB}$, and let $\alpha_A := \mathbb{I}_A \sqcap J;\top\!\!\!\top_{BA}$ so that $J = \alpha_A;\top\!\!\!\top_{AB}$ by Lemma 4.37 and $\alpha_A \neq \perp\!\!\!\perp_{AA}$ by Lemma 4.36 (3) holds. We obtain

$$\begin{aligned} J^{\uparrow} &= (\alpha_A;\top\!\!\!\top_{AB})^{\uparrow} && \text{see above} \\ &= (\alpha_A;\top\!\!\!\top_{AB}^{\uparrow})^{\uparrow} && \\ &= \alpha_A^{\uparrow};\top\!\!\!\top_{AB}^{\uparrow} && (10) \\ &= \mathbb{I}_A;\top\!\!\!\top_{AB} && \text{Axiom (5) since } \alpha_A \neq \perp\!\!\!\perp_{AA} \\ &= \top\!\!\!\top_{AB}. && \end{aligned}$$

(13) First of all, we have

$$\begin{aligned} X \sqsubseteq R^{\downarrow}{:}Q^{\uparrow} &\Leftrightarrow Q^{\uparrow} \sqcap X \sqsubseteq R^{\downarrow} && \text{definition :} \\ &\Leftrightarrow (Q^{\uparrow} \sqcap X)^{\uparrow} \sqsubseteq R && \text{Galois correspondence} \\ &\Leftrightarrow Q^{\uparrow} \sqcap X^{\uparrow} \sqsubseteq R && (11) \\ &\Leftrightarrow X^{\uparrow} \sqsubseteq R{:}Q^{\uparrow} && \text{definition :} \\ &\Leftrightarrow X \sqsubseteq (R{:}Q^{\uparrow})^{\downarrow} && \text{Galois correspondence} \end{aligned}$$

so that $R^{\downarrow}{:}Q^{\uparrow} = (R{:}Q^{\uparrow})^{\downarrow}$ follows. From Corollary 2.17 (5) we immediately conclude $(R{:}Q^{\uparrow})^{\downarrow} \sqsubseteq (R{:}Q)^{\downarrow}$. The last assertion follows from

$$\begin{aligned} Q^{\downarrow} \sqcap (R{:}Q)^{\uparrow} &= (Q^{\downarrow} \sqcap (R{:}Q))^{\uparrow} && \text{Axiom (4)} \\ &\sqsubseteq (Q \sqcap (R{:}Q))^{\uparrow} \\ &\sqsubseteq R^{\uparrow}. \end{aligned}$$

(14) First of all, we have

$$\begin{aligned} X \sqsubseteq Q^{\uparrow}\backslash T^{\downarrow} &\Leftrightarrow Q^{\uparrow}; X \sqsubseteq T^{\downarrow} && \text{definition } \backslash \\ &\Leftrightarrow (Q^{\uparrow}; X)^{\uparrow} \sqsubseteq T && \text{Galois correspondence} \\ &\Leftrightarrow Q^{\uparrow}; X^{\uparrow} \sqsubseteq T && (10) \\ &\Leftrightarrow X^{\uparrow} \sqsubseteq Q^{\uparrow}\backslash T && \text{definition } \backslash \\ &\Leftrightarrow X \sqsubseteq (Q^{\uparrow}\backslash T)^{\downarrow} && \text{Galois correspondence} \end{aligned}$$

so that $Q^{\uparrow}\backslash T^{\downarrow} = (Q^{\uparrow}\backslash T)^{\downarrow}$ follows. From Corollary 4.15 (5) we immediately conclude $(Q^{\uparrow}\backslash T)^{\downarrow} \sqsubseteq (Q\backslash T)^{\downarrow}$. The last assertion follows from

$$\begin{aligned} Q^{\downarrow}; (Q\backslash T)^{\uparrow} &= (Q^{\downarrow}; (Q\backslash T))^{\uparrow} && (9) \\ &\sqsubseteq (Q; (Q\backslash T))^{\uparrow} \\ &\sqsubseteq T^{\uparrow}. \end{aligned}$$

(15) This is shown analogously to (14). □

Notice that the previous lemma shows that R is crisp iff $R^{\downarrow} = R$ or $R^{\downarrow} = R^{\uparrow}$. In the rest of this book we will use the previous lemma without mentioning.

For Boolean arrow categories we are able to show additional properties.

Lemma 5.7 *Let $\mathcal{A}$ be a Boolean arrow category and $Q, R : A \to B$. Then we have*

(1) $\overline{Q^{\downarrow}} = \overline{Q}^{\uparrow}$ *and* $\overline{Q^{\uparrow}} = \overline{Q}^{\downarrow}$,

(2) $Q^{\uparrow} \sqcup R^{\downarrow} = (Q^{\uparrow} \sqcup R)^{\downarrow}$,

(3) $R^{\downarrow}{:}Q^{\uparrow} = (R^{\downarrow}{:}Q)^{\downarrow}$ *and* $(R{:}Q)^{\uparrow} = R^{\uparrow}{:}Q^{\downarrow}$.

Proof.

(1) Lemma 5.6 (13) gives us $\overline{Q^{\uparrow}} \sqsubseteq \overline{Q}^{\downarrow}$ and $\overline{Q}^{\uparrow} \sqsubseteq \overline{Q^{\downarrow}}$. From

$$\begin{aligned} Q^{\downarrow} &= \overline{\overline{Q^{\downarrow}}} \\ &\sqsubseteq \overline{\overline{Q}^{\uparrow}} && \text{see above} \\ &\sqsubseteq \overline{\overline{Q}}^{\downarrow} && \text{see above} \\ &= Q^{\downarrow} \end{aligned}$$

we conclude $Q^{\downarrow} = \overline{\overline{Q}^{\uparrow}}$, and, hence, $\overline{Q^{\downarrow}} = \overline{Q}^{\uparrow}$.

For $\overline{Q}$ instead of Q we get $\overline{\overline{Q}^{\downarrow}} = Q^{\uparrow}$, and, hence, $\overline{Q}^{\downarrow} = \overline{Q^{\uparrow}}$.

(2) The assertion follows immediately from

$$\begin{aligned}
Q^{\uparrow} \sqcup R^{\downarrow} &= \overline{\overline{Q^{\uparrow}} \sqcap \overline{R^{\downarrow}}} && \mathcal{A}[A,B] \text{ Boolean algebra} \\
&= \overline{\overline{Q}^{\downarrow} \sqcap \overline{R}^{\uparrow}} && (1) \\
&= \overline{(\overline{Q}^{\downarrow} \sqcap \overline{R})^{\uparrow}} \\
&= \overline{\overline{Q}^{\downarrow} \sqcap \overline{R}}^{\downarrow} && (1) \\
&= \left(\overline{\overline{Q}^{\downarrow}} \sqcup R\right)^{\downarrow} \\
&= (Q^{\uparrow} \sqcup R)^{\downarrow}. && (1)
\end{aligned}$$

(3) In a Boolean arrow category we have $S{:}T = \overline{T} \sqcup S$. We compute

$$\begin{aligned}
R^{\downarrow}{:}Q^{\uparrow} &= \overline{Q^{\uparrow}} \sqcup R^{\downarrow} && \text{see above} \\
&= \overline{Q}^{\downarrow} \sqcup R^{\downarrow} && (1) \\
&= (\overline{Q} \sqcup R^{\downarrow})^{\downarrow} && (2) \\
&= (R^{\downarrow}{:}Q)^{\downarrow}, \\
R^{\uparrow}{:}Q^{\downarrow} &= \overline{Q^{\downarrow}} \sqcup R^{\uparrow} && \text{see above} \\
&= \overline{Q}^{\uparrow} \sqcup R^{\uparrow} && (1) \\
&= (\overline{Q} \sqcup R)^{\uparrow} \\
&= (R{:}Q)^{\uparrow}.
\end{aligned}$$

□

As shown in the previous lemma in a Boolean arrow category we have $R^{\uparrow}{:}Q^{\downarrow} = (R{:}Q)^{\uparrow}$. On the other hand, $R^{\downarrow}{:}Q^{\uparrow} = (R^{\downarrow}{:}Q)^{\downarrow} \sqcup (R{:}Q^{\uparrow})^{\downarrow} \sqsubseteq (R{:}Q)^{\downarrow}$ by Lemma 5.6 (13) and the previous lemma. The corresponding equality is not valid as the following example shows:

Example 5.8 Let $\mathcal{B}_4 = \{0, a, b, 1\}$ be the Boolean algebra with 4 elements and $\overline{a} = b$. Consider the $1 \times 1 - \mathcal{B}_4$ matrices, i.e., the $\mathcal{B}_4$-fuzzy relations on a singleton set. Let Q and R be the matrices with coefficient a. Then we have $\overline{Q^{\uparrow}} \sqcup R^{\downarrow} = \perp\!\!\!\perp$ but $(\overline{Q} \sqcup R)^{\downarrow} = \top\!\!\!\top$. ◇

In Theorem 3.4 we have proved the so-called α-cut Theorem of fuzzy theory in $\mathcal{L}$-**Rel**. The next lemma states a weak version valid in any arrow category.

Lemma 5.9 *Let $\mathcal{A}$ be an arrow category and $R : A \to B$ be a relation. Then we have*

(1) $\displaystyle\bigsqcup_{\alpha_A \in \mathrm{Sc}_{\mathcal{A}}(A)} \alpha_A;(\alpha_A\backslash R)^{\downarrow} \sqsubseteq R,$

(2) $\displaystyle\bigsqcup_{\substack{\alpha_A \in \mathrm{Sc}_{\mathcal{A}}(A)\\ \alpha_A \neq \perp\!\!\!\perp_{AA}}} (\alpha_A\backslash R)^{\downarrow} \sqsubseteq R^{\uparrow}.$

Proof.

(1) The assertion follows immediately from

$$\bigsqcup_{\alpha_A \in \mathrm{Sc}_{\mathcal{A}}(A)} \alpha_A;(\alpha_A\backslash R)^{\downarrow} \sqsubseteq \bigsqcup_{\alpha_A \in \mathrm{Sc}_{\mathcal{A}}(A)} \alpha_A;(\alpha_A\backslash R) \sqsubseteq \bigsqcup_{\alpha_A \in \mathrm{Sc}_{\mathcal{A}}(A)} R = R.$$

(2) We immediately conclude

$$\begin{aligned}
\bigsqcup_{\substack{\alpha_A \in \mathrm{Sc}_{\mathcal{A}}(A)\\ \alpha_A \neq \perp\!\!\!\perp_{AA}}} (\alpha_A\backslash R)^{\downarrow} &= \bigsqcup_{\alpha_A \in \mathrm{Sc}_{\mathcal{A}}(A)} \alpha_A^{\uparrow};(\alpha_A\backslash R)^{\downarrow} \\
&= \bigsqcup_{\alpha_A \in \mathrm{Sc}_{\mathcal{A}}(A)} (\alpha_A;(\alpha_A\backslash R)^{\downarrow})^{\uparrow} && \text{Lemma 5.6 (9)} \\
&= \left(\bigsqcup_{\alpha_A \in \mathrm{Sc}_{\mathcal{A}}(A)} \alpha_A;(\alpha_A\backslash R)^{\downarrow}\right)^{\uparrow} && \text{Corollary 5.5 (4)} \\
&\sqsubseteq R^{\uparrow}. && \text{(1)}
\end{aligned}$$

□

Unfortunately, the general α-cut theorem is not necessarily valid in an arrow category. Let us consider the following examples:

Example 5.10 Let $\mathcal{L} := \{0, a, b, 1\}$ be the complete (linear) Brouwerian lattice, and $\mathcal{M}_1$ be the substructure of $\mathcal{L}$-fuzzy relations given in Figure 5.1.

$\mathcal{M}_1$ is closed under all operations, including $^{\uparrow}$ and $^{\downarrow}$, defined on $\mathcal{L}$-fuzzy relations, and, hence, an arrow category. But we have

$$\bigsqcup_{\alpha_A \in \mathrm{Sc}_{\mathcal{A}}(A)} \alpha_A;(\alpha_A\backslash R)^{\downarrow} = \begin{pmatrix} 1 & a \\ a & 1 \end{pmatrix} \neq R$$

for $R \in \left\{\begin{pmatrix} 1 & b \\ a & 1 \end{pmatrix}, \begin{pmatrix} 1 & a \\ b & 1 \end{pmatrix}, \begin{pmatrix} 1 & b \\ b & 1 \end{pmatrix}\right\}$. The reason is that the scalar $\begin{pmatrix} b & 0 \\ 0 & b \end{pmatrix}$ and the crisp relations $\begin{pmatrix} 1 & 0 \\ 1 & 1 \end{pmatrix}$ and $\begin{pmatrix} 1 & 1 \\ 0 & 1 \end{pmatrix}$ are not included in $\mathcal{M}_1$. The smallest set $\mathcal{N}_1$ of $\mathcal{L}$-fuzzy relations containing $\mathcal{M}_1$ and the three relations above, which is again closed under all operations contains 30 relations. In this arrow category the α-cut theorem is valid. Notice that in this first example the inclusion from Lemma 5.9 (2) is fact an equality. ◇

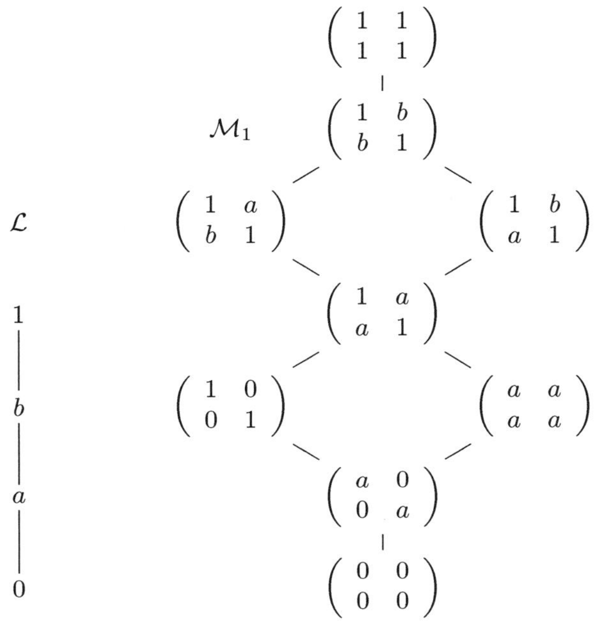

Figure 5.1. The lattice $\mathcal{L}$ and the structure $\mathcal{M}_1$.

Example 5.11 For this example consider the substructure $\mathcal{M}_2$ of $\mathcal{L}$-fuzzy relations given in Figure 5.2.

As above $\mathcal{M}_2$ is closed under all operations defined on $\mathcal{L}$-fuzzy relations, and, hence, an arrow category. Again, we have

$$\bigsqcup_{\alpha_A \in \mathrm{Sc}_{\mathcal{A}}(A)} \alpha_A; (\alpha_A \backslash R)^{\downarrow} \neq R$$

for $R \in \left\{ \begin{pmatrix} b & a \\ a & b \end{pmatrix}, \begin{pmatrix} 1 & a \\ a & 1 \end{pmatrix} \right\}$. This time the scalar $\begin{pmatrix} a & 0 \\ 0 & a \end{pmatrix}$ is missing. Furthermore, we have

$$\bigsqcup_{\substack{\alpha_A \in \mathrm{Sc}_{\mathcal{A}}(A) \\ \alpha_A \neq \perp\!\!\!\perp_{AA}}} (\alpha_A \backslash R)^{\downarrow} = \begin{pmatrix} 1 & 0 \\ 0 & 1 \end{pmatrix} \neq \begin{pmatrix} 1 & 1 \\ 1 & 1 \end{pmatrix} = R^{\uparrow}$$

for those relations proving that Lemma 5.9 (2) is not necessarily an equality. Notice that the set $\mathcal{N}_2 := \mathcal{M}_2 \cup \left\{ \begin{pmatrix} a & 0 \\ 0 & a \end{pmatrix}, \begin{pmatrix} a & a \\ a & a \end{pmatrix} \right\}$ is again an arrow category so that the α-cut theorem as well as Lemma 5.9 (2) is valid. ◇

In the next lemma we have summarized some further properties of arrow categories.

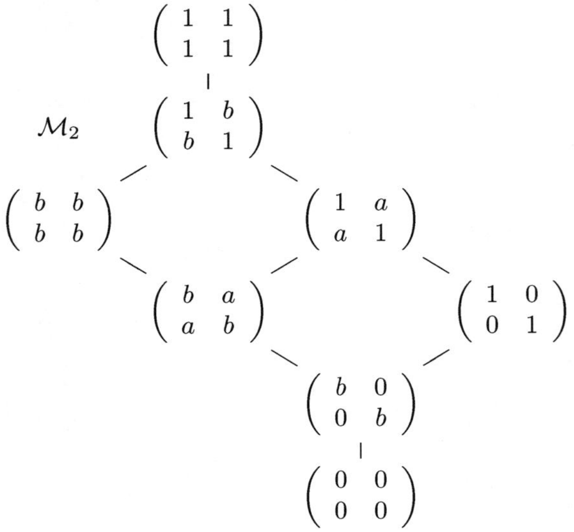

Figure 5.2. The structure $\mathcal{M}_2$.

Lemma 5.12 *Let $\mathcal{A}$ be an arrow category, $Q, R : A \to B$ relations and $\alpha_A \neq \perp\!\!\!\perp_{AA}$ a scalar. Then we have*

(1) $(\alpha_A \backslash R^{\uparrow})^{\downarrow} = R^{\uparrow}$,

(2) $(\mathbb{I}_A \sqcap \top\!\!\!\top_{AA}; R; \top\!\!\!\top_{BA})^{\uparrow} = \mathbb{I}_A \sqcap \top\!\!\!\top_{AA}; R^{\uparrow}; \top\!\!\!\top_{BA}$,

(3) $\top\!\!\!\top_{AB}; \top\!\!\!\top_{BC} = \top\!\!\!\top_{AC}$ *for all objects A, B and C, i.e., $\mathcal{A}$ is uniform,*

(4) if $R \neq \perp\!\!\!\perp_{AB}$, then $\top\!\!\!\top_{CA}; R^{\uparrow}; \top\!\!\!\top_{BD} = \top\!\!\!\top_{CD}$ *for all objects C and D.*

Proof.

(1) The assertion follows from

$$
\begin{aligned}
R^{\uparrow} &= R^{\uparrow\downarrow} \\
&= (\mathbb{I}_A \backslash R^{\uparrow})^{\downarrow} && \text{Lemma 4.16 (1)} \\
&\sqsubseteq (\alpha_A \backslash R^{\uparrow})^{\downarrow} && \text{Corollary 4.15 (4)} \\
&\sqsubseteq \bigsqcup_{\alpha_A \neq \perp\!\!\!\perp_{AA}} (\alpha_A \backslash R^{\uparrow})^{\downarrow} && \alpha_A \neq \perp\!\!\!\perp_{AA} \\
&\sqsubseteq R^{\uparrow\uparrow} && \text{Lemma 5.9 (2)} \\
&= R^{\uparrow}.
\end{aligned}
$$

(2) Consider the following computation:

$$\begin{aligned}(\mathbb{I}_A \sqcap \mathbb{T}_{AA};R;\mathbb{T}_{BA})^{\uparrow} &= (\mathbb{I}_A^{\uparrow} \sqcap \mathbb{T}_{AA};R;\mathbb{T}_{BA})^{\uparrow}\\ &= \mathbb{I}_A^{\uparrow} \sqcap (\mathbb{T}_{AA};R;\mathbb{T}_{BA})^{\uparrow}\\ &= \mathbb{I}_A \sqcap (\mathbb{T}_{AA}^{\uparrow};R;\mathbb{T}_{BA})^{\uparrow}\\ &= \mathbb{I}_A \sqcap \mathbb{T}_{AA}^{\uparrow};(R;\mathbb{T}_{BA})^{\uparrow}\\ &= \mathbb{I}_A \sqcap \mathbb{T}_{AA};(R;\mathbb{T}_{BA}^{\uparrow})^{\uparrow}\\ &= \mathbb{I}_A \sqcap \mathbb{T}_{AA};R^{\uparrow};\mathbb{T}_{BA}^{\uparrow}\\ &= \mathbb{I}_A \sqcap \mathbb{T}_{AA};R^{\uparrow};\mathbb{T}_{BA}.\end{aligned}$$

(3) The relation $\mathbb{T}_{AB};\mathbb{T}_{BA} = \mathbb{T}_{AA};\mathbb{T}_{AB};\mathbb{T}_{BA}$ is a nonzero ideal element on A by 4.36 (1) and (3). Using Lemma 5.6 (12) we get $(\mathbb{T}_{AB};\mathbb{T}_{BA})^{\uparrow} = \mathbb{T}_{AA}$. On the other hand we have

$$(\mathbb{T}_{AB};\mathbb{T}_{BA})^{\uparrow} = (\mathbb{T}_{AB}^{\uparrow};\mathbb{T}_{BA})^{\uparrow} = \mathbb{T}_{AB}^{\uparrow};\mathbb{T}_{BA}^{\uparrow} = \mathbb{T}_{AB};\mathbb{T}_{BA}.$$

Together we have $\mathbb{T}_{AC} = \mathbb{T}_{AA};\mathbb{T}_{AC} = \mathbb{T}_{AB};\mathbb{T}_{BA};\mathbb{T}_{AC} \sqsubseteq \mathbb{T}_{AB};\mathbb{T}_{BC}$.

(4) Since $R \neq \perp\!\!\!\perp_{AB}$ the composite $\mathbb{T}_{AA};R;\mathbb{T}_{BA}$ is a nonzero ideal on A by Lemma 4.36 (1) and (3). Using Lemma 5.6 (12) we have

$$\mathbb{T}_{AA} = (\mathbb{T}_{AA};R;\mathbb{T}_{BA})^{\uparrow} = \mathbb{T}_{AA};R^{\uparrow};\mathbb{T}_{BA}$$

and conclude that

$$\begin{aligned}\mathbb{T}_{CA};R^{\uparrow};\mathbb{T}_{BD} &= \mathbb{T}_{CA};\mathbb{T}_{AA};R^{\uparrow};\mathbb{T}_{BA};\mathbb{T}_{AD} && (3)\\ &= \mathbb{T}_{CA};\mathbb{T}_{AA};\mathbb{T}_{AB} && \text{see above}\\ &= \mathbb{T}_{CD}. && (3)\end{aligned}$$

□

In the next theorem we will show an important property of arrow categories. Notice that (3) of the previous lemma is essential.

Theorem 5.13 *Let $\mathcal{A}$ be an arrow category. For all objects A and B the complete Brouwerian lattices $\mathrm{Sc}_{\mathcal{G}}(A)$ and $\mathrm{Sc}_{\mathcal{G}}(B)$ are isomorphic.*

Proof. Define $f : \mathrm{Sc}_{\mathcal{G}}(A) \to \mathrm{Sc}_{\mathcal{G}}(B)$ and $g : \mathrm{Sc}_{\mathcal{G}}(B) \to \mathrm{Sc}_{\mathcal{G}}(A)$ by $f(\alpha_A) := \mathbb{I}_B \sqcap \mathbb{T}_{BA};\alpha_A;\mathbb{T}_{AB}$ and $g(\beta_B) := \mathbb{I}_A \sqcap \mathbb{T}_{AB};\beta_B;\mathbb{T}_{BA}$. As pointed out in the previous chapter it is sufficient that f is a complete lattice isomorphism. First of all, f and g are inverse, which follows from

$$\begin{aligned}g(f(\alpha_A)) &= \mathbb{I}_A \sqcap \mathbb{T}_{AB};(\mathbb{I}_B \sqcap \mathbb{T}_{BA};\alpha_A;\mathbb{T}_{AB});\mathbb{T}_{BA} && \text{definition } f \text{ and } g\\ &= \mathbb{I}_A \sqcap (\mathbb{T}_{AB};\mathbb{T}_{BA} \sqcap \mathbb{T}_{AA};\alpha_A;\mathbb{T}_{AA}) && \text{Lemma 4.23 (1)}\\ &= \mathbb{I}_A \sqcap (\mathbb{T}_{AA} \sqcap \mathbb{T}_{AA};\alpha_A;\mathbb{T}_{AA}) && \text{Lemma 5.12 (3)}\\ &= \mathbb{I}_A \sqcap \mathbb{T}_{AA};\alpha_A;\mathbb{T}_{AA} &&\\ &= \mathbb{I}_A \sqcap \alpha_A;\mathbb{T}_{AA} && \alpha_A \text{ scalar}\\ &= \alpha_A. && \text{Lemma 4.24 (1)}\end{aligned}$$

$f(g(\beta_B)) = \beta_B$ is shown analogously. By Lemma 2.11 it is sufficient to show that f is a complete lower and g a complete upper semilattice homomorphism. This is shown for partial identities $S_i : A \to A$ and relations $R_i : B \to B$ with $i \in I$ as follows:

$$\begin{aligned}
f\Big(\bigsqcap_{i\in I} S_i\Big) &= \mathbb{I}_B \sqcap \mathbb{T}_{BA};\Big(\bigsqcap_{i\in I} S_i\Big);\mathbb{T}_{AB} \\
&= \mathbb{I}_B \sqcap \bigsqcap_{i\in I}(\mathbb{T}_{BA};S_i;\mathbb{T}_{AB}) && \text{Lemma 4.24 (3)} \\
&= \bigsqcap_{i\in I}(\mathbb{I}_B \sqcap \mathbb{T}_{BA};S_i;\mathbb{T}_{AB}) \\
&= \bigsqcap_{i\in I} f(S_i), \\
g\Big(\bigsqcup_{i\in I} R_i\Big) &= \mathbb{I}_A \sqcap \mathbb{T}_{AB};\Big(\bigsqcup_{i\in I} R_i\Big);\mathbb{T}_{BA} \\
&= \mathbb{I}_A \sqcap \bigsqcup_{i\in I}(\mathbb{T}_{AB};R_i;\mathbb{T}_{BA}) \\
&= \bigsqcup_{i\in I}(\mathbb{I}_A \sqcap \mathbb{T}_{AB};R_i;\mathbb{T}_{BA}) && \text{completely upward-distributive} \\
&= \bigsqcup_{i\in I} g(R_i).
\end{aligned}$$ □

We will identify all sets of scalars and denote them by $\mathrm{Sc}[\mathcal{A}]$. An abstract element from $\mathrm{Sc}[\mathcal{A}]$ is denoted by α, i.e., without an index. The corresponding scalar on the object A is then denoted by α_A. By this convention, we have the following connection $\alpha_A = g(\alpha_B)$ and $\alpha_B = f(\alpha_A)$ for an $\alpha \in \mathrm{Sc}[\mathcal{A}]$ and all objects A and B where f and g are the isomorphisms from the previous lemma:

Lemma 5.14 *Let $\mathcal{A}$ be an arrow category. Then we have $\alpha_A;R = R;\alpha_B$ for all scalars $\alpha \in \mathrm{Sc}[\mathcal{A}]$ and relations $R : A \to B$.*

Proof. Using Lemma 4.23 (1) we have

$$\mathbb{T}_{AB};(\mathbb{I}_B \sqcap \mathbb{T}_{BA};\alpha_A;\mathbb{T}_{AB}) = \mathbb{T}_{AB} \sqcap \mathbb{T}_{AA};\alpha_A;\mathbb{T}_{AB} = \mathbb{T}_{AA};\alpha_A;\mathbb{T}_{AB}.$$

This implies

$$\begin{aligned}
\alpha_A;R &= \alpha_A;\mathbb{T}_{AB} \sqcap R && \text{Lemma 4.24 (2)} \\
&= \alpha_A;\mathbb{T}_{AA};\mathbb{T}_{AB} \sqcap R && \text{Lemma 4.21 (2)} \\
&= \mathbb{T}_{AA};\alpha_A;\mathbb{T}_{AB} \sqcap R && \alpha_A \text{ scalar} \\
&= \mathbb{T}_{AB};(\mathbb{I}_B \sqcap \mathbb{T}_{BA};\alpha_A;\mathbb{T}_{AB}) \sqcap R && \text{see above} \\
&= \mathbb{T}_{AB};\alpha_B \sqcap R && \text{convention} \\
&= R;\alpha_B. && \text{Lemma 4.24 (2)}
\end{aligned}$$ □

As an application of the previous lemma, we obtain the following lemma about the relationship of the α-cuts of Q and $Q^{\smile}$:

Lemma 5.15 *Let $\mathcal{A}$ be an arrow category. Then we have*

$$(\alpha_A \backslash Q)^{\downarrow\smile} = (\alpha_B \backslash Q^{\smile})^{\downarrow}$$

for all scalars $\alpha \in \mathrm{Sc}[\mathcal{A}]$ and relations $Q : A \to B$.

Proof. The assertion follows from

$$\begin{aligned}
X \sqsubseteq (\alpha_A \backslash Q)^{\downarrow\smile} &\Leftrightarrow X^{\smile} \sqsubseteq (\alpha_A \backslash Q)^{\downarrow} && \\
&\Leftrightarrow X^{\smile\uparrow} \sqsubseteq \alpha_A \backslash Q && \text{Galois correspondence} \\
&\Leftrightarrow \alpha_A; X^{\smile\uparrow} \sqsubseteq Q && \text{definition residual} \\
&\Leftrightarrow X^{\smile\uparrow}; \alpha_B \sqsubseteq Q && \text{Lemma 5.14} \\
&\Leftrightarrow X^{\uparrow\smile}; \alpha_B^{\smile} \sqsubseteq Q && \text{Lemma 4.9(1) and 5.6(8)} \\
&\Leftrightarrow \alpha_B; X^{\uparrow} \sqsubseteq Q^{\smile} && \\
&\Leftrightarrow X^{\uparrow} \sqsubseteq \alpha_B \backslash Q^{\smile} && \text{definition residual} \\
&\Leftrightarrow X \sqsubseteq (\alpha_B \backslash Q^{\smile})^{\downarrow}. && \text{Galois correspondence} \quad \Box
\end{aligned}$$

In the next lemma we have collected some closure properties of the class of crisp relations.

Lemma 5.16 *Let $\mathcal{A}$ be an arrow category and $Q_i, Q, T : A \to B$ for $i \in I$, $R : A \to C$, and $S : B \to C$ crisp relations. Then the following holds:*

(1) $\bigsqcup_{i \in I} Q_i$ and $\bigsqcap_{i \in I} Q_i$ are crisp.

(2) $Q^{\smile}$ is crisp.

(3) $Q; S$ is crisp.

(4) R/S and $Q \backslash R$ are crisp.

(5) $Q{:}T$ is crisp.

Proof. For the first three assertions consider the following computations:

(1) $(\bigsqcup_{i \in I} Q_i)^{\uparrow} = \bigsqcup_{i \in I} Q_i^{\uparrow} = \bigsqcup_{i \in I} Q_i$ and $(\bigsqcap_{i \in I} Q_i)^{\downarrow} = \bigsqcap_{i \in I} Q^{\downarrow}{}_i = \bigsqcap_{i \in I} Q_i$,

(2) $Q^{\smile\uparrow} = Q^{\uparrow\smile} = Q^{\smile}$,

(3) $(Q; S)^{\uparrow} = (Q; S^{\uparrow})^{\uparrow} = Q^{\uparrow}; S^{\uparrow} = Q; S$.

(4) From Lemma 5.6 (14) we conclude $(Q\backslash R)^{\uparrow} \sqsubseteq Q^{\downarrow}\backslash R^{\uparrow} = Q\backslash R$. The other assertion follows analogously.

(5) From Lemma 5.6 (13) we conclude $(Q{:}T)^{\uparrow} \sqsubseteq Q^{\uparrow}{:}T^{\downarrow} = Q{:}T$. □

The previous lemma, Lemma 5.6 (1) and (6) and Lemma 5.12 (4) give us the following corollary:

Corollary 5.17 *If $\mathcal{A}$ is an arrow category, then $\mathcal{A}^{\uparrow}$ is a simple Dedekind category with $\mathbb{T}_{AB} \neq \perp\!\!\!\perp_{AB}$.*

The substructure of crisp relations may satisfy additional properties.

Definition 5.18 *An arrow category $\mathcal{A}$ such that $\mathcal{A}^{\uparrow}$ is a Schröder category is called a Boolean-based arrow category.*

As already mentioned in Section 4.9 the crisp $\mathcal{L}$-fuzzy relations constitute a Schröder category so that **$\mathcal{L}$-Rel** is in fact a Boolean-based arrow category.

The inclusion $Q \subseteq R$ of $\mathcal{L}$-fuzzy relations has two aspects. First of all, there is the usual relational aspect. The set of all pairs (x, y) such that $Q(x, y) \neq \perp\!\!\!\perp_{AB}$ has to be a subset of the corresponding set of R. This may be expressed by the relational inclusion $Q^{\uparrow} \subseteq R^{\uparrow}$ of crisp relations. Furthermore, there is an aspect induced by the lattice $\mathcal{L}$. All values $Q(x, y)$ have to be less or equal to $R(x, y)$. The next lemma shows that these aspects of an inclusion can be found in all arrow categories.

Lemma 5.19 *Let $\mathcal{A}$ be an arrow category, $X, Y : A \to B$ be crisp relations and $\alpha_A, \beta_A \in \mathrm{Sc}_{\mathcal{A}}(A)$. Then we have*

$$\alpha_A; X \sqsubseteq \beta_A; Y \iff \alpha_A = \perp\!\!\!\perp_{AA} \text{ or } X = \perp\!\!\!\perp_{AB} \text{ or } (\alpha_A \sqsubseteq \beta_A \text{ and } X \sqsubseteq Y).$$

Proof. The implication $\Leftarrow$ is trivial. Now, suppose $\alpha_A; X \sqsubseteq \beta_A; Y$, $\alpha_A \neq \perp\!\!\!\perp_{AA}$ and $X \neq \perp\!\!\!\perp_{AB}$. Then we have $\alpha_A^{\uparrow} = \mathbb{I}_A$ and may conclude that

$$\begin{aligned}
X &= X^{\uparrow} && X \text{ crisp}\\
&= \alpha_A^{\uparrow}; X^{\uparrow} && \alpha_A^{\uparrow} = \mathbb{I}_A\\
&= (\alpha_A; X^{\uparrow})^{\uparrow} && \text{Lemma 5.6 (10)}\\
&= (\alpha_A; X)^{\uparrow} && X \text{ crisp}\\
&\sqsubseteq (\beta_A; Y)^{\uparrow} &&\\
&= (\beta_A; Y^{\uparrow})^{\uparrow} && Y \text{ crisp}\\
&= \beta_A^{\uparrow}; Y^{\uparrow} && \text{Lemma 5.6 (10)}\\
&\sqsubseteq Y^{\uparrow} &&\\
&= Y. && Y \text{ crisp}
\end{aligned}$$

From Lemma 5.12 (4) we obtain

$$\begin{aligned}
\alpha_A;\mathbb{T}_{AB} &= \alpha_A;\mathbb{T}_{AA};X;\mathbb{T}_{BB} && X \neq \mathbb{L}_{AB}\\
&= \mathbb{T}_{AA};\alpha_A;X;\mathbb{T}_{BB} && \alpha_A \text{ scalar}\\
&\sqsubseteq \mathbb{T}_{AA};\beta_A;Y;\mathbb{T}_{BB}\\
&= \beta_A;\mathbb{T}_{AA};Y;\mathbb{T}_{BB} && \beta_A \text{ scalar}\\
&\sqsubseteq \beta_A;\mathbb{T}_{AB},
\end{aligned}$$

and, hence,

$$\begin{aligned}
\alpha_A &= \mathbb{I}_A \sqcap \alpha_A;\mathbb{T}_{AA} && \text{Lemma 4.24 (1)}\\
&= \mathbb{I}_A \sqcap \alpha_A;\mathbb{T}_{AB};\mathbb{T}_{BA} && \text{Lemma 5.12 (3)}\\
&\sqsubseteq \mathbb{I}_A \sqcap \beta_A;\mathbb{T}_{AB};\mathbb{T}_{BA}\\
&= \mathbb{I}_A \sqcap \beta_A;\mathbb{T}_{AA} && \text{Lemma 5.12 (3)}\\
&= \beta_A. && \text{Lemma 4.24 (1)} \qquad \square
\end{aligned}$$

The previous lemma allows us to compute the α-cut of the composition from β with a crisp relation R.

Lemma 5.20 *Let $\mathcal{A}$ be an arrow category, $R : A \to B$ be a crisp relation and $\alpha_A, \beta_A \in \mathrm{Sc}_{\mathcal{A}}(A)$. Then we have*

$$(\alpha_A \backslash (\beta_A;R))^{\downarrow} = \begin{cases} \mathbb{T}_{AB} & \textit{iff } \alpha_A = \mathbb{L}_{AA},\\ R & \textit{iff } \alpha \neq \mathbb{L}_{AA} \textit{ and } \alpha_A \sqsubseteq \beta_A,\\ \mathbb{L}_{AB} & \textit{else.} \end{cases}$$

Proof. Using the previous lemma the assertion follows immediately from

$$\begin{aligned}
X \sqsubseteq (\alpha_A\backslash(\beta_A;R))^{\downarrow} &\Leftrightarrow X^{\uparrow} \sqsubseteq \alpha_A\backslash(\beta_A;R)\\
&\Leftrightarrow \alpha_A;X^{\uparrow} \sqsubseteq \beta_A;R\\
&\Leftrightarrow \alpha_A = \mathbb{L}_{AA} \text{ or } X^{\uparrow} = \mathbb{L}_{AB}\\
&\quad\ \text{or } (\alpha_A \sqsubseteq \beta_A \text{ and } X^{\uparrow} \sqsubseteq R) && \text{Lemma 5.19}\\
&\Leftrightarrow \alpha_A = \mathbb{L}_{AA} \text{ or } X = \mathbb{L}_{AB}\\
&\quad\ \text{or } (\alpha_A \sqsubseteq \beta_A \text{ and } X \sqsubseteq R). && \mathbb{L}_{AB} \text{ and } R \text{ crisp} \qquad \square
\end{aligned}$$

Let us consider the following operation in an arbitrary arrow category:

$$\varrho(R) := \bigsqcup_{\alpha\in\mathrm{Sc}[\mathcal{A}]} \alpha_A;(\alpha_A\backslash R)^{\downarrow}.$$

From Lemma 5.9 (1) we already know that $\varrho(R) \sqsubseteq R$. Furthermore, the examples have shown that the inclusion might be strict.

It is obvious that ϱ is monotone and the following computation shows that it is indeed a kernel operation:

$$\begin{aligned}\beta_A;(\beta_A\backslash R)^{\downarrow} \sqsubseteq \varrho(R) &\iff (\beta_A\backslash R)^{\downarrow} \sqsubseteq \beta_A\backslash\varrho(R)\\ &\iff (\beta_A\backslash R)^{\downarrow} \sqsubseteq (\beta_A\backslash\varrho(R))^{\downarrow}\\ &\implies \varrho(R) \sqsubseteq \varrho^2(R).\end{aligned}$$

Lemma 5.21 *Let $\mathcal{A}$ be an arrow category and $Q, R : A \to B, S : B \to C$. Then we have*

(1) $\varrho(Q^{\smile}) = \varrho(Q)^{\smile}$,

(2) $\varrho(Q \sqcap R) = \varrho(Q) \sqcap \varrho(R)$,

(3) $\varrho(R;S) = \varrho(R);\varrho(S)$.

Proof.

(1) Consider the following computation:

$$\begin{aligned}\varrho(Q^{\smile}) &= \bigsqcup_{\alpha\in\mathrm{Sc}[\mathcal{A}]} \alpha_B;(\alpha_B\backslash Q^{\smile})^{\downarrow} && \text{definition } \varrho\\ &= \bigsqcup_{\alpha\in\mathrm{Sc}[\mathcal{A}]} (\alpha_B\backslash Q^{\smile})^{\downarrow};\alpha_A && \text{Lemma 5.14}\\ &= \bigsqcup_{\alpha\in\mathrm{Sc}[\mathcal{A}]} (\alpha_A\backslash Q)^{\downarrow\smile};\alpha_A && \text{Lemma 5.15}\\ &= \bigsqcup_{\alpha\in\mathrm{Sc}[\mathcal{A}]} (\alpha_A;(\alpha_A\backslash Q)^{\downarrow})^{\smile} && \text{Lemma 4.9 (1)}\\ &= \Big(\bigsqcup_{\alpha\in\mathrm{Sc}[\mathcal{A}]} \alpha_A;(\alpha_A\backslash Q)^{\downarrow}\Big)^{\smile}\\ &= \varrho(Q)^{\smile}. && \text{definition } \varrho\end{aligned}$$

(2) Again, consider the following computation:

$$\begin{aligned}&\varrho(Q) \sqcap \varrho(R)\\ &= \Big(\bigsqcup_{\alpha\in\mathrm{Sc}[\mathcal{A}]} \alpha_A;(\alpha_A\backslash Q)^{\downarrow}\Big) \sqcap \Big(\bigsqcup_{\beta\in\mathrm{Sc}[\mathcal{A}]} \beta_A;(\beta_A\backslash R)^{\downarrow}\Big) && \text{definition } \varrho\\ &= \bigsqcup_{\alpha,\beta\in\mathrm{Sc}[\mathcal{A}]} \alpha_A;(\alpha_A\backslash Q)^{\downarrow}) \sqcap \beta_A;(\beta_A\backslash R)^{\downarrow})\\ &= \bigsqcup_{\alpha,\beta\in\mathrm{Sc}[\mathcal{A}]} (\alpha_A \sqcap \beta_A);((\alpha_A\backslash Q)^{\downarrow}) \sqcap (\beta_A\backslash R)^{\downarrow}) && \text{Lemma 4.9 (5)}\\ &\sqsubseteq \bigsqcup_{\alpha,\beta\in\mathrm{Sc}[\mathcal{A}]} (\alpha_A \sqcap \beta_A);(((\alpha_A \sqcap \beta_A)\backslash Q)^{\downarrow} \sqcap ((\alpha_A \sqcap \beta_A)\backslash R)^{\downarrow})\end{aligned}$$

$$
\begin{aligned}
&\sqsubseteq \bigsqcup_{\alpha\in \mathrm{Sc}[\mathcal{A}]} \alpha_A;((\alpha_A\backslash Q)^{\downarrow} \sqcap (\alpha_A\backslash R)^{\downarrow}) && \\
&= \bigsqcup_{\alpha\in \mathrm{Sc}[\mathcal{A}]} \alpha_A;((\alpha_A\backslash Q) \sqcap (\alpha_A\backslash R))^{\downarrow} && \text{Corollary 5.5 (4)}\\
&= \bigsqcup_{\alpha\in \mathrm{Sc}[\mathcal{A}]} \alpha_A;(\alpha_A\backslash (Q \sqcap R))^{\downarrow} && \text{Corollary 4.15 (6)}\\
&= \varrho(Q\sqcap R).
\end{aligned}
$$

The other inclusion is trivial since ϱ is a kernel operations.

(3) First of all, we have

$$
\begin{aligned}
\alpha_A;(\alpha_A\backslash R)^{\downarrow};(\alpha_B\backslash S)^{\downarrow} &= \alpha_A;\alpha_A;(\alpha_A\backslash R)^{\downarrow};(\alpha_B\backslash S)^{\downarrow} && \text{Lemma 4.9 (2)}\\
&= \alpha_A;(\alpha_A\backslash R)^{\downarrow};\alpha_B;(\alpha_B\backslash S)^{\downarrow} && \text{Lemma 5.14}\\
&\sqsubseteq \alpha_A;(\alpha_A\backslash R);\alpha_B;(\alpha_B\backslash S) &&\\
&\sqsubseteq R;S. &&
\end{aligned}
$$

This implies $(\alpha_A\backslash R)^{\downarrow};(\alpha_B\backslash S)^{\downarrow} \sqsubseteq \alpha_A\backslash(R;S)$ and since the left-hand side is crisp $(\alpha_A\backslash R)^{\downarrow};(\alpha_B\backslash S)^{\downarrow} \sqsubseteq (\alpha_A\backslash(R;S))^{\downarrow}$. We conclude

$$
\begin{aligned}
&\varrho(R);\varrho(S) && \\
&= \Big(\bigsqcup_{\alpha\in \mathrm{Sc}[\mathcal{A}]} \alpha_A;(\alpha_A\backslash R)^{\downarrow}\Big);\Big(\bigsqcup_{\beta\in \mathrm{Sc}[\mathcal{A}]} \beta_B;(\beta_B\backslash S)^{\downarrow}\Big) && \text{definition } \varrho\\
&= \bigsqcup_{\alpha,\beta\in \mathrm{Sc}[\mathcal{A}]} \alpha_A;(\alpha_A\backslash R)^{\downarrow};\beta_B;(\beta_B\backslash S)^{\downarrow} && \\
&= \bigsqcup_{\alpha,\beta\in \mathrm{Sc}[\mathcal{A}]} \alpha_A;\beta_A;(\alpha_A\backslash R)^{\downarrow};(\beta_B\backslash S)^{\downarrow} && \text{Lemma 5.14}\\
&= \bigsqcup_{\alpha,\beta\in \mathrm{Sc}[\mathcal{A}]} (\alpha_A\sqcap\beta_A);(\alpha_A\backslash R)^{\downarrow};(\beta_B\backslash S)^{\downarrow} && \text{Lemma 4.9 (3)}\\
&\sqsubseteq \bigsqcup_{\alpha,\beta\in \mathrm{Sc}[\mathcal{A}]} (\alpha_A\sqcap\beta_A);((\alpha_A\sqcap\beta_A)\backslash R)^{\downarrow};((\alpha_B\sqcap\beta_B)\backslash S)^{\downarrow} && \\
&\sqsubseteq \bigsqcup_{\alpha\in \mathrm{Sc}[\mathcal{A}]} \alpha_A;(\alpha_A\backslash R)^{\downarrow};(\alpha_B\backslash S)^{\downarrow} && \\
&\sqsubseteq \bigsqcup_{\alpha\in \mathrm{Sc}[\mathcal{A}]} \alpha_A;(\alpha_A\backslash(R;S))^{\downarrow} && \text{see above}\\
&= \varrho(R;S). &&
\end{aligned}
$$

Again, the other inclusion is trivial. □

As usual we are interested in the fixed points of the kernel operation ϱ.

Definition 5.22 *Let $\mathcal{A}$ be an arrow category. A relation $R : A \to B$ is called sliceable iff $\varrho(R) = R$.*

Notice that if the α-cut theorem is valid, all relations are sliceable. However, we have the following closure properties of the class of sliceable relations:

Theorem 5.23 *Let $\mathcal{A}$ be an arrow category. Then we have*

(1) All scalar relations are sliceable.

(2) All crisp relations are sliceable.

(3) If $Q : A \to B$ is sliceable, then so is $Q^{\smile}$.

(4) If $Q, R : A \to B$ are sliceable, then so is $Q \sqcap R$.

(5) If $R : A \to B$ and $S : B \to C$ are sliceable, then so is $R; S$.

Proof.

(1) Let β_A be a scalar. Then we immediately conclude

$$\begin{aligned} \varrho(\beta_A) &= \bigsqcup_{\alpha \in \mathrm{Sc}[\mathcal{A}]} \alpha_A; (\alpha_A \backslash \beta_A)^{\downarrow} \\ &= \bigsqcup_{\alpha_A \sqsubseteq \beta_A} \alpha_A && \text{Lemma 5.20} \\ &= \beta_A. \end{aligned}$$

(2) Let R be crisp and consider the following computation:

$$\begin{aligned} \varrho(R) &= \bigsqcup_{\alpha \in \mathrm{Sc}[\mathcal{A}]} \alpha_A; (\alpha_A \backslash R)^{\downarrow} \\ &= \bigsqcup_{\alpha \in \mathrm{Sc}[\mathcal{A}]} \alpha_A; (\alpha_A \backslash R^{\uparrow})^{\downarrow} && R \text{ crisp} \\ &= \bigsqcup_{\alpha \in \mathrm{Sc}[\mathcal{A}]} \alpha_A; R^{\uparrow} && \text{Lemma 5.12 (1)} \\ &= \Big(\bigsqcup_{\alpha \in \mathrm{Sc}[\mathcal{A}]} \alpha_A \Big); R && R \text{ crisp} \\ &= R. \end{aligned}$$

(3)–(5) follow from Lemma 5.21. □

We want to close this section by providing an example of an arrow category where ϱ does not preserve arbitrary meets. Obviously, the α-cut theorem cannot be valid in that category.

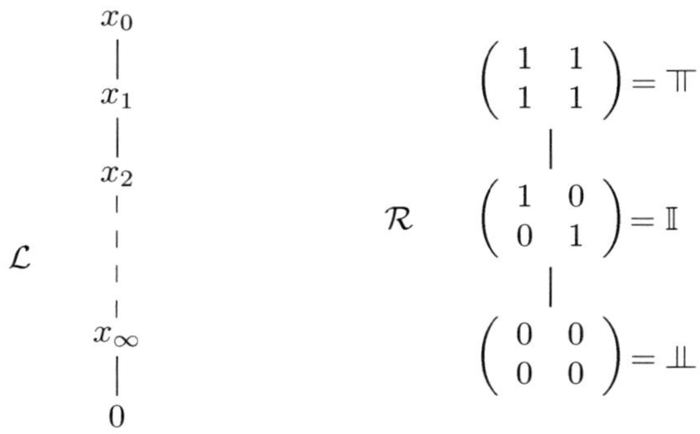

Figure 5.3. The lattice $\mathcal{L}$ and the simple Dedekind category $\mathcal{R}$.

Example 5.24 Consider the complete Brouwerian lattice $\mathcal{L}$ and the simple Dedekind category $\mathcal{R}$ given in Figure 5.3. Notice that $\mathcal{L}$ is the reversed order on $\mathbb{N}^\infty$ with an additional least element 0.

Since the least upper bound of each subset of $\mathcal{L}$ is in fact a maximum all antitone functions are antimorphisms and all operations in $\mathcal{R}^\mathcal{L}$ are computed componentwise. Notice that all relations in $\mathcal{R}$, and, hence, in $\mathcal{R}^\mathcal{L}$ are symmetric. The scalar g_i in $\mathcal{R}^\mathcal{L}$ corresponding to the element x_i ($i \in \mathbb{N}^\infty$) is given by

$$g_i(x) = \begin{cases} \top\!\!\!\top & \text{iff } x = 0 \\ \mathbb{I} & \text{iff } x \sqsubseteq x_i \\ \perp\!\!\!\perp & \text{otherwise} \end{cases}$$

Now, let $\mathcal{S}$ be the subset of antimorphisms fulfilling the property

$$\text{if } f(x_\infty) \neq \perp\!\!\!\perp, \text{ then there is an } i \in \mathbb{N} \text{ with } f(x_i) \neq \perp\!\!\!\perp.$$

It is easy to verify that the following properties are valid:

(1) if $f, g \in \mathcal{S}$, then so is $f;g$ and $f \sqcap g$,

(2) if $f_i \in \mathcal{S}$ for all $i \in I$, then so is $\bigsqcup_{i \in I} f_i$.

The conditions above show that $\mathcal{S}$ is an arrow category. But notice that the function g_∞, i.e, the scalar corresponding to x_∞, is not in $\mathcal{S}$ since $g_\infty(x_\infty) = \mathbb{I} \neq \perp\!\!\!\perp$ but $g_\infty(x_i) = \perp\!\!\!\perp$ for all $i \in \mathbb{N}$. Now, let f_i for $i \in \mathbb{N}^\infty$ be defined by

$$f_i(x) = \begin{cases} \top\!\!\!\top & \text{iff } x = 0 \text{ or } x \sqsubseteq x_i \\ \mathbb{I} & \text{otherwise} \end{cases}$$

Then $f_i \in \mathcal{S}$ for all $i \in \mathbb{N}^\infty$ and we have $\bigsqcap_{i \in \mathbb{N}} f_i = f_\infty$. It is easy to verify that for $i \in \mathbb{N}$ and $j \in \mathbb{N}^\infty$

$$(g_i \backslash f_j)^\downarrow = \begin{cases} \dot{\top\!\!\!\top} & \text{iff } j \leq i \\ \dot{\mathbb{I}} & \text{otherwise} \end{cases}$$

holds. Therefore, f_i is sliceable in $\mathcal{S}$ iff $i \in \mathbb{N}$, which shows that the α-cut theorem is not valid and that the set of sliceable relations is not closed under arbitrary meets. ◇

5.2 THE ARROW CATEGORY OF ANTIMORPHISMS

As shown in Theorem 4.33, the category $\mathcal{R}^{\mathcal{L}}$ is a Dedekind category. In order to establish that this structure is an arrow category, we first want to characterize the set of scalar elements in $\mathcal{R}^{\mathcal{L}}[A, A]$. Therefore, we need the following technical lemma:

Lemma 5.25 *Let $\mathcal{L}$ be a complete Brouwerian lattice, $\mathcal{R}$ be a Dedekind category, $f : \mathcal{L} \overset{\text{anti}}{\rightarrow} \mathcal{R}[A, A]$ be a partial identity in $\mathcal{R}^{\mathcal{L}}$ and $R : C \to A, S : A \to B$ relations from $\mathcal{R}$. Then we have*

(1) $\dot{R} \mathbin{;\!\!;} f = \dot{R}; f$,

(2) $f \mathbin{;\!\!;} \dot{S} = f; \dot{S}$.

Proof.

(1) First of all, we have

$$(\dot{R}; f)(0) = \dot{R}(0); f(0) = \mathbb{T}_{CA}; \mathbb{T}_{AA} = \mathbb{T}_{CA} = \tau(\dot{R}; f)(0) = (\dot{R} \mathbin{;\!\!;} f)(0)$$

since $\tau(\dot{R}; f)$ is an antimorphism. If $x \neq 0$ and $\bigvee M = x$, then the set $M \setminus \{0\}$ is not empty, and, hence, $\bigsqcap_{y \in M} f(y) = \bigsqcap_{0 \neq y \in M} f(y)$ since $f(0) = \mathbb{T}_{AA}$. Analogously, we have $\bigsqcap_{y \in M} (\dot{R}; f)(y) = \bigsqcap_{0 \neq y \in M} (\dot{R}; f)(y)$ and conclude

$$\begin{aligned}
\varphi(\dot{R}; f)(x) &= \bigsqcup_{\substack{M \subseteq \mathcal{L} \\ \bigvee M = x}} \bigsqcap_{y \in M} (\dot{R}; f)(y) && \text{definition } \varphi \\
&= \bigsqcup_{\substack{M \subseteq \mathcal{L} \\ \bigvee M = x}} \bigsqcap_{0 \neq y \in M} (\dot{R}; f)(y) && \text{see above} \\
&= \bigsqcup_{\substack{M \subseteq \mathcal{L} \\ \bigvee M = x}} \bigsqcap_{0 \neq y \in M} (R; f(y)) && \text{definition ; and } \dot{R} \\
&= \bigsqcup_{\substack{M \subseteq \mathcal{L} \\ \bigvee M = x}} R; \Big(\bigsqcap_{0 \neq y \in M} f(y) \Big) && \text{Lemma 4.24 (4)} \\
&= R; \Big(\bigsqcup_{\substack{M \subseteq \mathcal{L} \\ \bigvee M = x}} \bigsqcap_{0 \neq y \in M} f(y) \Big) \\
&= R; \Big(\bigsqcup_{\substack{M \subseteq \mathcal{L} \\ \bigvee M = x}} \bigsqcap_{y \in M} f(y) \Big) && \text{see above}
\end{aligned}$$

$$\begin{aligned} &= R;\varphi(f)(x) && \text{definition } \varphi \\ &= R;f(x) && f \text{ antimorphism} \\ &= (\dot{R};f)(x). && \text{definition ; and } \dot{R} \end{aligned}$$

Together we have $\varphi(\dot{R};f) = \dot{R};f$, and, hence, $\tau(\dot{R};f) \sqsubseteq \dot{R};f$. The other inclusion is trivial.

(2) is shown analogously. □

The previous lemma gives us the following:

Lemma 5.26 *Let $\mathcal{L}$ be a complete Brouwerian lattice, $\mathcal{R}$ be a Dedekind category and $\alpha_A : \mathcal{L} \overset{\text{anti}}{\to} \mathcal{R}[A,A]$ be a scalar in $\mathcal{R}^{\mathcal{L}}$. Then $\alpha_A(x)$ is a scalar for all $0 \neq x \in \mathcal{L}$.*

Proof. Suppose $x \neq 0$. Then $\alpha_A(x) \sqsubseteq \dot{\mathbb{I}}_A(x) = \mathbb{I}_A$ shows that $\alpha_A(x)$ is a partial identity for $x \neq 0$. Using the previous lemma we get

$$\begin{aligned} \alpha_A(x);\top\!\!\top_{AA} &= \alpha_A(x);\dot{\top\!\!\top}_{AA}(x) && \text{definition } \dot{\top\!\!\top}_{AA} \\ &= (\alpha_A;\dot{\top\!\!\top}_{AA})(x) && \text{definition ;} \\ &= (\alpha_A \mathbin{\dot{;}} \dot{\top\!\!\top}_{AA})(x) && \text{Lemma 5.25 (2)} \\ &= (\dot{\top\!\!\top}_{AA} \mathbin{\dot{;}} \alpha_A)(x) && \alpha_A \text{ scalar} \\ &= (\dot{\top\!\!\top}_{AA};\alpha_A)(x) && \text{Lemma 5.25 (1)} \\ &= \top\!\!\top_{AA};\alpha_A(x). && \text{definition ; and } \dot{\top\!\!\top}_{AA} \end{aligned}$$

□

For simple Dedekind categories we obtain the following result as an immediate consequence:

Corollary 5.27 *Let $\mathcal{L}$ be a complete Brouwerian lattice, $\mathcal{R}$ be a simple Dedekind category and $\alpha_A : \mathcal{L} \overset{\text{anti}}{\to} \mathcal{R}[A,A]$ be a scalar in $\mathcal{R}^{\mathcal{L}}$. Then $\alpha_A(x) \in \{\perp\!\!\perp_{AA}, \mathbb{I}_A\}$ for all $0 \neq x \in \mathcal{L}$.*

By the previous corollary and the fact that $\alpha_A(0) = \top\!\!\top_{AA}$ we may conclude that $\alpha_A(x) \in \{\perp\!\!\perp_{AA}, \mathbb{I}_A, \top\!\!\top_{AA}\}$ for all x and all scalars α_A in $\mathcal{R}^{\mathcal{L}}$ if $\mathcal{R}$ is simple.

We may define two functions $\gamma : \mathcal{L} \to \mathrm{Sc}_{\mathcal{R}^{\mathcal{L}}}(A)$ and $\delta : \mathrm{Sc}_{\mathcal{R}^{\mathcal{L}}}(A) \to \mathcal{L}$ between the underlying lattice of scalars over A in $\mathcal{R}^{\mathcal{L}}$ and $\mathcal{L}$ by

$$\begin{aligned} \gamma(x) &:= \bigsqcap\{\beta_A \in \mathrm{Sc}_{\mathcal{R}^{\mathcal{L}}}(A) \mid \beta_A(x) \neq \perp\!\!\perp_{AA}\} \\ \text{and} \quad \delta(\alpha_A) &:= \bigvee\{y \in \mathcal{L} \mid \alpha_A(y) \neq \perp\!\!\perp_{AA}\}. \end{aligned}$$

Notice that the sets on the right-hand side of the definitions above are not empty if $\top\!\!\top_{AB} \neq \perp\!\!\perp_{AB}$ for all objects A and B holds in $\mathcal{R}$. Furthermore, we have $\gamma(0) = \dot{\perp\!\!\perp}_{AA}$ and $\delta(\dot{\perp\!\!\perp}_{AA}) = 0$.

Lemma 5.28 *Let $\mathcal{L}$ be a complete Brouwerian lattice and $\mathcal{R}$ be a simple Dedekind category with $\mathbb{T}_{AB} \neq \perp\!\!\!\perp_{AB}$ for all objects A and B. Then for all $x, y \in \mathcal{L}$, and $\alpha_A, \beta_A \in \mathrm{Sc}_{\mathcal{R}^{\mathcal{L}}}(A)$ we have*

(1) $\gamma(x)(y) \neq \perp\!\!\!\perp_{AA} \iff y \leq x$,

(2) $\beta_A(\delta(\alpha_A)) \neq \perp\!\!\!\perp_{AA} \iff \alpha_A \sqsubseteq \beta_A$.

Proof.

(1) The case $x = 0$ is obvious. For $\Leftarrow$ suppose $y \leq x \neq 0$. Since every scalar is antitone, we immediately compute $\beta_A(x) \sqsubseteq \beta_A(y)$, and, hence, $\beta_A(y) \in \{\mathbb{I}_A, \mathbb{T}_{AA}\}$ for all β_A with $\beta_A(x) \neq \perp\!\!\!\perp_{AA}$. It follows

$$\gamma(x)(y) = \Big(\bigsqcap_{\beta_A(x) \neq \perp\!\!\!\perp_{AA}} \beta_A \Big)(y) = \bigsqcap_{\beta_A(x) \neq \perp\!\!\!\perp_{AA}} \beta_A(y) \neq \perp\!\!\!\perp_{AA}.$$

For the other implication we define $\hat{\beta}_A$ by

$$\hat{\beta}_A(z) := \begin{cases} \mathbb{T}_{AA} & \text{iff } z = 0, \\ \mathbb{I}_A & \text{iff } z \neq 0 \text{ and } z \leq x, \\ \perp\!\!\!\perp_{AA} & \text{iff } z \neq 0 \text{ and } z \not\leq x. \end{cases}$$

$\hat{\beta}_A$ is an antimorphism, which follows from

$$\begin{aligned} \bigsqcap_{z \in M} \hat{\beta}_A(z) &= \begin{cases} \mathbb{T}_{AA} & \text{iff } M = \emptyset \vee M = \{0\}, \\ \mathbb{I}_A & \text{iff } \forall z \in M : z \leq x \text{ and } \exists z \in M : z \neq 0, \\ \perp\!\!\!\perp_{AA} & \text{iff } \exists z \in M : z \neq 0 \text{ and } z \not\leq x. \end{cases} \\ &= \begin{cases} \mathbb{T}_{AA} & \text{iff } \bigvee M = 0, \\ \mathbb{I}_A & \text{iff } \bigvee M \neq 0 \text{ and } \bigvee M \leq x, \\ \perp\!\!\!\perp_{AA} & \text{iff } \bigvee M \neq 0 \text{ and } \bigvee M \not\leq x. \end{cases} \\ &= \hat{\beta}_A\Big(\bigvee M\Big). \end{aligned}$$

Furthermore, $\hat{\beta}_A$ is a scalar with $\hat{\beta}_A(x) \neq \perp\!\!\!\perp_{AA}$ by definition. Now, suppose $\gamma(x)(y) \neq \perp\!\!\!\perp_{AA}$. Then we have $\hat{\beta}_A(y) \neq \perp\!\!\!\perp_{AA}$, and, hence, $y \leq x$.

(2) First, the computation

$$\beta_A(\delta(\alpha_A)) = \beta_A\Big(\bigvee_{\alpha_A(y) \neq \perp\!\!\!\perp_{AA}} y \Big) = \bigsqcap_{\alpha_A(y) \neq \perp\!\!\!\perp_{AA}} \beta_A(y)$$

shows that $\beta_A(\delta(\alpha_A)) \neq \perp\!\!\!\perp_{AA}$ is equivalent to the property

$$\alpha_A(y) \neq \perp\!\!\!\perp_{AA} \Rightarrow \beta_A(y) \neq \perp\!\!\!\perp_{AA}$$

for all y since $\beta_A(y) \in \{\perp\!\!\!\perp_{AA}, \mathbb{I}_A, \mathbb{T}_{AA}\}$. The last property is equivalent to $\alpha_A \sqsubseteq \beta_A$ since $\alpha_A(z) = \mathbb{T}_{AA}$ iff $z = 0$ by Corollary 5.27. □

Now, we may characterize the set of scalars in $\mathcal{R}^{\mathcal{L}}[A, A]$ by the following theorem:

Theorem 5.29 *Let $\mathcal{L}$ be a complete Brouwerian lattice and $\mathcal{R}$ be a simple Dedekind category with $\mathbb{T}_{AB} \neq \mathbb{L}_{AB}$ for all objects A and B. Then $\mathcal{L}$ and* $\mathrm{Sc}_{\mathcal{R}^{\mathcal{L}}}(A)$ *are isomorphic.*

Proof. First, we show that γ and δ are inverse. Using the previous lemma this follows from

$$\begin{aligned}
\delta(\gamma(x)) &= \bigvee_{\gamma(x)(y) \neq \mathbb{L}_{AA}} y && \text{definition } \delta \\
&= \bigvee_{y \leq x} y && \text{Lemma 5.28 (1)} \\
&= x \\
\text{and } \gamma(\delta(\alpha_A)) &= \bigsqcap_{\beta_A(\delta(\alpha_A)) \neq \mathbb{L}_{AA}} \beta_A && \text{definition } \gamma \\
&= \bigsqcap_{\alpha_A \sqsubseteq \beta_A} \beta_A && \text{Lemma 5.28 (2)} \\
&= \alpha_A.
\end{aligned}$$

Since the notions of complete lattice isomorphisms and complete Brouwerian lattice isomorphisms are equivalent, it is sufficient to show that γ respects arbitrary intersections and unions. Let M be a subset of $\mathcal{L}$. Then we have

$$\begin{aligned}
\gamma\Big(\bigwedge M\Big)(y) \neq \mathbb{L}_{AA} &\Leftrightarrow y \leq \bigwedge M && \text{Lemma 5.28 (1)} \\
&\Leftrightarrow \forall x \in M : y \leq x \\
&\Leftrightarrow \forall x \in M : \gamma(x)(y) \neq \mathbb{L}_{AA} && \text{Lemma 5.28 (1)} \\
&\Leftrightarrow \bigsqcap_{x \in M} \gamma(x)(y) \neq \mathbb{L}_{AA} && \gamma(x)(y) \in \{\mathbb{I}_A, \mathbb{T}_{AA}\} \\
&\Leftrightarrow \Big(\bigsqcap_{x \in M} \gamma(x)\Big)(y) \neq \mathbb{L}_{AA}.
\end{aligned}$$

Since $\gamma(x)(y) = \mathbb{T}_{AA}$ iff $y = 0$ we conclude $\gamma(\bigwedge M)(y) = (\bigsqcap_{x \in M} \gamma(x))(y)$, and, hence, $\gamma(\bigwedge M) = \bigsqcap_{x \in M} \gamma(x)$.

It is sufficient to show that $\gamma(\bigvee M) \sqsubseteq \bigsqcup_{x \in M} \gamma(x)$ since γ is monotone as shown above. Suppose $\gamma(\bigvee M)(y) \neq \mathbb{L}_{AA}$, which is equivalent to $y \leq \bigvee M$ by Lemma 5.28 (1). Define $M_y := \{y \wedge x \mid x \in M\}$. Then we have $\bigvee M_y = y \wedge \bigvee M = y$ since $\mathcal{L}$ is a complete Brouwerian lattice. Furthermore, for all $z \in M_y$ there is an $x \in M$ such that $z \leq x$, which is equivalent to $\gamma(x)(z) \neq \perp\!\!\!\perp_{AA}$. This implies

$$\bigsqcap_{z \in M_y} \bigsqcup_{x \in M} \gamma(x)(z) \neq \perp\!\!\!\perp_{AA},$$

$$\text{and, hence,} \quad \varphi\Big(\bigsqcup_{x \in M} \gamma(x)\Big)(y) = \bigsqcup_{\bigvee N = y} \bigsqcap_{z \in N} \bigsqcup_{x \in M} \gamma(x)(z) \neq \perp\!\!\!\perp_{AA}.$$

Furthermore, $\varphi(\bigsqcup_{x \in M} \gamma(x))(0) = \bigsqcup \emptyset \sqcup \bigsqcup_{x \in M} \gamma(x)(0) = \top\!\!\!\top_{AA}$. Together we get $\gamma(\bigvee M) \sqsubseteq \varphi(\bigsqcup_{x \in M} \gamma(x))$, and, hence, $\gamma(\bigsqcup M) \sqsubseteq \varphi(\bigsqcup_{x \in M} \gamma(x)) \sqsubseteq \tau(\bigsqcup_{x \in M} \gamma(x)) = \dot{\bigsqcup}_{x \in M} \gamma(x)$. □

Now, we define an up- and down-operation in $\mathcal{R}^{\mathcal{L}}$ by

$$f^{\uparrow} := \dot{R} \text{ with } R = \bigsqcup_{y \neq 0} f(y) \qquad \text{and} \qquad f^{\downarrow} := \dot{f(1)}$$

or componentwise by

$$f^{\uparrow}(x) := \begin{cases} \top\!\!\!\top_{AB} & \text{iff } x = 0 \\ \bigsqcup_{y \neq 0} f(y) & \text{else,} \end{cases} \qquad\qquad f^{\downarrow}(x) := \begin{cases} \top\!\!\!\top_{AB} & \text{iff } x = 0 \\ f(1) & \text{else.} \end{cases}$$

Lemma 5.30 *Let $\mathcal{L}$ be a complete Brouwerian lattice, and $\mathcal{R}$ be a simple Dedekind category with $\top\!\!\!\top_{AB} \neq \perp\!\!\!\perp_{AB}$ for all objects A and B. Then for all $f, g_i : \mathcal{L} \to \mathcal{R}[A,B]$ with $i \in I$, $g : \mathcal{L} \overset{\text{anti}}{\to} \mathcal{R}[A,B]$ and $h : \mathcal{L} \overset{\text{anti}}{\to} \mathcal{R}[B,C]$ we have*

(1) $f^{\uparrow}$ and $f^{\downarrow}$ are antimorphisms,

(2) $\bigsqcup_{i \in I} g_i^{\uparrow} = (\bigsqcup_{i \in I} g_i)^{\uparrow}$,

(3) $(g; h^{\downarrow})^{\uparrow} = g^{\uparrow}; h^{\downarrow}$,

(4) $\varphi(f)^{\uparrow} = f^{\uparrow}$.

Proof.

(1) Let be $M \subseteq \mathcal{L}$. If $\bigsqcup M = 0$, the assertion is trivial. Now, suppose $\bigsqcup M \neq 0$. Then we immediately conclude that

$$f^{\uparrow}\Big(\bigsqcup M\Big) = \bigsqcup_{y \neq 0} f(y) = \bigsqcap_{x \in M} f^{\uparrow}(x)$$

$$\text{and } f^{\downarrow}\Big(\bigsqcup M\Big) = f(1) = \bigsqcap_{x \in M} f^{\downarrow}(x).$$

(2) If $x = 0$, we obtain

$$\Big(\bigsqcup_{i \in I} g_i^{\uparrow}\Big)(0) = \bigsqcup_{i \in I} g_i^{\uparrow}(0) = \top\!\!\!\top_{AB} = \Big(\bigsqcup_{i \in I} g_i\Big)^{\uparrow}(0).$$

Now, let $x \neq 0$. Then we have

$$\begin{aligned}
\left(\bigsqcup_{i\in I} g_i^{\uparrow}\right)(x) &= \bigsqcup_{i\in I} g_i^{\uparrow}(x) && \text{definition } \sqcup \\
&= \bigsqcup_{i\in I}\bigsqcup_{y\neq 0} g_i(y) && \text{definition } {}^{\uparrow} \\
&= \bigsqcup_{y\neq 0}\bigsqcup_{i\in I} g_i(y) \\
&= \left(\bigsqcup_{i\in I} g_i\right)^{\uparrow}(x). && \text{definition } {}^{\uparrow}
\end{aligned}$$

(3) First of all, $\mathbb{I}_B \neq \perp\!\!\!\perp_{BB}$ since $\top\!\!\!\top_{BB} \neq \perp\!\!\!\perp_{BB}$. For $x = 0$ we have

$$\begin{aligned}
(g;h^{\downarrow})^{\uparrow}(0) &= \top\!\!\!\top_{AC} && \text{definition } {}^{\uparrow} \\
&= \top\!\!\!\top_{AB};\top\!\!\!\top_{BC} && \mathcal{R} \text{ simple and } \mathbb{I}_B \neq \perp\!\!\!\perp_{BB} \\
&= g^{\uparrow}(0);h^{\downarrow}(0) = (g^{\uparrow};h^{\downarrow})(0).
\end{aligned}$$

If $x \neq 0$, we conclude that

$$\begin{aligned}
(g;h^{\downarrow})^{\uparrow}(x) &= \bigsqcup_{y\neq 0}(g;h^{\downarrow})(y) && \text{definition } {}^{\uparrow} \\
&= \bigsqcup_{y\neq 0} g(y);h^{\downarrow}(y) && \text{definition } ; \\
&= \bigsqcup_{y\neq 0} g(y);h(1) && \text{definition } {}^{\downarrow} \\
&= \left(\bigsqcup_{y\neq 0} g(y)\right);h(1) \\
&= g^{\uparrow}(x);h^{\downarrow}(x) && \text{definition } {}^{\uparrow} \\
&= (g^{\uparrow};h^{\downarrow})(x). && \text{definition } ;
\end{aligned}$$

(4) If $x = 0$, we get

$$\varphi(f)^{\uparrow}(0) = \top\!\!\!\top_{AB} = f^{\uparrow}(0).$$

Now, let $x \neq 0$. Then we conclude that $\varphi(f)^{\uparrow}(x) \sqsupseteq f^{\uparrow}(x)$ since φ is expanding and $^{\uparrow}$ monotone. For the other inclusion we have $\bigsqcap_{z\in M} f(z) \sqsubseteq \bigsqcup_{y\neq 0} f(y) = f^{\uparrow}(x)$ for all M such that $\bigsqcup M \neq 0$. This implies $\bigsqcup_{\substack{M\subseteq\mathcal{L}\\ \sqcup M = y}} \bigsqcap_{z\in M} f(z) \sqsubseteq f^{\uparrow}(x)$, and, hence, $\varphi(f)(y) \sqsubseteq f^{\uparrow}(x)$ for all $y \neq 0$. We conclude that $\bigsqcup_{y\neq 0} \varphi(f)(y) \sqsubseteq f^{\uparrow}(x)$, which is equivalent to $\varphi(f)^{\uparrow}(x) \sqsubseteq f^{\uparrow}(x)$. □

We are now ready to prove our main theorem in this section.

Theorem 5.31 *Let $\mathcal{L}$ be a complete Brouwerian lattice with $0 \neq 1$ and $\mathcal{R}$ be a simple Dedekind category with $\mathbb{T}_{AB} \neq \perp\!\!\!\perp_{AB}$ for all objects A and B. Then $\mathcal{R}^{\mathcal{L}}$ is an arrow category.*

Proof. We have already shown in Theorem 4.33 that $\mathcal{R}^{\mathcal{L}}$ is a Dedekind category. Since $0 \neq 1$ and $\mathbb{T}_{AB} \neq \perp\!\!\!\perp_{AB}$ the relations $\dot{\perp\!\!\!\perp}_{AB}$ and $\dot{\mathbb{T}}_{AB}$ are not equal. Axiom (1) is trivial and (2) follows from

$$\begin{aligned}
f^{\uparrow} \sqsubseteq g &\Leftrightarrow \forall x \neq 0 : f^{\uparrow}(x) \sqsubseteq g(x) && \text{since } f^{\uparrow}(0) = \mathbb{T}_{AB} = g(0)\\
&\Leftrightarrow \forall x \neq 0 : \bigsqcup_{y \neq 0} f(y) \sqsubseteq g(x) && \text{definition } {}^{\uparrow}\\
&\Leftrightarrow \bigsqcup_{y \neq 0} f(y) \sqsubseteq \bigsqcap_{z \in \mathcal{L}} g(z) && \text{since } g(0) = \mathbb{T}_{AB}\\
&\Leftrightarrow \forall x \neq 0 : f(x) \sqsubseteq \bigsqcap_{z \in \mathcal{L}} g(z) &&\\
&\Leftrightarrow \forall x \neq 0 : f(x) \sqsubseteq g\Big(\bigvee \mathcal{L}\Big) && g \text{ antimorphism}\\
&\Leftrightarrow \forall x \neq 0 : f(x) \sqsubseteq g(1) &&\\
&\Leftrightarrow \forall x \neq 0 : f(x) \sqsubseteq g^{\downarrow}(x) && \text{definition } {}^{\downarrow}\\
&\Leftrightarrow f \sqsubseteq g^{\downarrow}. && \text{since } f(0) = \mathbb{T}_{AB} = g^{\downarrow}(0)
\end{aligned}$$

Consider the following computation for $x \neq 0$:

$$\begin{aligned}
(f^{\uparrow\smile})(x) &= (f^{\uparrow}(x))^{\smile} && \text{definition } {}^{\smile}\\
&= \Big(\bigsqcup_{y \neq 0} f(y)\Big)^{\smile} && \text{definition } {}^{\uparrow}\\
&= \bigsqcup_{y \neq 0} f(y)^{\smile} &&\\
&= \bigsqcup_{y \neq 0} f^{\smile}(y) && \text{definition } {}^{\smile}\\
&= (f^{\smile\uparrow})(x). && \text{definition } {}^{\uparrow}
\end{aligned}$$

Since $f^{\uparrow\smile}$ and $f^{\smile\uparrow}$ are antimorphisms $f^{\uparrow\smile} = f^{\smile\uparrow}$ follows. In order to prove Axiom (3), we define the following predicate: $\mathfrak{P}(h, k) :\Leftrightarrow h^{\uparrow} = k$. This predicate is admissible since $\mathfrak{P}(h_i, k_i)$ for all $i \in I$ implies $\bigsqcup_{i \in I} h_i^{\uparrow} = \bigsqcup_{i \in I} k_i$, and, hence, $(\bigsqcup_{i \in I} h_i)^{\uparrow} = \bigsqcup_{i \in I} k_i$ by Lemma 5.30 (2), which is equivalent to $\mathfrak{P}(\bigsqcup_{i \in I} h_i, \bigsqcup_{i \in I} k_i)$. The base case $\mathfrak{P}(f;g^{\downarrow}, f^{\uparrow};g^{\downarrow})$ follows from Lemma 5.30 (3). Now, suppose $\mathfrak{P}(h, k)$. Then we conclude

$$\begin{aligned}
\varphi(h)^{\uparrow} &= h^{\uparrow} && \text{Lemma 5.30 (4)}\\
&= \varphi(h^{\uparrow}) && \text{Lemma 5.30 (1)}\\
&= \varphi(k) && \text{induction hypothesis}
\end{aligned}$$

The principle of fixed point induction gives us $\mathfrak{P}(\mu_\varphi(f;g^\downarrow),\mu_\varphi(f^\uparrow;g^\downarrow))$ and $\mathfrak{P}(\mu_\varphi(f\sqcap h^\downarrow),\mu_\varphi(f^\uparrow\sqcap h^\downarrow))$. Together we conclude

$$\begin{aligned}(f^\smile \mathbin{;\!\!\cdot} g^\downarrow)^\uparrow &= \tau(f^\smile;g^\downarrow)^\uparrow\\ &= \tau(f^{\smile\uparrow};g^\downarrow)\\ &= \tau(f^{\uparrow\smile};g^\downarrow) && \text{see above}\\ &= f^{\uparrow\smile} \mathbin{;\!\!\cdot} g^\downarrow,\end{aligned}$$

i.e, Axiom (3).

Consider the following computation for $x\neq 0$:

$$\begin{aligned}(f\sqcap h^\downarrow)^\uparrow(x) &= \bigsqcup_{y\neq 0}(f\sqcap h^\downarrow)(y)\\ &= \bigsqcup_{y\neq 0} f(y)\sqcap h(1)\\ &= \left(\bigsqcup_{y\neq 0} f(y)\right)\sqcap h(1) && \text{completely upward-distributive}\\ &= f^\uparrow(x)\sqcap h(1)\\ &= f^\uparrow(x)\sqcap h^\downarrow(x)\\ &= (f^\uparrow\sqcap h^\downarrow)(x).\end{aligned}$$

Again, $(f\sqcap h^\downarrow)^\uparrow$ and $f^\uparrow\sqcap h^\downarrow$ are antimorphisms so that Axiom (4) follows.

Let $\alpha_A\neq \dot{\perp\!\!\perp}_{AA}$ be a scalar. From Corollary 5.27 we conclude that $\alpha_A(x)\in\{\perp\!\!\perp_{AA},\mathbb{I}_A\}$ for all $x\neq 0$ and that there is at least one $y\neq 0$ such that $\alpha_A(y)=\mathbb{I}_A$. This implies $\alpha_A^\uparrow(x)=\bigsqcup_{y\neq 0}\alpha_A(y)=\mathbb{I}_A$ for $x\neq 0$, and, hence, $\alpha_A^\uparrow=\dot{\mathbb{I}}_A$, i.e., Axiom (5). □

Let $F:\mathcal{R}_1\to\mathcal{R}_2$ be a homomorphism between the Dedekind categories $\mathcal{R}_1$ and $\mathcal{R}_2$. Then we may define an extension $\hat{F}$ of F on the antitone functions from $\mathcal{L}$ to $\mathcal{R}_1[A,B]$ by

(1) $\hat{F}(A):=F(A)$ for all objects A,

(2) $\hat{F}(f)(x):=F(f(x))$ for all antitone functions $f:\mathcal{L}\overset{\sqsupseteq}{\to}\mathcal{R}_1[A,B]$ and $x\in\mathcal{L}$.

$\hat{F}(f)$ is antitone since $x\leq y$ implies $f(y)\leq f(x)$, and, hence, $F(f(y))\sqsubseteq F(f(x))$ by the monotonicity of F. Furthermore, we have the following lemma:

Lemma 5.32 *Let $F:\mathcal{R}_1\to\mathcal{R}_2$ be a homomorphism between the Dedekind categories $\mathcal{R}_1$ and $\mathcal{R}_2$, $\mathcal{L}$ be a complete Brouwerian lattice, $f:\mathcal{L}\overset{\geq}{\to}\mathcal{R}_1[A,B]$, $g:\mathcal{L}\overset{\geq}{\to}\mathcal{R}_1[B,C]$ and $f_i:\mathcal{L}\overset{\geq}{\to}\mathcal{R}_1[A,B]$ for all $i\in I$. Then we have*

(1) $\hat{F}(f;g) = \hat{F}(f);\hat{F}(g)$,

(2) $\hat{F}(\dot{\mathbb{I}}_A) = \dot{\mathbb{I}}_{\hat{F}(A)}$,

(3) $\hat{F}(\bigsqcup_{i\in I} f_i) = \bigsqcup_{i\in I} \hat{F}(f_i)$,

(4) $\hat{F}(\bigsqcap_{i\in I} f_i) = \bigsqcap_{i\in I} \hat{F}(f_i)$,

(5) $\hat{F}(f^{\smile}) = \hat{F}(f)^{\smile}$,

(6) $\hat{F}(f^{\downarrow}) = \hat{F}(f)^{\downarrow}$,

(7) $\hat{F}(f^{\uparrow}) = \hat{F}(f)^{\uparrow}$,

(8) $\tau(\hat{F}(f)) = \hat{F}(\tau(f))$.

Proof.

(1) The assertion follows immediately from

$$
\begin{aligned}
\hat{F}(f;g)(x) &= F((f;g)(x)) && \text{definition } \hat{F}\\
&= F(f(x);g(x)) && \text{definition };\\
&= F(f(x));F(g(x)) && F \text{ functor}\\
&= \hat{F}(f)(x);\hat{F}(g)(x) && \text{definition } \hat{F}\\
&= (\hat{F}(f);\hat{F}(g))(x). && \text{definition };
\end{aligned}
$$

(2)–(5) similar to (1).

(6) First, we have

$$
\begin{aligned}
\hat{F}(f^{\downarrow})(0) &= F(f^{\downarrow}(0)) && \text{definition } \hat{F}\\
&= F(\mathbb{T}_{AB}) && f^{\downarrow} \text{ antimorphism by Lemma 5.30 (1)}\\
&= \mathbb{T}_{F(A)F(B)} && F \text{ homomorphism}\\
&= \hat{F}(f)^{\downarrow}(0). && \hat{F}(f)^{\downarrow} \text{ antimorphism by Lemma 5.30 (1)}
\end{aligned}
$$

Now, suppose $x \neq 0$ and compute

$$
\begin{aligned}
\hat{F}(f^{\downarrow})(x) &= F(f^{\downarrow}(x)) && \text{definition } \hat{F}\\
&= F(f(1)) && \text{definition } {}^{\downarrow}\\
&= \hat{F}(f)(1) && \text{definition } \hat{F}\\
&= \hat{F}(f)^{\downarrow}(x). && \text{definition } {}^{\downarrow}
\end{aligned}
$$

(7) The case $x = 0$ follows similar to the corresponding case in (6). Now, suppose $x \neq 0$ and compute

$$
\begin{aligned}
\hat{F}(f^{\uparrow})(x) &= F(f^{\uparrow}(x)) && \text{definition } \hat{F}\\
&= F\Big(\bigsqcup_{y\neq 0} f(y)\Big) && \text{definition } {}^{\uparrow}
\end{aligned}
$$

$$= \bigsqcup_{y \neq 0} F(f(y)) \qquad F \text{ homomorphism}$$

$$= \bigsqcup_{y \neq 0} \hat{F}(f)(y) \qquad \text{definition } \mathcal{F}$$

$$= \hat{F}(f)^{\uparrow}(x). \qquad \text{definition } {}^{\uparrow}$$

(8) We prove the assertion by fixed point induction. Therefore, we define a predicate

$$\mathfrak{P}(g, h) \;:\Leftrightarrow\; g = \hat{F}(h).$$

This predicate is admissible since $\mathfrak{P}(g_i, h_i)$ for all $i \in I$ implies

$$\bigsqcup_{i \in I} g_i = \bigsqcup_{i \in I} \hat{F}(h_i) = \hat{F}\Big(\bigsqcup_{i \in I} h_i\Big)$$

by (3), and, hence, $\mathfrak{P}(\bigsqcup_{i \in I} g_i, \bigsqcup_{i \in I} h_i)$. The base case is trivial since we obviously have $\mathfrak{P}(\hat{F}(f), f)$. Now, suppose $\mathfrak{P}(g, h)$. Then we conclude

$$\varphi(g)(x) = \bigsqcup_{\bigvee M = x} \bigsqcap_{y \in M} g(y) \qquad \text{definition } \varphi$$

$$= \bigsqcup_{\bigvee M = x} \bigsqcap_{y \in M} \hat{F}(h)(y) \qquad \text{induction hypothesis}$$

$$= \bigsqcup_{\bigvee M = x} \bigsqcap_{y \in M} (F(h(y)) \qquad \text{definition } \hat{F}$$

$$= \bigsqcup_{\bigvee M = x} F\Big(\bigsqcap_{y \in M} h(y)\Big) \qquad F \text{ homomorphism}$$

$$= F\Big(\bigsqcup_{\bigvee M = x} \bigsqcap_{y \in M} h(y)\Big) \qquad F \text{ homomorphism}$$

$$= F(\varphi(h)(x)) \qquad \text{definition } \varphi$$

$$= \hat{F}(\varphi(h))(x), \qquad \text{definition } \hat{F}$$

and, hence, $\mathfrak{P}(\varphi(g), \varphi(h))$. From the principle of fixed point induction we get $\tau(\hat{F}(f)) = \hat{F}(\tau(f))$ for all antitone functions f. □

The previous lemma gives us the following theorem:

Theorem 5.33 *Let $\mathcal{R}_1$ and $\mathcal{R}_2$ be Dedekind categories with $\mathbb{T}_{AB} \neq \perp\!\!\!\perp_{AB}$ for all objects A and B, $\mathcal{L}$ a complete Brouwerian lattice with $0 \neq 1$ and $F : \mathcal{R}_1 \to \mathcal{R}_2$ a homomorphism. Then the restriction of $\hat{F}$ to antimorphisms is a homomorphism between the arrow categories $\mathcal{R}_1^{\mathcal{L}}$ and $\mathcal{R}_2^{\mathcal{L}}$. Furthermore, if F is faithful, then so is $\hat{F}$.*

Proof. First of all, $\hat{F}(f) = \hat{F}(\tau(f)) = \tau(\hat{F}(f))$ implies that $\hat{F}(f)$ is an antimorphism if f is. To show the first assertion we just prove that $\hat{F}$ preserves composition. All other properties are shown analogously using Lemma 5.32 (1)–(8)

$$\begin{aligned}
\hat{F}(f \mathbin{\dot{;}} g) &= \hat{F}(\tau(f;g)) && \text{definition } \dot{;} \\
&= \tau(\hat{F}(f;g)) && \text{Lemma 5.32(8)} \\
&= \tau(\hat{F}(f);\hat{F}(g)) && \text{Lemma 5.32(1)} \\
&= \hat{F}(f) \mathbin{\dot{;}} \hat{F}(g). && \text{definition } \dot{;}
\end{aligned}$$

Now, suppose F is faithful and $\hat{F}(f) = \hat{F}(g)$. Then we conclude $F(f(x)) = \hat{F}(f)(x) = \hat{F}(g)(x) = F(g(x))$, and, hence, $f(x) = g(x)$ for all $x \in \mathcal{L}$, which shows that $\hat{F}$ is faithful. □

5.3 ARROW CATEGORIES WITH CUTS

We have already seen that the α-cut theorem might not be valid in an arbitrary arrow category. In such a case, a relation, which is not sliceable cannot be represented by its cuts. The reason simply is, as shown in the examples of Section 5.1, that certain scalars or cuts are missing. But later on, we want to define new operations on relations based on their representation by cuts. Therefore, we consider the following structure:

Definition 5.34 *An arrow category with cuts $\mathcal{A}$ is an arrow category so that*

$$R \sqsubseteq \bigsqcup_{\alpha \in \mathrm{Sc}[\mathcal{A}]} \alpha_A;(\alpha_A \backslash R)^{\downarrow}$$

for all relations $R : A \to B$ holds.

In other words, an arrow category with cuts is an arrow category so that all relations are sliceable.

First of all, in an arrow category with cuts a stronger version of Lemma 5.9 is valid.

Theorem 5.35 (α-cut Theorem) *Let $\mathcal{A}$ be an arrow category with cuts and $R : A \to B$. Then we have*

(1) $R = \bigsqcup_{\alpha \in \mathrm{Sc}[\mathcal{A}]} (\alpha_A;(\alpha_A \backslash R)^{\downarrow}),$

(2) $R^{\uparrow} = \bigsqcup_{\substack{\alpha \in \mathrm{Sc}[\mathcal{A}] \\ \alpha_A \neq \perp\!\!\!\perp_{AA}}} (\alpha_A \backslash R)^{\downarrow}.$

Proof.

(1) follows immediately from Lemma 5.9(1).

(2) By Lemma 5.9(2) it remains to show the inclusion $\sqsubseteq$. Therefore, consider the following computation:

$$\begin{aligned}
R^{\uparrow} &= \Big(\bigsqcup_{\alpha\in \mathrm{Sc}[\mathcal{A}]} (\alpha_A; (\alpha_A \backslash R)^{\downarrow})\Big)^{\uparrow} && (1)\\
&= \bigsqcup_{\alpha\in \mathrm{Sc}[\mathcal{A}]} (\alpha_A; (\alpha_A \backslash R)^{\downarrow})^{\uparrow} && \text{Corollary 5.5 (4)}\\
&= \bigsqcup_{\alpha\in \mathrm{Sc}[\mathcal{A}]} \alpha_A^{\uparrow}; (\alpha_A \backslash R)^{\downarrow}\\
&= \bigsqcup_{\substack{\alpha\in \mathrm{Sc}[\mathcal{A}]\\ \alpha_A\neq \perp\!\!\!\perp_{AA}}} (\alpha_A \backslash R)^{\downarrow}.
\end{aligned}$$

□

Notice that the axioms of an arrow category with cuts are not independent. Axiom (4) of an arrow category can be derived as follows:

$$\begin{aligned}
Q^{\uparrow} \sqcap R^{\downarrow} &= \Big(\bigsqcup_{\alpha_A\neq \perp\!\!\!\perp_{AA}} (\alpha_A \backslash Q)^{\downarrow}\Big) \sqcap R^{\downarrow} && \text{Theorem 5.35 (2)}\\
&= \bigsqcup_{\alpha_A\neq \perp\!\!\!\perp_{AA}} (\alpha_A \backslash Q)^{\downarrow} \sqcap R^{\downarrow}\\
&= \bigsqcup_{\alpha_A\neq \perp\!\!\!\perp_{AA}} (\alpha_A \backslash Q)^{\downarrow} \sqcap R^{\downarrow\uparrow}\\
&= \bigsqcup_{\alpha_A\neq \perp\!\!\!\perp_{AA}} (\alpha_A \backslash Q)^{\downarrow} \sqcap (\alpha_A \backslash R^{\downarrow\uparrow})^{\downarrow} && \text{Lemma 5.12 (1)}\\
&= \bigsqcup_{\alpha_A\neq \perp\!\!\!\perp_{AA}} ((\alpha_A \backslash Q) \sqcap (\alpha_A \backslash R^{\downarrow}))^{\downarrow} && \text{Corollary 5.5 (4)}\\
&= \bigsqcup_{\alpha_A\neq \perp\!\!\!\perp_{AA}} (\alpha_A \backslash (Q \sqcap R^{\downarrow}))^{\downarrow} && \text{Corollary 4.15 (5)}\\
&= (Q \sqcap R^{\downarrow})^{\uparrow}. && \text{Theorem 5.35 (2)}
\end{aligned}$$

In a Boolean arrow category with cuts $Q^{\downarrow}$ can be expressed in terms of $.^{\uparrow}$ in a similar way as $Q^{\uparrow}$ can be expressed in terms of $.^{\downarrow}$ shown in Theorem 5.35 (2).

Theorem 5.36 *Let $\mathcal{A}$ be a Boolean arrow category with cuts. Then we have* $Q^{\downarrow} = \bigsqcap_{\alpha\in \mathrm{Sc}[\mathcal{A}]} (\alpha_A; Q)^{\uparrow}$.

Proof. Consider the following computation:

$$\begin{aligned}
Q^{\downarrow} &= \overline{\overline{Q}^{\uparrow}} && \text{Lemma 5.7 (1)}\\
&= \overline{\bigsqcup_{\alpha_A\neq \perp\!\!\!\perp_{AA}} (\alpha_A \backslash \overline{Q})^{\downarrow}} && \text{Theorem 5.35 (2)}
\end{aligned}$$

$$= \overline{\bigsqcup_{\alpha_A \neq \perp\!\!\!\perp_{AA}} \overline{(\alpha_A;Q)}^{\downarrow}} \qquad \text{Lemma 4.50 (1)}$$

$$= \bigsqcup_{\alpha_A \neq \perp\!\!\!\perp_{AA}} \overline{\overline{(\alpha_A;Q)}}^{\downarrow}$$

$$= \bigsqcap_{\substack{\alpha \in \mathrm{Sc}[\mathcal{A}] \\ \alpha_A \neq \perp\!\!\!\perp_{AA}}} (\alpha_A;Q)^{\uparrow} \qquad \text{Lemma 5.7 (1)}$$

$$= \bigsqcap_{\alpha \in \mathrm{Sc}[\mathcal{A}]} (\alpha_A;Q)^{\uparrow}. \qquad \Box$$

Again, the $\mathcal{L}$-fuzzy relations can be considered as the standard model of our theory.

Theorem 5.37 *Let $\mathcal{L}$ be a complete Brouwerian lattice with $0 \neq 1$. Then $\mathcal{L}$-**Rel** is an arrow category with cuts.*

Proof. By Theorem 5.3 $\mathcal{L}$-**Rel** is an arrow category. Lemma 3.3 (6) and Theorem 3.4 show the assertion. $\Box$

In the rest of this section we want to study the connection between crisp and s-crisp resp. l-crisp relations within an arbitrary arrow category with cuts. First of all, we need the following lemma:

Lemma 5.38 *Let $\mathcal{A}$ be an arrow category with cuts and $R : A \to B$. Then we have*

(1) if α_A is linear, then $R^{\uparrow} = (\alpha_A;R)^{\uparrow}$,

(2) $R^l \sqsubseteq R^{\uparrow} \sqsubseteq R^s$.

Proof.

(1) It is sufficient to show $R^{\uparrow} \sqsubseteq (\alpha_A;R)^{\uparrow}$. First, we have $(\alpha_A \sqcap \beta_A);(\beta_A\backslash R) = \alpha_A;\beta_A;(\beta_A\backslash R) \sqsubseteq \alpha_A;R$, which proves $\beta_A\backslash R \sqsubseteq (\alpha_A \sqcap \beta_A)\backslash(\alpha_A;R)$, and, hence, $(\beta_A\backslash R)^{\downarrow} \sqsubseteq ((\alpha_A \sqcap \beta_A)\backslash(\alpha_A;R))^{\downarrow}$. Since $\alpha_A \sqcap \beta_A \neq \perp\!\!\!\perp_{AA}$ iff $\beta_A \neq \perp\!\!\!\perp_{AA}$ and the set $M := \{\alpha_A \sqcap \beta_A \mid \perp\!\!\!\perp_{AA} \neq \beta_A \in \mathrm{Sc}_{\mathcal{G}}(A)\}$ is a subset of all nonzero scalars we obtain

$$R^{\uparrow} = \bigsqcup_{\beta_A \neq \perp\!\!\!\perp_{AA}} (\beta_A\backslash R)^{\downarrow} \qquad \text{Theorem 5.35 (2)}$$

$$\sqsubseteq \bigsqcup_{\beta_A \neq \perp\!\!\!\perp_{AA}} ((\alpha_A \sqcap \beta_A)\backslash(\alpha_A;R))^{\downarrow} \qquad \text{see above}$$

$$= \bigsqcup_{\gamma_A \in M} (\gamma_A\backslash(\alpha_A;R))^{\downarrow} \qquad \text{definition } M$$

$$\sqsubseteq \bigsqcup_{\gamma_A \neq \perp\!\!\!\perp_{AA}} (\gamma_A\backslash(\alpha_A;R))^{\downarrow} \qquad M \text{ subset of all nonzero scalars}$$

$$= (\alpha_A;R)^{\uparrow}. \qquad \text{Theorem 5.35 (2)}$$

(2) From the monotonicity of Φ_s we get

$$\begin{aligned} R^{\uparrow} &= \bigsqcup_{\alpha_A \neq \perp\!\!\!\perp_{AA}} (\alpha_A \backslash R)^{\downarrow} && \text{Theorem 5.35 (2)} \\ &\sqsubseteq \bigsqcup_{\alpha_A \neq \perp\!\!\!\perp_{AA}} (\alpha_A \backslash R) \\ &= \Phi_s(R) \\ &\sqsubseteq \Phi_s(\mu_{\Phi_s}(R)) && R \sqsubseteq \mu_{\Phi_s}(R) \\ &= \mu_{\Phi_s}(R) && \mu_{\Phi_s}(R) \text{ fixed point} \\ &= R^s. && \text{Theorem 4.41} \end{aligned}$$

Now, suppose α_A is linear. Then $\alpha_A;(\alpha_A\backslash R) \sqsubseteq R$ implies $(\alpha_A;(\alpha_A\backslash R))^{\uparrow} \sqsubseteq R^{\uparrow}$. By (1) we conclude that $(\alpha_A\backslash R)^{\uparrow} \sqsubseteq R^{\uparrow}$. Using the Galois correspondence we obtain $\alpha_A\backslash R \sqsubseteq R^{\uparrow\downarrow} = R^{\uparrow}$, and, hence, $\Phi_l(R) = \bigsqcup_{\alpha_A \text{ linear}} (\alpha_A\backslash R) \sqsubseteq R^{\uparrow}$. An easy fixed point induction shows $\mu_{\Phi_l}(R) \sqsubseteq R^{\uparrow}$, which is by Theorem 4.41 equivalent to the assertion. □

The previous lemma leads to the following connection between the three notions of crispness:

Theorem 5.39 *Let $\mathcal{A}$ be an arrow category with cuts. Then we have the following:*

(1) All s-crisp relations are crisp.

(2) All crisp relations are l-crisp.

Proof.

(1) Suppose R is s-crisp. Using Lemma 5.38 (2) we conclude $R^{\uparrow} \sqsubseteq R^s = R \sqsubseteq R^{\uparrow}$.

(2) Suppose R is crisp. Again, using Lemma 5.38 (2) we conclude $R^l \sqsubseteq R^{\uparrow} = R \sqsubseteq R^l$. □

The previous theorem is an abstract version of Lemma 4.44 and Lemma 4.46. Furthermore, we have a result similar to Lemma 4.45 and Lemma 4.47 concerning the characterization of those arrow categories with cuts where s-crispness resp. l-crispness and crispness coincide.

Theorem 5.40 *Let $\mathcal{A}$ be an arrow category with cuts. Then the following statements are equivalent:*

(1) $\mathcal{A}$ is linear.

(2) All crisp relations are s-crisp, i.e., $R^{\uparrow} = R^s$.

(3) All l-crisp are crisp, i.e., $R^{\uparrow} = R^l$.

Proof. (1) $\Rightarrow$ (2): Suppose R is crisp. Then by Theorem 5.39 (2) R is l-crisp, and, hence, s-crisp since all nonzero scalars are linear.
(2) $\Rightarrow$ (1): Let α_A be a nonzero scalar and β_A a scalar such that $\alpha_A \sqcap \beta_A = \perp\!\!\!\perp_{AA}$ holds. Then we have $\alpha_A;\beta_A = \alpha_A \sqcap \beta_A = \perp\!\!\!\perp_{AA}$ and conclude that $\beta_A = \perp\!\!\!\perp_{AA}$ since $\perp\!\!\!\perp_{AA}$ is crisp, and, hence, s-crisp.
(1) $\Rightarrow$ (3): Suppose R is l-crisp. Then R is s-crisp since all nonzero scalars are linear. Theorem 5.39 (1) shows that R is crisp.
(3) $\Rightarrow$ (1): Suppose there is a nonlinear scalar α_A, i.e., $\neg{:}\alpha_A \neq \perp\!\!\!\perp_{AA}$. Suppose $\beta_A;Q \sqsubseteq \neg{:}\alpha_A$ for a linear scalar β_A and a partial identity $Q : A \to A$. Then we conclude $\beta_A \sqcap Q = \beta_A;Q \sqsubseteq \neg{:}\alpha_A$, and, hence, $\alpha_A \sqcap \beta_A \sqcap Q \sqsubseteq \perp\!\!\!\perp_{AB}$. Since β_A is linear we get $\alpha_A \sqcap Q \sqsubseteq \perp\!\!\!\perp_{AB}$, and, hence, $Q \sqsubseteq \neg{:}\alpha_A$, which shows that $\neg{:}\alpha_A$ is l-crisp. On the other hand $\neg{:}\alpha_A$ is not crisp. We have $\neg{:}\alpha_A \neq \perp\!\!\!\perp_{AA}$ by the assumption and $\neg{:}\alpha_A \neq \mathbb{I}_A$ since otherwise we have $\perp\!\!\!\perp_{AA} = \alpha_A \sqcap \neg{:}\alpha_A = \alpha_A$, a contradiction to $\alpha_A \neq \perp\!\!\!\perp_{AA}$. □

5.4 THE ARROW CATEGORY WITH CUTS OF ANTIMORPHISMS

In this section we want to establish that the arrow category of antimorphisms is indeed an arrow category with cuts.

Theorem 5.41 *Let $\mathcal{L}$ be a complete Brouwerian lattice with $0 \neq 1$ and $\mathcal{R}$ be a simple Dedekind category with $\top\!\!\!\top_{AB} \neq \perp\!\!\!\perp_{AB}$ for all objects A and B. Then $\mathcal{R}^{\mathcal{L}}$ is an arrow category with cuts.*

Proof. By Lemma 5.31 $\mathcal{R}^{\mathcal{L}}$ is an arrow category. In order to prove the additional cut property, we define a function $h : \mathrm{Sc}[\mathcal{R}^{\mathcal{L}}] \to \mathcal{R}^{\mathcal{L}}[A,B]$ for a given $f \in \mathcal{R}^{\mathcal{L}}[A,B]$ by

$$h(\alpha)(x) := f(\delta(\alpha) \wedge x).$$

If $x = 0$, we conclude that $(\alpha_A;h(\alpha))(x) \sqsubseteq \top\!\!\!\top_{AB} = f(x)$. Suppose $\alpha_A(x) = \perp\!\!\!\perp_{AA}$. Then we get $(\alpha_A;h(\alpha))(x) = \alpha_A(x);h(\alpha)(x) = \perp\!\!\!\perp_{AA};h(\alpha)(x) = \perp\!\!\!\perp_{AB} \sqsubseteq f(x)$. Now, suppose $\alpha_A(x) \neq \perp\!\!\!\perp_{AA}$ and $x \neq 0$. Then we have $\gamma(\delta(\alpha))(x) \neq \perp\!\!\!\perp_{AA}$ by Theorem 5.29, and, hence, $x \leq \delta(\alpha)$ by Lemma 5.28 (1). This implies $h(\alpha)(x) = f(\delta(\alpha) \wedge x) = f(x)$, and, hence,

$$\begin{aligned}
(\alpha_A;h(\alpha))(x) &= \alpha_A(x);h(\alpha)(x) && \text{definition } ; \\
&= \mathbb{I}_A;h(\alpha)(x) && \text{Corollary 5.27} \\
&= f(x). && \text{see above}
\end{aligned}$$

Together we conclude that $\alpha_A;h(\alpha) \sqsubseteq f$, and, hence,

$$\begin{aligned}
\alpha_A \mathbin{\dot{;}} \tau(h(\alpha)) &= \tau(\alpha_A;\tau(h(\alpha))) && \text{definition } \dot{;} \\
&= \tau(\alpha_A;h(\alpha)) && \text{Lemma 4.31 (2)} \\
&\sqsubseteq \tau(f) && \text{see above} \\
&= f, && f \text{ antimorphism}
\end{aligned}$$

which shows $h(\alpha) \sqsubseteq \tau(h(\alpha)) \sqsubseteq \alpha_A \backslash f$ and $h(\alpha_A)^{\downarrow} \sqsubseteq (\alpha_A \backslash f)^{\downarrow}$. Furthermore, for $x = 0$ we have

$$\begin{aligned}
(\gamma(x); h(\gamma(x))^{\downarrow})(x) &= \gamma(x)(x); h(\gamma(x))^{\downarrow}(x) && \text{definition ;} \\
&= \dot{\perp\!\!\!\perp}_{AA}(x); h(\perp\!\!\!\perp_{AA})^{\downarrow}(x) && \gamma \text{ isomorphism} \\
&= \top\!\!\!\top_{AA}; \top\!\!\!\top_{AB} && \dot{\perp\!\!\!\perp}_{AA}(0) = \top\!\!\!\top_{AA} \\
& && \text{and } h(\perp\!\!\!\perp_{AA})^{\downarrow} \text{ antimorphism} \\
&= \top\!\!\!\top_{AB} \\
&= f(x) && f \text{ antimorphism}
\end{aligned}$$

and for $x \neq 0$

$$\begin{aligned}
(\gamma(x); h(\gamma(x))^{\downarrow})(x) &= \gamma(x)(x); h(\gamma(x))^{\downarrow}(x) && \text{definition ;} \\
&= \mathbb{I}_A; h(\gamma(x))^{\downarrow}(x) && \text{Lemma 5.28 (1)} \\
& && \text{and Corollary 5.27} \\
&= h(\gamma(x))^{\downarrow}(x) \\
&= h(\gamma(x))(1) && \text{definition } {}^{\downarrow} \\
&= f(\delta(\gamma(x)) \sqcap 1) && \text{definition } h \\
&= f(x). && \text{Theorem 5.29}
\end{aligned}$$

Together, this implies

$$\begin{aligned}
f(x) &= (\gamma(x); h(\gamma(x))^{\downarrow})(x) && \text{see above} \\
&\sqsubseteq \tau(\gamma(x); h(\gamma(x))^{\downarrow})(x) \\
&= (\gamma(x) \mathbin{\dot{;}} h(\gamma(x))^{\downarrow})(x) && \text{definition } \dot{;} \\
&\sqsubseteq (\gamma(x) \mathbin{\dot{;}} (\gamma(x)\backslash f)^{\downarrow})(x). && \text{see above}
\end{aligned}$$

Finally we conclude

$$\begin{aligned}
f &\sqsubseteq \bigsqcup_{\alpha_A \in \mathrm{Sc}[\mathcal{R}^{\mathcal{L}}]} (\alpha_A \mathbin{\dot{;}} (\alpha_A \backslash f)^{\downarrow}) \\
&\sqsubseteq \tau\Big(\bigsqcup_{\alpha_A \in \mathrm{Sc}[\mathcal{R}^{\mathcal{L}}]} (\alpha_A \mathbin{\dot{;}} (\alpha_A \backslash f)^{\downarrow}) \Big) \\
&= \dot{\bigsqcup_{\alpha_A \in \mathrm{Sc}[\mathcal{R}^{\mathcal{L}}]}} (\alpha_A \mathbin{\dot{;}} (\alpha_A \backslash f)^{\downarrow}).
\end{aligned}$$

□

5.5 GOGUEN CATEGORIES

In an arrow category with cuts all relations can be represented by their cuts. One might ask the question whether the converse is also valid. Does every antimorphism from the scalars to the crisp relations naturally give rise to a

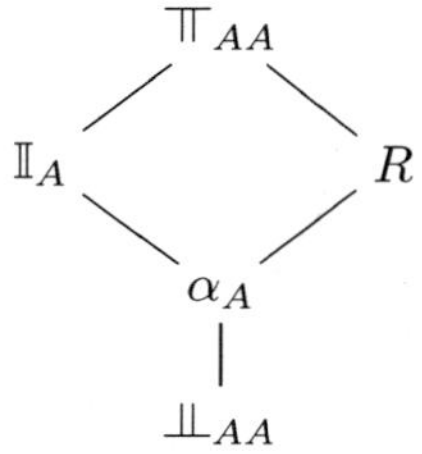

	$\cdot^{\smile}$	$\cdot^{\uparrow}$	$\cdot^{\downarrow}$
$\perp\!\!\!\perp_{AA}$	$\perp\!\!\!\perp_{AA}$	$\perp\!\!\!\perp_{AA}$	$\perp\!\!\!\perp_{AA}$
α_A	α_A	$\mathbb{I}_A$	$\perp\!\!\!\perp_{AA}$
$\mathbb{I}_A$	$\mathbb{I}_A$	$\mathbb{I}_A$	$\mathbb{I}_A$
R	R	$\top\!\!\!\top_{AA}$	$\perp\!\!\!\perp_{AA}$
$\top\!\!\!\top_{AA}$	$\top\!\!\!\top_{AA}$	$\top\!\!\!\top_{AA}$	$\top\!\!\!\top_{AA}$

;	$\perp\!\!\!\perp_{AA}$	α_A	$\mathbb{I}_A$	R	$\top\!\!\!\top_{AA}$
$\perp\!\!\!\perp_{AA}$	$\perp\!\!\!\perp_{AA}$	$\perp\!\!\!\perp_{AA}$	$\perp\!\!\!\perp_{AA}$	$\perp\!\!\!\perp_{AA}$	$\perp\!\!\!\perp_{AA}$
α_A	$\perp\!\!\!\perp_{AA}$	α_A	α_A	R	R
$\mathbb{I}_A$	$\perp\!\!\!\perp_{AA}$	α_A	$\mathbb{I}_A$	R	$\top\!\!\!\top_{AA}$
R	$\perp\!\!\!\perp_{AA}$	R	R	R	R
$\top\!\!\!\top_{AA}$	$\perp\!\!\!\perp_{AA}$	R	$\top\!\!\!\top_{AA}$	R	$\top\!\!\!\top_{AA}$

Figure 5.4. The arrow category $\mathcal{A}$.

relation in the category? Of course, such an antimorphism f can be map to the relation $\bigsqcup_{\alpha \in \mathrm{Sc}[\mathcal{G}]} \alpha_A; f(\alpha)$ but the question remains whether the set of cuts of this relation correspond to the image of the antimorphism f. Unfortunately, this is not the case as our example will show.

Example 5.42 Consider the one-object arrow category $\mathcal{A}$ induced by the definitions in Figure 5.4.

It is easy to verify that this structure is indeed an arrow category with cuts. Obviously, $\{\perp\!\!\!\perp_{AA}, \alpha_A, \mathbb{I}_A\}$ is the set of scalars, and $\{\perp\!\!\!\perp_{AA}, \mathbb{I}_A, \top\!\!\!\top_{AA}\}$ is the set of crisp relations. The function f defined by

$$f(\perp\!\!\!\perp_{AA}) := \top\!\!\!\top_{AA}, \qquad f(\alpha_A) := \top\!\!\!\top_{AA}, \qquad f(\mathbb{I}_A) := \mathbb{I}_A$$

is an antimorphism and we have

$$\bigsqcup_{\beta \in \mathrm{Sc}[\mathcal{A}]} \beta_A; f(\beta) = \perp\!\!\!\perp_{AA}; \top\!\!\!\top_{AA} \sqcup \alpha_A; \top\!\!\!\top_{AA} \sqcup \mathbb{I}_A; \mathbb{I}_A = \perp\!\!\!\perp_{AA} \sqcup R \sqcup \mathbb{I}_A = \top\!\!\!\top_{AA}.$$

This implies that the $\mathbb{I}$-cut of $\bigsqcup_{\beta \in \mathrm{Sc}[\mathcal{A}]} \beta_A; f(\beta)$ is $\top\!\!\!\top$. But, on the other hand, we have $\top\!\!\!\top_{AA} \not\sqsubseteq \mathbb{I}_A = f(\mathbb{I}_A)$. ◇

The observation above give rise to the following definition:

Definition 5.43 *A Goguen category $\mathcal{G}$ is an arrow category with cuts so that*

$$\beta_A; R^{\uparrow} \sqsubseteq \bigsqcup_{\alpha \in \mathrm{Sc}[\mathcal{G}]} \alpha_A; f(\alpha) \implies R \sqsubseteq f(\beta)$$

for all relations $R : A \to B$, *scalars* $\beta \in \mathrm{Sc}[\mathcal{G}]$ *and antimorphisms* $f : \mathrm{Sc}[\mathcal{G}] \to \mathcal{G}^{\uparrow}[A, B]$ *holds.*

The two additional properties of a Goguen category (with respect to an arrow category) can be expressed by a single equivalence. Notice that this equivalence was originally used to define Goguen categories [40, 41, 42, 43].

Lemma 5.44 *Let* $\mathcal{A}$ *be an arrow category. Then the following statements are equivalent:*

(1) $\mathcal{A}$ *is a Goguen category.*

(2) For all relations $R : A \to B$ *and antimorphisms* $f : \mathrm{Sc}[\mathcal{A}] \to \mathcal{A}^{\uparrow}[A, B]$ *we have*

$$R \sqsubseteq \bigsqcup_{\alpha \in \mathrm{Sc}[\mathcal{A}]} \alpha_A; f(\alpha) \iff (\beta_A \backslash R)^{\downarrow} \sqsubseteq f(\beta) \text{ for all } \beta \in \mathrm{Sc}[\mathcal{A}].$$

Proof. (1) $\Rightarrow$ (2) : Suppose $R \sqsubseteq \bigsqcup_{\alpha \in \mathrm{Sc}[\mathcal{A}]} \alpha_A; f(\alpha)$. Then we have

$$\begin{aligned}
X \sqsubseteq (\beta_A \backslash R)^{\downarrow} &\Leftrightarrow X^{\uparrow} \sqsubseteq \beta_A \backslash R && \text{Galois correspondence}\\
&\Leftrightarrow \beta_A; X^{\uparrow} \sqsubseteq R\\
&\Rightarrow \beta_A; X^{\uparrow} \sqsubseteq \bigsqcup_{\alpha \in \mathrm{Sc}[\mathcal{A}]} \alpha_A; f(\alpha)\\
&\Rightarrow X \sqsubseteq f(\beta), && \text{Goguen category}
\end{aligned}$$

and, hence, $(\beta_A \backslash R)^{\downarrow} \sqsubseteq f(\beta)$. In order to prove the other implication suppose $(\alpha_A \backslash R)^{\downarrow} \sqsubseteq f(\alpha)$ for all $\alpha \in \mathrm{Sc}[\mathcal{A}]$. Since $\mathcal{A}$ is an arrow category with cuts we conclude that

$$R \sqsubseteq \bigsqcup_{\alpha \in \mathrm{Sc}[\mathcal{A}]} \alpha_A; (\alpha_A \backslash R)^{\downarrow} \sqsubseteq \bigsqcup_{\alpha \in \mathrm{Sc}[\mathcal{A}]} \alpha_A; f(\alpha).$$

(2) $\Rightarrow$ (1) : Let be $R \in \mathcal{A}[A, B]$. Since $(\alpha_A \backslash R)^{\downarrow}$ is crisp and

$$\begin{aligned}
\bigsqcap_{\alpha \in M} (\alpha_A \backslash R)^{\downarrow} &= \Big(\bigsqcap_{\alpha \in M} (\alpha_A \backslash R)\Big)^{\downarrow} && \text{Corollary 5.5 (4)}\\
&= \Big(\Big(\bigsqcup M\Big) \backslash R\Big)^{\downarrow} && \text{Corollary 4.22 (4)}
\end{aligned}$$

the function $f : \mathrm{Sc}[\mathcal{A}] \to \mathcal{A}^{\uparrow}[A, B]$ defined by $f(\alpha) = (\alpha_A \backslash R)^{\downarrow}$ is an antimorphism. We conclude that $\mathcal{A}$ is an arrow category with cuts from 2. $\Leftarrow$.

Suppose $\beta_A; R^{\uparrow} \sqsubseteq \bigsqcup_{\alpha \in \mathrm{Sc}[\mathcal{A}]} \alpha_A; f(\alpha)$. If $\beta_A = \perp\!\!\!\perp_{AA}$, the assertion is trivial. Now, suppose $\beta_A \neq \perp\!\!\!\perp_{AA}$. Then 2. $\Rightarrow$ implies $(\beta_A \backslash (\beta_A; R^{\uparrow}))^{\downarrow} \sqsubseteq f(\beta)$. Lemma 5.20 gives us $(\beta \backslash (\beta; R^{\uparrow}))^{\downarrow} = R^{\uparrow}$, and, hence, $R \sqsubseteq R^{\uparrow} \sqsubseteq f(\beta)$. □

We will use Property 2. of the previous lemma as an alternative definition of Goguen categories without mentioning. The inclusions on both sides of the equivalence can be replaced by an equality as the next lemma shows.

Lemma 5.45 *Let $\mathcal{G}$ be a Goguen category. Then we have*

$$R = \bigsqcup_{\alpha \in \mathrm{Sc}[\mathcal{G}]} \alpha_A; f(\alpha) \iff (\beta_A \backslash R)^{\downarrow} = f(\beta) \text{ for all } \beta \in \mathrm{Sc}[\mathcal{G}].$$

for all relations $R : A \to B$ and antimorphisms $f : \mathrm{Sc}[\mathcal{G}] \to \mathcal{G}^{\uparrow}[A, B]$.

Proof. In order to prove the implication $\Rightarrow$ it is sufficient to show that $f(\beta) \sqsubseteq (\beta_A \backslash R)^{\downarrow}$ for all scalars β_A. We have $\beta_A; f(\beta) \sqsubseteq \bigsqcup_{\alpha \in \mathrm{Sc}[\mathcal{G}]} (\alpha_A; f(\alpha)) = R$, which implies $f(\beta) \sqsubseteq \beta_A \backslash R$. Since $f(\beta)$ is crisp we obtain $f(\beta)^{\uparrow} \sqsubseteq \beta_A \backslash R$, and, hence, $f(\beta) \sqsubseteq (\beta_A \backslash R)^{\downarrow}$.

$\Leftarrow$: It is sufficient to show that $\bigsqcup_{\alpha \in \mathrm{Sc}[\mathcal{G}]} (\alpha_A; f(\alpha)) \sqsubseteq R$. This follows from $\alpha_A; f(\alpha) = \alpha_A; (\alpha_A \backslash R)^{\downarrow} \sqsubseteq \alpha_A; (\alpha_A \backslash R) \sqsubseteq R$. □

One might ask whether an arrow category with cuts can be embedded into a suitable Goguen category. The general answer to this question is no.

Example 5.46 Consider again the arrow category with cuts $\mathcal{A}$ defined in Example 5.42. Suppose $\mathcal{A}$ can be embedded into a Goguen category $\mathcal{G}$. Then we identify $\mathcal{A}$ with its image in $\mathcal{G}$ and consider $\mathcal{A}$ to be a substructure of $\mathcal{G}$.

Now, consider the function $\hat{f} : \mathrm{Sc}[\mathcal{G}] \to \mathcal{G}^{\uparrow}[A, A]$ defined by

$$\hat{f}(\beta) = \begin{cases} \mathbb{T}_{AA} & \text{iff } \beta_A \sqsubseteq \alpha_A \\ \mathbb{I}_A & \text{otherwise} \end{cases}$$

Notice that the restriction of $\hat{f}$ to $\mathcal{A}$ is exactly the antimorphism f. It is easy to verify that $\hat{f}$ is also an antimorphism. As before, we have

$$\mathbb{T}_{AA} = R \sqcup \mathbb{I}_A = \alpha_A; \mathbb{T}_{AA} \sqcup \mathbb{I}_A; \mathbb{I}_A \sqsubseteq \bigsqcup_{\beta \in \mathrm{Sc}[\mathcal{G}]} \beta_A; \hat{f}(\beta)$$

so that $\mathbb{I}_A; \mathbb{T}^{\uparrow}_{AA} \sqsubseteq \bigsqcup_{\beta \in \mathrm{Sc}[\mathcal{G}]} \beta_A; \hat{f}(\beta)$ follows. But we have $\mathbb{T}_{AA} \not\sqsubseteq \mathbb{I}_A = \hat{f}(\mathbb{I}_A)$. ◇

We want to prove a lemma corresponding to Lemma 4.20. A homomorphism F between Goguen categories is a homomorphism between Dedekind categories so that the operation $.^{\uparrow}$ and $.^{\downarrow}$ are preserved, i.e., $F(R^{\uparrow}) = F(R)^{\uparrow}$ and $F(R^{\downarrow}) = F(R)^{\downarrow}$.

Lemma 5.47 *Let $F : \mathcal{G}_1 \to \mathcal{G}_2$ be a pre-functor between Goguen categories, which is full, faithful, and bijective on objects. Furthermore, suppose*

(1) either F or F^{-1} respects composition,

(2) either F or F^{-1} respects the converse operation,

(3) either F or F^{-1} respects the $^{\downarrow}$ operation,

(4) either F or F^{-1} is a complete lower semilattice homomorphism for every pair of objects, and

(5) either F or F^{-1} is an upper semilattice homomorphism for every pair of objects.

Then F is an isomorphism.

Proof. By Lemma 4.20, F is an isomorphism between Dedekind categories. Now, suppose without loss of generality that $F(R^{\downarrow}) = F(R)^{\downarrow}$ for all R in $\mathcal{G}_1$. Then the computation

$$\begin{aligned}
F(R^{\uparrow}) &= F\Big(\bigsqcup_{\alpha_A \neq \perp\!\!\!\perp_{AA}} (\alpha_A \backslash R)^{\downarrow}\Big) && \text{Lemma 5.35 (2)}\\
&= \bigsqcup_{\alpha_A \neq \perp\!\!\!\perp_{AA}} F((\alpha_A \backslash R)^{\downarrow}) && F \text{ homomorphism}\\
&= \bigsqcup_{\alpha_A \neq \perp\!\!\!\perp_{AA}} F(\alpha_A \backslash R)^{\downarrow} && \text{assumption}\\
&= \bigsqcup_{\alpha_A \neq \perp\!\!\!\perp_{AA}} (F(\alpha_A) \backslash F(R))^{\downarrow} && F \text{ homomorphism}\\
&= \bigsqcup_{\beta_A \neq \perp\!\!\!\perp_{AA}} (\beta_A \backslash F(R))^{\downarrow} && F \text{ bijective}\\
&= F(R)^{\uparrow}
\end{aligned}$$

shows that F preserves $^{\uparrow}$. From

$$\begin{aligned}
F^{-1}(S^{\uparrow}) &= F^{-1}(F(F^{-1}(S))^{\uparrow}) && F \text{ bijective}\\
&= F^{-1}(F(F^{-1}(S)^{\uparrow})) && F \text{ see above}\\
&= F^{-1}(S)^{\uparrow} && F \text{ bijective}
\end{aligned}$$

and a similar computation for $^{\downarrow}$ we conclude the assertion. □

5.6 THE GOGUEN CATEGORY OF ANTIMORPHISMS

In this section we want to establish that the arrow category of antimorphisms is indeed a Goguen category.

Theorem 5.48 *Let $\mathcal{L}$ be a complete Brouwerian lattice with $0 \neq 1$ and $\mathcal{R}$ be a simple Dedekind category with $\top\!\!\!\top_{AB} \neq \perp\!\!\!\perp_{AB}$ for all objects A and B. Then $\mathcal{R}^{\mathcal{L}}$ is a Goguen category.*

Proof. By Theorem 5.41 $\mathcal{R}^{\mathcal{L}}$ is an arrow category with cuts. Now, suppose $\beta_A \,\because\, f^{\uparrow} \sqsubseteq \bigsqcup\!\!\!\!\cdot_{\alpha_A \in \mathrm{Sc}_{\mathcal{R}^{\mathcal{L}}}(A)} (\alpha_A \,\because\, h(\alpha_A))$ for $h : \mathrm{Sc}_{\mathcal{R}^{\mathcal{L}}}(A) \overset{\text{anti}}{\rightarrow} \mathcal{R}^{\mathcal{L}}[A,B]$ such that $h(\alpha_A)$ is crisp for all $\alpha_A \in \mathrm{Sc}_{\mathcal{R}^{\mathcal{L}}}(A)$. If $\beta_A = \dot{\perp\!\!\!\perp}_{AA}$, the assertion is trivial. Suppose $\beta_A \neq \dot{\perp\!\!\!\perp}_{AA}$. Then we get

$$\begin{aligned}(\beta_A \,\because\, f^{\uparrow})(x) &= (\beta_A ; f^{\uparrow})(x) && \text{Lemma 5.25 (2)}\\ &= \beta_A(x); f^{\uparrow}(x), && \text{definition ;}\end{aligned}$$

such that

$$(\beta_A \,\because\, f^{\uparrow})(x) = \begin{cases} \top\!\!\!\top_{AB} & \text{iff } x = 0\\ \bigsqcup\limits_{y \neq 0} f(y) & \text{iff } \beta_A(x) = \mathbb{I}_A\\ \perp\!\!\!\perp_{AB} & \text{else.}\end{cases}$$

follows. Since $\beta_A \sqsubseteq \beta_A$ Lemma 5.28 (2) gives us $\beta_A(\delta(\beta_A)) \neq \perp\!\!\!\perp_{AA}$. Furthermore, $\delta(\beta_A) \neq 0$ since $\beta_A \neq \dot{\perp\!\!\!\perp}_{AA}$ and δ is an isomorphism. By Corollary 5.27 we conclude $\beta_A(\delta(\beta_A)) = \mathbb{I}_A$, and, hence, $(\beta_A \,\because\, f^{\uparrow})(\delta(\beta_A)) = \bigsqcup\limits_{y \neq 0} f(y)$.

Since $h(\alpha_A) = h(\alpha_A)^{\uparrow} = \dot{R}$ for $R = \bigsqcup\limits_{y\neq 0} h(\alpha_A)(y)$ we conclude

$$\begin{aligned}&\Big(\bigsqcup_{\alpha_A \in \mathrm{Sc}_{\mathcal{R}^{\mathcal{L}}}(A)} (\alpha_A \,\because\, h(\alpha_A))\Big)(x)\\ &= \bigsqcup_{\alpha_A \in \mathrm{Sc}_{\mathcal{R}^{\mathcal{L}}}(A)} (\alpha_A \,\because\, h(\alpha_A))(x) && \text{definition } \sqcup\\ &= \bigsqcup_{\alpha_A \in \mathrm{Sc}_{\mathcal{R}^{\mathcal{L}}}(A)} (\alpha_A ; h(\alpha_A))(x), && \text{Lemma 5.25 (2)}\end{aligned}$$

such that by Corollary 5.27

$$\Big(\bigsqcup_{\alpha_A \in \mathrm{Sc}_{\mathcal{R}^{\mathcal{L}}}(A)} (\alpha_A \,\because\, h(\alpha_A))\Big)(x) = \begin{cases} \top\!\!\!\top_{AB} & \text{iff } x = 0\\ \bigsqcup\limits_{\alpha_A(x) \neq \perp\!\!\!\perp_{AA}} h(\alpha_A)(x) & \text{else}\end{cases}$$

follows. Since $h(\alpha_A)$ is crisp and $0 \neq 1$ we have $h(\alpha_A)(x) = h(\alpha_A)(1)$ for all $x \neq 0$, and, hence, $\bigsqcup\limits_{\alpha_A \in \mathrm{Sc}_{\mathcal{R}^{\mathcal{L}}}(A)} (\alpha_A \,\because\, h(\alpha_A)) = \dot{Q}$ with $Q = \bigsqcup\limits_{\alpha_A(x) \neq \perp\!\!\!\perp_{AA}} h(\alpha_A)(1)$. Now, we want to show that $\dot{Q}(x) = h(\gamma(x))(1)$. Suppose $x = 0$. Then we have $h(\gamma(0))(1) = h(\dot{\perp\!\!\!\perp}_{AA})(1) = \dot{\top\!\!\!\top}_{AB}(1) = \top\!\!\!\top_{AB} = \dot{Q}(0)$ since γ is an isomorphism and h an antimorphism. If $x \neq 0$ and $\alpha_A(x) \neq \perp\!\!\!\perp_{AA}$, we conclude $\alpha_A(\delta(\gamma(x))) \neq \perp\!\!\!\perp_{AA}$ since γ and δ are inverse, and, hence, $\gamma(x) \sqsubseteq \alpha_A$ by Lemma 5.28 (2). This implies $h(\alpha_A) \sqsubseteq h(\gamma(x))$, and, hence, $Q = \bigsqcup\limits_{\alpha_A(x) \neq \perp\!\!\!\perp_{AA}} h(\alpha_A)(1) \sqsubseteq h(\gamma(x))(1)$. The other inclusion follows immediately from $\gamma(x)(x) = \mathbb{I}_A \neq \perp\!\!\!\perp_{AA}$. Together we have shown that $(\bigsqcup\limits_{\alpha_A \in \mathrm{Sc}_{\mathcal{R}^{\mathcal{L}}}(A)} (\alpha_A \,\because\, h(\alpha_A)))(x) = h(\gamma(x))(1)$.

Now, consider the following computation: Since γ is an isomorphism of complete lattices we have

$$\begin{aligned}
&\varphi\left(\bigsqcup_{\alpha_A\in \mathrm{Sc}_{\mathcal{RL}}(A)} (\alpha_A \,;\, h(\alpha_A))\right)(x) \\
&= \bigsqcup_{\bigvee M=x}\ \prod_{y\in M}\left(\bigsqcup_{\alpha_A\in \mathrm{Sc}_{\mathcal{RL}}(A)} (\alpha_A \,;\, h(\alpha_A))\right)(y) && \text{definition } \varphi \\
&= \bigsqcup_{\bigvee M=x}\ \prod_{y\in M} h(\gamma(y))(1) && \text{see above} \\
&= \bigsqcup_{\bigvee M=x} h\left(\bigsqcup_{y\in M}\gamma(y)\right)(1) && h \text{ antimorphism} \\
&= \bigsqcup_{\bigvee M=x} h\Big(\gamma\Big(\bigvee M\Big)\Big)(1) && \gamma \text{ homomorphism} \\
&= h(\gamma(x))(1) \\
&= \left(\bigsqcup_{\alpha_A\in \mathrm{Sc}_{\mathcal{RL}}(A)} (\alpha_A \,;\, h(\alpha_A))\right)(x), && \text{see above}
\end{aligned}$$

and, hence, $\dot{\bigsqcup}_{\alpha_A\in \mathrm{Sc}_{\mathcal{RL}}(A)} (\alpha_A \,;\, h(\alpha_A)) \sqsubseteq \bigsqcup_{\alpha_A\in \mathrm{Sc}_{\mathcal{RL}}(A)} (\alpha_A \,;\, h(\alpha_A))$.

Finally, we obtain the assertion as follows: The inclusion $f(0) \sqsubseteq h(\beta_A)(0)$ is trivial and for $x \neq 0$ we get

$$\begin{aligned}
f(x) &\sqsubseteq \bigsqcup_{y\neq 0} f(y) \\
&= (\beta_A \,;\, f^{\uparrow})(\delta(\beta_A)) && \text{see above} \\
&\sqsubseteq \left(\dot{\bigsqcup}_{\alpha_A\in \mathrm{Sc}_{\mathcal{RL}}(A)} (\alpha_A \,;\, h(\alpha_A))\right)(\delta(\beta_A)) && \text{assumption} \\
&\sqsubseteq \left(\bigsqcup_{\alpha_A\in \mathrm{Sc}_{\mathcal{RL}}(A)} (\alpha_A \,;\, h(\alpha_A))\right)(\delta(\beta_A)) && \text{see above} \\
&= h(\gamma(\delta(\beta_A)))(1) && \text{see above} \\
&= h(\beta_A)(1) && \gamma \text{ and } \delta \text{ are inverse} \\
&= h(\beta_A)^{\downarrow}(x) && \text{definition } {\downarrow} \\
&= h(\beta_A)(x). && h(\beta_A) \text{ crisp} \qquad \Box
\end{aligned}$$

5.7 REPRESENTATION OF GOGUEN CATEGORIES

Suppose $\mathcal{G}$ is a Goguen category. By Lemma 4.35 $\mathrm{Sc}[\mathcal{G}]$ is a complete Brouwerian lattice with $0 \neq 1$ since $\perp\!\!\!\perp_{AA} \neq \top\!\!\!\top_{AA}$ for all objects A. Furthermore, by Corollary 5.17 $\mathcal{G}^{\uparrow}$ is a simple Dedekind category with $\top\!\!\!\top_{AB} \neq \perp\!\!\!\perp_{AB}$ for all objects A and B. Theorem 5.48 shows that the category of antimorphisms $\mathcal{G}^{\uparrow^{\mathrm{Sc}[\mathcal{G}]}}$ is again a Goguen category. In this section, we want to prove that $\mathcal{G}$ and $\mathcal{G}^{\uparrow^{\mathrm{Sc}[\mathcal{G}]}}$ are isomorphic, i.e., we prove a pseudo-representation theorem for Goguen categories. Afterwards, we show that the representation theory of Goguen categories is equivalent to the representation theory of the simple Dedekind categories. This result allows us to transfer known representation results to the theory of Goguen categories.

Lemma 5.49 *Let $\mathcal{G}$ be a Goguen category and $f : \mathrm{Sc}_{\mathcal{G}}(A) \to \mathcal{G}^{\uparrow}[A, B]$. Then we have*

(1) $$\tau(f)(\beta_A) = \left(\beta_A \backslash \left(\bigsqcup_{\alpha_A \in \mathrm{Sc}_{\mathcal{G}}(A)} (\alpha_A; f(\alpha_A))\right)\right)^{\downarrow},$$

(2) $$\bigsqcup_{\alpha_A \in \mathrm{Sc}_{\mathcal{G}}(A)} (\alpha_A; \tau(f)(\alpha_A)) = \bigsqcup_{\alpha_A \in \mathrm{Sc}_{\mathcal{G}}(A)} (\alpha_A; f(\alpha_A)).$$

Proof.

(1) Let $\tilde{f}$ be defined by the right-hand side of the assertion, i.e.,

$$\tilde{f}(\beta_A) := \left(\beta_A \backslash \left(\bigsqcup_{\alpha_A \in \mathrm{Sc}_{\mathcal{G}}(A)} (\alpha_A; f(\alpha_A))\right)\right)^{\downarrow}.$$

Then $f \sqsubseteq \tilde{f}$ since

$$\begin{aligned}
&\beta_A; f(\beta_A) \sqsubseteq \bigsqcup_{\alpha_A \in \mathrm{Sc}_{\mathcal{G}}(A)} (\alpha_A; f(\alpha_A)) \\
\Leftrightarrow\ &\beta_A; f(\beta_A)^{\uparrow} \sqsubseteq \bigsqcup_{\alpha_A \in \mathrm{Sc}_{\mathcal{G}}(A)} (\alpha_A; f(\alpha_A)) && f(\beta_A) \text{ is crisp} \\
\Leftrightarrow\ &f(\beta_A)^{\uparrow} \sqsubseteq \beta_A \backslash \left(\bigsqcup_{\alpha_A \in \mathrm{Sc}_{\mathcal{G}}(A)} (\alpha_A; f(\alpha_A))\right) && \text{definition residual} \\
\Leftrightarrow\ &f(\beta_A) \sqsubseteq \left(\beta_A \backslash \left(\bigsqcup_{\alpha_A \in \mathrm{Sc}_{\mathcal{G}}(A)} (\alpha_A; f(\alpha_A))\right)\right)^{\downarrow}. && \text{Galois correspondence}
\end{aligned}$$

Furthermore, the computation

$$\bigsqcap_{\beta_A \in M} \tilde{f}(\beta_A) = \bigsqcap_{\beta_A \in M} \left(\beta_A \backslash \left(\bigsqcup_{\alpha_A \in \mathrm{Sc}_{\mathcal{G}}(A)} (\alpha_A; f(\alpha_A))\right)\right)^{\downarrow} \qquad \text{definition } \tilde{f}$$

$$= \left(\bigsqcap_{\beta_A \in M} \left(\beta_A \backslash \left(\bigsqcup_{\alpha_A \in \mathrm{Sc}_{\mathcal{G}}(A)} (\alpha_A; f(\alpha_A)) \right) \right) \right)^{\downarrow} \quad \text{Corollary 5.5 (4)}$$

$$= \left(\left(\bigsqcup M \right) \backslash \left(\bigsqcup_{\alpha_A \in \mathrm{Sc}_{\mathcal{G}}(A)} (\alpha_A; f(\alpha_A)) \right) \right)^{\downarrow} \quad \text{Corollary 4.22 (4)}$$

$$= \tilde{f}\left(\bigsqcup M \right) \quad \text{definition } \tilde{f}$$

shows that $\tilde{f}$ is an antimorphism. Together we have $\tau(f) \sqsubseteq \tau(\tilde{f}) = \tilde{f}$. For the other inclusion consider the following computation:

$$X \sqsubseteq \tilde{f}(\beta_A)$$

$$\Leftrightarrow X \sqsubseteq \left(\beta_A \backslash \left(\bigsqcup_{\alpha_A \in \mathrm{Sc}_{\mathcal{G}}(A)} (\alpha_A; f(\alpha_A)) \right) \right)^{\downarrow} \quad \text{definition } \tilde{f}$$

$$\Leftrightarrow X^{\uparrow} \sqsubseteq \beta_A \backslash \left(\bigsqcup_{\alpha_A \in \mathrm{Sc}_{\mathcal{G}}(A)} (\alpha_A; f(\alpha_A)) \right) \quad \text{Galois correspondence}$$

$$\Leftrightarrow \beta_A; X^{\uparrow} \sqsubseteq \bigsqcup_{\alpha_A \in \mathrm{Sc}_{\mathcal{G}}(A)} (\alpha_A; f(\alpha_A)) \quad \text{definition residual}$$

$$\Rightarrow \beta_A; X^{\uparrow} \sqsubseteq \bigsqcup_{\alpha_A \in \mathrm{Sc}_{\mathcal{G}}(A)} (\alpha_A; \tau(f)(\alpha_A)) \quad f \sqsubseteq \tau(f)$$

$$\Rightarrow X^{\uparrow} \sqsubseteq \tau(f)(\beta_A) \quad \text{Property (5b) for } \tau(f)$$

$$\Leftrightarrow X \sqsubseteq \tau(f)(\beta_A)^{\downarrow} \quad \text{Galois correspondence}$$

$$\Leftrightarrow X \sqsubseteq \tau(f)(\beta_A), \quad \tau(f)(\beta_A) \text{ is crisp}$$

which shows $\tilde{f} \sqsubseteq \tau(f)$.

(2) The inclusion $\sqsupseteq$ is trivial. The other inclusion is shown as follows:

$$\bigsqcup_{\alpha_A \in \mathrm{Sc}_{\mathcal{G}}(A)} (\alpha_A; \tau(f)(\alpha_A))$$

$$= \bigsqcup_{\alpha_A \in \mathrm{Sc}_{\mathcal{G}}(A)} \left(\alpha_A; \left(\alpha_A \backslash \left(\bigsqcup_{\beta_A \in \mathrm{Sc}_{\mathcal{G}}(A)} (\beta_A; f(\beta_A)) \right) \right) \right)^{\downarrow} \quad (1)$$

$$\sqsubseteq \bigsqcup_{\alpha_A \in \mathrm{Sc}_{\mathcal{G}}(A)} \left(\alpha_A; \left(\alpha_A \backslash \left(\bigsqcup_{\beta_A \in \mathrm{Sc}_{\mathcal{G}}(A)} (\beta_A; f(\beta_A) \right) \right) \right)$$

$$\sqsubseteq \bigsqcup_{\alpha_A \in \mathrm{Sc}_{\mathcal{G}}(A)} \left(\bigsqcup_{\beta_A \in \mathrm{Sc}_{\mathcal{G}}(A)} (\beta_A; f(\beta_A)) \right)$$

$$= \bigsqcup_{\alpha_A \in \mathrm{Sc}_{\mathcal{G}}(A)} (\alpha_A; f(\alpha_A)).$$

□

Now, we define the pseudo-representation functor $P_{\mathcal{G}} : \mathcal{G} \to \mathcal{G}{\uparrow}^{\mathrm{Sc}[\mathcal{G}]}$ by

$$\begin{aligned} P_{\mathcal{G}}(A) &:= A && \text{for all objects } A, \\ P_{\mathcal{G}}(R)(\alpha) &:= (\alpha_A \backslash R)^{\downarrow} && \text{for all } R : A \to B \text{ and } \alpha \in \mathrm{Sc}[\mathcal{G}], \end{aligned}$$

and its inverse $P_{\mathcal{G}}^{-1} : \mathcal{G}{\uparrow}^{\mathrm{Sc}[\mathcal{G}]} \to \mathcal{G}$ by

$$\begin{aligned} P_{\mathcal{G}}^{-1}(A) &:= A && \text{for all objects } A, \\ P_{\mathcal{G}}^{-1}(f) &:= \bigsqcup_{\alpha \in \mathrm{Sc}[\mathcal{G}]} (\alpha_A ; f(\alpha)) && \text{for all } f : \mathrm{Sc}[\mathcal{G}] \overset{\text{anti}}{\to} \mathcal{G}^{\uparrow}[A, B]. \end{aligned}$$

Using these definitions we are able to state our main theorem.

Theorem 5.50 (Pseudo-Representation Theorem) *Let $\mathcal{G}$ be a Goguen category. Then $\mathcal{G}$ and $\mathcal{G}{\uparrow}^{\mathrm{Sc}[\mathcal{G}]}$ are isomorphic via $P_{\mathcal{G}}$.*

Proof. Since

$$\begin{aligned} \bigsqcap_{\alpha_A \in M} P_{\mathcal{G}}(R)(\alpha) &= \bigsqcap_{\alpha_A \in M} (\alpha_A \backslash R)^{\downarrow} && \text{definition } P_{\mathcal{G}} \\ &= \left(\bigsqcap_{\alpha_A \in M} (\alpha_A \backslash R) \right)^{\downarrow} && \text{Corollary 5.5 (4)} \\ &= \left(\left(\bigsqcup M \right) \backslash R \right)^{\downarrow} && \text{Corollary 4.22 (4)} \\ &= P_{\mathcal{G}}(R) \left(\bigsqcup M \right) && \text{definition } P_{\mathcal{G}} \end{aligned}$$

$P_{\mathcal{G}}(R)$ is an antimorphism, and, hence, $P_{\mathcal{G}}$ well-defined. Suppose $P_{\mathcal{G}}(R) = P_{\mathcal{G}}(S)$. Then we have

$$\begin{aligned} R &= \bigsqcup_{\alpha \in \mathrm{Sc}[\mathcal{G}]} (\alpha_A ; (\alpha_A \backslash R)^{\downarrow}) && \text{Theorem 5.35} \\ &= \bigsqcup_{\alpha \in \mathrm{Sc}[\mathcal{G}]} (\alpha_A ; P_{\mathcal{G}}(R)(\alpha)) && \text{definition } P_{\mathcal{G}} \\ &= \bigsqcup_{\alpha \in \mathrm{Sc}[\mathcal{G}]} (\alpha_A ; P_{\mathcal{G}}(S)(\alpha)) && \\ &= \bigsqcup_{\alpha \in \mathrm{Sc}[\mathcal{G}]} (\alpha_A ; (\alpha_A \backslash S)^{\downarrow}) && \text{definition } P_{\mathcal{G}} \\ &= S, && \text{Theorem 5.35} \end{aligned}$$

which shows that $P_{\mathcal{G}}$ is faithful. Now, suppose $f : \mathrm{Sc}[\mathcal{G}] \overset{\mathrm{anti}}{\to} \mathcal{G}^{\uparrow}[A,B]$ and compute

$$\begin{aligned}
P_{\mathcal{G}}\left(\bigsqcup_{\alpha\in \mathrm{Sc}[\mathcal{G}]}(\alpha_A; f(\alpha))\right)(\beta) &= \left(\beta_A\backslash\left(\bigsqcup_{\alpha\in \mathrm{Sc}[\mathcal{G}]}(\alpha_A; f(\alpha))\right)\right)^{\downarrow} && \text{definition } P_{\mathcal{G}}\\
&= \tau(f)(\beta) && \text{Lemma 5.49 (1)}\\
&= f(\beta) && f \text{ antimorphism}
\end{aligned}$$

for every scalar $\beta \in \mathrm{Sc}[\mathcal{G}]$, which shows that $P_{\mathcal{G}}$ is full and that the inverse of $P_{\mathcal{G}}$ is indeed $P_{\mathcal{G}}^{-1}$. Now, we want to show five properties required by Lemma 5.47.

(1) First, the following computation:

$$\begin{aligned}
&\bigsqcup_{\alpha\in \mathrm{Sc}[\mathcal{G}]}(\alpha_A; f(\alpha); g(\alpha))\\
&= \bigsqcup_{\alpha\in \mathrm{Sc}[\mathcal{G}]}(\alpha_A; f(\alpha); \alpha_B; g(\alpha)) && \text{Lemma 5.14}\\
&\sqsubseteq \left(\bigsqcup_{\alpha\in \mathrm{Sc}[\mathcal{G}]}(\alpha_A; f(\alpha))\right); \left(\bigsqcup_{\beta\in \mathrm{Sc}[\mathcal{G}]}(\beta_B; g(\beta))\right)\\
&= \bigsqcup_{\alpha\in \mathrm{Sc}[\mathcal{G}]}\left(\alpha_A; f(\alpha); \left(\bigsqcup_{\beta\in \mathrm{Sc}[\mathcal{G}]}(\beta_B; g(\beta))\right)\right)\\
&= \bigsqcup_{\alpha,\beta\in \mathrm{Sc}[\mathcal{G}]}(\alpha_A; f(\alpha); \beta_B; g(\beta))\\
&= \bigsqcup_{\alpha,\beta\in \mathrm{Sc}[\mathcal{G}]}(\alpha_A; \beta_A; f(\alpha); g(\beta)) && \text{Lemma 5.14}\\
&= \bigsqcup_{\alpha,\beta\in \mathrm{Sc}[\mathcal{G}]}((\alpha_A \sqcap \beta_A); f(\alpha); g(\beta))\\
&\sqsubseteq \bigsqcup_{\alpha,\beta\in \mathrm{Sc}[\mathcal{G}]}((\alpha_A \sqcap \beta_A); f(\alpha\sqcap\beta); g(\alpha\sqcap\beta)) && f \text{ and } g \text{ are antitone}\\
&= \bigsqcup_{\alpha\in \mathrm{Sc}[\mathcal{G}]}(\alpha_A; f(\alpha); g(\alpha))
\end{aligned}$$

implies $\bigsqcup_{\alpha\in \mathrm{Sc}[\mathcal{G}]}(\alpha_A; f(\alpha); g(\alpha)) = (\bigsqcup_{\alpha\in \mathrm{Sc}[\mathcal{G}]}(\alpha_A; f(\alpha))); (\bigsqcup_{\beta\in \mathrm{Sc}[\mathcal{G}]}(\beta_B; g(\beta)))$.

We conclude

$$\begin{aligned}
P_{\mathcal{G}}^{-1}(f \mathbin{\ddot{;}} g) &= \bigsqcup_{\alpha\in\mathrm{Sc}[\mathcal{G}]} (\alpha_A; (f \mathbin{\ddot{;}} g)(\alpha)) && \text{definition } P_{\mathcal{G}}^{-1}\\
&= \bigsqcup_{\alpha\in\mathrm{Sc}[\mathcal{G}]} (\alpha_A; \tau(f;g)(\alpha)) && \text{definition } \ddot{;}\\
&= \bigsqcup_{\alpha\in\mathrm{Sc}[\mathcal{G}]} (\alpha_A; (f;g)(\alpha)) && \text{Lemma 5.49 (2)}\\
&= \bigsqcup_{\alpha\in\mathrm{Sc}[\mathcal{G}]} (\alpha_A; f(\alpha); g(\alpha)) && \text{definition ;}\\
&= \left(\bigsqcup_{\alpha\in\mathrm{Sc}[\mathcal{G}]} (\alpha_A; f(\alpha))\right); \left(\bigsqcup_{\beta\in\mathrm{Sc}[\mathcal{G}]} (\beta_B; g(\beta))\right) && \text{see above}\\
&= P_{\mathcal{G}}^{-1}(f); P_{\mathcal{G}}^{-1}(g). && \text{definition } P_{\mathcal{G}}^{-1}
\end{aligned}$$

(2) We immediately conclude that

$$\begin{aligned}
P_{\mathcal{G}}(Q^{\smile})(\alpha) &= (\alpha_A \backslash Q^{\smile})^{\downarrow} && \text{definition } P_{\mathcal{G}}\\
&= (\alpha_B \backslash Q)^{\downarrow\smile} && \text{Lemma 5.15}\\
&= (P_{\mathcal{G}}(Q)(\alpha))^{\smile} && \text{definition } P_{\mathcal{G}}\\
&= P_{\mathcal{G}}(Q)^{\smile}(\alpha). && \text{definition } {}^{\smile}
\end{aligned}$$

(3) First of all, we have

$$P_{\mathcal{G}}(Q^{\downarrow})(\perp\!\!\!\perp) = \top\!\!\!\top_{AB} = P_{\mathcal{G}}(Q)^{\downarrow}(\perp\!\!\!\perp)$$

since both functions are antimorphisms. Now, suppose $\alpha \neq \perp\!\!\!\perp$. Then we have

$$\begin{aligned}
P_{\mathcal{G}}(Q^{\downarrow})(\alpha) &= (\alpha_A \backslash Q^{\downarrow})^{\downarrow} && \text{definition } P_{\mathcal{G}}\\
&= Q^{\downarrow} && \text{Lemma 5.12 (1)}\\
&= (\mathbb{I}_A \backslash Q)^{\downarrow} && \text{Lemma 4.16 (1)}\\
&= P_{\mathcal{G}}(Q)(\mathbb{I}) && \text{definition } P_{\mathcal{G}}\\
&= P_{\mathcal{G}}(Q)^{\downarrow}(\alpha). && \text{definition } {}^{\downarrow}
\end{aligned}$$

(4) We immediately conclude that

$$
\begin{aligned}
P_{\mathcal{G}}\left(\bigsqcap_{i\in I} R_i\right)(\alpha) &= \left(\alpha_A \backslash \left(\bigsqcap_{i\in I} R_i\right)\right)^{\downarrow} && \text{definition } P_{\mathcal{G}} \\
&= \left(\bigsqcap_{i\in I} (\alpha_A \backslash R_i)\right)^{\downarrow} && \text{Corollary 4.22 (3)} \\
&= \bigsqcap_{i\in I} (\alpha_A \backslash R_i)^{\downarrow} && \text{Corollary 5.5 (4)} \\
&= \bigsqcap_{i\in I} P_{\mathcal{G}}(R_i)(\alpha). && \text{definition } P_{\mathcal{G}}
\end{aligned}
$$

(5) Again, we immediately conclude that

$$
\begin{aligned}
P_{\mathcal{G}}^{-1}\left(\dot{\bigsqcup_{i\in I}} f_i\right) &= \bigsqcup_{\alpha\in \mathrm{Sc}[\mathcal{G}]} \left(\alpha_A ; \left(\dot{\bigsqcup_{i\in I}} f_i\right)(\alpha)\right) && \text{definition } P_{\mathcal{G}}^{-1} \\
&= \bigsqcup_{\alpha\in \mathrm{Sc}[\mathcal{G}]} \left(\alpha_A ; \tau\left(\bigsqcup_{i\in I} f_i\right)(\alpha)\right) && \text{definition } \dot{\sqcup} \\
&= \bigsqcup_{\alpha\in \mathrm{Sc}[\mathcal{G}]} \left(\alpha_A ; \left(\bigsqcup_{i\in I} f_i(\alpha)\right)\right) && \text{Lemma 5.49 (2)} \\
&= \bigsqcup_{\alpha\in \mathrm{Sc}[\mathcal{G}]} \bigsqcup_{i\in I} (\alpha_A ; f_i(\alpha)) \\
&= \bigsqcup_{i\in I} \bigsqcup_{\alpha\in \mathrm{Sc}[\mathcal{G}]} (\alpha_A ; f_i(\alpha)) \\
&= \bigsqcup_{i\in I} P_{\mathcal{G}}^{-1}(f_i). && \text{definition } P_{\mathcal{G}}^{-1} \qquad \square
\end{aligned}
$$

The extension $\hat{P}_{\mathcal{G}}$ of the pseudo-representation functor gives us the following:

Theorem 5.51 *A Goguen category $\mathcal{G}$ is representable iff $\mathcal{G}^{\uparrow}$ is representable.*

Proof. The implication $\Rightarrow$ is trivial since crisp relations are represented by 0-1 crisp relations. Now, suppose there is an embedding $F : \mathcal{G}^{\uparrow} \to \mathbf{Rel}$. Then Theorem 5.33 implies that $\hat{F}$ is an embedding between ${\mathcal{G}^{\uparrow}}^{\mathrm{Sc}[\mathcal{G}]}$ and $\mathbf{Rel}^{\mathrm{Sc}[\mathcal{G}]}$. By Theorem 5.50 $\mathcal{G}$ and ${\mathcal{G}^{\uparrow}}^{\mathrm{Sc}[\mathcal{G}]}$ as well as $\mathbf{Rel}^{\mathrm{Sc}[\mathcal{G}]}$ and $\mathrm{Sc}[\mathcal{G}]$-$\mathbf{Rel}$ are isomorphic such that $P_{\mathcal{G}} \circ \hat{F} \circ P_{\mathrm{Sc}[\mathcal{G}]\text{-}\mathbf{Rel}}^{-1}$ is an embedding from $\mathcal{G}$ to $\mathrm{Sc}[\mathcal{G}]$-$\mathbf{Rel}$. $\square$

5.8 BOOLEAN-BASED GOGUEN CATEGORIES

The axioms of an arrow category, and, hence, of a Goguen category are somehow asymmetric. The property $(\sqcap^{\uparrow})$ $Q^{\uparrow} \sqcap R^{\downarrow} = (Q \sqcap R^{\downarrow})^{\uparrow}$ is an axiom of this theory

$$z_i := \{(j,j) \mid 0 < j \leq i\} \cup \{(j,k) \mid j,k > i\}$$
$$y_i := z_i \cup \{(0,j) \mid j \geq 0\} \cup \{(j,0) \mid j \geq 0\}$$

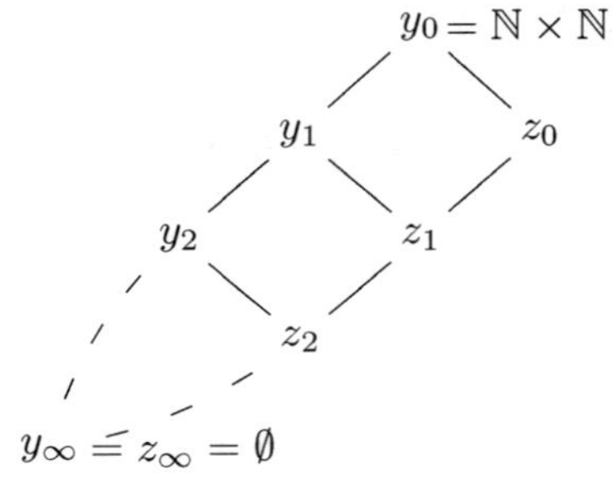

Figure 5.5. The relations y_i and z_i.

but the dual property ($\sqcup^{\downarrow}$) $Q^{\uparrow} \sqcup R^{\downarrow} = (Q^{\uparrow} \sqcup R)^{\downarrow}$ is not. The main reason is that the theory of complete Brouwerian lattices, which serves as a foundation of arrow categories, is also asymmetric. The infinite distribution law $x \wedge \bigvee_{i\in I} y_i = \bigvee_{i\in I}(x \wedge y_i)$ is valid but its dual version $x \vee \bigwedge_{i\in I} y_i = \bigwedge_{i\in I}(x \vee y_i)$ might not. Based on that observation we construct an example where ($\sqcup^{\downarrow}$) fails to hold.

Example 5.52 For each $k \in \mathbb{N}$ let be $\mathcal{R}_k := \{R \subseteq \mathbb{N} \times \mathbb{N} \mid \forall i,j \geq k : iRj\}$, i.e., the set of all binary relations on $\mathbb{N}$ such that all elements greater or equal to k are related. It is not hard to verify that the following properties:

(1) if $R \in \mathcal{R}_k$, then so is R^{T},

(2) if $R_1 \in \mathcal{R}_{k_1}$ and $R_2 \in \mathcal{R}_{k_2}$, then $R_1 \cap R_2 \in \mathcal{R}_{\max(k_1,k_2)}$,

(3) if $R_1 \in \mathcal{R}_{k_1}$ and $R_2 \in \mathcal{R}_{k_2}$, then $R_1 \circ R_2 \in \mathcal{R}_{\max(k_1,k_2)}$,

(4) if $R_i \in \mathcal{R}_{k_i}$ for all $i \in I$ and $k = \min\{k_i \mid i \in I\}$, then $\bigcup_{i\in I} R_i \in \mathcal{R}_k$,

The properties above show that $\mathcal{R}_\infty := \{\emptyset\} \cup \bigcup_{k\in\mathbb{N}} \mathcal{R}_k$ together with $\cap, \cup, .^{\mathsf{T}}$ and $\circ$ is a simple Dedekind category. Notice that in this category infinite meets and the residuals do not coincide with the corresponding operation on $\mathcal{P}(\mathbb{N} \times \mathbb{N})$.

Let y_i, z_i with $i \in \mathbb{N}$ be the relations defined in Figure 5.5.

The relations above show that the dual version of the infinite distribution law is not valid. Furthermore, the infinite meet y_∞ of the y_i's does not correspond to their set-theoretic intersection – the relation $\{(0,j) \mid j \geq 0\} \cup \{(j,0) \mid j \geq 0\}$.

Now, consider the Goguen category $\mathcal{R}_\infty^{\mathbb{N}^\infty}$, i.e., the antimorphisms from the natural numbers extended by a greatest element to $\mathcal{R}_\infty$. Furthermore, let be $f := \dot{z}_0$ and $g(k) := y_k$ for all $k \in \mathbb{N}^\infty$. Obviously f and g are antimorphisms. Since

$$(f \sqcup g)(k) = f(k) \sqcup g(k) \sqsupseteq z_0 \sqcup y_k = \mathbb{N} \times \mathbb{N} = y_0$$

for all $k \in \mathbb{N}^\infty$ we have $f \sqcup\!\!\!\cdot\, g = \dot{y_0}$. This implies

$$\begin{aligned}(f^\uparrow \sqcup\!\!\!\cdot\, g)^\downarrow &= (f \sqcup\!\!\!\cdot\, g)^\downarrow && f \text{ is crisp}\\ &= \dot{y_0}^\downarrow && \text{see above}\\ &= \dot{y_0}. && \dot{y_0} \text{ is crisp}\end{aligned}$$

On the other hand, $g^\downarrow(k) = g(\dot{\infty}) = y_\infty$ for $k \neq 0$, and, hence, $f^\uparrow \sqcup\!\!\!\cdot\, g^\downarrow = \dot{z_0} \sqcup\!\!\!\cdot\, \dot{y_\infty} = \dot{z_0}$. ◇

We have already shown in Lemma 5.7 (2) that in a Boolean arrow category ($\sqcup\!\!\!\cdot^\downarrow$) is valid. In the remainder of this section we want to show that the theory of Boolean-based Goguen categories is already strong enough to prove this property.

Recall that a Boolean-based Goguen category is Goguen category $\mathcal{G}$ so that the substructure of crisp relations $\mathcal{G}^\uparrow$ is a Schröder category.

Due to our pseudo-representation theorem (Theorem 5.50 it is sufficient to show ($\sqcup\!\!\!\cdot^\downarrow$) for antimorphisms.

Theorem 5.53 *Let $\mathcal{R}^\mathcal{L}$ be a Boolean-based Goguen category. Then we have $f^\uparrow \sqcup\!\!\!\cdot\, g^\downarrow = (f^\uparrow \sqcup\!\!\!\cdot\, g)^\downarrow$ for all f, g in $\mathcal{R}^\mathcal{L}[A, B]$.*

Proof. First of all, we show that $\dot{Q} \sqcup g$ is an antimorphism, and, hence, that $\dot{Q} \sqcup\!\!\!\cdot\, g = \dot{Q} \sqcup g$ holds. Assume $x \neq 0$ and consider the following computation:

$$\begin{aligned}\varphi(\dot{Q} \sqcup g)(x) &= \bigsqcup_{\bigvee M = x} \bigsqcap_{y \in M} (\dot{Q} \sqcup g)(y) && \text{definition } \varphi\\ &= \bigsqcup_{\bigvee M = x} \bigsqcap_{y \in M} (\dot{Q}(y) \sqcup g(y))\\ &= \bigsqcup_{\bigvee M = x} \bigsqcap_{0 \neq y \in M} (\dot{Q}(y) \sqcup g(y)) && x \neq 0\\ &= \bigsqcup_{\bigvee M = x} \bigsqcap_{0 \neq y \in M} (Q \sqcup g(y))\\ &= \bigsqcup_{\bigvee M = x} \left(Q \sqcup \bigsqcap_{0 \neq y \in M} g(y)\right) && \text{Theorem 2.28}\\ &= \bigsqcup_{\bigvee M = x} (Q \sqcup g(x)) && g \text{ antimorphism}\\ &= Q \sqcup g(x)\\ &= \dot{Q}(x) \sqcup g(x) && x \neq 0\\ &= (\dot{Q} \sqcup g)(x).\end{aligned}$$

For $x = 0$ we have

$$\begin{aligned}
\varphi(\dot{Q} \sqcup g)(x) &= \bigsqcup_{\bigvee M = 0} \bigsqcap_{y \in M} (\dot{Q} \sqcup g)(y) && \text{definition } \varphi \\
&= (\dot{Q} \sqcup g)(x). && \text{since } M = \emptyset \text{ or } M = \{0\}
\end{aligned}$$

So, we have shown that $\varphi(\dot{Q} \sqcup g) = \dot{Q} \sqcup g$, which implies that $\dot{Q} \sqcup g$ is an antimorphism.

For $x \neq 0$ we have

$$\begin{aligned}
(\dot{Q} \sqcup g)^{\downarrow}(x) &= (\dot{Q} \sqcup g)(1) && \text{definition } .^{\downarrow} \\
&= \dot{Q}(1) \sqcup g(1) \\
&= \dot{Q}(x) \sqcup g^{\downarrow}(x) && \text{definition } .^{\downarrow} \\
&= (\dot{Q} \sqcup g^{\downarrow})(x)
\end{aligned}$$

and for $x = 0$ obviously $(\dot{Q} \sqcup g)^{\downarrow}(x) = \top\!\!\!\top_{AB} = (\dot{Q} \sqcup g^{\downarrow})(x)$ so that $(\dot{Q} \sqcup g)^{\downarrow} = \dot{Q} \sqcup g^{\downarrow}$ follows.

Now, let $Q := \bigsqcup_{x \neq 0} f(x)$. Then the assertion follows from

$$\begin{aligned}
(f^{\uparrow} \dot{\sqcup} g)^{\downarrow} &= (\dot{Q} \dot{\sqcup} g)^{\downarrow} && \text{definition } f^{\uparrow} \\
&= (\dot{Q} \sqcup g)^{\downarrow} && \text{see above} \\
&= \dot{Q} \sqcup g^{\downarrow} && \text{see above} \\
&= \dot{Q}^{\uparrow} \dot{\sqcup} g^{\downarrow} && \text{see above} \\
&= f^{\uparrow} \dot{\sqcup} g^{\downarrow}. && \text{definition } f^{\uparrow}
\end{aligned}$$

□

Finally, we obtain the following:

Corollary 5.54 *Let $\mathcal{G}$ be a Boolean-based Goguen category. Then we have $Q^{\uparrow} \sqcup R^{\downarrow} = (Q^{\uparrow} \sqcup R)^{\downarrow}$ for all $Q, R : A \to B$.*

5.9 EQUATIONS IN GOGUEN CATEGORIES

A Goguen category may provide some relational constructions as products, sums, or splittings (cf. Section 4.6). Such a construction is given by an object together with a set of relations fulfilling some equations. One may expect that the pairing $Q;\pi^{\smile} \sqcap R;\rho^{\smile}$ of two crisp relations Q and R is crisp too. If the projections are crisp, then this is the case since the class of crisp relations is closed under the usual relational operations. Especially in applications, such a property seems to be essential. For example, if the input domain of a fuzzy controller is a product with noncrisp projection, there would be a fuzzification, which is not an integral part of the controller. This fuzzification arises from the specific choice of the product. In this case, reasoning about the controller using a suitable relation of a Goguen category seems to be impossible or at least difficult. Unfortunately, there may exist such noncrisp projections. Consider the Boolean lattice $\mathcal{B}_4 := \{0, a, b, 1\}$ and the following relations represented as $\mathcal{B}_4$-valued matrices:

$$\pi_1 := \begin{pmatrix} 1 & 0 \\ a & b \\ b & a \\ 0 & 1 \end{pmatrix}, \quad \rho_1 := \begin{pmatrix} 1 & 0 \\ b & a \\ a & b \\ 0 & 1 \end{pmatrix}, \quad \pi_2 := \begin{pmatrix} 1 & 0 \\ 1 & 0 \\ 0 & 1 \\ 0 & 1 \end{pmatrix}, \quad \rho_2 := \begin{pmatrix} 1 & 0 \\ 0 & 1 \\ 1 & 0 \\ 0 & 1 \end{pmatrix}.$$

Both pairs (π_1, ρ_1) and (π_2, ρ_2) constitute a product of two copies of a set with two elements, i.e., they fulfill the equations required for a product. The second pair of relations is the usual pair of crisp projections. The first pair is not crisp. But, this example also indicates that in $\mathcal{B}_4$-**Rel** for any pair of projections there is also a crisp version of the corresponding product, i.e., there are crisp relations between the same objects fulfilling the equations required for a product. In our example, one may require without loss of generality that the projections are crisp.

In this chapter, we will investigate when the validity of a set of equations S within a Goguen category $\mathcal{G}$ implies the validity of S in $\mathcal{G}^{\uparrow}$. The application to products, sums and splittings of crisp relations then is obvious. If one of these constructions exists in $\mathcal{G}$, then it exists in $\mathcal{G}^{\uparrow}$, i.e., the corresponding relations may be chosen to be crisp.

Throughout this chapter $\mathcal{L}$ is supposed to be a proper lattice, i.e., a lattice with at least one complete prime filter. We start with a lemma on the function ϑ introduced in Section 2.8.

Lemma 5.55 *Let $\mathcal{L}$ be a complete Brouwerian lattice, and $\mathcal{R}$ be a Dedekind category. For all antitone functions $f : \mathcal{L} \overset{\geq}{\to} \mathcal{R}[A,B]$ and $g : \mathcal{L} \overset{\geq}{\to} \mathcal{R}[B,C]$ we have*

(1) $\vartheta(f;g) = \vartheta(f);\vartheta(g)$,

(2) $\vartheta(f^{\smile}) = \vartheta(f)^{\smile}$.

Proof.

(1) First, we show that $\bigsqcup\limits_{\mathfrak{M}\subseteq\psi(x)} (f(x);g(x)) = (\bigsqcup\limits_{\mathfrak{M}\subseteq\psi(x)} f(x));(\bigsqcup\limits_{\mathfrak{M}\subseteq\psi(x)} g(x))$. The inclusion $\sqsubseteq$ is trivial. Suppose $\mathfrak{M} \subseteq \psi(x)$ and $\mathfrak{M} \subseteq \psi(y)$. Then $\mathfrak{M} \subseteq \psi(x) \cap \psi(y) = \psi(x \wedge y)$. Furthermore, $f(x);g(y) \sqsubseteq f(x \wedge y);g(x \wedge y)$

since f and g are antitone. We conclude that

$$\begin{aligned}
&(\bigsqcup_{\mathfrak{M}\subseteq\psi(x)} f(x));\left(\bigsqcup_{\mathfrak{M}\subseteq\psi(x)} g(x)\right)\\
&= \bigsqcup_{\mathfrak{M}\subseteq\psi(x)} (f(x);\left(\bigsqcup_{\mathfrak{M}\subseteq\psi(x)} g(x)\right)\\
&= \bigsqcup_{\mathfrak{M}\subseteq\psi(x)} \bigsqcup_{\mathfrak{M}\subseteq\psi(y)} (f(x);g(y))\\
&\sqsubseteq \bigsqcup_{\mathfrak{M}\subseteq\psi(x\wedge y)} (f(x\wedge y);g(x\wedge y)) && \text{computation above}\\
&= \bigsqcup_{\mathfrak{M}\subseteq\psi(x)} (f(x);g(x)).
\end{aligned}$$

Now, consider the following computation:

$$\begin{aligned}
(\vartheta(f;g))(\mathfrak{M}) &= \bigsqcup_{\mathfrak{M}\subseteq\psi(x)} (f;g)(x) && \text{definition } \vartheta\\
&= \bigsqcup_{\mathfrak{M}\subseteq\psi(x)} (f(x);g(x)) && \text{definition of ;}\\
&= \left(\bigsqcup_{\mathfrak{M}\subseteq\psi(x)} f(x)\right);\left(\bigsqcup_{\mathfrak{M}\subseteq\psi(x)} g(x)\right) && \text{computation above}\\
&= \vartheta(f)(\mathfrak{M});\vartheta(g)(\mathfrak{M}) && \text{definition } \vartheta\\
&= (\vartheta(f);\vartheta(g))(\mathfrak{M}). && \text{definition of ;}
\end{aligned}$$

(2) The assertion follows immediately from

$$\begin{aligned}
(\vartheta(f^\smile))(\mathfrak{M}) &= \bigsqcup_{\mathfrak{M}\subseteq\psi(x)} f^\smile(x) && \text{definition } \vartheta\\
&= \bigsqcup_{\mathfrak{M}\subseteq\psi(x)} (f(x))^\smile && \text{definition } ^\smile\\
&= \left(\bigsqcup_{\mathfrak{M}\subseteq\psi(x)} f(x)\right)^\smile\\
&= (\vartheta(f)(\mathfrak{M}))^\smile && \text{definition } \vartheta\\
&= (\vartheta(f)^\smile)(\mathfrak{M}). && \text{definition } ^\smile
\end{aligned}$$

□

In the next lemma we have summarized the essential properties of the validity of equations within several categories introduced so far.

Lemma 5.56 *Let $\mathcal{R}^{\mathcal{L}}$ be a Goguen category, t be a term in the language of distributive allegories with greatest elements, σ be an environment over $\mathcal{R}^{\mathcal{L}}$ and σ' be an environment over $\mathcal{R}^{\mathcal{L}}_{\geq}$. Then we have*

(1) $\mathcal{V}_{\mathcal{R}^{\mathcal{L}}}(t)(\sigma) = \tau(\mathcal{V}_{\mathcal{R}^{\mathcal{L}}_{\geq}}(t)(\sigma))$,

(2) $\vartheta(\mathcal{V}_{\mathcal{R}^{\mathcal{L}}_{\geq}}(t)(\sigma')) = \mathcal{V}_{\mathcal{R}^{\mathcal{P}(\mathcal{F}_{\mathcal{L}})}_{\geq}}(t)(\sigma'')$ *where* $\sigma''(a) := \sigma'(a)$ *for all object variables* a *and* $\sigma''(r : a \to b) := \vartheta(\sigma'(r : a \to b))$ *for all relational variables* $r : a \to b$,

(3) $\mathcal{V}_{\mathcal{R}^{\mathcal{L}}_{\geq}}(t)(\sigma')(x) = \mathcal{V}_{\mathcal{R}}(t)(\sigma''')$ *where* $\sigma'''(a) := \sigma'(a)$ *for all object variables* a *and* $\sigma'''(r : a \to b) := \sigma'(r : a \to b)(x)$ *for all relational variables* $r : a \to b$,

(4) *if* $\sigma(r : a \to b)$ *is crisp for all* $r : a \to b \in RV(t)$, *then* $\mathcal{V}_{\mathcal{R}^{\mathcal{L}}}(t)(\sigma)$ *is crisp and we have* $\mathcal{V}_{\mathcal{R}^{\mathcal{L}}}(t)(\sigma) = \dot{R}$ *with* $R := \mathcal{V}_{\mathcal{R}^{\mathcal{L}}_{\geq}}(t)(\sigma)(x)$ *for an arbitrary* $x \neq 0$.

Proof.

(1) We prove the assertion by structural induction.

$t = \perp\!\!\!\perp_{ab}$: We immediately conclude that

$$\begin{aligned} \mathcal{V}_{\mathcal{R}^{\mathcal{L}}}(\perp\!\!\!\perp_{ab})(\sigma) &= \dot{\perp\!\!\!\perp}_{\sigma(a)\sigma(b)} && \text{definition } \mathcal{V}_{\mathcal{R}^{\mathcal{L}}} \\ &= \tau(\perp\!\!\!\perp_{\sigma(a)\sigma(b)}) && \text{definition } \dot{\perp\!\!\!\perp}_{\sigma(a)\sigma(b)} \\ &= \tau(\mathcal{V}_{\mathcal{R}^{\mathcal{L}}_{\geq}}(\perp\!\!\!\perp_{ab})(\sigma)). && \text{definition } \mathcal{V}_{\mathcal{R}^{\mathcal{L}}_{\geq}} \end{aligned}$$

$t \in \{\mathbb{I}_a, \top\!\!\!\top_{ab}\}$: is shown analogously.

$t = r : a \to b$: We immediately conclude that

$$\begin{aligned} &\mathcal{V}_{\mathcal{R}^{\mathcal{L}}}(r : a \to b)(\sigma) \\ &= \sigma(r : a \to b) && \text{definition } \mathcal{V}_{\mathcal{R}^{\mathcal{L}}} \\ &= \tau(\sigma(x)) && \sigma(r : a \to b) \text{ antimorphism} \\ &= \tau(\mathcal{V}_{\mathcal{R}^{\mathcal{L}}_{\geq}}(r : a \to b)(\sigma)). && \text{definition } \mathcal{V}_{\mathcal{R}^{\mathcal{L}}_{\geq}} \end{aligned}$$

$t = t_1 \sqcap t_2$: Again, we immediately conclude that

$$\begin{aligned} &\mathcal{V}_{\mathcal{R}^{\mathcal{L}}}(t_1 \sqcap t_2)(\sigma) \\ &= \mathcal{V}_{\mathcal{R}^{\mathcal{L}}}(t_1)(\sigma) \sqcap \mathcal{V}_{\mathcal{R}^{\mathcal{L}}}(t_2)(\sigma) && \text{definition } \mathcal{V}_{\mathcal{R}^{\mathcal{L}}} \\ &= \tau(\mathcal{V}_{\mathcal{R}^{\mathcal{L}}_{\geq}}(t_1)(\sigma)) \sqcap \tau(\mathcal{V}_{\mathcal{R}^{\mathcal{L}}_{\geq}}(t_2)(\sigma)) && \text{induction hypothesis} \\ &= \tau(\mathcal{V}_{\mathcal{R}^{\mathcal{L}}_{\geq}}(t_1)(\sigma) \sqcap \mathcal{V}_{\mathcal{R}^{\mathcal{L}}_{\geq}}(t_2)(\sigma)) && \text{Lemma 2.46 (2)} \\ &= \tau(\mathcal{V}_{\mathcal{R}^{\mathcal{L}}_{\geq}}(t_1 \sqcap t_2)(\sigma)). && \text{definition } \mathcal{V}_{\mathcal{R}^{\mathcal{L}}_{\geq}} \end{aligned}$$

$t = t_1 \sqcup t_2$: Consider the following computation:

$$\begin{aligned} &\mathcal{V}_{\mathcal{R}^{\mathcal{L}}}(t_1 \sqcup t_2)(\sigma) \\ &= \mathcal{V}_{\mathcal{R}^{\mathcal{L}}}(t_1)(\sigma) \dot{\sqcup} \mathcal{V}_{\mathcal{R}^{\mathcal{L}}}(t_2)(\sigma) && \text{definition } \mathcal{V}_{\mathcal{R}^{\mathcal{L}}} \\ &= \tau(\mathcal{V}_{\mathcal{R}^{\mathcal{L}}}(t_1)(\sigma) \sqcup \mathcal{V}_{\mathcal{R}^{\mathcal{L}}}(t_2)(\sigma)) && \text{definition } \dot{\sqcup} \\ &= \tau(\mathcal{V}_{\mathcal{R}^{\mathcal{L}}_{\geq}}(t_1)(\sigma) \sqcup \mathcal{V}_{\mathcal{R}^{\mathcal{L}}_{\geq}}(t_2)(\sigma)) && \text{induction hypothesis} \\ &= \tau(\mathcal{V}_{\mathcal{R}^{\mathcal{L}}_{\geq}}(t_1 \sqcup t_2)(\sigma)). && \text{definition } \mathcal{V}_{\mathcal{R}^{\mathcal{L}}_{\geq}} \end{aligned}$$

$t = t_1; t_2$**:** Again, consider the following computation:

$$\begin{aligned}
\mathcal{V}_{\mathcal{R}^{\mathcal{L}}}(t_1;t_2)(\sigma) &= \mathcal{V}_{\mathcal{R}^{\mathcal{L}}}(t_1)(\sigma) \mathbin{\breve{;}} \mathcal{V}_{\mathcal{R}^{\mathcal{L}}}(t_2)(\sigma) && \text{definition } \mathcal{V}_{\mathcal{R}^{\mathcal{L}}} \\
&= \tau(\mathcal{V}_{\mathcal{R}^{\mathcal{L}}}(t_1)(\sigma); \mathcal{V}_{\mathcal{R}^{\mathcal{L}}}(t_2)(\sigma)) && \text{definition } \breve{;} \\
&= \tau(\mathcal{V}_{\mathcal{R}^{\mathcal{L}}_{\geq}}(t_1)(\sigma); \mathcal{V}_{\mathcal{R}^{\mathcal{L}}_{\geq}}(t_2)(\sigma)) && \text{induction hypothesis} \\
&= \tau(\mathcal{V}_{\mathcal{R}^{\mathcal{L}}_{\geq}}(t_1;t_2)(\sigma)). && \text{definition } \mathcal{V}_{\mathcal{R}^{\mathcal{L}}_{\geq}}
\end{aligned}$$

$t = t_1^{\smile}$**:** Last but not least, the following computation shows the assertion:

$$\begin{aligned}
\mathcal{V}_{\mathcal{R}^{\mathcal{L}}}(t_1^{\smile})(\sigma) &= (\mathcal{V}_{\mathcal{R}^{\mathcal{L}}}(t_1)(\sigma))^{\smile} && \text{definition } \mathcal{V}_{\mathcal{R}^{\mathcal{L}}} \\
&= \tau(\mathcal{V}_{\mathcal{R}^{\mathcal{L}}_{\geq}}(t_1)(\sigma)))^{\smile} && \text{induction hypothesis} \\
&= \tau((\mathcal{V}_{\mathcal{R}^{\mathcal{L}}_{\geq}}(t_1)(\sigma))^{\smile}) && \text{Lemma 4.32 (2)} \\
&= \tau(\mathcal{V}_{\mathcal{R}^{\mathcal{L}}_{\geq}}(t_1^{\smile})(\sigma)). && \text{definition } \mathcal{V}_{\mathcal{R}^{\mathcal{L}}_{\geq}}
\end{aligned}$$

(2) Again, the assertion is proved by structural induction.

$t = \perp\!\!\!\perp_{ab}$**:** We immediately conclude that

$$\begin{aligned}
&\vartheta(\mathcal{V}_{\mathcal{R}^{\mathcal{L}}_{\geq}}(\perp\!\!\!\perp_{ab})(\sigma'))(\mathfrak{M}) \\
&= \bigvee_{\mathfrak{M}\subseteq\psi(x)} \mathcal{V}_{\mathcal{R}^{\mathcal{L}}_{\geq}}(\perp\!\!\!\perp_{ab})(\sigma')(x) && \text{definition } \vartheta() \\
&= \perp\!\!\!\perp_{\sigma'(a)\sigma'(b)} && \text{definition } \mathcal{V}_{\mathcal{R}^{\mathcal{L}}_{\geq}} \\
&= \mathcal{V}_{\mathcal{R}^{\mathcal{P}(\mathcal{F}_{\mathcal{L}})}_{\geq}}(\perp\!\!\!\perp_{ab})(\sigma'')(\mathfrak{M}). && \text{definition } \mathcal{V}_{\mathcal{R}^{\mathcal{P}(\mathcal{F}_{\mathcal{L}})}_{\geq}}, \\
& && \sigma'(a) = \sigma''(a) \text{ and } \sigma'(b) = \sigma''(b)
\end{aligned}$$

$t \in \{\mathbb{I}_a, \top\!\!\!\top_{ab}\}$ **:** is shown analogously.

$t = r : a \to b$**:** follows immediately from the required property of σ''.

$t = t_1 \sqcap t_2$**:** We immediately conclude that

$$\begin{aligned}
&\vartheta(\mathcal{V}_{\mathcal{R}^{\mathcal{L}}_{\geq}}(t_1 \sqcap t_2)(\sigma')) \\
&= \vartheta((\mathcal{V}_{\mathcal{R}^{\mathcal{L}}_{\geq}}(t_1)(\sigma') \sqcap \mathcal{V}_{\mathcal{R}^{\mathcal{L}}_{\geq}}(t_2)(\sigma'))) && \text{definition } \mathcal{V}_{\mathcal{R}^{\mathcal{L}}_{\geq}} \\
&= \vartheta((\mathcal{V}_{\mathcal{R}^{\mathcal{L}}_{\geq}}(t_1)(\sigma')) \sqcap \vartheta(\mathcal{V}_{\mathcal{R}^{\mathcal{L}}_{\geq}}(t_2)(\sigma'))) && \text{Lemma 2.63 (3)} \\
&= \mathcal{V}_{\mathcal{R}^{\mathcal{P}(\mathcal{F}_{\mathcal{L}})}_{\geq}}(t_1)(\sigma'') \sqcap \mathcal{V}_{\mathcal{R}^{\mathcal{P}(\mathcal{F}_{\mathcal{L}})}_{\geq}}(t_2)(\sigma'') && \text{induction hypothesis} \\
&= \mathcal{V}_{\mathcal{R}^{\mathcal{P}(\mathcal{F}_{\mathcal{L}})}_{\geq}}(t_1 \sqcap t_2)(\sigma''). && \text{definition } \mathcal{V}_{\mathcal{R}^{\mathcal{P}(\mathcal{F}_{\mathcal{L}})}_{\geq}}
\end{aligned}$$

$t \in \{t_1 \sqcup t_2, t_1; t_2, t_1^{\smile}\}$**:** is shown analogously by applying Lemma 2.63 (2), Lemma 5.55 (1) and Lemma 5.55 (2), respectively.

(3) The assertion is trivial since all operations and constants are defined componentwise.

(4) We define an environment over $\mathcal{R}$ by

$$\begin{aligned} \sigma_x(a) &:= \sigma(a) && \text{for all object variables } a, \\ \sigma_x(r : a \to b) &:= \sigma(r : a \to b)(x) && \text{for all relational variables } r : a \to b. \end{aligned}$$

Since crisp relations in $\mathcal{R}^{\mathcal{L}}$ are of the form $\dot{Q}$ for a suitable relation Q in $\mathcal{R}$ we conclude that $\sigma_x(r : a \to b) = \sigma_y(r : a \to b)$ for all $r : a \to b \in \mathrm{RV}(t)$ and $x \neq 0$ and $y \neq 0$. Theorem 4.53 implies $\mathcal{V}_{\mathcal{R}}(t)(\sigma_x) = \mathcal{V}_{\mathcal{R}}(t)(\sigma_y)$, and, hence, $\mathcal{V}_{\mathcal{R}^{\mathcal{L}}_{\geq}}(t)(\sigma)(x) = \mathcal{V}_{\mathcal{R}^{\mathcal{L}}_{\geq}}(t)(\sigma)(y)$ by (3) of this lemma. With other words $\mathcal{V}_{\mathcal{R}^{\mathcal{L}}_{\geq}}(t)(\sigma)$ is apart from 0 the constant function returning R. Consequently, $\tau(\mathcal{V}_{\mathcal{R}^{\mathcal{L}}_{\geq}}(t)(\sigma)) = \dot{R}$, which shows the assertion using (1) of this lemma. □

Now, we are ready to prove our main theorem in this chapter.

Theorem 5.57 *Let $\mathcal{L}$ be a proper Brouwerian lattice with $0 \neq 1$, $\mathcal{R}$ a simple Dedekind category with $\perp\!\!\!\perp_{AB} \neq \top\!\!\!\top_{AB}$ for all objects A and B, $S = \{t_1^i = t_2^i \mid i \in I\}$ be a set of equations in the language of distributive allegories with greatest elements, $V = \{r_1 : a_1 \to b_1, \ldots, r_n : a_n \to b_n\}$ a set of relational variables, σ an environment over $\mathcal{R}^{\mathcal{L}}$ such that $\sigma(r : a \to b)$ is crisp for all relational variables $r : a \to b \in RV(S) \setminus V$, and $f_1, \ldots, f_n$ be elements of $\mathcal{R}^{\mathcal{L}}$ such that*

$$\mathcal{R}^{\mathcal{L}} \models_{\sigma[f_1/r_1:a_1\to b_1,\ldots,f_n/r_n:a_n\to b_n]} t_1^i = t_2^i$$

for all $i \in I$. Then for $U_j := \bigsqcup_{x \in F} f_j(x)$ with $1 \leq j \leq n$ and an arbitrary $F \in \mathcal{F}_{\mathcal{L}}$ we have for all $i \in I$

$$\mathcal{R}^{\mathcal{L}} \models_{\sigma[\dot{U}_1/r_1:a_1\to b_1,\ldots,\dot{U}_n/r_n:a_n\to b_n]} t_1^i = t_2^i.$$

Proof. For brevity, let $\tilde{\sigma} := \sigma[f_1/r_1 : a_1 \to b_1, \ldots, f_n/r_n : a_n \to b_n]$,

$$\begin{aligned} \tilde{\sigma}'(a) &:= \sigma(a) && \text{for all object variables } a, \\ \tilde{\sigma}'(r : a \to b) &:= \vartheta(\tilde{\sigma}(r : a \to b)) && \text{for all relational variables } r : a \to b, \\ \tilde{\sigma}''(a) &:= \tilde{\sigma}'(a) = \sigma(a) && \text{for all object variables } a, \\ \tilde{\sigma}''(r : a \to b) &:= \tilde{\sigma}'(r : a \to b)(\{F\}) && \text{for all relational variables } r : a \to b \end{aligned}$$

and $h_j^i := \mathcal{V}_{\mathcal{R}^{\mathcal{L}}_{\geq}}(t_j^i)(\tilde{\sigma})$ for $j = 1, 2$ and $i \in I$. Then we have

$$\begin{aligned} & \mathcal{V}_{\mathcal{R}^{\mathcal{L}}}(t_1^i)(\tilde{\sigma}) = \mathcal{V}_{\mathcal{R}^{\mathcal{L}}}(t_2^i)(\tilde{\sigma}) \\ \Leftrightarrow\ & \tau(h_1^i) = \tau(h_2^i) && \text{Lemma 5.56 (1)} \\ \Rightarrow\ & \vartheta(\tau(h_1^i)) = \vartheta(\tau(h_2^i)) \end{aligned}$$

$$
\begin{aligned}
&\Rightarrow \tau(\vartheta(\tau(h_1^i))) = \tau(\vartheta(\tau(h_2^i))) && \\
&\Leftrightarrow \tau(\vartheta(h^i)_1) = \tau(\vartheta(h^i)_2) && \text{Lemma 2.64} \\
&\Leftrightarrow \tau(\mathcal{V}_{\mathcal{R}_{\geq}^{\mathcal{P}(\mathcal{F}_{\mathcal{L}})}}(t_1^i)(\tilde{\sigma}')) = \tau(\mathcal{V}_{\mathcal{R}_{\geq}^{\mathcal{P}(\mathcal{F}_{\mathcal{L}})}}(t_2^i)(\tilde{\sigma}')) && \text{Lemma 5.56 (2)} \\
&\Rightarrow \tau(\mathcal{V}_{\mathcal{R}_{\geq}^{\mathcal{P}(\mathcal{F}_{\mathcal{L}})}}(t_1^i)(\tilde{\sigma}'))(\{F\}) = \tau(\mathcal{V}_{\mathcal{R}_{\geq}^{\mathcal{P}(\mathcal{F}_{\mathcal{L}})}}(t_2^i)(\tilde{\sigma}'))(\{F\}) && \\
&\Leftrightarrow (\mathcal{V}_{\mathcal{R}_{\geq}^{\mathcal{P}(\mathcal{F}_{\mathcal{L}})}}(t_1^i)(\tilde{\sigma}'))(\{F\}) = (\mathcal{V}_{\mathcal{R}_{\geq}^{\mathcal{P}(\mathcal{F}_{\mathcal{L}})}}(t_2^i)(\tilde{\sigma}'))(\{F\}) && \text{Lemma 2.63 (4)} \\
&\Leftrightarrow \mathcal{V}_{\mathcal{R}}(t_1^i)(\tilde{\sigma}'') = \mathcal{V}_{\mathcal{R}}(t_2^i)(\tilde{\sigma}''). && \text{Lemma 5.56 (3)}
\end{aligned}
$$

Now, define $\delta := \sigma[\dot{U}_1/r_1 : a_1 \to b_1, \ldots, \dot{U}_n/r_n : a_n \to b_n]$ and

$$
\begin{aligned}
\delta'(a) &:= \delta(a) = \sigma(a) && \text{for all object variables } a, \\
\delta'(r : a \to b) &:= \delta(r : a \to b)(x) && \text{for all relational variables } r : a \to b
\end{aligned}
$$

First of all, we have

$$\mathcal{V}_{\mathcal{R}^{\mathcal{L}}}(t_1^i)(\delta)(0) = \mathbb{T} = \mathcal{V}_{\mathcal{R}^{\mathcal{L}}}(t_2^i)(\delta)(0)$$

since both functions are antimorphisms. Suppose $x \neq 0$. Then $\delta(r : a \to b)$ is crisp for all relational variables $r : a \to b \in \mathrm{RV}(S)$ and Lemma 5.56 (4) implies that $\mathcal{V}_{\mathcal{R}^{\mathcal{L}}}(t_j^i)(\delta)$ is crisp and $\mathcal{V}_{\mathcal{R}^{\mathcal{L}}}(t_j^i)(\delta)(x) = \mathcal{V}_{\mathcal{R}_{\geq}^{\mathcal{L}}}(t_j^i)(\delta)(x)$ since $x \neq 0$. Furthermore, for a relational variable $r : a \to b \in \mathrm{RV}(S) \setminus V$ we have

$$
\begin{aligned}
\tilde{\sigma}''(r : a \to b) &= \tilde{\sigma}'(r : a \to b)(\{F\}) && \text{definition } \tilde{\sigma}'' \\
&= \vartheta(\tilde{\sigma}(r : a \to b))(\{F\}) && \text{definition } \tilde{\sigma}' \\
&= \bigsqcup_{y \in F} \tilde{\sigma}(r : a \to b)(y) && \text{Lemma 2.63 (4)} \\
&= \bigsqcup_{y \in F} \sigma(r : a \to b)(y) && r : a \to b \in \mathrm{RV}(S) \setminus V \text{ and definition } \tilde{\sigma} \\
&= \sigma(r : a \to b)(x) && \sigma(r : a \to b) \text{ is crisp, } 0 \notin F \text{ and } x \neq 0 \\
&= \delta(r : a \to b)(x) && r : a \to b \in \mathrm{RV}(S) \setminus V \text{ and definition } \delta \\
&= \delta'(r : a \to b) && \text{definition } \delta'
\end{aligned}
$$

and for $r_i : a_i \to b_i \in R$ with $i \in I$

$$
\begin{aligned}
\tilde{\sigma}''(r_i : a_i \to b_i) &= \tilde{\sigma}'(r_i : a_i \to b_i)(\{F\}) && \text{definition } \tilde{\sigma}'' \\
&= \vartheta(\tilde{\sigma}(r_i : a_i \to b_i))(\{F\}) && \text{definition } \tilde{\sigma}' \\
&= \vartheta(f_i)(\{F\}) && r_i : a_i \to b_i \in V \\
&= \bigsqcup_{y \in F} f_i(y) && \text{Lemma 2.63 (4)}
\end{aligned}
$$

$$
\begin{aligned}
&= U_i && \text{definition } U_i \\
&= \dot{U}_i(x) && x \neq 0 \\
&= \delta(r_i : a_i \to b_i)(x) && \text{definition } \delta \text{ and} \\
& && r_i : a_i \to b_i \in R \\
&= \delta'(r_i : a_i \to b_i) && \text{definition } \delta'
\end{aligned}
$$

such that $\tilde{\sigma}''$ and δ' are equal for all relational variables from $\mathrm{RV}(S)$. We obtain

$$
\begin{aligned}
\mathcal{V}_{\mathcal{R}^{\mathcal{L}}}(t_j^i)(\delta)(x) &= \mathcal{V}_{\mathcal{R}^{\mathcal{L}}_{\geq}}(t_j^i)(\delta)(x) && \text{see above} \\
&= \mathcal{V}_{\mathcal{R}}(t_j^i)(\delta') && \text{Lemma 5.56 (3)} \\
&= \mathcal{V}_{\mathcal{R}}(t_j^i)(\tilde{\sigma}''). && \text{Theorem 4.53 and computation above}
\end{aligned}
$$

Finally, we have

$$
\begin{aligned}
\mathcal{V}_{\mathcal{R}^{\mathcal{L}}}(t_1^i)(\delta)(x) &= \mathcal{V}_{\mathcal{R}}(t_1^i)(\tilde{\sigma}'') \\
&= \mathcal{V}_{\mathcal{R}}(t_2^i)(\tilde{\sigma}'') \\
&= \mathcal{V}_{\mathcal{R}^{\mathcal{L}}}(t_2^i)(\delta)(x),
\end{aligned}
$$

and, hence, $\mathcal{R}^{\mathcal{L}} \models_{\sigma[\dot{U}_1/r_1:a_1\to b_1,\ldots,\dot{U}_n/r_n:a_n\to b_n]} t_1^i = t_2^i$. □

Using the pseudo-representation functor $P_{\mathcal{G}}$ the previous theorem may be transferred to arbitrary Goguen categories. For a relation R fulfilling a set of equations S we may define the corresponding antimorphism by $f(\alpha) := P_{\mathcal{G}}(R)(\alpha) = (\alpha_A \backslash R)^{\downarrow}$. By the previous theorem we obtain $U = \bigsqcup_{\alpha\in F} f(\alpha) = \bigsqcup_{\alpha\in F} (\alpha_A\backslash R)^{\downarrow}$, and, hence, a crisp relation Q fulfilling S by

$$
\begin{aligned}
Q &:= P_{\mathcal{G}}^{-1}(\dot{U}) \\
&= \bigsqcup_{\beta\in\mathrm{Sc}[\mathcal{G}]} (\beta_A; \dot{U}(\beta)) && \text{definition } P_{\mathcal{G}}^{-1} \\
&= \bigsqcup_{\perp\!\!\!\perp\neq\beta\in\mathrm{Sc}[\mathcal{G}]} (\beta_A; \dot{U}(\beta)) \\
&= \bigsqcup_{\perp\!\!\!\perp\neq\beta\in\mathrm{Sc}[\mathcal{G}]} \left(\beta_A; \left(\bigsqcup_{\alpha\in F} (\alpha_A\backslash R)^{\downarrow}\right)\right) && \text{definition } \dot{U} \\
&= \left(\bigsqcup_{\perp\!\!\!\perp\neq\beta\in\mathrm{Sc}[\mathcal{G}]} \beta_A\right); \left(\bigsqcup_{\alpha\in F} (\alpha_A\backslash R)^{\downarrow}\right) \\
&= \bigsqcup_{\alpha\in F} (\alpha_A\backslash R)^{\downarrow}.
\end{aligned}
$$

Compare the last expression with representation of $R^{\uparrow}$ by its cuts. Our relation Q is computed similar by restricting the scalars to elements of the complete prime filter F.

We aim at the following corollary:

Corollary 5.58 *Let $\mathcal{G}$ be a Goguen category with a proper underlying lattice* $\mathrm{Sc}[\mathcal{G}]$, $S = \{t_1^i = t_2^i \mid i \in I\}$ *be a set of equations in the language of distributive allegories with greatest elements,* $V = \{r_1 : a_1 \to b_1, \ldots, r_n : a_n \to b_n\}$ *a set of relational variables,* σ *an environment over* $\mathcal{G}$ *such that* $\sigma(r : a \to b)$ *is crisp for all relational variables* $r : a \to b \in RV(S) \setminus V$, *and* $R_1, \ldots, R_n$ *be relations such that*

$$\mathcal{G} \models_{\sigma[R_1/r_1:a_1 \to b_1, \ldots, R_n/r_n:a_n \to b_n]} t_1^i = t_2^i$$

for all $i \in I$. *Then for* $Q_j := \bigsqcup_{\alpha \in F} (\alpha_{\sigma(a_j)} \backslash R_j)^{\downarrow}$ *with* $1 \leq j \leq n$ *and an arbitrary* $F \in \mathcal{F}_{\mathrm{Sc}[\mathcal{G}]}$ *we have for all* $i \in I$

$$\mathcal{G} \models_{\sigma[Q_1/r_1:a_1 \to b_1, \ldots, Q_n/r_n:a_n \to b_n]} t_1^i = t_2^i.$$

Since products, sums, and splittings induced by crisp symmetric idempotents are defined by equations in the sense of the previous corollary, we may require in a Goguen category with a proper underlying lattice $\mathrm{Sc}[\mathcal{G}]$ without loss of generality that the related relations are crisp.

Unfortunately, we were just able to prove Theorem 5.57 for Goguen categories $\mathcal{R}^{\mathcal{L}}$ with a proper lattice $\mathcal{L}$. On the other hand, we did not find a counterexample to this theorem in general. This observation may motivate the following conjecture:

Conjecture 5.59 *The existential part of Theorem 5.57 is true for all Goguen categories of the form* $\mathcal{R}^{\mathcal{L}}$.

Obviously, if the previous conjecture is proved, the result could be transferred to arbitrary Goguen categories in a similar way.

5.10 OPERATIONS DERIVED FROM LATTICE-ORDERED SEMIGROUPS

In Chapter 3 we have defined some $*$-based operations for a loos $(\mathcal{L}, *, e, z)$ on $\mathcal{L}$-fuzzy relations. Now, we want to investigate an abstract counterpart of these operations within an arbitrary Goguen category and a loos $(\mathrm{Sc}[\mathcal{G}], *, \epsilon, \zeta)$ on the scalars of $\mathcal{G}$.

Throughout this section, unless otherwise stated, let $\mathcal{G}$ be a Goguen category and $*$ an operation such that $(\mathrm{Sc}[\mathcal{G}], *, \epsilon, \zeta)$ is a loos. Furthermore, suppose $\otimes$ is a binary operation on relations such that

(1) $\otimes$ is defined for all pairs of relations from $\mathcal{G}[A, A]$ for all objects A and its value is within $\mathcal{G}[B, B]$ for a suitable B and if $Q \otimes R$ is defined for $Q : A \to B$ and $R : C \to D$, then $\otimes$ is defined for all pairs of relations from $\mathcal{G}[A, B]$ and $\mathcal{G}[C, D]$ and its value is within $\mathcal{G}[E, F]$ for suitable E and F,

(2) if $Q \otimes R$ is defined for $Q : A \to B$ and $R : C \to D$ and within $\mathcal{G}[E, F]$, then $Q \otimes \perp\!\!\!\perp_{CD} = \perp\!\!\!\perp_{AB} \otimes R = \perp\!\!\!\perp_{EF}$,

(3) if $\mathbb{T}_{AB} \otimes \mathbb{T}_{CD}$ is defined and within $\mathcal{G}[E,F]$, then $\mathbb{T}_{AB} \otimes \mathbb{T}_{CD} = \mathbb{T}_{EF}$,

(4) $\otimes$ distributes over arbitrary unions in both arguments, i.e., for all relations Q, Q_i, R, R_i with $i \in I$ we have

$$Q \otimes \left(\bigsqcup_{i\in I} R_i\right) = \bigsqcup_{i\in I}(Q \otimes R_i) \quad \text{and} \quad \left(\bigsqcup_{i\in I} Q_i\right) \otimes R = \bigsqcup_{i\in I}(Q_i \otimes R)$$

whenever the application of $\otimes$ is defined,

(5) for all $\alpha, \beta \in \mathrm{Sc}[\mathcal{G}]$ and relations $Q : A \to B, R : C \to D$ such that $Q \otimes R$ is defined and within $\mathcal{G}[E,F]$ we have

$$(\alpha_E \sqcap \beta_E); (Q \otimes R) = (\alpha_A; Q) \otimes (\beta_C; R),$$

(6) $\otimes$ is closed on $\mathcal{G}^{\uparrow}$, i.e., for all crisp relations Q, R such that $Q \otimes R$ is defined $Q \otimes R$ is crisp.

Notice that $\sqcap$ and ; satisfy the properties above. (1),(2), and (4) follow immediately from the definition of a Dedekind category. For meet property (3) is trivial and for composition it follows from the fact that $\mathcal{G}$ is uniform. Property (6) is true since the crisp relations are closed under the relational operations. Finally, property (5) is shown as follows:

$$\begin{aligned}
(\alpha_A \sqcap \beta_A); (Q \sqcap R) &= (\alpha_A \sqcap \beta_A); \mathbb{T}_{AB} \sqcap Q \sqcap R && \text{Lemma 4.24 (2)}\\
&= \alpha_A; \mathbb{T}_{AB} \sqcap \beta_A; \mathbb{T}_{AB} \sqcap Q \sqcap R && \text{Lemma 4.24 (3)}\\
&= \alpha_A; Q \sqcap \beta_A; R && \text{Lemma 4.24 (2),}\\
(\alpha_A \sqcap \beta_A); Q; S &= \alpha_A; \beta_A; Q; S && \text{Lemma 4.9 (3)}\\
&= \alpha_A; Q; \beta_B; S && \text{Lemma 5.14}
\end{aligned}$$

Now, we may define the $*$-based operation $Q \otimes_* R$ as follows: It is defined via the cut representation of Q and R.

Definition 5.60 *Let $Q : A \to B, R : C \to D$ be relations such that $Q \otimes R$ is defined and within $\mathcal{G}[E,F]$. Then we define*

$$Q \otimes_* R := \bigsqcup_{\alpha,\beta\in \mathrm{Sc}[\mathcal{G}]} (\alpha * \beta)_E; ((\alpha_A \backslash Q)^{\downarrow} \otimes (\beta_C \backslash R)^{\downarrow}).$$

Notice that $(\alpha * \beta)_E$ in the definition above denotes the corresponding scalar $\alpha * \beta \in \mathrm{Sc}[\mathcal{G}]$ on the object E. Furthermore, by our convention on the notion of scalars we have $(\alpha \sqcap \beta)_A = \alpha_A \sqcap \beta_A$ and $(\alpha \sqcup \beta)_A = \alpha_A \sqcup \beta_A$.

Since $\otimes$ and the left residual in the second argument are monotone the operation $\otimes_*$ is also monotone in both arguments.

For $\mathcal{L}$-fuzzy relations the lattice $\mathcal{L}$ and the lattice of scalar elements are isomorphic. Therefore, the operation $*$ may be considered as to be defined on $\mathcal{L}$ or on the scalar elements. If we identify these lattices, α_A^{x*y} and $(\alpha^x * \alpha^y)_A$ denote the same scalar on the set A. Theorem 3.7 shows that for $\mathcal{L}$-fuzzy relations and $\otimes \in \{\sqcap, \circ\}$ the definitions given in Chapter 3 are special cases of the abstract definition above.

Now, we want to give an alternative definition of $Q \otimes_* R$.

Lemma 5.61 *Let $Q : A \to B, R : C \to D$ be relations such that $Q \otimes R$ is defined and within $\mathcal{G}[E, F]$. Then we have*

$$Q \otimes_* R = \bigsqcup_{\alpha \in \mathrm{Sc}[\mathcal{G}]} \alpha_E; \left(\bigsqcup_{\substack{\beta,\gamma \in \mathrm{Sc}[\mathcal{G}] \\ \beta * \gamma \sqsupseteq \alpha}} ((\beta_A \backslash Q)^{\downarrow} \otimes (\gamma_C \backslash R)^{\downarrow}) \right).$$

Proof. This may be obtained from

$$\begin{aligned}
Q \otimes_* R &= \bigsqcup_{\alpha,\beta \in \mathrm{Sc}[\mathcal{G}]} (\alpha * \beta)_E; ((\alpha_A \backslash Q)^{\downarrow} \otimes (\beta_C \backslash R)^{\downarrow}) && \text{definition } \otimes_* \\
&= \bigsqcup_{\alpha \in \mathrm{Sc}[\mathcal{G}]} \alpha_E; \left(\bigsqcup_{\substack{\beta,\gamma \in \mathrm{Sc}[\mathcal{G}] \\ \beta * \gamma = \alpha}} ((\beta_A \backslash Q)^{\downarrow} \otimes (\gamma_C \backslash R)^{\downarrow}) \right) \\
&= \bigsqcup_{\alpha \in \mathrm{Sc}[\mathcal{G}]} \alpha_E; \left(\bigsqcup_{\substack{\beta,\gamma \in \mathrm{Sc}[\mathcal{G}] \\ \beta * \gamma \sqsupseteq \alpha}} ((\beta_A \backslash Q)^{\downarrow} \otimes (\gamma_C \backslash R)^{\downarrow}) \right),
\end{aligned}$$

where the last equality is shown as follows: The inclusion $\sqsubseteq$ is trivial and $\sqsupseteq$ is implied by $\alpha_E; ((\beta_A \backslash Q)^{\downarrow} \otimes (\gamma_C \backslash R)^{\downarrow}) \sqsubseteq (\beta * \gamma)_E; ((\beta_A \backslash Q)^{\downarrow} \otimes (\gamma_C \backslash R)^{\downarrow})$ for all $\beta * \gamma \sqsupseteq \alpha$ in $\mathrm{Sc}[\mathcal{G}]$. □

There is a connection between the previous lemma and the α-cut representation of $Q \otimes_* R$. Define $f : \mathrm{Sc}[\mathcal{G}] \to \mathcal{G}^{\uparrow}[E, F]$ by

$$f(\alpha) := \bigsqcup_{\substack{\beta,\gamma \in \mathrm{Sc}[\mathcal{G}] \\ \beta * \gamma \sqsupseteq \alpha}} ((\beta_A \backslash Q)^{\downarrow} \otimes (\gamma_C \backslash R)^{\downarrow}).$$

From the following computation with $\alpha \sqsubseteq \alpha'$

$$\begin{aligned}
f(\alpha') &= \bigsqcup_{\substack{\beta,\gamma \in \mathrm{Sc}[\mathcal{G}] \\ \beta * \gamma \sqsupseteq \alpha'}} ((\beta_A \backslash Q)^{\downarrow} \otimes (\gamma_C \backslash R)^{\downarrow}) && \text{definition } f \\
&\sqsubseteq \bigsqcup_{\substack{\beta,\gamma \in \mathrm{Sc}[\mathcal{G}] \\ \beta * \gamma \sqsupseteq \alpha}} ((\beta_A \backslash Q)^{\downarrow} \otimes (\gamma_C \backslash R)^{\downarrow}) && \alpha \sqsubseteq \alpha' \sqsubseteq \beta * \gamma \\
&= f(\alpha) && \text{definition } f
\end{aligned}$$

we conclude that f is antitone. By Lemma 5.49 (2) and the previous lemma

$$Q \otimes_* R = \bigsqcup_{\alpha \in \mathrm{Sc}[\mathcal{G}]} (\alpha_E; \tau(f)(\alpha))$$

follows. From Lemma 5.45 we conclude $\tau(f)(\alpha) = (\alpha_E \backslash Q \otimes_* R)^{\downarrow}$.

Unfortunately, $\otimes_*$ is not an operation on scalars since for $\epsilon = \mathbb{I}, \zeta = \perp\!\!\!\perp$ and $\otimes =;$ we have

$$\begin{aligned}
\alpha_A;_* \perp\!\!\!\perp_{AA} &= \bigsqcup_{\gamma,\delta\in\mathrm{Sc}[\mathcal{G}]} ((\gamma * \delta)_A; (\gamma_A\backslash\alpha_A)^{\downarrow}; (\delta_A\backslash\perp\!\!\!\perp_{AA})^{\downarrow}) && \text{definition } ;_* \\
&= \bigsqcup_{\substack{\gamma,\delta\in\mathrm{Sc}[\mathcal{G}]\\ \gamma\neq\perp\!\!\!\perp}} ((\gamma * \delta)_A; (\gamma_A\backslash\alpha_A)^{\downarrow}; (\delta_A\backslash\perp\!\!\!\perp_{AA})^{\downarrow}) && \text{since } \zeta = \perp\!\!\!\perp \\
&= \bigsqcup_{\substack{\gamma,\delta\in\mathrm{Sc}[\mathcal{G}]\\ \perp\!\!\!\perp\neq\gamma\sqsubseteq\alpha}} ((\gamma * \delta)_A; (\delta_A\backslash\perp\!\!\!\perp_{AA})^{\downarrow}) && \text{Lemma 5.20} \\
&= \bigsqcup_{\substack{\gamma,\delta\in\mathrm{Sc}[\mathcal{G}]\\ \perp\!\!\!\perp\neq\gamma\sqsubseteq\alpha}} ((\gamma * \delta)_A; \top\!\!\!\top_{AA}) && \text{definition residual} \\
&= \left(\bigsqcup_{\substack{\gamma,\delta\in\mathrm{Sc}[\mathcal{G}]\\ \perp\!\!\!\perp\neq\gamma\sqsubseteq\alpha}} (\gamma * \delta)_A \right); \top\!\!\!\top_{AA} \\
&= (\alpha * \mathbb{I})_A; \top\!\!\!\top_{AA} && * \text{ monotone} \\
&= \alpha_A; \top\!\!\!\top_{AA}. && \epsilon = \mathbb{I}
\end{aligned}$$

Therefore, we define a new operation for scalars by

$$\alpha_A \,\tilde{\otimes}_*\, \beta_A := ((\alpha_A; \top\!\!\!\top_{AA}) \otimes_* (\beta_A; \top\!\!\!\top_{AA})) \sqcap \mathbb{I}_B.$$

By Property (1) of $\otimes$ the operation $\tilde{\otimes}_*$ is well-defined.

Lemma 5.62 *Let α and β be scalars such that $\alpha_A \otimes \beta_A$ is defined and within $\mathcal{G}[B, B]$. Then we have*

(1) $(\alpha_A; \top\!\!\!\top_{AA}) \otimes_* (\beta_A; \top\!\!\!\top_{AA}) = (\alpha * \beta)_B; \top\!\!\!\top_{BB}$,

(2) $(\alpha_A; \top\!\!\!\top_{AA}) \otimes_* (\beta_A; \top\!\!\!\top_{AA}) = ((\alpha_A; \top\!\!\!\top_{AA}) \otimes_* (\beta_A; \top\!\!\!\top_{AA})); \top\!\!\!\top_{BB}$.

Proof.

(1) For brevity, let $R := (\gamma_A\backslash(\alpha_A; \top\!\!\!\top_{AA}))^{\downarrow} \otimes (\delta_A\backslash(\beta_A; \top\!\!\!\top_{AA}))^{\downarrow}$. Then we immediately conclude that

$$\begin{aligned}
&(\alpha_A; \top\!\!\!\top_{AA}) \otimes_* (\beta_A; \top\!\!\!\top_{AA}) \\
&= \bigsqcup_{\gamma,\delta\in\mathrm{Sc}[\mathcal{G}]} ((\gamma * \delta)_B; R) && \text{definition } \otimes_* \\
&= \bigsqcup_{\substack{\gamma\sqsubseteq\alpha\\ \delta\sqsubseteq\beta}} ((\gamma * \delta)_B; (\top\!\!\!\top_{AA} \otimes \top\!\!\!\top_{AA})) && \text{Lemma 5.20}
\end{aligned}$$

$$= \bigsqcup_{\substack{\gamma \sqsubseteq \alpha \\ \delta \sqsubseteq \beta}} ((\gamma * \delta)_B ; \mathbb{T}_{BB}) \qquad \text{Property (3) of } \otimes$$

$$= \left(\bigsqcup_{\substack{\gamma \sqsubseteq \alpha \\ \delta \sqsubseteq \beta}} (\gamma * \delta)_B \right) ; \mathbb{T}_{BB}$$

$$= (\alpha * \beta)_B ; \mathbb{T}_{BB} \qquad \text{monotonicity of } *$$

(2) The computation

$$\begin{aligned}
&(\alpha_A ; \mathbb{T}_{AA}) \otimes_* (\beta_A ; \mathbb{T}_{AA}) \\
&= (\alpha * \beta)_B ; \mathbb{T}_{BB} && \text{(1) of this lemma} \\
&= (\alpha * \beta)_B ; \mathbb{T}_{BB} ; \mathbb{T}_{BB} && \text{Lemma 4.21 (2)} \\
&= (\alpha_A ; \mathbb{T}_{AA}) \otimes_* (\beta_A ; \mathbb{T}_{AA}) ; \mathbb{T}_{BB} && \text{(1) of this lemma}
\end{aligned}$$

shows the assertion. □

Using $\tilde{\otimes}_*$ we may compare $*$ with the corresponding $*$-based operation as follows:

Lemma 5.63 *Let α and β be scalars such that $\alpha_A \otimes \beta_A$ is defined and within $\mathcal{G}[B,B]$. Then $\alpha_A \tilde{\otimes}_* \beta_A = (\alpha * \beta)_B$.*

Proof. We immediately conclude that

$$\begin{aligned}
\alpha_A \tilde{\otimes}_* \beta_A &= ((\alpha_A ; \mathbb{T}_{AA}) \otimes_* (\beta_A ; \mathbb{T}_{AA})) \sqcap \mathbb{I}_B && \text{definition } \tilde{\otimes}_* \\
&= (\alpha * \beta)_B ; \mathbb{T}_{BB} \sqcap \mathbb{I}_B && \text{Lemma 5.62 (1)} \\
&= (\alpha * \beta)_B . && \text{Lemma 4.24 (1)}
\end{aligned}$$ □

By Lemma 2.66 (2) $\sqcap$ is the strongest t-norm-like operation. This leads to the following property of the corresponding $*$-based operation:

Lemma 5.64 *Suppose $\otimes$ is defined on $\mathcal{G}[A,B]$ and $\mathcal{G}[C,D]$ and its value is within $\mathcal{G}[E,F]$. Then we have $\otimes_* = \otimes$ iff $* = \sqcap$, i.e., $Q \otimes_* R = Q \otimes R$ for all $Q : A \to B$ and $R : C \to D$ iff $* = \sqcap$.*

Proof. The implication $\Leftarrow$ follows from

$$\begin{aligned}
&Q \otimes_\sqcap R \\
&= \bigsqcup_{\alpha,\beta \in \mathrm{Sc}[\mathcal{G}]} ((\alpha \sqcap \beta)_E ; ((\alpha_A \backslash Q)^\downarrow \otimes (\beta_C \backslash R)^\downarrow)) && \text{definition } \otimes_*
\end{aligned}$$

$$= \bigsqcup_{\alpha,\beta\in \mathrm{Sc}[\mathcal{G}]} ((\alpha_E \sqcap \beta_E);((\alpha_A\backslash Q)^{\downarrow} \otimes (\beta_C\backslash R)^{\downarrow}))$$

$$= \bigsqcup_{\alpha,\beta\in \mathrm{Sc}[\mathcal{G}]} ((\alpha_A;(\alpha_A\backslash Q)^{\downarrow}) \otimes (\beta_C;(\beta_C\backslash R)^{\downarrow})) \qquad \text{Property (5) of } \otimes$$

$$= \left(\bigsqcup_{\alpha\in \mathrm{Sc}[\mathcal{G}]} (\alpha_A;(\alpha_A\backslash Q)^{\downarrow})\right) \otimes \left(\bigsqcup_{\beta\in \mathrm{Sc}[\mathcal{G}]} (\beta_C;(\beta_C\backslash R)^{\downarrow})\right) \qquad \text{Property (4) of } \otimes$$

$$= Q \otimes R. \qquad \text{Theorem 5.35}$$

The computation

$$\begin{aligned}
(\alpha * \beta)_B &= \alpha_A \,\tilde{\otimes}_*\, \beta_A && \text{Lemma 5.63}\\
&= ((\alpha_A;\mathbb{T}_{AA}) \otimes_* (\beta_A;\mathbb{T}_{AA})) \sqcap \mathbb{I}_B && \text{definition } \tilde{\otimes}_*\\
&= ((\alpha_A;\mathbb{T}_{AA}) \otimes (\beta_A;\mathbb{T}_{AA})) \sqcap \mathbb{I}_B && \text{assumption}\\
&= ((\alpha_A;\mathbb{T}_{AA}) \otimes_\sqcap (\beta_A;\mathbb{T}_{AA})) \sqcap \mathbb{I}_B && \text{as shown above}\\
&= \alpha_A \,\tilde{\otimes}_\sqcap\, \beta_A && \text{definition } \tilde{\otimes}_\sqcap\\
&= (\alpha \sqcap \beta)_B && \text{Lemma 5.63}
\end{aligned}$$

proves the other implication. □

Since $\sqcup$ is the weakest t-conorm-like operation by Lemma 2.67 (2) we get a similar result in the special case $\otimes = \sqcap$.

Lemma 5.65 *We have* $\sqcap_* = \sqcup$ *iff* $* = \sqcup$, *i.e.,* $Q \sqcap_* R = Q \sqcup R$ *for all* $Q, R : A \to B$ *iff* $* = \sqcup$.

Proof. The implication $\Leftarrow$ follows from

$$Q \sqcap_\sqcup R$$

$$= \bigsqcup_{\alpha,\beta\in \mathrm{Sc}[\mathcal{G}]} ((\alpha \sqcup \beta)_A;((\alpha_A\backslash Q)^{\downarrow} \sqcap (\beta_A\backslash R)^{\downarrow})) \qquad \text{definition } \sqcap_\sqcup$$

$$= \bigsqcup_{\alpha,\beta\in \mathrm{Sc}[\mathcal{G}]} ((\alpha_A \sqcup \beta_A);((\alpha_A\backslash Q)^{\downarrow} \sqcap (\beta_A\backslash R)^{\downarrow}))$$

$$= \bigsqcup_{\alpha,\beta\in \mathrm{Sc}[\mathcal{G}]} (\alpha_A;((\alpha_A\backslash Q)^{\downarrow} \sqcap (\beta_A\backslash R)^{\downarrow})$$

$$\sqcup\ \beta_A;((\alpha_A\backslash Q)^{\downarrow} \sqcap (\beta_A\backslash R)^{\downarrow}))$$

$$\sqsubseteq \bigsqcup_{\alpha,\beta\in \mathrm{Sc}[\mathcal{G}]} (\alpha_A;(\alpha_A\backslash Q)^{\downarrow} \sqcup \beta_A;(\beta_A\backslash R)^{\downarrow})$$

$$= \left(\bigsqcup_{\alpha\in \mathrm{Sc}[\mathcal{G}]} (\alpha_A;(\alpha_A\backslash Q)^{\downarrow})\right) \sqcup \left(\bigsqcup_{\beta\in \mathrm{Sc}[\mathcal{G}]} (\beta_A;(\beta_A\backslash R)^{\downarrow})\right)$$

$$= Q \sqcup R \qquad \text{Theorem 5.35}$$

$$= \left(\bigsqcup_{\alpha \in \mathrm{Sc}[\mathcal{G}]} (\alpha_A; ((\alpha_A \backslash Q)^{\downarrow} \sqcap \mathbb{T}_{AB})) \right) \qquad \text{Theorem 5.35}$$

$$\sqcup \left(\bigsqcup_{\beta \in \mathrm{Sc}[\mathcal{G}]} (\beta_A; (\mathbb{T}_{AB} \sqcap (\beta_A \backslash R)^{\downarrow})) \right)$$

$$= \left(\bigsqcup_{\alpha \in \mathrm{Sc}[\mathcal{G}]} ((\alpha_A \sqcup \mathbb{\perp}_{AA}); ((\alpha_A \backslash Q)^{\downarrow} \sqcap (\mathbb{\perp}_{AA} \backslash R)^{\downarrow})) \right) \qquad \text{definition residual}$$

$$\sqcup \left(\bigsqcup_{\beta \in \mathrm{Sc}[\mathcal{G}]} ((\mathbb{\perp}_{AA} \sqcup \beta_A); ((\mathbb{\perp}_{AA} \backslash Q)^{\downarrow} \sqcap (\beta_A \backslash R)^{\downarrow})) \right)$$

$$\sqsubseteq \bigsqcup_{\alpha, \beta \in \mathrm{Sc}[\mathcal{G}]} ((\alpha_A \sqcup \beta_A); ((\alpha_A \backslash Q)^{\downarrow} \sqcap (\beta_A \backslash R)^{\downarrow}))$$

$$= \bigsqcup_{\alpha, \beta \in \mathrm{Sc}[\mathcal{G}]} ((\alpha \sqcup \beta)_A; ((\alpha_A \backslash Q)^{\downarrow} \sqcap (\beta_A \backslash R)^{\downarrow}))$$

$$= Q \sqcap_{\sqcup} R. \qquad \text{definition } \sqcap_{\sqcup}$$

The computation

$$\begin{aligned}
(\alpha * \beta)_A &= \alpha_A \tilde{\sqcap}_* \beta_A && \text{Lemma 5.63} \\
&= ((\alpha_A; \mathbb{T}_{AA}) \sqcap_* (\beta_A; \mathbb{T}_{AA})) \sqcap \mathbb{I}_A && \text{definition } \sqcap_* \\
&= ((\alpha_A; \mathbb{T}_{AA}) \sqcup (\beta_A; \mathbb{T}_{AA})) \sqcap \mathbb{I}_A && \text{assumption} \\
&= (\alpha_A; \mathbb{T}_{AA} \sqcap \mathbb{I}_A) \sqcup (\beta_A; \mathbb{T}_{AA} \sqcap \mathbb{I}_A) && \\
&= \alpha_A \sqcup \beta_A && \text{Lemma 4.24 (1)} \\
&= (\alpha \sqcup \beta)_A && \text{see above}
\end{aligned}$$

proves the other implication. □

Suppose $(\mathcal{L}, *, 1, 0)$ is a loos and R is a crisp $\mathcal{L}$-fuzzy relation. Then we have

$$(Q \sqcap_* R)(x, y) = Q(x, y) * R(x, y) = Q(x, y) \sqcap R(x, y) = (Q \sqcap R)(x, y).$$

The next lemma shows that this property is true in general.

Lemma 5.66 *Let $\epsilon = \mathbb{I}$, and $Q : A \to B$ and $R : C \to D$ be relations such that $Q \otimes R$ is defined and within $\mathcal{G}[E, F]$. If Q or R is crisp, then we have $Q \otimes_* R = Q \otimes R$.*

Proof. Suppose R is crisp. The computation

$$\begin{aligned}
Q \otimes_* R &= \bigsqcup_{\alpha, \beta \in \mathrm{Sc}[\mathcal{G}]} ((\alpha * \beta)_E; ((\alpha_A \backslash Q)^{\downarrow} \otimes (\beta_A \backslash R)^{\downarrow})) && \text{definition } \otimes_* \\
&= \bigsqcup_{\substack{\alpha \in \mathrm{Sc}[\mathcal{G}] \\ \beta \neq \mathbb{\perp}}} ((\alpha * \beta)_E; ((\alpha_A \backslash Q)^{\downarrow} \otimes (\beta_C \backslash R)^{\downarrow})) && \text{Lemma 2.66 (1)}
\end{aligned}$$

$$
\begin{aligned}
&= \bigsqcup_{\substack{\alpha\in\mathrm{Sc}[\mathcal{G}]\\ \beta\neq\perp\!\!\!\perp}} ((\alpha*\beta)_E;((\alpha_A\backslash Q)^{\downarrow}\otimes R)) && \text{Lemma 5.12 (1)}\\
&= \bigsqcup_{\alpha\in\mathrm{Sc}[\mathcal{G}]} \left(\left(\bigsqcup_{\beta\neq\perp\!\!\!\perp}(\alpha*\beta)_E\right);((\alpha_A\backslash Q)^{\downarrow}\otimes R)\right)\\
&= \bigsqcup_{\alpha\in\mathrm{Sc}[\mathcal{G}]} ((\alpha*\mathbb{I})_E;((\alpha_A\backslash Q)^{\downarrow}\otimes R)) && * \text{ is monotone}\\
&= \bigsqcup_{\alpha\in\mathrm{Sc}[\mathcal{G}]} (\alpha_E;((\alpha_A\backslash Q)^{\downarrow}\otimes R)) && \epsilon=\mathbb{I}\\
&= \bigsqcup_{\alpha\in\mathrm{Sc}[\mathcal{G}]} ((\alpha_E\sqcap\mathbb{I}_E);((\alpha_A\backslash Q)^{\downarrow}\otimes R))\\
&= \bigsqcup_{\alpha\in\mathrm{Sc}[\mathcal{G}]} ((\alpha_A;(\alpha\backslash Q)^{\downarrow})\otimes R) && \text{Property (5) of }\otimes\\
&= \left(\bigsqcup_{\alpha\in\mathrm{Sc}[\mathcal{G}]} (\alpha_A;(\alpha_A\backslash Q)^{\downarrow})\right)\otimes R && \text{Property (4) of }\otimes\\
&= Q\otimes R && \text{Theorem 5.35}
\end{aligned}
$$

shows the assertion. The second assertion is shown analogously. □

Lemma 2.66 may also be lifted to the $*$-based operations as follows:

Lemma 5.67 *Let $\epsilon=\mathbb{I}$, and $Q:A\to B$ and $R:C\to D$ be relations such that $Q\otimes R$ is defined and within $\mathcal{G}[E,F]$. Then we have*

(1) $Q\otimes_* \perp\!\!\!\perp_{CD} = \perp\!\!\!\perp_{AB}\otimes_* R = \perp\!\!\!\perp_{EF}$,

(2) $Q\sqcap_* \top\!\!\!\top_{AB} = Q$ *and* $\top\!\!\!\top_{CD}\sqcap_* R = R$,

(3) $Q\otimes_{\circledast} R\sqsubseteq Q\otimes_* R\sqsubseteq Q\otimes R$.

Proof.

(1) The assertion follows immediately from

$$
\begin{aligned}
Q\otimes_*\perp\!\!\!\perp_{CD} &= Q\otimes\perp\!\!\!\perp_{CD} && \text{Lemma 5.66}\\
&= \perp\!\!\!\perp_{EF}. && \text{Property (2) of }\otimes
\end{aligned}
$$

The second assertion is shown analogously.

(2) Consider the computation

$$
\begin{aligned}
Q\sqcap_*\top\!\!\!\top_{AB} &= Q\sqcap\top\!\!\!\top_{AB} && \text{Lemma 5.66}\\
&= Q.
\end{aligned}
$$

Again, the second assertion is shown analogously.

(3) follows immediately from Lemma 2.66 and Lemma 5.64. □

Replacing $\mathbb{I}$ by $\perp\!\!\!\perp$ we obtain a slightly modified dual version of the previous two lemmata.

Lemma 5.68 *Let $\epsilon = \perp\!\!\!\perp$, and $Q : A \to B$ and $R : C \to D$ be relations such that $Q \otimes R$ is defined and within $\mathcal{G}[E,F]$. If Q or R is crisp, then $Q \otimes_* R = (Q \otimes \top\!\!\!\top_{CD}) \sqcup (\top\!\!\!\top_{AB} \otimes R)$.*

Proof. Suppose R is crisp. Consider the computations

$$\begin{aligned}
&\bigsqcup_{\alpha\in\mathrm{Sc}[\mathcal{G}]} ((\alpha * \perp\!\!\!\perp)_E; ((\alpha_A\backslash Q)^{\downarrow} \otimes \top\!\!\!\top_{CD})) \\
&= \bigsqcup_{\alpha\in\mathrm{Sc}[\mathcal{G}]} (\alpha_E; ((\alpha_A\backslash Q)^{\downarrow} \otimes \top\!\!\!\top_{CD})) && \text{Lemma 2.67 (1)} \\
&= \bigsqcup_{\alpha\in\mathrm{Sc}[\mathcal{G}]} ((\alpha_E \sqcap \mathbb{I}_E); ((\alpha_A\backslash Q)^{\downarrow} \otimes \top\!\!\!\top_{CD})) \\
&= \bigsqcup_{\alpha\in\mathrm{Sc}[\mathcal{G}]} ((\alpha_A; (\alpha_A\backslash Q)^{\downarrow}) \otimes \top\!\!\!\top_{CD}) && \text{Property (5) of } \otimes \\
&= \left(\bigsqcup_{\alpha\in\mathrm{Sc}[\mathcal{G}]} (\alpha_A; (\alpha_A\backslash Q)^{\downarrow})\right) \otimes \top\!\!\!\top_{CD} && \text{Property (4) of } \otimes \\
&= Q \otimes \top\!\!\!\top_{CD}, && \text{Theorem 5.35}
\end{aligned}$$

$$\begin{aligned}
&\bigsqcup_{\substack{\alpha\in\mathrm{Sc}[\mathcal{G}] \\ \beta\neq\perp\!\!\!\perp}} ((\alpha * \beta)_E; ((\alpha_A\backslash Q)^{\downarrow} \otimes R)) \\
&= \bigsqcup_{\alpha\in\mathrm{Sc}[\mathcal{G}]} \left(\left(\bigsqcup_{\beta\neq\perp\!\!\!\perp} (\alpha * \beta)_E\right); ((\alpha_A\backslash Q)^{\downarrow} \otimes R)\right) \\
&= \bigsqcup_{\alpha\in\mathrm{Sc}[\mathcal{G}]} (\alpha * \mathbb{I})_E; ((\alpha_A\backslash Q)^{\downarrow} \otimes R) && * \text{ is monotone} \\
&= \bigsqcup_{\alpha\in\mathrm{Sc}[\mathcal{G}]} ((\alpha_A\backslash Q)^{\downarrow} \otimes R) && \text{Lemma 2.67 (1)} \\
&= \left(\bigsqcup_{\alpha\in\mathrm{Sc}[\mathcal{G}]} (\alpha_A\backslash Q)^{\downarrow}\right) \otimes R && \text{Property (4) of } \otimes \\
&= ((\perp\!\!\!\perp_{AA}\backslash Q)^{\downarrow}) \otimes R && \text{Corollary 4.15 (4)} \\
&= \top\!\!\!\top^{\downarrow}{}_{AB} \otimes R && \text{definition residual} \\
&= \top\!\!\!\top_{AB} \otimes R.
\end{aligned}$$

Together this implies

$$\begin{aligned}
Q \otimes_* R &= \bigsqcup_{\alpha,\beta\in\mathrm{Sc}[\mathcal{G}]} ((\alpha * \beta)_E; ((\alpha_A\backslash Q)^{\downarrow} \otimes (\beta_C\backslash R)^{\downarrow})) && \text{definition } \otimes_* \\
&= \bigsqcup_{\alpha\in\mathrm{Sc}[\mathcal{G}]} ((\alpha * \perp\!\!\!\perp)_E; ((\alpha_A\backslash Q)^{\downarrow} \otimes (\perp\!\!\!\perp_{CC}\backslash R)^{\downarrow}))
\end{aligned}$$

$$\sqcup \bigsqcup_{\substack{\alpha \in \mathrm{Sc}[\mathcal{G}] \\ \beta \neq \perp\!\!\!\perp}} ((\alpha * \beta)_E; ((\alpha_A \backslash Q)^{\downarrow} \otimes (\beta_C \backslash R)^{\downarrow}))$$

$$= \bigsqcup_{\alpha \in \mathrm{Sc}[\mathcal{G}]} ((\alpha * \perp\!\!\!\perp)_E; ((\alpha_A \backslash Q)^{\downarrow} \otimes \top\!\!\!\top_{CD})) \qquad \text{definition residual}$$

$$\sqcup \bigsqcup_{\substack{\alpha \in \mathrm{Sc}[\mathcal{G}] \\ \beta \neq \perp\!\!\!\perp}} ((\alpha * \beta)_E; ((\alpha_A \backslash Q)^{\downarrow} \otimes R)) \qquad \text{Lemma 5.12 (1)}$$

$$= (Q \otimes \top\!\!\!\top_{CD}) \sqcup (\top\!\!\!\top_{AB} \otimes R). \qquad \text{see above}$$

The second assertion is shown analogously. □

The next lemma is again a lifting of a corresponding result (Lemma 2.67) for loos's.

Lemma 5.69 *Let $\epsilon = \perp\!\!\!\perp$, and $Q : A \to B$ and $R : C \to D$ be relations such that $Q \otimes R$ is defined and within $\mathcal{G}[E, F]$. Then we have*

(1) $Q \otimes_* \top\!\!\!\top_{CD} = \top\!\!\!\top_{AB} \otimes_* R = \top\!\!\!\top_{EF}$,

(2) $Q \sqcap_* \perp\!\!\!\perp_{AB} = Q$ and $\perp\!\!\!\perp_{CD} \sqcap_* R = R$,

(3) $Q \otimes_{\sqcup} R \sqsubseteq Q \otimes_* R \sqsubseteq Q \otimes_{\boxplus} R$.

Proof.

(1) The assertion follows immediately from

$$\begin{aligned} Q \otimes_* \top\!\!\!\top_{CD} &= (Q \otimes \top\!\!\!\top_{CD}) \sqcup (\top\!\!\!\top_{AB} \otimes \top\!\!\!\top_{CD}) && \text{Lemma 5.68} \\ &= (Q \otimes \top\!\!\!\top_{CD}) \sqcup \top\!\!\!\top_{EF} && \text{Property (3) of } \otimes \\ &= \top\!\!\!\top_{EF}. \end{aligned}$$

The second assertion is shown analogously.

(2) Consider the computation

$$\begin{aligned} Q \sqcap_* \perp\!\!\!\perp_{AB} &= (Q \sqcap \top\!\!\!\top_{AB}) \sqcup (\top\!\!\!\top_{AB} \sqcap \perp\!\!\!\perp_{AB}) && \text{Lemma 5.68} \\ &= Q. \end{aligned}$$

Again, the second assertion is shown analogously.

(3) follows immediately from Lemma 2.67. □

In the rest of this section we want to prove some basic properties of the $*$-based operations and the structures induced by them. We start with the following theorem:

Theorem 5.70 *Let $\otimes$ be commutative. Then the operation $\otimes_*$ is commutative iff $(\mathrm{Sc}[\mathcal{G}], *, \epsilon, \zeta)$ is a commutative loos.*

Proof. The implication $\Leftarrow$ follows from

$$\begin{aligned} Q \otimes_* R &= \bigsqcup_{\alpha,\beta \in \mathrm{Sc}[\mathcal{G}]} ((\alpha * \beta)_E; ((\alpha_A \backslash Q)^{\downarrow} \otimes (\beta_C \backslash R)^{\downarrow})) && \text{definition } \otimes_* \\ &= \bigsqcup_{\alpha,\beta \in \mathrm{Sc}[\mathcal{G}]} ((\beta * \alpha)_E; ((\beta_C \backslash R)^{\downarrow} \otimes (\alpha_A \backslash Q)^{\downarrow}) && \otimes \text{ and } * \text{ commutative} \\ &= R \otimes_* Q. && \text{definition } \otimes_* \end{aligned}$$

The computation

$$\begin{aligned} (\alpha * \beta)_B &= \alpha_A \tilde{\otimes}_* \beta_A && \text{Lemma 5.63} \\ &= ((\alpha_A; \mathbb{T}_{AA}) \otimes_* (\beta_A; \mathbb{T}_{AA})) \sqcap \mathbb{I}_B && \text{definition } \tilde{\otimes}_* \\ &= ((\beta_A; \mathbb{T}_{AA}) \otimes_* (\alpha_A; \mathbb{T}_{AA})) \sqcap \mathbb{I}_B && \text{assumption} \\ &= \beta_A \tilde{\otimes}_* \alpha_A && \text{definition } \tilde{\otimes}_* \\ &= (\beta * \alpha)_B && \text{Lemma 5.63} \end{aligned}$$

shows the other implication. □

Next, we want to focus on associativity. Therefore, we need the following technical lemma:

Lemma 5.71 *Let* $(\mathrm{Sc}[\mathcal{G}], *, \epsilon, \zeta)$ *be a cloos,* $g : \mathrm{Sc}[\mathcal{G}] \to \mathcal{G}^{\uparrow}[A, B]$ *be antitone,* $h : \mathrm{Sc}[\mathcal{G}] \to \mathcal{G}^{\uparrow}[C, D]$ *an antimorphism and* $\otimes$ *defined on* $\mathcal{G}[A, B]$ *and* $\mathcal{G}[C, D]$*. Furthermore, let*

$$f(\alpha) := \bigsqcup_{\substack{\beta,\gamma \in \mathrm{Sc}[\mathcal{G}] \\ \beta * \gamma \sqsupseteq \alpha}} (\tau(g)(\beta) \otimes h(\gamma)), \qquad \bar{f}(\alpha) := \bigsqcup_{\substack{\beta,\gamma \in \mathrm{Sc}[\mathcal{G}] \\ \beta * \gamma \sqsupseteq \alpha}} (g(\beta) \otimes h(\gamma)).$$

Then we have $\tau(f) = \tau(\bar{f})$.

Proof. The inclusion $\sqsupseteq$ is trivial since $g \sqsubseteq \tau(g)$ and $\otimes, \sqcup$ and τ are monotone.

Obviously, $\bar{f}$ is antitone and by Property (6) of $\otimes$ a function from $\mathrm{Sc}[\mathcal{G}]$ to $\mathcal{G}^{\uparrow}[E, F]$ for suitable objects E and F. Therefore, we may prove the other inclusion by fixed point induction. We define a predicate

$$\mathfrak{P}(k, l) \;:\Longleftrightarrow\; \forall \alpha \in \mathrm{Sc}[\mathcal{G}] : \bigsqcup_{\substack{\beta,\gamma \in \mathrm{Sc}[\mathcal{G}] \\ \beta * \gamma \sqsupseteq \alpha}} (k(\beta) \otimes h(\gamma)) \sqsubseteq l(\alpha).$$

This predicate is admissible since $\mathfrak{P}(k_i, l_i)$ for all $i \in I$ implies

$$\begin{aligned} &\forall \alpha \in \mathrm{Sc}[\mathcal{G}] : \bigsqcup_{i \in I} \bigsqcup_{\beta * \gamma \sqsupseteq \alpha} (k_i(\beta) \otimes h(\gamma)) \sqsubseteq \bigsqcup_{i \in I} l_i(\alpha) \\ \Leftrightarrow\; &\forall \alpha \in \mathrm{Sc}[\mathcal{G}] : \bigsqcup_{\beta * \gamma \sqsupseteq \alpha} \bigsqcup_{i \in I} (k_i(\beta) \otimes h(\gamma)) \sqsubseteq \left(\bigsqcup_{i \in I} l_i \right)(\alpha) && \text{definition } \sqcup \end{aligned}$$

$$\Leftrightarrow \forall\alpha \in \mathrm{Sc}[\mathcal{G}] : \bigsqcup_{\beta*\gamma\sqsupseteq\alpha} \left(\left(\bigsqcup_{i\in I} k_i(\beta)\right) \otimes h(\gamma)\right) \sqsubseteq \left(\bigsqcup_{i\in I} l_i\right)(\alpha) \quad \text{Prop. (4) of } \otimes$$

$$\Leftrightarrow \forall\alpha \in \mathrm{Sc}[\mathcal{G}] : \bigsqcup_{\beta*\gamma\sqsupseteq\alpha} \left(\left(\bigsqcup_{i\in I} k_i\right)(\beta) \otimes h(\gamma)\right) \sqsubseteq \left(\bigsqcup_{i\in I} l_i\right)(\alpha) \quad \text{definition } \sqcup$$

$$\Leftrightarrow \mathfrak{P}\left(\bigsqcup_{i\in I} k_i, \bigsqcup_{i\in I} l_i\right). \quad \text{definition } \mathfrak{P}$$

The base case $\mathfrak{P}(g, \bar{f})$ is trivial. In order to prove the induction step, we want to show the following property:

$$(*) \qquad \bigsqcup_{\beta*\gamma\sqsupseteq\alpha} \bigsqcup_{\sqcup M=\beta} \bigsqcap_{\delta\in M} (k(\delta) \otimes h(\gamma)) \sqsubseteq \bigsqcup_{\sqcup N\sqsupseteq\alpha} \bigsqcap_{\eta\in N} \bigsqcup_{\mu*\nu\sqsupseteq\eta} (k(\mu) \otimes h(\nu)).$$

Suppose $\beta * \gamma \sqsupseteq \alpha$ and $\bigsqcup M = \beta$. If $M = \emptyset$, the left side of $(*)$ equals $\perp\!\!\!\perp_{EF}$ and the inclusion is trivial. Therefore, let $M \neq \emptyset$. Then we define $N_\gamma := \{\delta * \gamma \mid \delta \in M\}$ and conclude that

$$\begin{aligned}
\bigsqcup N_\gamma &= \bigsqcup_{\delta\in M} (\delta * \gamma) && \text{definition } N_\gamma \\
&= \left(\left(\bigsqcup M\right) * \gamma\right) && * \text{ is continuous and } M \neq \emptyset \\
&= \beta * \gamma && \bigsqcup M = \beta \\
&\sqsupseteq && \alpha.
\end{aligned}$$

Furthermore, we have $k(\delta) \otimes h(\gamma) \sqsubseteq \bigsqcup_{\mu*\nu\sqsupseteq\delta*\gamma} (k(\mu) \otimes h(\nu))$ for all $\delta \in M$ since $\delta * \gamma \sqsupseteq \delta * \gamma$. This implies $\bigsqcap_{\delta\in M} (k(\delta) \otimes h(\gamma)) \sqsubseteq \bigsqcap_{\eta\in N_\gamma} \bigsqcup_{\mu*\nu\sqsupseteq\eta} (k(\mu) \otimes h(\nu))$, and, hence, $(*)$. Now, suppose $\mathfrak{P}(k, l)$. Then we conclude for $\alpha \in \mathrm{Sc}[\mathcal{G}]$

$$\begin{aligned}
&\bigsqcup_{\beta*\gamma\sqsupseteq\alpha} (\varphi(k)(\beta) \otimes h(\gamma)) \\
&= \bigsqcup_{\beta*\gamma\sqsupseteq\alpha} \left(\left(\bigsqcup_{\sqcup M=\beta} \bigsqcap_{\delta\in M} k(\delta)\right) \otimes h(\gamma)\right) && \text{definition } \varphi \\
&= \bigsqcup_{\beta*\gamma\sqsupseteq\alpha} \bigsqcup_{\sqcup M=\beta} \left(\left(\bigsqcap_{\delta\in M} k(\delta)\right) \otimes h(\gamma)\right) && \text{Property (4) of } \otimes \\
&\sqsubseteq \bigsqcup_{\beta*\gamma\sqsupseteq\alpha} \bigsqcup_{\sqcup M=\beta} \bigsqcap_{\delta\in M} (k(\delta) \otimes h(\gamma)) && \otimes \text{ monotone} \\
&\sqsubseteq \bigsqcup_{\sqcup N\sqsupseteq\alpha} \bigsqcap_{\eta\in N} \bigsqcup_{\mu*\nu\sqsupseteq\eta} (k(\mu) \otimes h(\nu)) && \text{by } (*) \\
&\sqsubseteq \bigsqcup_{\sqcup N\sqsupseteq\alpha} \bigsqcap_{\eta\in N} l(\eta) && \text{induction hypothesis} \\
&= \varphi(l)(\alpha), && \text{Lemma 2.42}
\end{aligned}$$

and, hence, $\mathfrak{P}(\varphi(k),\varphi(l))$. The principle of fixed point induction gives us $f \sqsubseteq \tau(\bar{f})$, which implies $\tau(f) \sqsubseteq \tau^2(\bar{f}) = \tau(\bar{f})$. $\square$

Notice that a version of the previous lemma, where $h(\gamma)$ and $g(\beta)$ resp. $\tau(g)(\beta)$ are exchanged, may also be proved.

Lemma 5.72 *Let* $(\mathrm{Sc}[\mathcal{G}], *_1, \epsilon_1, \zeta_1)$ *and* $(\mathrm{Sc}[\mathcal{G}], *_2, \epsilon_2, \zeta_2)$ *be clooses. Furthermore, suppose* $Q : A \to B, R : C \to D$ *and* $S : E \to F$ *and* $Q \otimes R : G \to H, R \otimes S : I \to J$ *and* $(Q \otimes R) \otimes S, Q \otimes (R \otimes S) : K \to L$. *Then we have*

(1) $(Q \otimes_{*_1} R) \otimes_{*_2} S$
$$= \bigsqcup_{\alpha,\beta,\gamma \in \mathrm{Sc}[\mathcal{G}]} (((\alpha *_1 \beta) *_2 \gamma)_K; (((\alpha_A \backslash Q)^{\downarrow} \otimes (\beta_C \backslash R)^{\downarrow}) \otimes (\gamma_E \backslash S)^{\downarrow})),$$

(2) $Q \otimes_{*_1} (R \otimes_{*_2} S)$
$$= \bigsqcup_{\alpha,\beta,\gamma \in \mathrm{Sc}[\mathcal{G}]} ((\alpha *_1 (\beta *_2 \gamma))_K; ((\alpha_A \backslash Q)^{\downarrow} \otimes ((\beta_C \backslash R)^{\downarrow} \otimes (\gamma_E \backslash S)^{\downarrow}))).$$

Proof.

(1) Define the following functions:

$$g(\alpha) := \bigsqcup_{\substack{\beta,\gamma \in \mathrm{Sc}[\mathcal{G}] \\ \beta *_1 \gamma \sqsupseteq \alpha}} ((\beta_A \backslash Q)^{\downarrow} \otimes (\gamma_C \backslash R)^{\downarrow}),$$
$$h(\alpha) := (\alpha_E \backslash S)^{\downarrow},$$
$$f(\alpha) := \bigsqcup_{\substack{\beta,\gamma \in \mathrm{Sc}[\mathcal{G}] \\ \beta *_2 \gamma \sqsupseteq \alpha}} ((\beta_G \backslash (Q \otimes_{*_1} R))^{\downarrow} \otimes h(\gamma)),$$
$$\bar{f}(\alpha) := \bigsqcup_{\substack{\beta,\gamma \in \mathrm{Sc}[\mathcal{G}] \\ \beta *_2 \gamma \sqsupseteq \alpha}} (g(\beta) \otimes h(\gamma)).$$

$f, \bar{f}$ and g are antitone and by Property (6) of $\otimes$ functions from $\mathrm{Sc}[\mathcal{G}]$ to crisp relations. Furthermore, h is an antimorphism, and we have

$$\begin{aligned}
& f(\alpha) \\
&= \bigsqcup_{\beta *_2 \gamma \sqsupseteq \alpha} ((\beta_G \backslash (Q \otimes_{*_1} R))^{\downarrow} \otimes h(\gamma)) && \text{definition } f \\
&= \bigsqcup_{\beta *_2 \gamma \sqsupseteq \alpha} \left(\left(\beta_G \backslash \left(\bigsqcup_{\delta \in \mathrm{Sc}[\mathcal{G}]} (\delta_G; g(\delta)) \right) \right)^{\downarrow} \otimes h(\gamma) \right) && \text{Lemma 5.61} \\
&= \bigsqcup_{\beta *_2 \gamma \sqsupseteq \alpha} (\tau(g)(\beta_G) \otimes h(\gamma)) && \text{Lemma 5.49 (1),} \\
& \bar{f}(\alpha) \\
&= \bigsqcup_{\beta *_2 \gamma \sqsupseteq \alpha} (g(\beta) \otimes h(\gamma)) && \text{definition } \bar{f}
\end{aligned}$$

$$= \bigsqcup_{\beta *_2 \gamma \sqsupseteq \alpha} \left(\left(\bigsqcup_{\mu *_1 \nu \sqsupseteq \beta} ((\mu_A \backslash Q)^{\downarrow} \otimes (\nu_C \backslash R)^{\downarrow}) \right) \otimes h(\gamma) \right) \qquad \text{definition } g$$

$$= \bigsqcup_{\beta *_2 \gamma \sqsupseteq \alpha} \bigsqcup_{\mu *_1 \nu \sqsupseteq \beta} (((\mu_A \backslash Q)^{\downarrow} \otimes (\nu_C \backslash R)^{\downarrow}) \otimes h(\gamma)) \qquad \text{Prop. (4) of } \otimes$$

$$= \bigsqcup_{\beta *_2 \gamma \sqsupseteq \alpha} \bigsqcup_{\mu *_1 \nu \sqsupseteq \beta} (((\mu_A \backslash Q)^{\downarrow} \otimes (\nu_C \backslash R)^{\downarrow}) \otimes (\gamma_E \backslash S)^{\downarrow}) \qquad \text{definition } h$$

$$= \bigsqcup_{(\mu *_1 \nu) *_2 \gamma \sqsupseteq \alpha} (((\mu_A \backslash Q)^{\downarrow} \otimes (\nu_C \backslash R)^{\downarrow}) \otimes (\gamma_E \backslash S)^{\downarrow}),$$

$$\bigsqcup_{\alpha \in \mathrm{Sc}[\mathcal{G}]} (\alpha_K ; \bar{f}(\alpha))$$

$$= \bigsqcup_{\alpha \in \mathrm{Sc}[\mathcal{G}]} \left(\alpha_K ; \left(\bigsqcup_{(\mu *_1 \nu) *_2 \gamma \sqsupseteq \alpha} (((\mu_A \backslash Q)^{\downarrow} \otimes (\nu_C \backslash R)^{\downarrow}) \otimes (\gamma_E \backslash S)^{\downarrow}) \right) \right)$$

$$= \bigsqcup_{\alpha \in \mathrm{Sc}[\mathcal{G}]} \left(\alpha_K ; \left(\bigsqcup_{(\mu *_1 \nu) *_2 \gamma = \alpha} (((\mu_A \backslash Q)^{\downarrow} \otimes (\nu_C \backslash R)^{\downarrow}) \otimes (\gamma_E \backslash S)^{\downarrow}) \right) \right)$$

$$= \bigsqcup_{\alpha, \beta, \gamma \in \mathrm{Sc}[\mathcal{G}]} (((\alpha *_1 \beta) *_2 \gamma)_K ; (((\alpha_A \backslash Q)^{\downarrow} \otimes (\beta_C \backslash R)^{\downarrow}) \otimes (\gamma_E \backslash S)^{\downarrow})),$$

where the second equality is shown as follows: The inclusion $\sqsupseteq$ is trivial and $\sqsubseteq$ is implied by

$$\alpha_K ; (((\mu_A \backslash Q)^{\downarrow} \otimes (\nu_C \backslash R)^{\downarrow}) \otimes (\gamma_E \backslash S)^{\downarrow})$$
$$\sqsubseteq ((\mu *_1 \nu) *_2 \gamma) ; (((\mu_A \backslash Q)^{\downarrow} \otimes (\nu_C \backslash R)^{\downarrow}) \otimes (\gamma_E \backslash S)^{\downarrow})$$

for all $(\mu *_1 \nu) *_2 \gamma \sqsupseteq \alpha$ in $\mathrm{Sc}[\mathcal{G}]$. Finally, we have

$$(Q \otimes_{*_1} R) \otimes_{*_2} S = \bigsqcup_{\alpha \in \mathrm{Sc}[\mathcal{G}]} (\alpha_K ; f(\alpha)) \qquad \text{Lemma 5.61}$$

$$= \bigsqcup_{\alpha \in \mathrm{Sc}[\mathcal{G}]} (\alpha_K ; \tau(f)(\alpha)) \qquad \text{Lemma 5.49 (2)}$$

$$= \bigsqcup_{\alpha \in \mathrm{Sc}[\mathcal{G}]} (\alpha_K ; \tau(\bar{f})(\alpha)) \qquad \text{Lemma 5.71 and the first computation above}$$

$$= \bigsqcup_{\alpha \in \mathrm{Sc}[\mathcal{G}]} (\alpha_K ; \bar{f}(\alpha)) \qquad \text{Lemma 5.49 (2),}$$

such that the assertion follows from the computations above.

(2) is shown analogously. □

Now, we are ready to state our theorem about associativity of $\otimes_*$.

Theorem 5.73 *Let $\otimes$ be associative, and $(\mathrm{Sc}[\mathcal{G}], *, \epsilon, \zeta)$ be complete. Then $\otimes_*$ is associative iff $(\mathrm{Sc}[\mathcal{G}], *, \epsilon, \zeta)$ is a losg.*

Proof. The implication $\Leftarrow$ follows immediately from Lemma 5.72. Suppose $\otimes_*$ is associative. Then $\otimes$ maps pairs of relations from $\mathcal{G}[A,A]$ to $\mathcal{G}[A,A]$ and we have

$$
\begin{aligned}
&(\alpha_A \tilde{\otimes}_* \beta_A);\mathbb{T}_{AA} \\
&= (((\alpha_A;\mathbb{T}_{AA}) \otimes_* (\beta_A;\mathbb{T}_{AA})) \sqcap \mathbb{I}_A);\mathbb{T}_{BB} && \text{definition } \tilde{\otimes}_* \\
&= (((\alpha_A;\mathbb{T}_{AA}) \otimes_* (\beta_A;\mathbb{T}_{AA}));\mathbb{T}_{AA} \sqcap \mathbb{I}_A);\mathbb{T}_{AA} && \text{Lemma 5.62 (2)} \\
&= ((\alpha_A;\mathbb{T}_{AA}) \otimes_* (\beta_A;\mathbb{T}_{AA}));\mathbb{T}_{AA} \sqcap \mathbb{T}_{AA} && \text{Lemma 4.23 (1)} \\
&= (\alpha_A;\mathbb{T}_{AA}) \otimes_* (\beta_A;\mathbb{T}_{AA}). && \text{Lemma 5.62 (2)}
\end{aligned}
$$

Then for all $\alpha, \beta, \gamma \in \mathrm{Sc}[\mathcal{G}]$ we conclude that

$$
\begin{aligned}
&((\alpha * \beta) * \gamma)_A \\
&= (\alpha * \beta)_A \tilde{\otimes}_* \gamma_A && \text{Lemma 5.63} \\
&= (\alpha_A \tilde{\otimes}_* \beta_A) \tilde{\otimes}_* \gamma_A && \text{Lemma 5.63} \\
&= (((\alpha_A \tilde{\otimes}_* \beta_A);\mathbb{T}_{AA}) \otimes_* (\gamma_A;\mathbb{T}_{AA})) \sqcap \mathbb{I}_A && \text{definition } \tilde{\otimes}_* \\
&= ((\alpha_A;\mathbb{T}_{AA}) \otimes_* (\beta_A;\mathbb{T}_{AA})) \otimes_* (\gamma_A;\mathbb{T}_{AA})) \sqcap \mathbb{I}_A. && \text{see above}
\end{aligned}
$$

The equality $(\alpha * (\beta * \gamma))_A = ((\alpha_A;\mathbb{T}_{AA}) \otimes_* ((\beta_A;\mathbb{T}_{AA}) \otimes_* (\gamma_A;\mathbb{T}_{AA}))) \sqcap \mathbb{I}_A$ follows analogously. □

If $\otimes$ is composition, one may ask for the categorical structure induced by $;_*$. The answer is given in the next theorem.

Theorem 5.74 *Let* $(\mathrm{Sc}[\mathcal{G}], *, \epsilon, \zeta)$ *be complete and suppose that there is an object* A *in* $\mathcal{G}$ *such that* $\mathbb{T}_{AA} \neq \mathbb{I}_A$*. Then* $\mathcal{G}$ *together with composition* $;_*$ *and identity morphisms* ϵ *is a category iff* $(\mathrm{Sc}[\mathcal{G}], *, \epsilon, \zeta)$ *is a losg with* $\zeta = \perp\!\!\!\perp$.

Proof. First of all, we have

$$
\begin{aligned}
Q;_* \epsilon_B &= \bigsqcup_{\alpha,\beta \in \mathrm{Sc}[\mathcal{G}]} ((\alpha * \beta)_A; (\alpha_A \backslash Q)^{\downarrow}; (\beta_B \backslash \epsilon_B)^{\downarrow}) && \text{definition } ;_* \\
&= \left(\bigsqcup_{\substack{\alpha,\beta \in \mathrm{Sc}[\mathcal{G}] \\ \beta \neq \perp\!\!\!\perp}} ((\alpha * \beta)_A; (\alpha_A \backslash Q)^{\downarrow}; (\beta_B \backslash \epsilon_B)^{\downarrow}) \right) \\
&\quad \sqcup \left(\bigsqcup_{\alpha \in \mathrm{Sc}[\mathcal{G}]} ((\alpha * \perp\!\!\!\perp)_A; (\alpha_A \backslash Q)^{\downarrow}; \mathbb{T}_{BB}) \right) && \text{definition residual} \\
&= \left(\bigsqcup_{\substack{\alpha,\beta \in \mathrm{Sc}[\mathcal{G}] \\ \perp\!\!\!\perp \neq \beta \sqsubseteq \epsilon}} ((\alpha * \beta)_A; (\alpha_A \backslash Q)^{\downarrow}) \right) && \text{Lemma 5.20} \\
&\quad \sqcup \left(\bigsqcup_{\alpha \in \mathrm{Sc}[\mathcal{G}]} ((\alpha * \perp\!\!\!\perp)_A; (\alpha_A \backslash Q)^{\downarrow}; \mathbb{T}_{BB}) \right)
\end{aligned}
$$

$$= \left(\bigsqcup_{\alpha \in \mathrm{Sc}[\mathcal{G}]} \left(\left(\bigsqcup_{\perp\!\!\!\perp \neq \beta \sqsubseteq \epsilon} (\alpha * \beta)_A \right) ; (\alpha_A \backslash Q)^{\downarrow} \right) \right)$$

$$\sqcup \left(\bigsqcup_{\alpha \in \mathrm{Sc}[\mathcal{G}]} ((\alpha * \perp\!\!\!\perp)_A ; (\alpha_A \backslash Q)^{\downarrow} ; \top\!\!\!\top_{BB}) \right)$$

$$= \left(\bigsqcup_{\alpha \in \mathrm{Sc}[\mathcal{G}]} ((\alpha * \epsilon)_A ; (\alpha_A \backslash Q)^{\downarrow}) \right) \qquad * \text{ monotone}$$

$$\sqcup \left(\bigsqcup_{\alpha \in \mathrm{Sc}[\mathcal{G}]} ((\alpha * \perp\!\!\!\perp)_A ; (\alpha_A \backslash Q)^{\downarrow} ; \top\!\!\!\top_{BB}) \right)$$

$$= \left(\bigsqcup_{\alpha \in \mathrm{Sc}[\mathcal{G}]} (\alpha_A ; (\alpha_A \backslash Q)^{\downarrow}) \right) \qquad \epsilon \text{ neutral element}$$

$$\sqcup \left(\bigsqcup_{\alpha \in \mathrm{Sc}[\mathcal{G}]} ((\alpha * \perp\!\!\!\perp)_A ; (\alpha_A \backslash Q)^{\downarrow} ; \top\!\!\!\top_{BB}) \right)$$

$$= Q \sqcup \left(\bigsqcup_{\alpha \in \mathrm{Sc}[\mathcal{G}]} ((\alpha * \perp\!\!\!\perp)_A ; (\alpha_A \backslash Q)^{\downarrow} ; \top\!\!\!\top_{BB}) \right). \qquad \text{Theorem 5.35}$$

Analogously, we get $\epsilon_A ;_* Q = Q \sqcup (\bigsqcup_{\alpha \in \mathrm{Sc}[\mathcal{G}]} ((\perp\!\!\!\perp * \alpha)_A ; \top\!\!\!\top_{AA} ; (\alpha_B \backslash Q)^{\downarrow}))$. Using Theorem 5.73, we know that for $\Leftarrow$ it is sufficient to show that ϵ is the identity. This follows for $\zeta = \perp\!\!\!\perp$ immediately from the computation above.

Again, using Theorem 5.73 it is sufficient for $\Rightarrow$ to show that $\zeta = \perp\!\!\!\perp$. Suppose ϵ is the identity and A is an object with $\top\!\!\!\top_{AA} \neq \mathbb{I}_A$. Then we have

$$\gamma_A = \gamma_A ;_* \epsilon_A$$

$$= \gamma_A \sqcup \left(\bigsqcup_{\alpha \in \mathrm{Sc}[\mathcal{G}]} ((\alpha * \perp\!\!\!\perp)_A ; (\alpha_A \backslash \gamma_A)^{\downarrow} ; \top\!\!\!\top_{AA}) \right) \qquad \text{computation above}$$

$$= \gamma_A \sqcup \left(\bigsqcup_{\alpha \sqsubseteq \gamma} ((\alpha * \perp\!\!\!\perp)_A ; \top\!\!\!\top_{AA}) \right) \qquad \text{Lemma 5.20}$$

$$= \gamma_A \sqcup \left(\bigsqcup_{\alpha \sqsubseteq \gamma} (\alpha * \perp\!\!\!\perp)_A \right) ; \top\!\!\!\top_{AA}$$

$$= \gamma_A \sqcup (\gamma * \perp\!\!\!\perp)_A ; \top\!\!\!\top_{AA}, \qquad * \text{ monotone}$$

which is equivalent to $(\gamma * \perp\!\!\!\perp)_A ; \top\!\!\!\top_{AA} \sqsubseteq \gamma_A$. From Lemma 5.19 we conclude that $(\gamma * \perp\!\!\!\perp)_A = \perp\!\!\!\perp_{AA}$ since $\top\!\!\!\top_{AA} \neq \perp\!\!\!\perp_{AA}$ and $\top\!\!\!\top_{AA} \not\sqsubseteq \mathbb{I}_A$. $(\perp\!\!\!\perp * \gamma)_A = \perp\!\!\!\perp_{AA}$ is shown analogously such that $\zeta = \perp\!\!\!\perp$ follows. □

Since the converse operation is well-behaved we get the following theorem:

Theorem 5.75 *Let* $(\mathrm{Sc}[\mathcal{G}], *, \epsilon, \zeta)$ *be a closg. Then* $(Q;_* R)^\smile = R^\smile;_* Q^\smile$ *for all* $Q : A \to B$ *and* $R : B \to C$.

Proof. The computation

$$\begin{aligned}
(Q;_* R)^\smile &= \left(\bigsqcup_{\alpha,\beta \in \mathrm{Sc}[\mathcal{G}]} ((\alpha * \beta)_A; (\alpha_A \backslash Q)^\downarrow; (\beta_B \backslash R)^\downarrow) \right)^\smile && \text{definition } ;_* \\
&= \bigsqcup_{\alpha,\beta \in \mathrm{Sc}[\mathcal{G}]} ((\beta_B \backslash R)^{\downarrow\smile}; (\alpha_A \backslash Q)^{\downarrow\smile}; (\alpha * \beta)_A^\smile) \\
&= \bigsqcup_{\alpha,\beta \in \mathrm{Sc}[\mathcal{G}]} ((\beta_B \backslash R)^{\downarrow\smile}; (\alpha_A \backslash Q)^{\downarrow\smile}; (\alpha * \beta)_A) && (\alpha * \beta)_A \text{ partial identity} \\
&= \bigsqcup_{\alpha,\beta \in \mathrm{Sc}[\mathcal{G}]} ((\alpha * \beta)_C; (\beta_B \backslash R)^{\downarrow\smile}; (\alpha_A \backslash Q)^{\downarrow\smile}) && \text{Lemma 5.14} \\
&= \bigsqcup_{\alpha,\beta \in \mathrm{Sc}[\mathcal{G}]} ((\alpha * \beta)_C; (\beta_C \backslash R^\smile)^\downarrow; (\alpha_B \backslash Q^\smile)^\downarrow) && \text{Lemma 5.15} \\
&= R^\smile;_* Q^\smile && \text{definition } ;_*
\end{aligned}$$

shows the assertion. □

Finally, we will focus on continuity of $\otimes_*$.

Theorem 5.76 *Let* $(\mathrm{Sc}[\mathcal{G}], *, \epsilon, \zeta)$ *be a cloos. Then we have*

$$\left(\bigsqcup_{i \in I} Q_i \right) \otimes_* R = \bigsqcup_{i \in I} (Q_i \otimes_* R) \quad \text{and} \quad Q \otimes_* \left(\bigsqcup_{i \in I} R_i \right) = \bigsqcup_{i \in I} (Q \otimes_* R_i)$$

for all Q, Q_i, R, R_i *with* $i \in I$ *whenever the application of* $\otimes_*$ *is defined.*

Proof. Define $g(\alpha) := \bigsqcup_{i \in I} (\alpha_A \backslash Q_i)^\downarrow$. Then g is antitone and a function from $\mathrm{Sc}[\mathcal{G}]$ to $\mathcal{G}^\uparrow[A, B]$. Furthermore, we have

$$\begin{aligned}
\bigsqcup_{i \in I} Q_i &= \bigsqcup_{i \in I} \bigsqcup_{\alpha \in \mathrm{Sc}[\mathcal{G}]} (\alpha_A; (\alpha_A \backslash Q_i)^\downarrow) && \text{Theorem 5.35} \\
&= \bigsqcup_{\alpha \in \mathrm{Sc}[\mathcal{G}]} \left(\alpha_A; \left(\bigsqcup_{i \in I} (\alpha_A \backslash Q_i)^\downarrow \right) \right) \\
&= \bigsqcup_{\alpha \in \mathrm{Sc}[\mathcal{G}]} (\alpha_A; g(\alpha)), && \text{definition } g
\end{aligned}$$

and, hence, $(\beta_A\backslash(\bigsqcup_{i\in I} Q_i))^{\downarrow} = \tau(g)(\beta)$ for all $\beta \in \mathrm{Sc}[\mathcal{G}]$ by Lemma 5.49 (2). Furthermore, let

$$f(\alpha) := \bigsqcup_{\beta*\gamma\sqsupseteq\alpha} (\tau(g)(\beta) \otimes (\gamma\backslash R)^{\downarrow}) \quad \text{and} \quad \bar{f}(\alpha) := \bigsqcup_{\beta*\gamma\sqsupseteq\alpha} (g(\beta) \otimes (\gamma\backslash R)^{\downarrow}).$$

Then we conclude that

$$\begin{aligned}
&\left(\bigsqcup_{i\in I} Q_i\right) \otimes_* R \\
&= \bigsqcup_{\alpha\in\mathrm{Sc}[\mathcal{G}]} \left(\alpha_E;\left(\bigsqcup_{\beta*\gamma\sqsupseteq\alpha} ((\beta_A\backslash(\bigsqcup_{i\in I} Q_i))^{\downarrow} \otimes (\gamma_C\backslash R)^{\downarrow})\right)\right) && \text{Lemma 5.61} \\
&= \bigsqcup_{\alpha\in\mathrm{Sc}[\mathcal{G}]} \left(\alpha_E;\left(\bigsqcup_{\beta*\gamma\sqsupseteq\alpha} (\tau(g)(\beta) \otimes (\gamma_C\backslash R)^{\downarrow})\right)\right) && \text{computation above} \\
&= \bigsqcup_{\alpha\in\mathrm{Sc}[\mathcal{G}]} (\alpha_E; f(\alpha)) && \text{definition } f \\
&= \bigsqcup_{\alpha\in\mathrm{Sc}[\mathcal{G}]} (\alpha_E; \tau(f)(\alpha)) && \text{Lemma 5.49 (2)} \\
&= \bigsqcup_{\alpha\in\mathrm{Sc}[\mathcal{G}]} (\alpha_E; \tau(\bar{f})(\alpha)) && \text{Lemma 5.71} \\
&= \bigsqcup_{\alpha\in\mathrm{Sc}[\mathcal{G}]} (\alpha_E; \bar{f}(\alpha)) && \text{Lemma 5.49 (2)} \\
&= \bigsqcup_{\alpha\in\mathrm{Sc}[\mathcal{G}]} \left(\alpha_E;\left(\bigsqcup_{\beta*\gamma\sqsupseteq\alpha} (g(\beta) \otimes (\gamma_C\backslash R)^{\downarrow})\right)\right) && \text{definition } \bar{f} \\
&= \bigsqcup_{\alpha\in\mathrm{Sc}[\mathcal{G}]} \left(\alpha_E;\left(\bigsqcup_{\beta*\gamma\sqsupseteq\alpha} \left(\left(\bigsqcup_{i\in I}(\beta_A\backslash Q_i)^{\downarrow}\right) \otimes (\gamma_C\backslash R)^{\downarrow}\right)\right)\right) && \text{definition } g \\
&= \bigsqcup_{\alpha\in\mathrm{Sc}[\mathcal{G}]} \left(\alpha_E;\left(\bigsqcup_{\beta*\gamma\sqsupseteq\alpha} \bigsqcup_{i\in I} ((\beta\backslash Q_i)^{\downarrow} \otimes (\gamma\backslash R)^{\downarrow})\right)\right) && \text{Property (4) of } \otimes \\
&= \bigsqcup_{i\in I} \bigsqcup_{\alpha\in\mathrm{Sc}[\mathcal{G}]} \left(\alpha_E;\left(\bigsqcup_{\beta*\gamma\sqsupseteq\alpha} ((\beta\backslash Q_i)^{\downarrow} \otimes (\gamma\backslash R)^{\downarrow})\right)\right) \\
&= \bigsqcup_{i\in I} (Q_i \otimes_* R). && \text{Lemma 5.61}
\end{aligned}$$

The second equality is shown analogously. □

The previous theorem and Corollary 2.19 show that $\otimes_*$ is a lower adjoint of a triple of residuated operations.

Corollary 5.77 *Let* $(\mathrm{Sc}[\mathcal{G}], *, \epsilon, \zeta)$ *be a cloos. Then there are operations* $\lhd_*^{\otimes}$, $\rhd_*^{\otimes}$ *and* $\mathrm{syQ}_*^{\otimes}(.,.)$ *such that*

$$\begin{aligned} Q \otimes_* X \sqsubseteq R &\iff X \sqsubseteq Q \lhd_*^{\otimes} R, \\ Y \otimes_* S \sqsubseteq R &\iff Y \sqsubseteq R \rhd_*^{\otimes} S \\ \textit{and} \quad Q \otimes_* X \sqsubseteq R \textit{ and } X \otimes_* R^{\smile} \sqsubseteq Q^{\smile} &\iff X \sqsubseteq \mathrm{syQ}_*^{\otimes}(Q, R), \end{aligned}$$

whenever the application of $\otimes_*$ *is defined.*

If $\otimes$ is composition, we usually omit the superscript $\otimes$ resp. ;.

The previous corollary shows that an inclusion $Q;_* X \sqsubseteq R$ has a greatest solution in X, namely $Q \lhd_* R$. Furthermore, the equation $Q;_* X = R$ has a solution ($X = Q \lhd_* R$) iff $Q;_* (Q \lhd_* R) = R$.

Notice that we have $Q \lhd_*^{\otimes} R = Q\backslash R$, $R \rhd_*^{\otimes} S = R/S$ and $\mathrm{syQ}_*^{\otimes}(Q, R) = \mathrm{syQ}(Q, R)$ if $\otimes =;$ and $* = \sqcap$ since $;_{\sqcap} =;$ by Lemma 5.64.

6

FUZZY CONTROLLERS IN GOGUEN CATEGORIES

Following our mathematical investigation on the theory of Goguen categories, we now want to focus on an applications in computer science. Throughout this chapter, we will use the notations of Goguen categories even if the relations are concrete $\mathcal{L}$-fuzzy relations. Furthermore, $*$ is considered to be an operation from a closg $(\mathrm{Sc}[\mathcal{G}], *, \mathbb{I}, \zeta)$ unless otherwise stated.

6.1 THE MAMDANI APPROACH TO FUZZY CONTROLLERS

We want to show that a fuzzy controller may be described by a simple term in the language of Goguen categories. This may be used in at least two ways. First of all, we get in some sense a denotational semantics of fuzzy controllers, and, hence, a mathematical theory to reason about notions like correctness versus a given specification, safety properties, and so on. One may prove such properties of a controller using the calculus of Goguen categories developed so far. Furthermore, a system, which is able to compute relational terms, may be used to obtain a prototype of the controller. There are two suitable systems, the RELVIEW system developed at the Christian-Albrechts-University of Kiel and the RATH system developed at the University of the Federal Armed Forces Munich [19]. The latter system is in fact a library of Haskell modules that allows to explore relational structures as relation algebras, Dedekind categories, allegories, and so on by providing different means to construct such algebras and to compute relational expressions in a given one. In the diploma thesis by Triebsess [38] certain modules containing the theory of Goguen categories

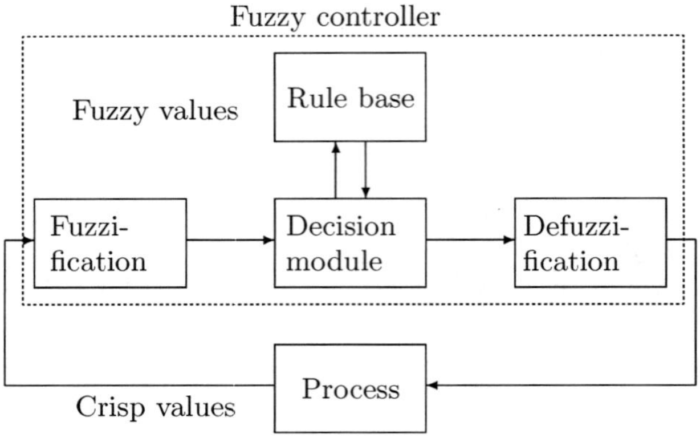

Figure 6.1. Components of a fuzzy controller.

were developed. Furthermore, a special module allows the user to construct and execute $\mathcal{L}$-fuzzy controllers in a given Goguen category.

We want to concentrate on the method of Mamdani [25] for constructing a fuzzy controller summarized in Figure 6.1. In this approach a fuzzy controller consists of a rule base, a decision module, a fuzzification, and a defuzzification. Notice that our fuzzy controllers are not limited to use coefficients from the unit interval $[0, 1]$ of the real numbers. In fact, our running example throughout this chapter will be a controller with values from a nonlinear ordering.

6.2 LINGUISTIC ENTITIES AND VARIABLES

A fuzzy controller is usually formulated using linguistic entities, i.e., abstract notions represented by common words from every day language (like: "extremely high speed", "hot water", "very heavy rain", etc.). Variables ranging over those abstract entities are called linguistic variables. They are understood as variables over suitable $\mathcal{L}$-fuzzy sets. As usual in the theory of relations we describe a subset of A by a relation $M : \mathrm{I} \to A$, where I is a unit of the corresponding relational category. In the case of Goguen categories, such a relation is an abstract notion of an $\mathcal{L}$-fuzzy subset as required for the interpretation of linguistic variables.

As indicated above, linguistic entities are often built up from two components. First of all, there is a basic notion of an abstract entity as "high speed." This basic notion may be modified by an adverb as "very" or "extremely." On a suitable level of abstraction, these adverbs may be seen as linguistic modifiers, i.e., functions mapping $\mathcal{L}$-fuzzy sets to $\mathcal{L}$-fuzzy sets. We will study ordering-based, weakening, and intensifying modifiers (cf. [6, 7]).

Suppose E is an ordering relation, i.e., $\mathbb{I}_A \sqsubseteq E$ (E reflexive), $E;E \sqsubseteq E$ (E transitive), and $E \sqcap E^{\smile} = \mathbb{I}_A$ (E antisymmetric). The well-known concept and its relational description of upper and/or lower bounds of a subset $M : \mathrm{I} \to A$ (cf. [32]) may be used to model the linguistic modifiers "greater than" and "less

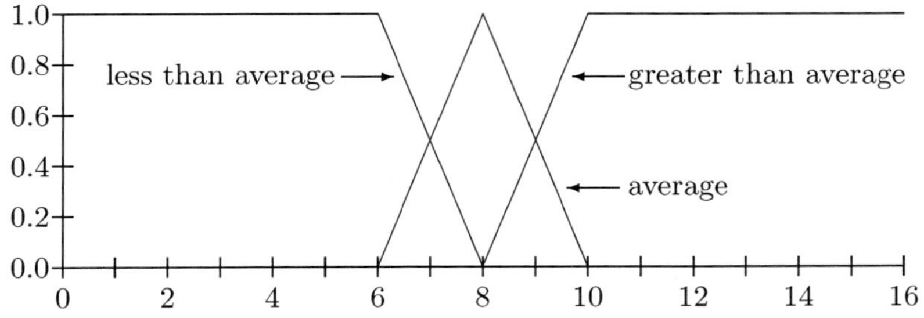

Figure 6.2. Ordering-based modifiers.

than" with respect to a semigroup operation $*$. We define

$$\begin{aligned} \text{greater than}_*(E, M) &:= (E^\smile \rhd_* M)^\smile, \\ \text{less than}_*(E, M) &:= (E \rhd_* M)^\smile. \end{aligned}$$

Example 6.1 We want to illustrate the definitions above within fuzzy sets using Łukasiewicz t-norm $t_L(x, y) := \max\{0, x + y - 1\}$ for $*$. Suppose that the mean score of a test is 8. The fuzzy set "average" in the universe of scores $[0, 16]$ may be represented by a triangular fuzzy set shown in Figure 6.2.

Let E be the natural (crisp) ordering on $[0, 16]$. Then we get the fuzzy set "greater than average" as indicated in the same figure. Notice that this set is greatest solution X of $\text{average}^\smile ;_{t_L} X \sqsubseteq E$. Therefore, the degree of membership x of 9 has to be 0.5. If z is a value with $9 < z \leq 10$, then $E(z, 9) = 0$, and, hence, $x + y$ with y the degree of membership of z in "average" has to be less or equal to 1. ◇

Another interesting class of modifiers originates from relations that model approximate equalities. Such a relation Ξ should be reflexive $\mathbb{I}_A \sqsubseteq \Xi$ and symmetric $\Xi^\smile \sqsubseteq \Xi$. In a first attempt one would also require transitivity. This may lead to a counterintuitive result. To illustrate this, we recall an example given in [8]:

> In everyday life we usually do not feel a difference in temperature between 0° and 1°, neither between 1° and 2°, between 35° and 36° and so on. For a human being, those degrees are approximately equal. Obviously, the corresponding relation is not transitive since otherwise all temperatures would be approximately equal, which is a counter-intuitive result.

Such approximate equality may be used to model weakening and intensifying modifiers as "extremely", "very", "more or less", and "roughly". The following intuitive inclusions should be guaranteed:

$$\text{extremely}(M) \subseteq \text{very}(M) \subseteq M \subseteq \text{more or less}(M) \subseteq \text{roughly}(M)$$

for all $\mathcal{L}$-fuzzy sets M. We define

$$\begin{aligned}
\text{extremely}_*(\Xi, M) &:= (M \rhd_* \Xi) \rhd_* \Xi,\\
\text{very}_*(\Xi, M) &:= M \rhd_* \Xi,\\
\text{more or less}_*(\Xi, M) &:= M;_* \Xi,\\
\text{roughly}_*(\Xi, M) &:= (M;_* \Xi);_* \Xi.
\end{aligned}$$

or more generally

$$\begin{aligned}
\text{very}^1_*(\Xi, M) &:= \text{very}_*(\Xi, M),\\
\text{very}^{i+1}_*(\Xi, M) &:= \text{very}_*(\Xi, \text{very}^i(\Xi, M)),\\
\text{roughly}^1_*(\Xi, M) &:= \text{more or less}_*(\Xi, M),\\
\text{roughly}^{i+1}_*(\Xi, M) &:= \text{more or less}_*(\Xi, \text{roughly}^i(\Xi, M))
\end{aligned}$$

for all $i \geq 1$.

Lemma 6.2 *Suppose $\Xi : A \to A$ is a reflexive relation and define $\Xi^1 := \Xi$ and $\Xi^{i+1} := \Xi^i;_* \Xi$. Then we have*

(1) if $;_*$ is associative, then $\text{very}^i_*(\Xi, M) = \text{very}_*(\Xi^i, M)$ and $\text{roughly}^i_*(\Xi, M) = \text{more or less}_*(\Xi^i, M)$,

(2) $\text{very}^{i+1}_*(\Xi, M) \sqsubseteq \text{very}^i_*(\Xi, M) \sqsubseteq M$ for all $i \geq 1$,

(3) $M \sqsubseteq \text{roughly}^i_*(\Xi, M) \sqsubseteq \text{roughly}^{i+1}_*(\Xi, M)$ for all $i \geq 1$.

Proof.

(1) The second assertion is trivial and the first one follows from

$$\begin{aligned}
X \sqsubseteq \text{very}_*(\Xi, \text{very}(\Xi, M)) &\Leftrightarrow X \sqsubseteq (M \rhd_* \Xi) \rhd_* \Xi && \text{definition very}\\
&\Leftrightarrow X;_* \Xi \sqsubseteq M \rhd_* \Xi && \text{residuated operation}\\
&\Leftrightarrow (X;_* \Xi);_* \Xi \sqsubseteq M && \text{residuated operation}\\
&\Leftrightarrow X;_* \Xi^2 \sqsubseteq M && ;_* \text{ associative}\\
&\Leftrightarrow X \sqsubseteq M \rhd_* \Xi^2 && \text{residuated operation}\\
&\Leftrightarrow X \sqsubseteq \text{very}_*(\Xi^2, M). && \text{definition very}
\end{aligned}$$

(2) The assertion follows from $\text{very}_*(\Xi, M) \sqsubseteq M$. This is shown by

$$\begin{aligned}
X \sqsubseteq \text{very}_*(\Xi, M) &\Leftrightarrow X \sqsubseteq M \rhd_* \Xi && \text{definition very}\\
&\Leftrightarrow X;_* \Xi \sqsubseteq M && \text{residuated operation}\\
&\Rightarrow X \sqsubseteq X;_* \Xi \sqsubseteq M. && ;_* \text{ is monotonic and } \mathbb{I}_A \sqsubseteq \Xi
\end{aligned}$$

(3) follows immediately from the reflexivity of Ξ. □

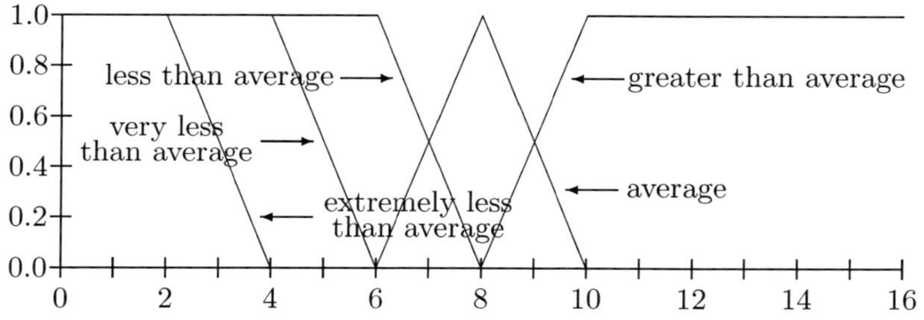

Figure 6.3. Weakening and intensifying modifiers.

The previous lemma gives another reason not to require that Ξ is transitive. In that case all very$^i_*$ resp. roughly$^i_*$ would be equal.

Example 6.3 Again, we want to illustrate the definitions above within fuzzy sets and the Łukasiewicz t-norm. We define

$$\Xi(x, y) := \min(1, \max(0, 1.2 - 0.1|x - y|)).$$

Intuitively, two values are considered as equal (with degree 1) if they are within a range less or equal to 2. The result is shown in Figure 6.3. ◇

The interpretation of the linguistic entities now consists of a suitable choice of $\mathcal{L}$-fuzzy subsets of the input resp. output domain A, i.e., by relations $Q : \mathrm{I} \to A$, for any linguistic entity that occurs within the controller. The abstract set of linguistic entities itself is modelled within an arbitrary Goguen category by a suitable disjoint union of several copies of a unit I. Last but not least, the whole interpretation L^{in} for the input resp. L^{out} for the output is given by the corresponding disjoint union of the relations above. For example, if A is the set of temperatures and the input domain of the controller, the set of linguistic entities is given by the set $\{\text{very cold}, \text{cold}, \text{medium}, \text{hot}, \text{very hot}\}$ and their interpretation by relations $Q_i : \mathrm{I} \to A$ for $1 \leq i \leq 5$ then we have

$$L^{in} := \left(\bigsqcup_{1 \leq i \leq 5} (\iota_i^{\smile} ; Q_i) \right) : \mathrm{I} + \mathrm{I} + \mathrm{I} + \mathrm{I} + \mathrm{I} \to A,$$

where ι_i for $1 \leq i \leq 5$ are the crisp injections from I to $\mathrm{I} + \mathrm{I} + \mathrm{I} + \mathrm{I} + \mathrm{I}$.

Notice that it is essential that the injections are crisp. If the injections are noncrisp, there would be a fuzzification, which is not an integral part of the definition of the controller. This fuzzification arises from the specific choice of the sum. In this case, reasoning about the controller using the term above seems to be impossible or at least difficult.

Example 6.4 As a running example in this chapter we want to construct a temperature controller. It has to control the temperature in a room with two different colonies of bacteria. These colonies need a slightly different temperature for optimal growth. The first one needs about 24° and the second one about 25.5°. Both colonies will die if the temperature is less than 5° or greater than 45° for a while. The input of the controller are temperatures taken from the left-closed/right-open interval $A := [0.0 \ldots 50.0[$. The output is a value from $B := \{-20, -19, -18, \ldots, 18, 19, 20\}$, the adjusting values of the heating, or a special signal "AL" to indicate an alert. Therefore, the controller will be a relation $C : A \to B + \mathrm{I}$. The linguistic entities for the input resp. output are given by

OT $\hat{=}$ optimal temperature
SW $\hat{=}$ slightly too warm
SC $\hat{=}$ slightly too cold
LW $\hat{=}$ little bit too warm
LC $\hat{=}$ little bit too cold
TW $\hat{=}$ too warm
TC $\hat{=}$ too cold
MW $\hat{=}$ much too warm
MC $\hat{=}$ much too cold

NC $\hat{=}$ no change
PS $\hat{=}$ positive small
NS $\hat{=}$ negative small
PM $\hat{=}$ positive medium
NM $\hat{=}$ negative medium
PB $\hat{=}$ positive big
NB $\hat{=}$ negative big
AL $\hat{=}$ alert

Since a temperature may be optimal with a certain degree in two senses, namely for the first and the second colony, we choose the lattice $\mathcal{L}$ to be $[0,1] \times [0,1]$. We will denote the $\mathcal{L}$-fuzzy relations corresponding to the linguistic entities as shown in the following table:

OT	Q_0			NC	S_0	AL	S_4
SW	Q_1	SC	Q_{-1}	PS	S_1	NS	S_{-1}
LW	Q_2	LC	Q_{-2}	PM	S_2	NM	S_{-2}
TW	Q_3	TC	Q_{-3}	PB	S_3	NB	S_{-3}
MW	Q_4	MC	Q_{-4}				

We start our interpretation of the linguistic entities with two $\mathcal{L}$-fuzzy relations $e_{24}, e_{25.5} : \mathrm{I} \to A$ defined by

$$e_{24}(1,x) := \begin{cases} (1,0) \text{ iff } x = 24, \\ (0,0) \text{ iff } x \neq 24 \end{cases} \quad \text{and} \quad e_{25.5}(1,x) := \begin{cases} (0,1) \text{ iff } x = 25.5, \\ (0,0) \text{ iff } x \neq 25.5, \end{cases}$$

denoting the optimal temperature for the first and second colony. Furthermore, we define an approximate equality Ξ_A by

$$\Xi_A(x,y) := (\min(1, \max(0, a_1 - b_1|x-y|)), \min(1, \max(0, a_2 - b_2|x-y|)))$$

for suitable a_1, a_2, b_1 and b_2. Ξ_A expresses, which temperatures are considered as equal in respect to the first (coefficients a_1 and b_1) and to the second (coefficients a_2 and b_2) colony. By weakening e_{24} resp. $e_{25.5}$ and combining the results we obtain the $\mathcal{L}$-fuzzy set

$$Q_0 := \text{more or less}(\Xi_A, e_{24}) \sqcup \text{more or less}(\Xi_A, e_{25.5}).$$

Notice that we use $\sqcap$ for $*$ in the definition above. As an example, we want to compute $Q_0(1, 24.8)$ with $a_1 = a_2 = 1.2, b_1 = 0.35$ and $b_2 = 0.25$

$$
\begin{aligned}
& Q_0(1, 24.8) \\
&= (e_{24}; \Xi_A)(1, 24.8) \vee (e_{25.5}; \Xi_A)(1, 24.8) && \text{definition } Q_0 \\
&= ((1,0) \wedge \Xi_A(24, 24.8)) \vee ((0,1) \wedge \Xi_A(25.5, 24.8)) && \text{def. } e_{24}, e_{25.5} \text{ and ;} \\
&= ((1,0) \wedge (0.92, 1)) \vee ((0,1) \wedge (0.965, 1)) && \text{definition } \Xi_A \\
&= (0.92, 1).
\end{aligned}
$$

The relations for SW, ..., TC are computed by shifting Q_0 to the left resp. to the right. This may be achieved using a suitable crisp bijection $s_A : A \to A$. For example, for a suitable u let s_A be defined by $s_A(x, y) = (1, 1)$ if $y = (x + u)$ mod 50.0 and $s_A(x, y) = (0, 0)$ otherwise. It seems to be unnatural to require that s_A is a bijection. But this property will make the proofs in Section 6.7 much more easier. Furthermore, s_A fulfills a special kind of a monotonicity property. Suppose E_A is the linear ordering on A. An element is in the domain of the univalent and injective relation $s_A \sqcap E_A$ iff it is expanded by s_A. Analogously, an element is in the range of that relation iff it is contracted by s_A. Between its domain and range, $s_A \sqcap E$ is an order isomorphism such that we have

$$E_A; (s_A \sqcap E_A) = (s_A \sqcap E_A); E_A.$$

Now, we define

$$Q_{i+1} := Q_i; s_A \quad \text{and} \quad Q_{-(i+1)} := Q_{-i}; s_A^{\smile}$$

for $0 \leq i \leq 2$. Finally, Q_4 and Q_{-4} are defined by the order-based modifiers. Suppose E_A is the ordering on A and $*$ is the Łukasiewicz t-norm extended to pairs, i.e., $(x_1, x_2) * (y_1, y_2) := (t_L(x_1, y_1), t_L(x_2, y_2))$. Then we obtain

$$Q_4 := \text{greater than}_*(E_A, Q_3) \quad \text{and} \quad Q_{-4} := \text{less than}_*(E_A, Q_{-3}).$$

The interpretation of the output linguistic entities is done analogously. We start with the crisp relation $e_0 : \mathrm{I} \to B$ defined by $e_0(1, 0) = (1, 1)$ and $e_0(1, x) = (0, 0)$ otherwise. Furthermore, we define an approximate equality Ξ_B on B by

$$\Xi_B(x, y) := (\min(1, \max(0, a - b|x - y|)), \min(1, \max(0, a - b|x - y|)))$$

for suitable a and b. Together with a suitable crisp bijection $s_B : B \to B$ for shifting we define

$$S'_0 := \text{more or less}(\Xi_B, e_0), \qquad S'_{i+1} := S'_i; s_B \quad \text{and} \quad S'_{-(i+1)} := S'_{-i}; s_B^{\smile}$$

for $0 \leq i \leq 2$. Finally, using the crisp injections ι and κ from B resp. I to $B + \mathrm{I}$ we get $S_i := S'_i; \iota$ for $-3 \leq i \leq 3$, $S_4 := \kappa$, and, hence,

$$L^{in} := \bigsqcup_{-4 \leq i \leq 4} \iota_i^{\smile}; Q_i \qquad \text{and} \qquad L^{out} := \bigsqcup_{-3 \leq i \leq 4} \iota_i^{\smile}; S_i. \qquad \diamond$$

6.3 FUZZIFICATION

The fuzzification part of a controller consists of an operation $F(x)$ mapping each input value x to an $\mathcal{L}$-fuzzy set. In our approach the input values from A are interpreted by relational elements or points, i.e., by crisp functions $x : \mathrm{I} \to A$. Therefore, the easiest fuzzification operation is the identity since points are special $\mathcal{L}$-fuzzy sets. Naturally, other operations are possible. For example, one may map such a point to another $\mathcal{L}$-fuzzy sets using the weakening operators from Section 6.2.

A suitable choice hardly depends on the application. Usually, the fuzzification part is used to validate the controller. Therefore, some arbitrary values are chosen for the possible parameters in a first attempt. By testing the controller for suitable inputs those parameters are modified until a desired behavior can be observed.

Example 6.5 In our example we will use the identity as fuzzification. ◇

6.4 THE RULE BASE

A control rule is usually formulated as a conditional expression using the linguistic variables, i.e., it is of the form

$$\textbf{if } x \textbf{ is } \mathrm{M}, \textbf{ then } y = N,$$

where x and y are linguistic variables considered as the input resp. as the output and M and N are fuzzy sets. These sets are built up from basic linguistic entities and some $*$-based operations. We may require without loss of generality that M and N are indeed basic linguistic entities. If not, we introduce a new entity for the corresponding expression. With this convention a control rule may be seen as pair of such linguistic entities.

A rule base, i.e., a finite list of control rules, may be described by a crisp relation R between the given sets of linguistic entities. As mentioned above, in an arbitrary Goguen category these sets are modelled by a suitable disjoint union of several copies of a unit I. R is given by the corresponding relation between them. For example the rule base

$$\begin{aligned} &\textbf{if } x \textbf{ is } M_1, \textbf{ then } y = N_1,\\ &\textbf{if } x \textbf{ is } M_2, \textbf{ then } y = N_1,\\ &\textbf{if } x \textbf{ is } M_3, \textbf{ then } y = N_2 \end{aligned}$$

is modelled by a relation $R : \mathrm{I}+\mathrm{I}+\mathrm{I} \to \mathrm{I}+\mathrm{I}$ defined by

$$R := \iota_1^\smile ; \iota_1 \sqcup \iota_2^\smile ; \iota_1 \sqcup \iota_3^\smile ; \iota_2,$$

where $\iota_1, \iota_2, \iota_3$ resp. ι_1, ι_2 are the crisp injections from I to $\mathrm{I}+\mathrm{I}+\mathrm{I}$ resp. $\mathrm{I}+\mathrm{I}$. R may be also represented by the following matrix:

$$R = \begin{pmatrix} 1 & 0 \\ 1 & 0 \\ 0 & 1 \end{pmatrix}$$

In general, if $R(i)$ denotes the set of indices of output linguistic entities related by the rule base to the input linguistic entity i, the relation R is of the from

$$R = \bigsqcup_{\substack{i\in I\\ j\in R(i)}} (\iota_i^{\smile};\iota_j).$$

If we combine the interpretation of the rule base and of the linguistic entities for input and output, we obtain the following relational terms $T : A \to B$ for the core of the controller:

$$T := (L^{in\smile};_{*_1} R);_{*_2} L^{out} \quad \text{or} \quad T := L^{in\smile};_{*_1} (R;_{*_2} L^{out}),$$

where $(\mathrm{Sc}[\mathcal{G}], *_1, \mathbb{I}, \zeta)$ and $(\mathrm{Sc}[\mathcal{G}], *_2, \mathbb{I}, \zeta)$ are closgs. The following and a similar computation for the second term show that just one closg is really needed:

$$\begin{aligned}
& L^{in\smile};_* (R;_{*'} L^{out}) \\
&= L^{in\smile};_* \left(R;_{*'} \left(\bigsqcup_{j\in J}(\iota_j^{\smile};S_j)\right)\right) && \text{definition } L^{out} \\
&= L^{in\smile};_* \left(R; \left(\bigsqcup_{j\in J}(\iota_j^{\smile};S_j)\right)\right) && \text{Lemma 5.66} \\
&= L^{in\smile};_* \left(\left(\bigsqcup_{\substack{i\in I\\ j\in R(i)}} (\iota_i^{\smile};\iota_j)\right); \left(\bigsqcup_{j\in J}(\iota_j^{\smile};S_j)\right)\right) && \text{interpretation } R \\
&= L^{in\smile};_* \left(\bigsqcup_{\substack{i\in I\\ j\in R(i)}} (\iota_i^{\smile};S_j)\right) && \text{definition injections} \\
&= \left(\bigsqcup_{i\in I}(Q_i^{\smile};\iota_i)\right);_* \left(\bigsqcup_{\substack{i\in I\\ j\in R(i)}} (\iota_i^{\smile};S_j)\right) && \text{definition } L^{in} \\
&= \bigsqcup_{l\in I} \bigsqcup_{\substack{i\in I\\ j\in R(i)}} ((Q_l^{\smile};\iota_l);_* (\iota_i^{\smile};S_j)) && ;_* \text{ continuous} \\
&= \bigsqcup_{l\in I} \bigsqcup_{\substack{i\in I\\ j\in R(i)}} ((Q_l^{\smile};_*\iota_l);_* (\iota_i^{\smile};_*S_j)) && \text{Lemma 5.66} \\
&= \bigsqcup_{l\in I} \bigsqcup_{\substack{i\in I\\ j\in R(i)}} (Q_l^{\smile};_* (\iota_l;_*\iota_i^{\smile});_* S_j) && \text{Theorem 5.73} \\
&= \bigsqcup_{l\in I} \bigsqcup_{\substack{i\in I\\ j\in R(i)}} (Q_l^{\smile};_* (\iota_l;\iota_i^{\smile});_* S_j) && \text{Lemma 5.66} \\
&= \bigsqcup_{\substack{i\in I\\ j\in R(i)}} (Q_i^{\smile};_* S_j),
\end{aligned}$$

where the last equality follows from the definition of the injections and $Q;_* \mathbb{I}_B = Q;\mathbb{I}_B = Q$ and $Q;_* \perp\!\!\!\perp_{BC} = Q;\perp\!\!\!\perp_{BC} = \perp\!\!\!\perp_{AC}$ for all $Q : A \to B$ since $\mathbb{I}_B$ and $\perp\!\!\!\perp_{BC}$ are crisp.

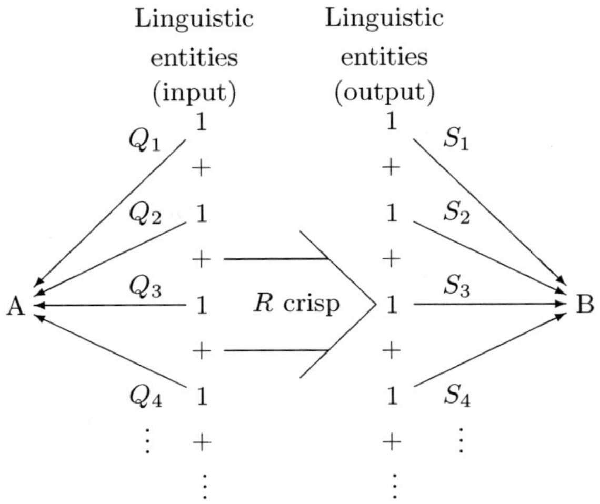

Figure 6.4. Core of a fuzzy controller.

The core $T : A \to B$ of a fuzzy controller is visualized in Figure 6.4. Notice again that we do not require that the underlying lattice $\mathcal{L}$ is the unit interval.

Example 6.6 Now, we want to return to our running example. Consider the following rule base and its interpretation by a matrix:

if x **is** OT, **then** y = NC,
if x **is** SW, **then** y = NS,
if x **is** SC, **then** y = PS,
if x **is** LW, **then** y = NM,
if x **is** LC, **then** y = PM,
if x **is** TW, **then** y = NB,
if x **is** TC, **then** y = PB,
if x **is** MW, **or** x **is** MC, **then** y = AL.

$$R = \begin{pmatrix} 1 & 0 & 0 & 0 & 0 & 0 & 0 & 0 \\ 0 & 1 & 0 & 0 & 0 & 0 & 0 & 0 \\ 0 & 0 & 1 & 0 & 0 & 0 & 0 & 0 \\ 0 & 0 & 0 & 1 & 0 & 0 & 0 & 0 \\ 0 & 0 & 0 & 0 & 1 & 0 & 0 & 0 \\ 0 & 0 & 0 & 0 & 0 & 1 & 0 & 0 \\ 0 & 0 & 0 & 0 & 0 & 0 & 1 & 0 \\ 0 & 0 & 0 & 0 & 0 & 0 & 0 & 1 \\ 0 & 0 & 0 & 0 & 0 & 0 & 0 & 1 \end{pmatrix}$$

If we denote the crisp injections by ι_i^{in} for $-4 \le i \le 4$ and ι_i^{out} for $-3 \le i \le 4$, the relational term for R is given by

$$R := \left(\bigsqcup_{-3 \le i \le 4} (\iota_i^{in\smile} ; \iota_i^{out}) \right) \sqcup \iota_{-4}^{in\smile} ; \iota_4^{out}$$

We choose $\sqcap$ for $*$ and get the following core of the controller $T : A \to B + \mathrm{I}$:

$$\begin{aligned} T &:= \left(\bigsqcup_{-4 \le i \le 4} (Q_i^{\smile} ; \iota_i^{in}) \right) ; R; \left(\bigsqcup_{-3 \le i \le 4} (\iota_i^{out\smile} ; S_i) \right) \\ &= \bigsqcup_{-3 \le i \le 4} Q_i^{\smile} ; S_i \sqcup Q_{-4}^{\smile} ; S_4. \qquad \text{computation above} \quad \diamond \end{aligned}$$

6.5 DECISION MODULE

The decision module describes to which degree a rule of the controller is activated for a given input. In our approach this corresponds to the question of how to combine the result of the fuzzification $F(x)$ with the core of the controller T.

Usually, a so-called optimistic view is taken (cf. [14]). Using the unit interval the degree of activation of a rule

$$\textbf{if } x \textbf{ is } M, \textbf{ then } y = N$$

for a fuzzy set P is computed in respect to a given t-norm by the expression

$$\sup_{x \in A} t(P(x), M(x)),$$

i.e., as the supremum of the combined degrees of membership within P and M for all suitable x. This corresponds exactly to a $*$-based composition within Goguen categories such that we usually use $U(x) := F(x);_* T$ as the fuzzy part of the controller.

Also, a more pessimistic view may be chosen. Such an approach corresponds to a relation U based on some residuals instead of $;_*$. For example, one may choose $U(x) := F(x)^{\smile} \rhd_* T$ or quite more pessimistic $U(x) := \mathrm{syQ}_*(F(x)^{\smile}, T)$. These expressions compute the degree of inclusion resp. the degree of equality of $F(x)$ and the corresponding M. But, as mentioned in [14] none of those pessimistic views has been used for any fuzzy controller so far.

Example 6.7 In our example we choose the optimistic view with $* = \sqcap$ such that

$$U(x) := F(x); T = x; T = x; \left(\bigsqcup_{-3 \leq i \leq 4} (Q_i^{\smile}; S_i) \sqcup Q_{-4}^{\smile}; S_4 \right). \qquad \diamond$$

6.6 DEFUZZIFICATION

In the defuzzification part of controller the fuzzy output is transformed back into a crisp value. In our approach we need an operation $\mathcal{D}$ mapping the $\mathcal{L}$-fuzzy relation $U(x) : \mathrm{I} \to B$ to a crisp relation $\mathcal{D}(U(x)) : \mathrm{I} \to B$. There are several proposals for $\mathcal{D}$ throughout the literature (e.g., cf. [15]). Most of them are closely related to the unit interval $[0, 1]$ and the operations defined there. Therefore, the choice of $\mathcal{D}$ depends usually on the lattice $\mathcal{L}$, which is used to model the degree of membership within the controller. But, at least one class of methods may be used for all lattices, methods arising from the cut operation. Given an operation Θ_I, which maps any x to a scalar $\Theta_\mathrm{I}(x)$ on I we define

$$\mathcal{D}(U(x)) := (\Theta_\mathrm{I}(x) \backslash U(x))^{\downarrow}.$$

The most simple definition for Θ_I would be a constant function mapping any x to a given scalar α_I, i.e., $\Theta_\mathrm{I}(x) := \alpha_\mathrm{I}$. Another suitable choice for Θ_I may be the scalar of the maximal degree of membership. Within $\mathcal{L}$-fuzzy relations consider the partial identity $\Theta_{\mathrm{I}}(x) := U(x) \circ \mathbb{T}_{B\mathrm{I}} \sqcap \mathbb{I}_{\mathrm{I}}$ and compute

$$\begin{aligned}
\Theta_{\mathrm{I}}(x)(1,1) &= (U(x) \circ \mathbb{T}_{B\mathrm{I}} \sqcap \mathbb{I}_{\mathrm{I}})(1,1) && \text{definition } \Theta_{\mathrm{I}}(x) \\
&= (U(x) \circ \mathbb{T}_{B\mathrm{I}})(1,1) && \text{definition } \sqcap \text{ and } \mathbb{I}_{\mathrm{I}} \\
&= \bigvee_{v \in B} (U(x)(1,v) \wedge \mathbb{T}_{B\mathrm{I}}(v,1)) && \text{definition } \circ \\
&= \bigvee_{v \in B} U(x)(1,v). && \text{definition } \mathbb{T}_{B\mathrm{I}}
\end{aligned}$$

With other words, this relation computes the supremum w of all degrees of membership of elements $v \in B$ related to x within $U(x)$.

Under some circumstances the controller $\mathcal{D}(U(x))$ may be expressed in quite a nice way. Suppose Θ_{I} fulfills $x^{\smile};\Theta_{\mathrm{I}}(x) = S_A;x^{\smile}$ for all $x : \mathrm{I} \to A$ and a suitable partial identity $S_A : A \to A$. Furthermore, suppose $F(x)$ is some weakening of x, i.e., $F(x) = x;_{*'}\Xi$ for some closg and relation Ξ, and, hence, $F(x) = x;\Xi$ since x is crisp. Then we have in the optimistic approach

$$\begin{aligned}
U(x) &= F(x);_* T && \text{definition of } U(x) \\
&= (x;\Xi);_* T && \text{definition of } F(x) \\
&= (x;_* \Xi);_* T && \text{Lemma 5.66} \\
&= x;_* (\Xi;_* T) && \text{Theorem 5.73} \\
&= x;(\Xi;_* T). && \text{Lemma 5.66}
\end{aligned}$$

If we use the abbreviation $T' := \Xi;_* T$, the computation above implies

$$\begin{aligned}
Y \sqsubseteq \mathcal{D}(U(x)) &\Leftrightarrow Y \sqsubseteq (\Theta_{\mathrm{I}}(x)\backslash U(x))^{\downarrow} && \text{definition } \mathcal{D}(U(x)) \\
&\Leftrightarrow Y \sqsubseteq (\Theta_{\mathrm{I}}(x)\backslash (x;T'))^{\downarrow} && \text{computation above} \\
&\Leftrightarrow Y^{\uparrow} \sqsubseteq \Theta_{\mathrm{I}}(x)\backslash (x;T') && \text{Galois correspondence} \\
&\Leftrightarrow \Theta_{\mathrm{I}}(x);Y^{\uparrow} \sqsubseteq x;T' && \text{definition residual} \\
&\Leftrightarrow x^{\smile};\Theta_{\mathrm{I}}(x);Y^{\uparrow} \sqsubseteq T' && \text{Lemma 4.8 (2)} \\
&\Leftrightarrow S_A;x^{\smile};Y^{\uparrow} \sqsubseteq T' && \text{property of } \Theta_{\mathrm{I}} \\
&\Leftrightarrow x^{\smile};Y^{\uparrow} \sqsubseteq S_A\backslash T' && \text{definition residual} \\
&\Leftrightarrow x^{\smile\downarrow};Y^{\uparrow} \sqsubseteq S_A\backslash T' && x \text{ crisp} \\
&\Leftrightarrow (x^{\smile\downarrow};Y)^{\uparrow} \sqsubseteq S_A\backslash T' && \text{Lemma 5.6 (9)} \\
&\Leftrightarrow x^{\smile\downarrow};Y \sqsubseteq (S_A\backslash T')^{\downarrow} && \text{Galois correspondence} \\
&\Leftrightarrow x^{\smile};Y \sqsubseteq (S_A\backslash T')^{\downarrow} && x \text{ crisp} \\
&\Leftrightarrow Y \sqsubseteq x;(S_A\backslash T')^{\downarrow}, && \text{Lemma 4.8 (2)}
\end{aligned}$$

and, hence, $\mathcal{D}(U(x)) = x; (S_A \backslash T')^{\downarrow}$. Consequently, the controller is given by a simple relational term $C := (S_A \backslash T')^{\downarrow}$. Its action on arguments $\mathcal{D}(U(x))$ is just the usual relational application $x; C$ of C on x.

The constant function as well as the operation of maximal degree fulfills the property above. First, suppose $\Theta_{\mathrm{I}}(x) = \alpha_{\mathrm{I}}$ for a given scalar α_{I}. Then we have

$$\begin{aligned} x^{\smile}; \Theta_{\mathrm{I}}(x) &= x^{\smile}; \alpha_{\mathrm{I}} && \text{definition } \Theta_{\mathrm{I}} \\ &= \alpha_A; x^{\smile}. && \text{Lemma 5.14} \end{aligned}$$

Second, suppose $\Theta_{\mathrm{I}}(x) = U(x); \mathbb{T}_{B\mathrm{I}} \sqcap \mathbb{I}_{\mathrm{I}}$. Then we have

$$\begin{aligned} x^{\smile}; \Theta_{\mathrm{I}}(x) &= x^{\smile}; (U(x); \mathbb{T}_{B\mathrm{I}} \sqcap \mathbb{I}_{\mathrm{I}}) && \text{definition } \Theta_{\mathrm{I}} \\ &= x^{\smile}; (x; T'; \mathbb{T}_{B\mathrm{I}} \sqcap \mathbb{I}_{\mathrm{I}}) && \text{computation above} \\ &= T'; \mathbb{T}_{B\mathrm{I}} \sqcap x^{\smile} && \text{Lemma 4.7 (2)} \\ &= T'; \mathbb{T}_{BA}; x^{\smile} \sqcap x^{\smile} && x \text{ total} \\ &= (T'; \mathbb{T}_{BA} \sqcap \mathbb{I}_A); x^{\smile}. && \text{Lemma 4.7 (1)} \end{aligned}$$

Usually, a controller defined using a cut as defuzzification is not a function. For example, there may be none or more than one possible values with maximal degree of membership for a given input x. But, in applications it is usually essential that the controller codes a function. Otherwise, it would not be clear which action, if any, should be done. Therefore, the cut approach has to be modified. Within the defuzzification operation one has to select a specific element as the result. This may be done by several operations. For example, if there is an ordering on the output domain, one could choose the greatest or least element among the set of results. Also, some weighted mean could be taken if the output domain offers such an operation.

A general approach for selecting a specific element may be as follows: Suppose $f : \mathcal{P}_\emptyset(B) \to B$ is a crisp function mapping each (crisp) nonempty subset of B to an element of B. For example, any mean function and the order-based operations may be represented in that way. The class of mean functions shows that the empty set has to be excluded. A controller derived from an extension of a mean function to the empty set usually does not grasp the intended behavior of the system. The abstract description of the object $\mathcal{P}_\emptyset(B)$ within an arbitrary Goguen category $\mathcal{G}$ is given by a total relational power, introduced in [39], in the Dedekind category $\mathcal{G}^{\uparrow}$ of crisp relations. This construction is defined by a crisp relation $\varepsilon_B^\emptyset : B \to \mathcal{P}_\emptyset(B)$ such that

$$\begin{aligned} \mathrm{syQ}(\varepsilon_B^\emptyset, \varepsilon_B^\emptyset) &\sqsubseteq \mathbb{I}_{\mathcal{P}_\emptyset(B)}, \\ \mathrm{syQ}(X^{\smile}, \varepsilon_B^\emptyset); \mathbb{T}_{\mathcal{P}_\emptyset(B)C} &= X; \mathbb{T}_{BC} \qquad \text{for all crisp relations } X : A \to B. \end{aligned}$$

For a total relation $X : A \to B$ the relation $\mathrm{syQ}(X^{\smile}, \varepsilon_B^\emptyset)$ corresponds to the map, which maps every $x \in A$ to the image under X, i.e., the set of all $y \in B$, which are related to x. Now, we define a defuzzification by

$$\mathcal{D}(U(x)) := \mathrm{syQ}((\Theta_{\mathrm{I}}(x) \backslash U(x))^{\downarrow \smile}, \varepsilon_B^\emptyset); f.$$

Again, if Θ_{I} and F fulfill the properties above, the controller may be represented by a simple relational term, i.e., we have $\mathcal{D}(U(x)) = x;C$ where $C : A \to B$ is given by

$$\begin{aligned} \mathcal{D}(U(x)) &= \mathrm{syQ}((x;(S_A\backslash T')^{\downarrow})^{\smile}, \varepsilon^{\emptyset}_B);f && \text{definition } \mathcal{D} \text{ and } U \\ &= \mathrm{syQ}((S_A\backslash T')^{\downarrow\smile};x^{\smile}, \varepsilon^{\emptyset}_B);f \\ &= x;\mathrm{syQ}((S_A\backslash T')^{\downarrow\smile}, \varepsilon^{\emptyset}_B);f. && \text{Lemma 4.17 (1)} \end{aligned}$$

Example 6.8 Now, we want to return to our running example. We use the cut approach with a constant operation Θ_{I} and an arbitrary mean function for selecting a result. It seems not to be ingenious to use the maximal degree of membership operation since our underlying lattice $\mathcal{L}$ is not linear. In fact, the interpretation of OT, the relation Q_0, shows that there is no temperature, which is optimal for both colonies. This implies that, in general, we will not find an element with maximal degree of membership within the set of possible results.

Suppose $f : \mathcal{P}_{\emptyset}(B+\mathrm{I}) \to B+\mathrm{I}$ is a function. We require that f maps a set containing the "AL" element to that element. This property may be expressed by the following relational expression:

$$(\varepsilon^{\emptyset\smile}_{B+\mathrm{I}};\kappa^{\smile};\mathbb{T}_{\mathrm{I}B+\mathrm{I}} \sqcap \mathbb{I}_{B+\mathrm{I}});f = (\varepsilon^{\emptyset\smile}_{B+\mathrm{I}};\kappa^{\smile};\mathbb{T}_{\mathrm{I}B+\mathrm{I}} \sqcap \mathbb{I}_{B+\mathrm{I}});\mathbb{T}_{B+\mathrm{I}\mathrm{I}};\kappa.$$

The partial identity $\varepsilon^{\emptyset\smile}_{B+\mathrm{I}};\kappa^{\smile};\mathbb{T}_{\mathrm{I}B+\mathrm{I}} \sqcap \mathbb{I}_{B+\mathrm{I}}$ describes those sets containing "AL." Applied to this subset f should be the constant function $\mathbb{T}_{B+\mathrm{I}\mathrm{I}};\kappa$ mapping each set to "AL."

In Section 6.7 we will investigate properties of the scalar α_{I} (definition of the defuzzification), the parameter u_A, u_B (definition of the shifting functions s_A resp. s_B), and a, b (definition of the approximate equality Ξ_B on B) in respect to given values a_1, a_2, b_1, b_2 (definition of the approximate equality Ξ_A on A) such that our controller $C = \mathrm{syQ}((\alpha_A\backslash T)^{\downarrow\smile}, \varepsilon^{\emptyset}_{B+\mathrm{I}});f$ is indeed a mapping. ◇

6.7 PROVING PROPERTIES OF A CONTROLLER

Since our interpretation of a controller is an operation within a suitable Goguen category we are able to prove a lot of theorems about it by reasoning in the abstract theory of Goguen categories. Since this theory is basically equational and element-free it seems to be advantageous not to involve special properties of the underlying lattice $\mathcal{L}$ as far as possible.

As indicated in the previous section, we want to find some properties of the parameters within our running example such that C is indeed a function. Suppose C is a controller defined by

$$C := \mathrm{syQ}\left(\left(\alpha_A\backslash\left(\bigsqcup_{i\in I} T_i\right)\right)^{\downarrow\smile}, \varepsilon^{\emptyset}_B\right);f \quad \text{with} \quad T_i := \bigsqcup_{j\in R(i)} (Q_i^{\smile};_* S_j).$$

We will use the abbreviation $V_i := (\alpha_A \backslash T_i)^{\downarrow}$.

Lemma 6.9 *If* $\bigsqcup_{i\in I}(V_i; \mathbb{T}_{B\mathrm{I}}) = \mathbb{T}_{A\mathrm{I}}$, *then* C *is a mapping.*

Proof. First of all, we want to prove that every relation of the specific form $\mathrm{syQ}(X^{\smile}, \varepsilon_B^{\emptyset}); f$ is univalent. This follows from

$$\begin{aligned}
&(\mathrm{syQ}(X^{\smile}, \varepsilon_B^{\emptyset})^{\smile}; f); \mathrm{syQ}(X^{\smile}, \varepsilon_B^{\emptyset}); f \\
&= f^{\smile}; \mathrm{syQ}(\varepsilon_B^{\emptyset}, X^{\smile}); \mathrm{syQ}(X^{\smile}, \varepsilon_B^{\emptyset}); f && \text{Lemma 4.17 (2)} \\
&\sqsubseteq f^{\smile}; \mathrm{syQ}(\varepsilon_B^{\emptyset}, \varepsilon_B^{\emptyset}); f && \text{Lemma 4.17 (3)} \\
&\sqsubseteq f^{\smile}; f && \text{definition } \varepsilon_B^{\emptyset} \\
&\sqsubseteq \mathbb{I}_B. && f \text{ univalent}
\end{aligned}$$

Since the operation $^{\downarrow}$ and the left residual in the second argument are monotonic we get $\bigsqcup_{i\in I} V_i \sqsubseteq (\alpha_A \backslash (\bigsqcup_{i\in I} T_i))^{\downarrow}$, and, hence, for all objects D

$$\begin{aligned}
\mathbb{T}_{AD} &= \mathbb{T}_{A\mathrm{I}}; \mathbb{T}_{\mathrm{I}D} && \text{Lemma 5.12 (5)} \\
&= \bigsqcup_{i\in I}(V_i; \mathbb{T}_{B\mathrm{I}}); \mathbb{T}_{\mathrm{I}D} && \text{assumption} \\
&= \left(\bigsqcup_{i\in I} V_i\right); \mathbb{T}_{B\mathrm{I}}; \mathbb{T}_{\mathrm{I}D} \\
&= \left(\bigsqcup_{i\in I} V_i\right); \mathbb{T}_{BD} && \text{Lemma 5.12 (5)} \\
&\sqsubseteq \left(\alpha_A \backslash \left(\bigsqcup_{i\in I} T_i\right)\right)^{\downarrow}; \mathbb{T}_{BD}. && \text{see above}
\end{aligned}$$

This immediately implies

$$\begin{aligned}
&\left(\alpha_A \backslash \left(\bigsqcup_{i\in I} T_i\right)\right)^{\downarrow}; \mathbb{T}_{BD} = \mathbb{T}_{AD} \\
&\Leftrightarrow \mathrm{syQ}\left(\left(\alpha_A \backslash \left(\bigsqcup_{i\in I} T_i\right)\right)^{\downarrow\smile}, \varepsilon_B^{\emptyset}\right); \mathbb{T}_{\mathcal{P}_{\emptyset}(B)D} = \mathbb{T}_{AD} && \text{definition } \varepsilon_B^{\emptyset} \\
&\Leftrightarrow \mathrm{syQ}\left(\left(\alpha_A \backslash \left(\bigsqcup_{i\in I} T_i\right)\right)^{\downarrow\smile}, \varepsilon_B^{\emptyset}\right); f; \mathbb{T}_{BD} = \mathbb{T}_{AD} && f \text{ total} \\
&\Leftrightarrow C; \mathbb{T}_{BD} = \mathbb{T}_{AD}. && \text{definition } C \quad \square
\end{aligned}$$

In the next lemma we want to investigate the relation between V_{i+1} and V_i resp. $V_{-(i+1)}$ and V_{-i} for $0 \leq i \leq 2$ within our controller. Notice that it is essential that the shifting function s_A and s_B are chosen as bijections.

Lemma 6.10 *For all* $0 \leq i \leq 2$ *we have* $V_{i+1} = s_A^{\smile}; V_i; \hat{s}_B$ *and* $V_{-(i+1)} = s_A; V_{-i}; \hat{s}_B^{\smile}$ *with* $\hat{s}_B := \iota^{\smile}; s_B; \iota \sqcup \kappa^{\smile}; \kappa$.

Proof. We just show the first assertion. First of all, $\hat{s}_B$ is a bijection, which follows from

$$\begin{aligned}
\hat{s}_B^{\smile}; \hat{s}_B &= (\iota^{\smile}; s_B^{\smile}; \iota \sqcup \kappa^{\smile}; \kappa); (\iota^{\smile}; s_B; \iota \sqcup \kappa^{\smile}; \kappa) && \text{definition } \hat{s}_B \\
&= \iota^{\smile}; s_B^{\smile}; s_B; \iota \sqcup \kappa^{\smile}; \kappa && \text{definition injections} \\
&= \iota^{\smile}; \iota \sqcup \kappa^{\smile}; \kappa && s_B \text{ bijection} \\
&= \mathbb{I}_{B+\mathrm{I}}, && \text{definition injections} \\
\hat{s}_B; \hat{s}_B^{\smile} &= (\iota^{\smile}; s_B; \iota \sqcup \kappa^{\smile}; \kappa); (\iota^{\smile}; s_B^{\smile}; \iota \sqcup \kappa^{\smile}; \kappa) && \text{definition } \hat{s}_B \\
&= \iota^{\smile}; s_B; s_B^{\smile}; \iota \sqcup \kappa^{\smile}; \kappa && \text{definition injections} \\
&= \iota^{\smile}; \iota \sqcup \kappa^{\smile}; \kappa && s_B \text{ bijection} \\
&= \mathbb{I}_{B+\mathrm{I}}. && \text{definition injections}
\end{aligned}$$

Furthermore, we have

$$\iota; \hat{s}_B = \iota; (\iota^{\smile}; s_B; \iota \sqcup \kappa^{\smile}; \kappa) = s_B; \iota.$$

Finally, the assertion follows immediately from

$$\begin{aligned}
& X \sqsubseteq V_{i+1} \\
\Leftrightarrow\ & X \sqsubseteq (\alpha_A \backslash T_{i+1})^{\downarrow} && \text{definition } V_{i+1} \\
\Leftrightarrow\ & X^{\uparrow} \sqsubseteq \alpha_A \backslash T_{i+1} && \text{Galois correspondence} \\
\Leftrightarrow\ & \alpha_A; X^{\uparrow} \sqsubseteq T_{i+1} && \text{definition residual} \\
\Leftrightarrow\ & \alpha_A; X^{\uparrow} \sqsubseteq Q_{i+1}^{\smile};_* S_{i+1} && \text{definition } T_{i+1} \\
\Leftrightarrow\ & \alpha_A; X^{\uparrow} \sqsubseteq (s_A^{\smile}; Q_i^{\smile});_* (S_i'; s_B; \iota) && \text{definition } Q_{i+1} \text{ and } S_{i+1} \\
\Leftrightarrow\ & \alpha_A; X^{\uparrow} \sqsubseteq (s_A^{\smile}; Q_i^{\smile});_* (S_i'; \iota; \hat{s}_B) && \text{see above} \\
\Leftrightarrow\ & \alpha_A; X^{\uparrow} \sqsubseteq (s_A^{\smile}; Q_i^{\smile});_* (S_i; \hat{s}_B) && \text{definition } S_i \\
\Leftrightarrow\ & \alpha_A; X^{\uparrow} \sqsubseteq (s_A^{\smile};_* Q_i^{\smile});_* (S_i;_* \hat{s}_B) && \text{Lemma 5.66} \\
\Leftrightarrow\ & \alpha_A; X^{\uparrow} \sqsubseteq s_A^{\smile};_* (Q_i^{\smile};_* S_i);_* \hat{s}_B && \text{Theorem 5.73} \\
\Leftrightarrow\ & \alpha_A; X^{\uparrow} \sqsubseteq s_A^{\smile}; (Q_i^{\smile};_* S_i); \hat{s}_B && \text{Lemma 5.66} \\
\Leftrightarrow\ & \alpha_A; X^{\uparrow} \sqsubseteq s_A^{\smile}; T_i; \hat{s}_B && \text{definition } T_i \\
\Leftrightarrow\ & s_A; \alpha_A; X^{\uparrow}; \hat{s}_B^{\smile} \sqsubseteq T_i && \text{Lemma 4.8 (1)–(2)} \\
\Leftrightarrow\ & \alpha_A; s_A; X^{\uparrow}; \hat{s}_B^{\smile} \sqsubseteq T_i && \text{Lemma 5.14} \\
\Leftrightarrow\ & s_A; X^{\uparrow}; \hat{s}_B^{\smile} \sqsubseteq \alpha_A \backslash T_i && \text{definition residual} \\
\Leftrightarrow\ & s_A^{\uparrow}; X^{\uparrow}; \hat{s}_B^{\smile\uparrow} \sqsubseteq \alpha_A \backslash T_i && s_A \text{ and } s_B; \iota \text{ crisp} \\
\Leftrightarrow\ & (s_A^{\uparrow}; X; \hat{s}_B^{\smile\uparrow})^{\uparrow} \sqsubseteq \alpha_A \backslash T_i && \text{Lemma 5.6 (10)}
\end{aligned}$$

$$\Leftrightarrow (s_A; X; \hat{s}_B^{\smile})^{\uparrow} \sqsubseteq \alpha_A \backslash T_i \qquad s_A \text{ and } s_B; \iota \text{ crisp}$$
$$\Leftrightarrow s_A; X; \hat{s}_B^{\smile} \sqsubseteq (\alpha_A \backslash T_i)^{\downarrow} \qquad \text{Galois correspondence}$$
$$\Leftrightarrow s_A; X; \hat{s}_B^{\smile} \sqsubseteq V_i \qquad \text{definition } V_i$$
$$\Leftrightarrow X \sqsubseteq s_A^{\smile}; V_i; \hat{s}_B. \qquad \text{Lemma 4.8(1)–(2)}$$
□

As a first property, we will require that the domain of V_0 is an interval. An interval may be described within the language of relations as follows: Suppose $x, y : \mathrm{I} \to A$ are crisp mappings such that $y \sqsubseteq x; E_A$, i.e., the element given by x is less or equal to the element given by y. Notice that the property above is equivalent to $x \sqsubseteq y; E_A^{\smile}$ by Lemma 4.8. The corresponding interval is described by $x; E_A \sqcap y; E_A^{\smile}$. For brevity, we will use the notation $[x, y]$ for intervals. Notice that a term $[x, y]$ should always imply the required order property for x and y. Therefore, our requirement for V_0 may be formalized by

$$V_0; \mathbb{T}_{(B+\mathrm{I})\mathrm{I}} = [x, y]^{\smile}$$

for suitable crisp mappings $x, y : \mathrm{I} \to A$.

First, we want to show that the domain of V_0 may be described by the $\mathcal{L}$-fuzzy set Q_0.

Lemma 6.11 *Suppose $V = (\alpha_A \backslash (Q^{\smile};_* S))^{\downarrow}$ for relations $Q : \mathrm{I} \to A$ and $S : \mathrm{I} \to B$ such that $S^{\downarrow}$ is total. Then we have $V; \mathbb{T}_{B\mathrm{I}} = (\alpha_\mathrm{I} \backslash Q)^{\downarrow\smile}$.*

Proof. To prove the inclusion $\sqsubseteq$ notice that we have $\mathbb{T}_{\mathrm{II}} = \mathbb{T}_{\mathrm{I}B}; S^{\downarrow\smile} \sqsubseteq \mathbb{T}_{\mathrm{I}B}; S^{\smile}$ since $S^{\downarrow}$ is total, and, hence, $\mathbb{T}_{\mathrm{I}B}; S^{\smile} = \mathbb{I}_\mathrm{I}$ since I is a unit. We conclude

$$\begin{aligned}
\alpha_\mathrm{I}; \mathbb{T}_{\mathrm{I}B}; V^{\smile} &= \mathbb{T}_{\mathrm{I}B}; \alpha_B; V^{\smile} && \text{definition scalar}\\
&= \mathbb{T}_{\mathrm{I}B}; \alpha_B; (\alpha_A \backslash (Q^{\smile};_* S))^{\downarrow\smile} && \text{definition } V\\
&\sqsubseteq \mathbb{T}_{\mathrm{I}B}; \alpha_B; (\alpha_A \backslash (Q^{\smile};_* S))^{\smile} && \text{Corollary 5.5 (2)}\\
&= \mathbb{T}_{\mathrm{I}B}; \alpha_B; (\alpha_B \backslash (Q^{\smile};_* S)^{\smile}) && \text{Lemma 5.15}\\
&\sqsubseteq \mathbb{T}_{\mathrm{I}B}; (Q^{\smile};_* S)^{\smile} && \text{Corollary 4.15 (2)}\\
&= \mathbb{T}_{\mathrm{I}B}; (S^{\smile};_* Q) && \text{Theorem 5.75}\\
&= \mathbb{T}_{\mathrm{I}B};_* (S^{\smile};_* Q) && \text{Lemma 5.66}\\
&= (\mathbb{T}_{\mathrm{I}B};_* S^{\smile});_* Q && \text{Theorem 5.73}\\
&= (\mathbb{T}_{\mathrm{I}B}; S^{\smile});_* Q && \text{Lemma 5.66}\\
&= \mathbb{I}_\mathrm{I};_* Q && \text{see above}\\
&= \mathbb{I}_\mathrm{I}; Q && \text{Lemma 5.66}\\
&= Q.
\end{aligned}$$

By the definition of the residuals $V;\mathbb{T}_{BI} \sqsubseteq (\alpha_{\mathrm{I}}\backslash Q)^{\downarrow\smile}$ follows. For the other inclusion notice again that $S^{\downarrow};\mathbb{T}_{BI} = \mathbb{I}_{\mathrm{I}}$. We obtain

$$\begin{aligned}
(\alpha_{\mathrm{I}}\backslash Q)^{\downarrow\smile} &= (\alpha_{\mathrm{I}}\backslash Q)^{\downarrow\smile};S^{\downarrow};\mathbb{T}_{BI} && \text{see above}\\
&= (\alpha_A\backslash Q^{\smile})^{\downarrow};S^{\downarrow};\mathbb{T}_{BI} && \text{Lemma 5.15}\\
&= ((\alpha_A\backslash Q^{\smile})^{\downarrow};S^{\downarrow})^{\downarrow};\mathbb{T}_{BI} && \text{Lemma 5.16 (3)}\\
&\sqsubseteq ((\alpha_A\backslash Q^{\smile});S^{\downarrow})^{\downarrow};\mathbb{T}_{BI} && \text{Corollary 5.5 (2)}\\
&\sqsubseteq (\alpha_A\backslash (Q^{\smile};S^{\downarrow}))^{\downarrow};\mathbb{T}_{BI} && \text{Lemma 4.16 (2)}\\
&= (\alpha_A\backslash (Q^{\smile};_* S^{\downarrow}))^{\downarrow};\mathbb{T}_{BI} && \text{Lemma 5.66}\\
&\sqsubseteq (\alpha_A\backslash (Q^{\smile};_* S))^{\downarrow};\mathbb{T}_{BI} && ;_* \text{ and } \backslash \text{ monotonic}\\
&= V;\mathbb{T}_{BI}. && \text{definition } V
\end{aligned}$$

□

The previous lemma may be applied to our controller.

Lemma 6.12 *We have* $V_i;\mathbb{T}_{(B+\mathrm{I})\mathrm{I}} = (\alpha_{\mathrm{I}}\backslash Q_i)^{\downarrow\smile}$ *for all* $-4 \le i \le 4$.

Proof. First of all, we have

$$\begin{aligned}
\mathbb{T}_{\mathrm{I}D} &= e_0;\iota;\mathbb{T}_{(B+\mathrm{I})D} && e_0 \text{ and } \iota \text{ are total}\\
&\sqsubseteq e_0;\iota;\Xi^{\downarrow}{}_B;\mathbb{T}_{(B+\mathrm{I})D} && \mathbb{I}_B \sqsubseteq \Xi_B\\
&= (e_0;\iota;\Xi^{\downarrow}{}_B)^{\downarrow};\mathbb{T}_{(B+\mathrm{I})D} && \text{Lemma 5.16}\\
&\sqsubseteq (e_0;\iota;\Xi_B)^{\downarrow};\mathbb{T}_{(B+\mathrm{I})D} && \text{Corollary 5.5 (2)}\\
&= S_0{}^{\downarrow};\mathbb{T}_{(B+\mathrm{I})D}, && \text{definition } S_0
\end{aligned}$$

such that the assertion is true for $i = 0$ by Lemma 6.11. The other cases are deduced by induction as follows: Suppose $i \ge 0$. Then we conclude the assertion from

$$\begin{aligned}
V_{i+1};\mathbb{T}_{(B+\mathrm{I})\mathrm{I}} &= s_A^{\smile};V_i;\hat{s}_B;\mathbb{T}_{(B+\mathrm{I})\mathrm{I}} && \text{Lemma 6.10}\\
&= s_A^{\smile};V_i;\mathbb{T}_{(B+\mathrm{I})\mathrm{I}} && \hat{s}_B \text{ total}\\
&= s_A^{\smile};(\alpha_{\mathrm{I}}\backslash Q_i)^{\downarrow\smile} && \text{induction hypothesis}\\
&= ((\alpha_{\mathrm{I}}\backslash Q_i)^{\downarrow};s_A)^{\smile} && \\
&= (\alpha_{\mathrm{I}}\backslash (Q_i;s_A))^{\downarrow\smile} && \text{Lemma 4.16 (3)}\\
&= (\alpha_{\mathrm{I}}\backslash Q_{i+1})^{\downarrow\smile}, && \text{definition } Q_{i+1}
\end{aligned}$$

$$
\begin{aligned}
V_{-(i+1)}; \top\!\!\top_{(B+\mathrm{I})\mathrm{I}} &= s_A; V_{-i}; \hat{s}_B^{\smile}; \top\!\!\top_{(B+\mathrm{I})\mathrm{I}} && \text{Lemma 6.10}\\
&= s_A; V_{-i}; \top\!\!\top_{(B+\mathrm{I})\mathrm{I}} && \hat{s}_B^{\smile} \text{ total}\\
&= s_A; (\alpha_\mathrm{I} \backslash Q_{-i})^{\downarrow\smile} && \text{induction hypothesis}\\
&= ((\alpha_\mathrm{I} \backslash Q_{-i})^{\downarrow}; s_A^{\smile})^{\smile} &&\\
&= (\alpha_\mathrm{I} \backslash (Q_{-i}; s_A^{\smile}))^{\downarrow\smile} && \text{Lemma 4.16 (3)}\\
&= (\alpha_\mathrm{I} \backslash Q_{-(i+1)})^{\downarrow\smile}. && \text{definition } Q_{-(i+1)} \qquad \square
\end{aligned}
$$

Now, we want to prove two technical lemmata on elements and intervals within our application, i.e., E_A and s_A fulfil $E_A; (s_A \sqcap E_A) = (s_A \sqcap E_A); E_A$.

Lemma 6.13 *Suppose $y : \mathrm{I} \to A$ is a map such that $y; s_A \sqsubseteq y; E_A$. Then we have*

(1) $\mathbb{I}_A \sqcap E_A; y^{\smile}; y; E_A^{\smile} \sqsubseteq \mathbb{I}_A \sqcap E_A; s_A^{\smile}$,

(2) if $\mathbb{I}_A \sqcap R^{\smile}; R \sqsubseteq \mathbb{I}_A \sqcap E_A; y^{\smile}; y; E_A^{\smile}$, *then* $R; s_A = R; (s_A \sqcap E_A)$,

(3) if $y \sqsubseteq x; E_A$, *then* $x; s_A \sqsubseteq x; E_A$,

(4) if $[x, y]$ *is an interval, then so is* $[x; s_A, y; s_A]$ *and* $[x, y]; s_A = [x; s_A, y; s_A]$.

Proof.

(1) First of all, we have

$$
\begin{aligned}
y &= y \sqcap y; s_A; s_A^{\smile} && s_A \text{ bijection}\\
&\sqsubseteq y \sqcap y; E_A; s_A^{\smile} && \text{assumption}\\
&= y; (\mathbb{I}_A \sqcap E_A; s_A^{\smile}). && y \text{ map}
\end{aligned}
$$

By Lemma 4.8 (2) we conclude $y^{\smile}; y \sqsubseteq \mathbb{I}_A \sqcap E_A; s_A^{\smile}$, and, hence,

$$y^{\smile}; y = (y^{\smile}; y)^{\smile} \sqsubseteq (\mathbb{I}_A \sqcap E_A; s_A^{\smile})^{\smile} = \mathbb{I}_A \sqcap s_A; E_A^{\smile}.$$

Now, the assertion follows from

$$
\begin{aligned}
&\mathbb{I}_A \sqcap E_A; y^{\smile}; y; E_A^{\smile}\\
&\sqsubseteq \mathbb{I}_A \sqcap E_A; (\mathbb{I}_A \sqcap s_A; E_A^{\smile}); E_A^{\smile} && \text{see above}\\
&\sqsubseteq \mathbb{I}_A \sqcap E_A; (E_A \sqcap s_A); E_A^{\smile}; E_A^{\smile} && \text{modular law}\\
&\sqsubseteq \mathbb{I}_A \sqcap E_A; (E_A \sqcap s_A); E_A^{\smile} && E_A \text{ transitive}\\
&= \mathbb{I}_A \sqcap (E_A \sqcap s_A); E_A; E_A^{\smile} && \text{property of } s_A \sqcap E_A\\
&\sqsubseteq \mathbb{I}_A \sqcap (E_A \sqcap s_A); \top\!\!\top_{AA} &&\\
&= \mathbb{I}_A \sqcap (E_A \sqcap s_A); (E_A \sqcap s_A)^{\smile} && \text{Lemma 4.23 (2)}\\
&\sqsubseteq \mathbb{I}_A \sqcap E_A; s_A^{\smile}.
\end{aligned}
$$

(2) We immediately conclude that

$$\begin{aligned} R;s_A &= R;(\mathbb{I}_A \sqcap R^{\smile};R);s_A && \text{Lemma 4.5 (8)} \\ &\sqsubseteq R;(\mathbb{I}_A \sqcap E_A;y^{\smile};y;E_A^{\smile});s_A && \text{assumption} \\ &\sqsubseteq R;(\mathbb{I}_A \sqcap E_A;s_A^{\smile});s_A && \text{by (1)} \\ &= R;(s_A \sqcap E_A). && \text{Lemma 4.7 (2)} \end{aligned}$$

The other inclusion is trivial.

(3) First of all, we have $\mathbb{I}_A \sqcap x^{\smile};x \sqsubseteq \mathbb{I}_A \sqcap E_A;y^{\smile};y;E_A^{\smile}$, which implies $x;s_A = x;(s_A \sqcap E_A)$ by (2). We get

$$\begin{aligned} x;s_A &= x;(s_A \sqcap E_A) && \text{by (2)} \\ &= x;s_A \sqcap x;E_A && x \text{ map}, \end{aligned}$$

and, hence, $x;s_A \sqsubseteq x;E_A$.

(4) First of all, we have to show $y;s_A \sqsubseteq x;s_A;E_A$. Notice that we have $y \sqsubseteq x;E_A$ and $x \sqsubseteq y;E_A^{\smile}$ since $[x,y]$ is an interval. We obtain

$$\begin{aligned} y;s_A &= y;s_A \sqcap y;E_A && \text{assumption} \\ &= y;(s_A \sqcap E_A) && y \text{ map} \\ &\sqsubseteq x;E_A;(s_A \sqcap E_A) && \text{see above} \\ &= x;(s_A \sqcap E_A);E_A && \text{property of } s_A \sqcap E_A \\ &\sqsubseteq x;s_A;E_A. \end{aligned}$$

Furthermore, we have $\mathbb{I}_A \sqcap x^{\smile};x \sqsubseteq \mathbb{I}_A \sqcap E_A;y^{\smile};y;E_A^{\smile}$ and

$$\begin{aligned} &\mathbb{I}_A \sqcap [x,y]^{\smile};[x,y] \\ &= \mathbb{I}_A \sqcap (E_A^{\smile};x^{\smile} \sqcap E_A;y^{\smile});(x;E_A \sqcap y;E_A^{\smile}) && \text{definition } [x,y] \\ &\sqsubseteq \mathbb{I}_A \sqcap E_A;y^{\smile};y;E_A^{\smile}, \end{aligned}$$

such that $x;(s_A \sqcap E_A) = x;s_A$ and $[x,y];(s_A \sqcap E_A) = [x,y];s_A$ follows from (2). We have

$$\begin{aligned} y;E_A^{\smile} &= (y \sqcap y;s_A;E_A^{\smile});E_A^{\smile} && \text{assumption on } y \\ &= (y;s_A;s_A^{\smile} \sqcap y;s_A;E_A^{\smile});E_A^{\smile} && s_A \text{ bijection} \\ &= y;s_A;(s_A^{\smile} \sqcap E_A^{\smile});E_A^{\smile} && y;s_A \text{ map} \\ &= y;s_A;(s_A \sqcap E_A)^{\smile};E_A^{\smile} \\ &= y;s_A;E_A^{\smile};(s_A \sqcap E_A)^{\smile}. && \text{property } E_A \end{aligned}$$

Finally, the assertion follows from

$$
\begin{aligned}
&[x,y];s_A \\
&= [x,y];(s_A \sqcap E_A) && \text{see above}\\
&= (x;E_A \sqcap y;E_A^{\smile});(s_A \sqcap E_A) && \text{definition } [x,y]\\
&= (x;E_A \sqcap y;s_A;E_A^{\smile};(s_A \sqcap E_A)^{\smile});(s_A \sqcap E_A) && \text{see above}\\
&= x;E_A;(s_A \sqcap E_A) \sqcap y;s_A;E_A^{\smile} && \text{Lemma 4.7 (2)}\\
&= x;(s_A \sqcap E_A);E_A \sqcap y;s_A;E_A^{\smile} && \text{property } E_A\\
&= x;s_A;E_A \sqcap y;s_A;E_A^{\smile} && \text{see above}\\
&= [x;s_A,y;s_A]. && \text{definition } [x;s_A,y;s_A] \quad \square
\end{aligned}
$$

If we use $s_A^{\smile}$ instead of s_A, we get similar results. We have summarized these properties in the next corollary without a proof.

Corollary 6.14 *Suppose $x : \mathrm{I} \to A$ is a map such that $x \sqsubseteq x;s_A^{\smile};E_A$. Then we have*

(1) $\mathbb{I}_A \sqcap E_A^{\smile};x^{\smile};x;E_A \sqsubseteq \mathbb{I}_A \sqcap E_A^{\smile};s_A$,

(2) if $\mathbb{I}_A \sqcap R^{\smile};R \sqsubseteq \mathbb{I}_A \sqcap E_A^{\smile};x^{\smile};x;E_A$, *then* $R;s_A^{\smile} = R;(s_A \sqcap E_A)^{\smile}$,

(3) if $y \sqsubseteq x;E_A$, *then* $y \sqsubseteq y;s_A^{\smile};E_A$,

(4) if $[x,y]$ *is an interval, then so is* $[x;s_A^{\smile},y;s_A^{\smile}]$ *and* $[x,y];s_A^{\smile} = [x;s_A^{\smile},y;s_A^{\smile}]$.

Before we return to our example we state a lemma about the union of intervals. Obviously, the union of two intervals is again an interval if they overlap.

Lemma 6.15 *If $v \sqsubseteq [t,u]$ and $u \sqsubseteq [v,w]$, then $[t,u] \sqcup [v,w] = [t,w]$.*

Proof. First of all, $u \sqsubseteq t;E_A$ and $u \sqsubseteq [v,w]$ implies $w \sqsubseteq u;E_A \sqsubseteq t;E_A$ such that $[t,w]$ is indeed an interval. Furthermore, $v \sqsubseteq [t,u] \sqsubseteq t;E_A$ and $u \sqsubseteq [v,w] \sqsubseteq w;E_A^{\smile}$ implies $t;E_A \sqcup v;E_A = t;E_A$ and $u;E_A^{\smile} \sqcup w;E_A^{\smile} = w;E_A^{\smile}$, respectively, and we have

$$
\begin{aligned}
\top\!\!\top_{\mathrm{I}A} &= u;\top\!\!\top_{AA} && u \text{ total}\\
&= u;(E_A \sqcup E_A^{\smile}) && E_A \text{ linear ordering}\\
&= u;E_A \sqcup u;E_A^{\smile} &&\\
&\sqsubseteq v;E_A \sqcup u;E_A^{\smile}. && u \sqsubseteq [v,w]
\end{aligned}
$$

The assertion follows from

$$
\begin{aligned}
&[t,u] \sqcup [v,w] \\
&= (t;E_A \sqcap u;E_A^{\smile}) \sqcup (v;E_A \sqcap w;E_A^{\smile}) && \text{definition interval} \\
&= (t;E_A \sqcup v;E_A) \sqcap (t;E_A \sqcup w;E_A^{\smile}) \\
&\quad \sqcap\ (u;E_A^{\smile} \sqcup v;E_A) \sqcap (u;E_A^{\smile} \sqcup w;E_A^{\smile}) \\
&= t;E_A \sqcap w;E_A^{\smile} \sqcap (t;E_A \sqcup w;E_A^{\smile}) && \text{see above} \\
&= t;E_A \sqcap w;E_A^{\smile} \\
&= [t,w]. && \text{definition interval} \quad \square
\end{aligned}
$$

Now, let $s_A^0 := \mathbb{I}_A$ and $s_A^{i+1} := s_A^i; s_A$ resp. $s_A^{0\,\smile} := \mathbb{I}_A$ and $s_A^{i+1\,\smile} := s_A^{i\,\smile}; s_A^{\smile}$. We may summarize our attempt so far as follows:

Lemma 6.16 *If* $V_0; \mathbb{T}_{(B+\mathrm{I})\mathrm{I}} = [x,y]^{\smile}$ *such that*

$$
x; s_A^{i\,\smile} \sqsubseteq x; s_A^{i+1\,\smile}; E_A, \qquad y; s_A^{i+1} \sqsubseteq y; s_A^i; E_A \qquad \textit{and} \qquad y; s_A^i \sqsubseteq x; s_A^{i+1}; E_A
$$

for all $0 \leq i \leq 2$, *then we have* $\bigsqcup\limits_{-3 \leq i \leq 3} (V_i; \mathbb{T}_{(B+\mathrm{I})\mathrm{I}}) = [x; s_A^{3\,\smile}, y; s_A^3]^{\smile}$.

Proof. First of all, we show

$$
V_i; \mathbb{T}_{(B+\mathrm{I})\mathrm{I}} = [x; s_A^i, y; s_A^i]^{\smile} \qquad \text{and} \qquad V_{-i}; \mathbb{T}_{(B+\mathrm{I})\mathrm{I}} = [x; s_A^{i\,\smile}, y; s_A^{i\,\smile}]^{\smile}
$$

for $0 \leq i \leq 3$. The first assertion follows by induction from

$$
\begin{aligned}
V_{i+1}; \mathbb{T}_{(B+\mathrm{I})\mathrm{I}} &= s_A^{\smile}; V_i; \hat{s}_B; \mathbb{T}_{(B+\mathrm{I})\mathrm{I}} && \text{Lemma 6.10} \\
&= s_A^{\smile}; V_i; \mathbb{T}_{B\mathrm{I}} && \hat{s}_B \text{ total} \\
&= s_A^{\smile}; [x; s_A^i, y; s_A^i]^{\smile} && \text{induction hypothesis} \\
&= [x; s_A^{i+1}, y; s_A^{i+1}]^{\smile}, && \text{Lemma 6.13}
\end{aligned}
$$

and the second is shown analogously. The required order properties give us the possibility to apply Lemma 6.15 such that the assertion follows. $\square$

Since E_A has a least element 0 and greatest element 50.0 the intervals $[0, x]$ and $[x, 50.0]$ are given by the relations $x; E_A^{\smile}$ and $x; E_A$, respectively. The remaining parts of the domain of C are exactly the intervals $[0, x; s_A^{3\,\smile}]$ and $[y; s_A^3, 50.0]$. In the next lemma we want to investigate a property such that the domain of V_{-4} resp. of V_4 fills this gap.

Lemma 6.17 *Suppose* $V_0; \mathbb{T}_{(B+\mathrm{I})\mathrm{I}} = [x,y]^{\smile}$,

$$
x; s_A^{i\,\smile} \sqsubseteq x; s_A^{i+1\,\smile}; E_A \qquad \textit{and} \qquad y; s_A^{i+1} \sqsubseteq y; s_A^i; E_A
$$

for all $0 \leq i \leq 2$. *Then* $\alpha_{\mathrm{I}};_* Q_0 \sqsubseteq [x,y]$ *implies* $[0, x; s_A^{3\smile}]^\smile \sqsubseteq V_{-4}; \mathbb{T}_{(B+\mathrm{I})\mathrm{I}}$ *and* $[y; s_A^3, 50.0]^\smile \sqsubseteq V_4; \mathbb{T}_{(B+\mathrm{I})\mathrm{I}}$.

Proof. For brevity, let $u := x; s_A^{3\smile}$. Using the order properties on x we may apply Corollary 6.14 (4) and conclude $[x,y]; s_A^{3\smile} = [x; s_A^{3\smile}, y; s_A^{3\smile}]$. This implies

$$\begin{aligned}
\alpha_{\mathrm{I}}; Q_{-3} &= \alpha_{\mathrm{I}}; Q_0; s_A^{3\smile} && \text{definition } Q_{-3}\\
&\sqsubseteq [x,y]; s_A^{3\smile} && \text{assumption}\\
&= [x; s_A^{3\smile}, y; s_A^{3\smile}] && \text{Corollary 6.14 (4)}\\
&\sqsubseteq x; s_A^{3\smile}; E_A.
\end{aligned}$$

The following computation shows the first assertion:

$$\begin{aligned}
&\alpha_{\mathrm{I}};_* Q_{-3} \sqsubseteq u; E_A\\
&\Leftrightarrow u^\smile; (\alpha_{\mathrm{I}};_* Q_{-3}) \sqsubseteq E_A && \text{Lemma 4.8 (2)}\\
&\Rightarrow E_A; u^\smile; (\alpha_{\mathrm{I}};_* Q_{-3}) \sqsubseteq E_A && E_A \text{ transitive}\\
&\Leftrightarrow (E_A; u^\smile);_* (\alpha_{\mathrm{I}};_* Q_{-3}) \sqsubseteq E_A && \text{Lemma 5.66}\\
&\Leftrightarrow ((E_A; u^\smile);_* \alpha_{\mathrm{I}});_* Q_{-3} \sqsubseteq E_A && \text{Theorem 5.73}\\
&\Leftrightarrow (E_A; u^\smile; \alpha_{\mathrm{I}});_* Q_{-3} \sqsubseteq E_A && \text{Lemma 5.66}\\
&\Leftrightarrow E_A; u^\smile; \alpha_{\mathrm{I}} \sqsubseteq E_A \rhd_* Q_{-3} && \text{definition } \rhd_*\\
&\Leftrightarrow E_A; u^\smile; \alpha_{\mathrm{I}} \sqsubseteq Q_{-4}^\smile && \text{definition } Q_{-4}\\
&\Leftrightarrow \alpha_A; E_A; u^\smile \sqsubseteq Q_{-4}^\smile && \text{Lemma 5.14}\\
&\Leftrightarrow E_A; u^\smile \sqsubseteq \alpha_A \backslash Q_{-4}^\smile && \text{definition residual}\\
&\Leftrightarrow E_A; u^\smile \sqsubseteq (\alpha_A \backslash Q_{-4}^\smile)^\downarrow && E_A; u^\smile \text{ crisp}\\
&\Leftrightarrow E_A; u^\smile \sqsubseteq (\alpha_A \backslash Q_{-4}^\smile)^\downarrow; \mathbb{T}_{\mathrm{II}} && \mathbb{T}_{\mathrm{II}} = \mathbb{I}_{\mathrm{I}}\\
&\Leftrightarrow E_A; u^\smile \sqsubseteq (\alpha_A \backslash Q_{-4}^\smile)^\downarrow; \kappa; \mathbb{T}_{(B+\mathrm{I})\mathrm{I}} && \kappa \text{ total}\\
&\Leftrightarrow E_A; u^\smile \sqsubseteq ((\alpha_A \backslash Q_{-4}^\smile)^\downarrow; \kappa)^\downarrow; \mathbb{T}_{(B+\mathrm{I})\mathrm{I}} && \text{Lemma 5.16}\\
&\Rightarrow E_A; u^\smile \sqsubseteq ((\alpha_A \backslash Q_{-4}^\smile); \kappa)^\downarrow; \mathbb{T}_{(B+\mathrm{I})\mathrm{I}} && R^\downarrow \sqsubseteq R\\
&\Rightarrow E_A; u^\smile \sqsubseteq (\alpha_A \backslash (Q_{-4}^\smile; \kappa))^\downarrow; \mathbb{T}_{(B+\mathrm{I})\mathrm{I}} && \text{Lemma 4.16 (2)}\\
&\Leftrightarrow E_A; u^\smile \sqsubseteq (\alpha_A \backslash T_{-4})^\downarrow; \mathbb{T}_{(B+\mathrm{I})\mathrm{I}} && \text{definition } T_{-4}\\
&\Leftrightarrow [0,u]^\smile \sqsubseteq V_{-4}; \mathbb{T}_{(B+\mathrm{I})\mathrm{I}}. && \text{definition } V_{-4} \text{ and } [0,u]
\end{aligned}$$

The second assertion is shown analogously. □

We want to interpret the property above. Suppose α is the scalar given by the element $(a_0, b_0) \in [0,1] \times [0,1]$. Then the previous lemma requires that for any element z, which is not in the interval $[x, y]$ but in the $\mathcal{L}$-fuzzy set Q_0 with a degree (a, b), i.e., $Q_0(1, z) = (a, b)$, we have $(a_0, b_0) * (a, b) = (0, 0)$, which is equivalent to $a_0 + a \leq 1$ and $b_0 + b \leq 1$. Notice that $(a, b) \leq (a_0, b_0)$ since z is not in the domain $[x, y]$ of V_0 and V_0 is defined by an α-cut. We may choose $a_0, b_0 \leq \frac{1}{2}$ and conclude

$$a_0 + a \leq a_0 + a_0 = 2a_0 \leq 1 \quad \text{and} \quad b_0 + b \leq b_0 + b_0 = 2b_0 \leq 1.$$

Now, we want to summarize the requirements on the controller on the level of elements. Again, suppose α is the scalar given by the element $(a_0, b_0) \in [0, 1] \times [0, 1]$ with $a_0 > 0$ and $b_0 > 0$.

(1) $V_0; \mathbb{T}_{(B+\mathrm{I})\mathrm{I}} = [x, y]^{\smile}$. By Lemma 6.12 this is equivalent to $(\alpha_{\mathrm{I}} \backslash Q_0)^{\downarrow} = [x, y]$ and on the level of elements to

$$z \in [x, y] \Leftrightarrow (\alpha_{\mathrm{I}} \backslash Q_0)^{\downarrow}(1, z)$$

for all $z \in A$. The right side may be computed as follows:

$$\begin{aligned}
&(\alpha_{\mathrm{I}} \backslash Q_0)^{\downarrow}(1, z) \\
&\Leftrightarrow Q_0(1, z) \geq (a_0, b_0) && \text{Lemma 3.3 (5)} \\
&\Leftrightarrow \min(1, \max(0, a_1 - b_1|24 - z|)) \geq a_0 && \text{definition } Q_0 \\
&\text{and } \min(1, \max(0, a_2 - b_2|25.5 - z|)) \geq b_0 \\
&\Leftrightarrow a_1 - b_1|24 - z| \geq a_0 \text{ and } a_2 - b_2|25.5 - z| \geq b_0 && a_0, b_0 \in [0, 1] \\
&\Leftrightarrow \frac{a_1 - a_0}{b_1} \geq |24 - z| \text{ and } \frac{a_2 - b_0}{b_2} \geq |25.5 - z| && b_1, b_2 \geq 0 \\
&\Leftrightarrow z \in [24 - \frac{a_1 - a_0}{b_1}, 24 + \frac{a_1 - a_0}{b_1}] \\
&\text{and } z \in [25.5 - \frac{a_2 - b_0}{b_2}, 25.5 + \frac{a_2 - b_0}{b_2}]
\end{aligned}$$

Consequently, x resp. y is the least resp. greatest element of A such that

$$\begin{aligned}
\max(24 - \frac{a_1 - a_0}{b_1}, 25.5 - \frac{a_2 - b_0}{b_2}) &\leq x \\
\text{and} y \leq \min(24 + \frac{a_1 - a_0}{b_1}, 25.5 + \frac{a_2 - b_0}{b_2}).
\end{aligned}$$

(2) $x; s_A^{i\,\smile} \sqsubseteq x; s_A^{i+1\,\smile}; E_A$, $y; s_A^{i+1} \sqsubseteq y; s_A^i; E_A$ and $y; s_A^i \sqsubseteq x; s_A^{i+1}; E_A$ for all $0 \leq i \leq 2$. If we choose the u in the definition of s_A such that $3u \leq \min(50.0 - y, x)$, these properties are fulfilled.

(3) $\alpha_{\mathrm{I}};_* Q_0 \sqsubseteq [x, y]$. As indicated above, this property is fulfilled if $a_0, b_0 \leq \frac{1}{2}$.

As a last requirement we will demand that our controller permits an AL-signal if the temperature is less than or equal to 5° or greater than or equal to 45°. In the language of relations this may be expressed by

$$e_5 \sqsubseteq u; E_A \text{ or } u \sqsubseteq e_{45}; E_A \text{ implies } u; C = \mathrm{AL}.$$

In the next lemma we give a sufficient condition for that property.

Lemma 6.18 *Suppose* $x; s_A^{3\smile} \sqsubseteq e_5; E_A$ *and* $e_{45} \sqsubseteq y; s_A^3; E_A$. *Then* $e_5 \sqsubseteq u; E_A$ *or* $u \sqsubseteq e_{45}; E_A$ *implies* $u; C = \mathrm{AL}$.

Proof. From $u \sqsubseteq e_5; E_A^{\smile}$ we conclude using Lemma 6.17 and Lemma 6.12

$$u \sqsubseteq [0, x; s_A^{3\smile}] \sqsubseteq (V_{-4}; \mathbb{T}_{\mathrm{I}(B+\mathrm{I})})^{\smile} = \alpha_{\mathrm{I}} \backslash Q_{-4}.$$

Furthermore, we have

$$\begin{aligned}
(Q_{-4}^{\smile};_* \kappa); \kappa^{\smile} &= (Q_{-4}^{\smile};_* \kappa);_* \kappa^{\smile} && \text{Lemma 5.66}\\
&= Q_{-4}^{\smile};_* (\kappa;_* \kappa^{\smile}) && \text{Theorem 5.73}\\
&= Q_{-4}^{\smile};_* (\kappa; \kappa^{\smile}) && \text{Lemma 5.66}\\
&= Q_{-4}^{\smile};_* \mathbb{I}_{\mathrm{I}} && \text{definition } \kappa\\
&= Q_{-4}^{\smile}; \mathbb{I}_{\mathrm{I}} && \text{Lemma 5.66}\\
&= Q_{-4}^{\smile}.
\end{aligned}$$

Together, we obtain

$$\begin{aligned}
u \sqsubseteq \alpha_{\mathrm{I}} \backslash Q_{-4} &\Leftrightarrow \alpha_{\mathrm{I}}; u \sqsubseteq Q_{-4} && \text{definition residual}\\
&\Leftrightarrow u^{\smile}; \alpha_{\mathrm{I}} \sqsubseteq Q_{-4}^{\smile} &&\\
&\Leftrightarrow \alpha_A; u^{\smile} \sqsubseteq Q_{-4}^{\smile} && \text{Lemma 5.14}\\
&\Leftrightarrow \alpha_A; u^{\smile} \sqsubseteq (Q_{-4}^{\smile};_* \kappa); \kappa^{\smile} && \text{see above}\\
&\Leftrightarrow \alpha_A; u^{\smile}; \kappa \sqsubseteq Q_{-4}^{\smile};_* \kappa && \text{Lemma 4.8 (1)}\\
&\Leftrightarrow u^{\smile}; \kappa \sqsubseteq \alpha_A \backslash (Q_{-4}^{\smile};_* \kappa) && \text{definition residual}\\
&\Leftrightarrow u^{\smile}; \kappa \sqsubseteq (\alpha_A \backslash (Q_{-4}^{\smile};_* \kappa))^{\downarrow} && u \text{ and } \kappa \text{ crisp}\\
&\Leftrightarrow u^{\smile}; \kappa \sqsubseteq V_{-4} && \text{definition } V_{-4}\\
&\Leftrightarrow \kappa \sqsubseteq u; V_{-4}. && \text{Lemma 4.8 (2)}
\end{aligned}$$

This immediately implies

$$\begin{aligned}
\mathbb{T}_{\mathrm{I}(B+\mathrm{I})} &= \kappa; \kappa^{\smile}; \mathbb{T}_{\mathrm{I}(B+\mathrm{I})} && \text{definition } \kappa\\
&\sqsubseteq u; V_{-4}; \kappa^{\smile}; \mathbb{T}_{\mathrm{I}(B+\mathrm{I})} && \text{see above}\\
&\sqsubseteq u; \left(\alpha_A \backslash \left(\bigsqcup_{-4 \leq i \leq 4} T_i\right)\right)^{\downarrow}; \kappa^{\smile}; \mathbb{T}_{\mathrm{I}(B+\mathrm{I})}. && \text{definition } V_{-4}
\end{aligned}$$

For brevity, let $R := u; \mathrm{syQ}\left(\left(\alpha_A \backslash \left(\bigsqcup_{-4 \leq i \leq 4} T_i\right)\right)^{\downarrow\smile}, \varepsilon_{B+\mathrm{I}}^{\emptyset}\right)$. Then we have

$$\begin{aligned}
&R; (\varepsilon_{B+\mathrm{I}}^{\emptyset\smile}; \kappa^{\smile}; \mathbb{T}_{\mathrm{I}(B+\mathrm{I})} \sqcap \mathbb{I}_{B+\mathrm{I}})\\
&= R; \varepsilon_{B+\mathrm{I}}^{\emptyset\smile}; \kappa^{\smile}; \mathbb{T}_{\mathrm{I}(B+\mathrm{I})} \sqcap R && \text{Lemma 4.7 (1)}
\end{aligned}$$

$$= u; \left(\alpha_A \backslash \left(\bigsqcup_{-4 \leq i \leq 4} T_i\right)\right)^{\downarrow}; \kappa^{\smile}; \mathbb{T}_{\mathrm{I}(B+\mathrm{I})} \sqcap R \qquad \text{property } \varepsilon^{\emptyset}$$

$$= R, \qquad \text{see above}$$

and, hence, the first assertion from

$$
\begin{aligned}
u; C &= R; f && \text{definition } C \\
&= R; (\varepsilon^{\emptyset\,\smile}_{B+\mathrm{I}}; \kappa^{\smile}; \mathbb{T}_{\mathrm{I}(B+\mathrm{I})} \sqcap \mathbb{I}_{B+\mathrm{I}}); f && \text{see above} \\
&= R; (\varepsilon^{\emptyset\,\smile}_{B+\mathrm{I}}; \kappa^{\smile}; \mathbb{T}_{\mathrm{I}(B+\mathrm{I})} \sqcap \mathbb{I}_{B+\mathrm{I}}); \mathbb{T}_{(B+\mathrm{I})\mathrm{I}}; \kappa && \text{definition } f \\
&= R; \mathbb{T}_{(B+\mathrm{I})\mathrm{I}}; \kappa && \text{see above} \\
&= \mathbb{T}_{\mathrm{II}}; \kappa && R \text{ total} \\
&= \kappa && \mathrm{I} \text{ unit} \\
&= \mathrm{AL}. && \text{definition AL}
\end{aligned}
$$

The second assertion follows analogously. □

Since we do not want an AL-signal too often we choose $x; s^{3\,\smile}_A$ as small and $y; s^3_A$ as great as possible. On the element level, we have to choose u as great as possible such that $5 \leq x - 3u$ and $y + 3u \leq 45$, or equivalently $3u \leq \min(x-5, 45-y)$, holds.

Let us consider an example. Suppose $a_1 = a_2 = 1.2, b_1 = 0.35$ and $b_2 = 0.25$. As indicated in (3) above, we choose let $a_0 = b_0 = \frac{1}{2}$. Using (1) we get

$$
\begin{aligned}
\max(24 - \frac{a_1 - a_0}{b_1}, 25.5 - \frac{a_2 - b_0}{b_2}) &= \max(24 - 2, 25.5 - 2.8) = 22.7, \\
\min(24 + \frac{a_1 - a_0}{b_1}, 25.5 + \frac{a_2 - b_0}{b_2}) &= \min(24 + 2, 25.5 + 2.8) = 26,
\end{aligned}
$$

and, hence, $x = 22.7$ and $y = 26$. Furthermore, the previous property above gives us $\min(x-5, 45-y) = \min(17.7, 19) = 17.7$ such that we choose $u = 5.9$.

6.8 DISCUSSION OF THE APPROACH

Our approach has several advantages. We want to discuss them in detail.

Of course, it is possible to implement the controller by using the unit interval $[0,1]$ as underlying lattice instead of $[0,1] \times [0,1]$. But, in that case, we have to fix a temperature t_0, or at least a set of temperatures, in advance, which is good with respect to both colonies. The controller would try to keep the actual temperature closely to t_0. Selecting a suitable t_0 is a nontrivial problem. It either has to be computed once the parameters are fixed or be chosen by an expert. In our approach this is not necessary. The controller will find that temperature on its own depending on the chosen parameters.

During the development process of the controller we have selected specific semigroup operations in several places in advance. We kept the controller parametric by not fixing the parameters of that operation. From an abstract proof we then derived several properties that have to be satisfied by the parameters of the controller to ensure totality. Finally, we haven chosen suitable values to aim at a concrete controller. Notice that the abstract proof does not use any specific property of the selected semigroup operations so that the whole approach is in fact parametric in almost all those operations. The bottom line is that the abstract approach allows to make decisions as late as possible, which may save a considerable amount of money and effort. It is well known that early mistakes detected late are most painful.

Last but not least, the relational term derived in the previous section can be used as a prototype of the controller. This was actually done using the RATH system [19] and its extension for Goguen categories [38].

INDEX

SYMBOLS

REFERENCES

[1] Asperti A., Longo G.: Categories, Types and Structures. The MIT Press, Cambridge, Massachusetts (1991).

[2] Belohlávek, R.: Fuzzy Relational Systems: Foundations and Principles. IFSR International Series on System Science and Engineering, Vol. 20, Kluwer Academic/Plenum Press, New York (2002).

[3] Berghammer R., Gritzner T., Schmidt G.: Prototyping relational specifications using higher-order objects. In: Heering, J., Meinke, K., Möller, B., Nipkow, T. (eds.): Proc. International Workshop on Higher Order Algebra, Logic and Term Rewriting (HOA '93), LNCS 816, Springer, 56–75 (1994).

[4] Birkhoff G.: Lattice Theory, American Mathematical Society Colloquium Publications, Providence, Rhode Island Vol. XXV, 3rd edition. (1968).

[5] Chin L.H., Tarski A.: Distributive and Modular Laws in the Arithmetic of Relation Algebras. University of California Press, Berkeley, California (1951).

[6] De Cock M., Kerre E.E.: A New Class of Fuzzy Modifiers. In: Proceedings of ISMVL2000, IEEE Computer Society, 121–126 (2000).

[7] De Cock M., Bodenhofer U., Kerre E.E.: Modelling Linguistic Expressions Using Fuzzy Relations. In: Proceedings 6th Int. Conf. on Soft Computing (IIZUKA2000), 353–360 (2000).

[8] De Cock M., Radzikowska A.M., Kerre E.E.: Modelling Linguistic Modifiers Using Fuzzy-Rough Structures. In: Proceedings of IPMU2000, Vol. III, 1735–1742 (2000).

[9] Fodor J., Roubens M.: Fuzzy Preference Modelling and Multicriteria Decision Support. Kluwer Academic Publishers, Dordrecht, The Netherlands (1994).

[10] Freyd P., Scedrov A.: Categories, Allegories. North-Holland, Amsterdam (1990).

[11] Furusawa, H.: Algebraic Formalizations of Fuzzy Relations and Their Representation Theorems. Ph.D. Thesis, Department of Informatics, Kyushu University, Japan (1998).

[12] Goguen J.A.: $\mathcal{L}$-fuzzy sets. J. Math. Anal. Appl. 18, 145–157 (1967).

[13] Goldberg, D.E.: Genetic Algorithms in Search, Optimization & Machine Learning. Addison-Wesley, Reading, Massachusetts (1989).

[14] Gottwald, S.: Fuzzy Sets and Fuzzy Logic. Foundations of Application – from a Mathematical Point of View. Vieweg, Braunschweig, Weisbaden (1993).

[15] Grauel, A.: Fuzzy-Logik. Einführung in die Grundlagen mit Anwendungen. Wissenschaftsverlag Mannheim, Germany (1995).

[16] Grätzer, G.: General Lattice Theory. 2nd edition, Birkhäuser, Basel, Switzerland (1998).

[17] Jónsson B., Tarski A.: Boolean Algebras with Operators, I & II. Amer. J. Math. 73 (1951) 891–939, 74 (1952) 127–162.

[18] Jech, T.: Set Theory. Academic Press, London (1978).

[19] Kahl, W., Schmidt G.: Exploring (Finite) Relation Algebras Using Tools Written in Haskell. University of the Federal Armed Forces Munich, Report No. 2000–02 (2000).

[20] Kawahara, Y., Furusawa H.: Crispness and Representation Theorems in Dedekind Categories. DOI-TR 143, Kyushu University, Japan (1997).

[21] Kawahara, Y., Furusawa H.: An Algebraic Formalization of Fuzzy Relations. Fuzzy Set Syst 101, 125–135 (1999).

[22] Klaua, D.: Über einen Ansatz zur mehrwertigen Mengenlehre. Monatsb. Deutsch. Akad. Wiss. Berlin 7, 859–867 (1965).

[23] Klaua, D.: Ein Ansatz zur mehrwertigen Mengenlehre. Math. Nachr. 33, 273–296 (1967).

[24] Kitainik, L.: Fuzzy Decision Procedures with Binary Relations – Towards a Unified Theory. Kluwer Academic Publisher Boston, Massachusetts (1993).

[25] Mamdani, E.H., Gaines, B.R.: Fuzzy Reasoning and its Application. Academic Press, London (1987).

[26] Novak, N., Perfilieva, I., Mockor J.: Mathematical Principles of Fuzzy Logic. Kluwer Academic Publishers, London (1999).

[27] Olivier J.P., Serrato D.: Catégories de Dedekind. Morphismes dans les Catégories de Schröder. C.R. Acad. Sci. Paris 290, 939–941 (1980).

[28] Olivier J.P., Serrato D.: Squares and Rectangles in Relational Categories – Three Cases: Semilattice, Distributive lattice and Boolean Non-unitary. Fuzzy Set Syst 72, 167–178 (1995).

[29] Priestley, H.A., Davey, B.A.: Introduction to Lattices and Order. Cambridge University Press, Cambridge (1990).

[30] Ross, B.J., Zhu, H.: Procedural Texture Evolution Using Multiobjective Optimization. New Generat Comput 22(3), 271–293 (2004).

[31] Schaffer J.D.: Multiple objective optimization with vector evaluated genetic algorithms. In: Proceedings of an International Conference on Genetic Algorithms and Their Applications. Lawrence Erlbaum Hillsdale, New Jersey, 74–79 (1985).

[32] Schmidt G., Ströhlein T.: Relationen und Graphen. Springer (1989); English version: Relations and Graphs. Discrete Mathematics for Computer Scientists, EATCS Monographs on Theoret. Comput. Sci., Springer (1993).

[33] Schmidt G., Hattensperger C., Winter M.: Heterogeneous Relation Algebras. In: Brink C., Kahl W., Schmidt G. (eds.), Relational Methods in Computer Science, Advances in Computing Science. Springer, Vienna (1997).

[34] Schröder, E.: Algebra der Logik, 3. Band. Teubner, Leipzig (1895).

[35] Tarski, A.: On the Calculus of Relations. J. Symbolic Logic 6, 73–89 (1941).

[36] Tarski, A.: A Formalization of Set Theory without Variables. J. Symbolic Logic 18 (1953).

[37] Tarski, A. and Givant, S.: A Formalization of Set Theory without Variables. Amer. Math. Soc. Colloq. Publ. 41 (1987).

[38] Triebsees, T.: Extending RATH by Goguen Categories. Diploma Thesis. University of the Federal Armed Forces Munich (2002).

[39] Winter M.: Strukturtheorie heterogener Relationenalgebren mit Anwendung auf Nichtdetermismus in Programmiersprachen. Dissertationsverlag NG Kopierladen GmbH, München (1998).

[40] Winter M.: A new Algebraic Approach to L-Fuzzy Relations Convenient to Study Crispness. INS Information Science 139, 233–252 (2001).

[41] Winter M.: Representation Theory of Goguen Categories. Fuzzy Set. Syst. 138, 85–126 (2003).

[42] Winter M.: Relational Constructions in Goguen Categories. In: Relational Methods in Computer Science, 6th Int. Conf. RelMiCS, LNCS 2561, 212–227 (2002)

[43] Winter M.: Derived Operations in Goguen Categories. TAC Theory and Applications of Categories 10(11), 220–247 (2002).

[44] Zadeh L.A.: Fuzzy sets. Inform Control 8, 338–353 (1965).

TRENDS IN LOGIC

1. G. Schurz: *The Is-Ought Problem.* An Investigation in Philosophical Logic. 1997 ISBN 0-7923-4410-3
2. E. Ejerhed and S. Lindström (eds.): *Logic, Action and Cognition.* Essays in Philosophical Logic. 1997 ISBN 0-7923-4560-6
3. H. Wansing: *Displaying Modal Logic.* 1998 ISBN 0-7923-5205-X
4. P. Hájek: *Metamathematics of Fuzzy Logic.* 1998 ISBN 0-7923-5238-6
5. H.J. Ohlbach and U. Reyle (eds.): *Logic, Language and Reasoning.* Essays in Honour of Dov Gabbay. 1999 ISBN 0-7923-5687-X
6. K. Došen: *Cut Elimination in Categories.* 2000 ISBN 0-7923-5720-5
7. R.L.O. Cignoli, I.M.L. D'Ottaviano and D. Mundici: *Algebraic Foundations of many-valued Reasoning.* 2000 ISBN 0-7923-6009-5
8. E.P. Klement, R. Mesiar and E. Pap: *Triangular Norms.* 2000 ISBN 0-7923-6416-3
9. V.F. Hendricks: *The Convergence of Scientific Knowledge.* A View From the Limit. 2001 ISBN 0-7923-6929-7
10. J. Czelakowski: *Protoalgebraic Logics.* 2001 ISBN 0-7923-6940-8
11. G. Gerla: *Fuzzy Logic.* Mathematical Tools for Approximate Reasoning. 2001 ISBN 0-7923-6941-6
12. M. Fitting: *Types, Tableaus, and Gödel's God.* 2002 ISBN 1-4020-0604-7
13. F. Paoli: *Substructural Logics: A Primer.* 2002 ISBN 1-4020-0605-5
14. S. Ghilardi and M. Zawadowki: *Sheaves, Games, and Model Completions.* A Categorical Approach to Nonclassical Propositional Logics. 2002 ISBN 1-4020-0660-8
15. G. Coletti and R. Scozzafava: *Probabilistic Logic in a Coherent Setting.* 2002 ISBN 1-4020-0917-8; Pb: 1-4020-0970-4
16. P. Kawalec: *Structural Reliabilism.* Inductive Logic as a Theory of Justification. 2002 ISBN 1-4020-1013-3
17. B. Löwe, W. Malzkorn and T. Räsch (eds.): *Foundations of the Formal Sciences II.* Applications of Mathematical Logic in Philosophy and Linguistics, Papers of a conference held in Bonn, November 10-13, 2000. 2003 ISBN 1-4020-1154-7
18. R.J.G.B. de Queiroz (ed.): *Logic for Concurrency and Synchronisation.* 2003 ISBN 1-4020-1270-5
19. A. Marcja and C. Toffalori: *A Guide to Classical and Modern Model Theory.* 2003 ISBN 1-4020-1330-2; Pb 1-4020-1331-0
20. S.E. Rodabaugh and E.P. Klement (eds.): *Topological and Algebraic Structures in Fuzzy Sets.* A Handbook of Recent Developments in the Mathematics of Fuzzy Sets. 2003 ISBN 1-4020-1515-1; Pb 1-4020-1516-X

21. V.F. Hendricks and J. Malinowski: *Trends in Logic*. 50 Years Studia Logica. 2003 ISBN 1-4020-1601-8

22. M. Dalla Chiara, R. Giuntini and R Greechie: *Reasoning in Quantum Theory*. Sharp and Unsharp Quantum Logics. 2004 ISBN 1-4020-1978-5

23. B. Löwe, B. Piwinger and T. Räsch (eds.): *Classical and New Paradigms of Computation and their Complexity Hierarchies*. Papers of the conference "Foundations of the Formal Sciences III" held in Vienna, September 21–24, 2001 ISBN 1-4020-2775-3

24. G. Jäger: *Anaphora and Type Logical Grammar*. 2005 ISBN 978-1-4020-3904-1

25. M. Winter: *Goguen Categories*. A Categorical Approach to L-fuzzy Relations. 2007 ISBN 978-1-4020-6163-9